THE
MODERN FAMILY
AND THE CHURCH

THE
MODERN FAMILY
AND
THE CHURCH

by

REGINA WESTCOTT WIEMAN

HARPER & BROTHERS

NEW YORK   LONDON

To my father

HENRY HANSON
Man of integrity

whose sense and vision of the social good
permitted no easy complacency
wherever was needed a
fighter or builder

CONTENTS

viii   *Contents*
                        Part IV

FACING INTO THE FUTURE

INTRODUCTION

THE impetus to study at deeper levels the relation of family and church has derived from three sources chiefly. The first of these is long-continued work with certain groups of parents. These fathers and mothers were disturbed concerning the place of religion and the church in family living. The second is the various groups of pastors and other religious workers who are seeking a way to connect religion significantly and dynamically with other major human interests while still conserving the true nature of religion. The third is an increasing concern that the basic human values which have been secured in the home and church of the past be fostered again amidst the wider complexities of modern living.

The immediate occasion which prompted this present undertaking was work done as a member of the staff of a Pastors' Institute sponsored by one of the universities. There were convened leaders from all parts of the country. For this reason it provided opportunity to sense the conditions which are most universal and disturbing among workers in the field of religion. Conspicuous among them was the increasing degree to which problems of marriage and family life have become insistent calls upon the attention of the staff of the church. Connected with this situation was the realization, disturbing to the leaders, that the church weakens as family life weakens. These and related findings have heightened their professional interest in this area. Consequently concern for family life has moved into a major place in the program of such churches as have sensitive and creative leadership.

Parents, singly and in groups, frequently voice their perplexity about God, religion, and the church. With some of them it is primarily a reluctance to give up an interest traditionally established. With a few it is selfish concern lest they suffer some penalty in neglecting these interests. But with the far greater majority, it is a genuine concern to understand, soundly evaluate, and respond constructively and rationally to this profound interest, the growth of meaning and value. To this end they want to define the relation of the family to the church.

Change in social outlook and in the form of the major human interests occurs so swiftly in these powerfully instrumentalized days that there is a widening divergence between the generation of parents and that of youth. There is a veritable chasm between that of the ruling officers of the average church and that of its youth. This leaves parents in a very uncomfortable and bewildering position. Above all else they are aligned with their children. They seek for these the most out of life. A vast number of parents still feel that this "most out of life" must give to God the controlling place in human living. But they do not see how to promote this interest in their families with honesty, effectiveness, and enthusiasm. More and more of them are asking, "Shall our children attend Sunday School?" or "How can we develop interest in religion?" or "Has religion any longer a justifiable claim upon our attention? And, if not, to what forces should we turn for the needed resources in invigorating and progressively integrating the cultural growth of the family?"

Many parents are troubled because their particular churches seem to impede or injure rather than foster and guide. Or perhaps they exhibit indifference to the family except in the matter of exploiting the family to meet its obligations to the church. Most parents, however, feel that their particular churches are ready to do all that is possible for the growth of the family, but both parents and church workers are floundering through a great deal of activity in which there is not much real progress.

Whatever the following studies have to contribute to this culturally crucial problem is the outcome of these years of work with families on the one hand and with religious leaders on the other. Through study, experimentation, and cooperative evaluating of findings, group after group has worked its way a little farther toward understanding and effectiveness. Some of these groups have been study groups of parents or leaders or both. Some of them have been individual families treated in private professional practice over a great number of years. Some have been staffs of religious institutions seeking guidance for more constructive approach to their actual daily work. The insistence of these earnest groups has forced a deeper analysis of the bases for the interfunctioning of family and church.

The very natures of these two institutions are such that a bond unites them which is essential to the vitality of each. Unless this basic bond between the two is discovered and its requirements understood, they cannot join together in that cooperative union which their respective functions require. This book endeavors to locate and illuminate this bond, and then to suggest measures by which, in mutual support, the family and the church can abundantly contribute to the fulfillment of human life.

The building up of such a cooperative union upon this basic bond is a long-term problem and involves the reshaping of both institutions. Nothing less than this, however, can conserve their cultural functions. Those young people who are thinking about these interests at all seriously already seem to be feeling their way toward sounder foundations. The fact that so many individuals and institutions are ready and eager for a unifying and strengthening program of a sort which merits their intellectual respect and their loyal devotion provides a powerful factor for clearing the way for sounder and more creative developments.

It was at first planned to present a rather fully representative survey of the specific developments being sponsored by the churches of this country in the interest of the family. To this end, contact was made with many institutions and individuals, all of whom manifested active interest in the undertaking. But the reports indicated that the work is as yet too near its beginnings to make such a survey possible. Therefore the plan has had to be changed to one which seeks to indicate the beginnings and the trends in general. The focus of attention is upon what is developing rather than upon who is instituting it.

Because a number of parents and religious workers who learned that this study was going on expressed an urgent wish that it be made usable by classes in parent education, a guiding outline has been incorporated.

Pausing to voice appreciation of those influences which have furthered this study opens up a wide span of life. First is the contribution to my own development made by the significant communion of family life and of a succession of church fellowships during the maturing years. Both the resources and limitations of these experiences in communion have yielded insight as well as enriched growth more than can be readily expressed. Next come the groups met in professional work, previously mentioned. With them there has been much creative interaction concerning this problem. More recently involved are the many organizations which have lent their interest and made their reports of present developments in their own groups. These find further mention in the body of the book. They include the national headquarters of major church divisions and denominations, national headquarters of many educational organizations, a number of municipal and local institutions and many individual officers and leaders whose work is related to this field. My friends among the young people have also been generous with their cooperation, most of these through sharing some of their pertinent experiences and some through making available to me the formulations of the rituals they have developed in preparation for marriage. To these organizations and persons, all and severally, warm gratitude is herewith expressed. Particularly meaningful appreciation I extend to my husband, Henry N. Wieman, for his active cooperation in my undertaking.

Part I

THE FAMILY IN THE LIFE OF TODAY

Introduction

THE title of this book indicates its first interest as that of the interfunctioning relations between the family and the church. This must be a thin and superficial process if it is undertaken without some understanding of the intricacy and scope of the social web into which the family as a basic social institution is being woven. The church cannot function without the family. But it can function effectively with the family only when it sees the family in its total cultural setting. Consequently it is of first importance that the church consider all the conditions necessary for effective family life, together with the possibilities of cooperation between all the institutions that shape these conditions. The church, no more than the family, can draw boundary lines to mark the limits of its domain these days. There must be limits certainly when it comes to distinctive functions, methods, and plans of procedures, but as regards the scope of its interests there can be none. Therefore, when we essay to discover what we can of the relations of family and church, it must be in this intricate pattern of social interweaving that we seek them.

Just now the threads for the weaving are in a bad snarl. It is important to trace these threads as best we can. This is attempted in Chapter I. Then there are certain difficulties in weaving its distinctive social pattern which existed in the family a long time before this snarl occurred. Some of the more persistent of these long-term problems are discussed in Chapter II. The primary functions of the modern family are set into their cultural connections in Chapter III.

3

Chapter 1

THE CRISIS FOR THE FAMILY

THE family is the orphan institution among the organizations of modern civilization. It is regularly utilized, exploited, disrupted, or despoiled as an incident in the climb to power or to wealth which are the obsessions of this ruthlessly competitive, individualistic age. The single family is a tiny, relatively short-lived institution which has increasing difficulty in establishing and maintaining sufficient social status to permit the fulfilling of its functions.

It is easy to see the helplessness of the very small, autonomous countries of the world pieced into the map altogether too close to the large, covetous, competitive nations. It is impossible for these small nations to attain either full economic independence or political power equal to that of the major nations. They sense that they may be disrupted, bullied, or even gobbled up by some stronger nation turned ravenous. History gruesomely illustrates the possibility.

The modern family wedged in between the powerful institutions of the modern world is in a more hopeless situation than these small countries. The world knows the names of these tiny national units, and much about them. In theory, at any rate, it recognizes that they have rights which should be respected and protected. There are standards of mutual responsibility and of justice governing dealings with them, however often these may be ignored in practice. The whole world knows that certain values that distinguish culture from barbarism are at stake when some larger nation reverts to wolfishness and violates these rights. But there is not this vivid universal recognition of the cultural values at stake when the family unit is subjected to overmaster-

5

ing pressures from more powerful social organizations which are covetous, competitive, and calloused.

Not so long ago, the American family was, in the main, economically independent. Further, the size, prestige, and power of the well-established family were factors that had to be reckoned with in community enterprises and maneuverings. Blood-loyalty and the tendency to cluster made the family loom large in a community still small enough to be personal, and to be more of an aggregate than a centralized organization. Indeed everyone lived in a home—his own or that of a relative—and all the industries and professions which developed were, first of all, communal answers to the needs of the family. The conspicuous and most significant aspect of the typical colonial American community was its group of landed homes, some extensive, some limited. Located near the center of the group was to be found The Common. Encircling it there grew up other conveniences, industrial and cultural, for the *common* use of the families making up the community. In later developments, Main Street was laid out to serve the surrounding families. These families who made up the community were the important concern. Their condition, progress, standards, interests, activities, needs, losses, gains, sorrows, joys, and achievements were of great moment.

Beyond this position of prominence given to the family by the community there was a consciousness of family within the family itself. Pervading the institution there was a sense of the sacredness which must not be violated. Pride in one's family, sacrifice for it, loyalty to it, whole-family cooperation in many events and undertakings, familiarity with its records, deeply ingrained sentiments toward its symbols and relics, long residence in the same house or locality, and direct personal relations between many of its members vivified the sense of family into a dominant control in all living. One of the most potent appeals in matters of conduct and of ambition was that of keeping the family name unblemished. One of the most arousing incentives to industrious striving was the possibility of adding to the splendor of the family. "Who are you?" meant "What of your family?"

Two dioramas recently exhibited in Chicago dramatized this sense. They showed the family one hundred years ago and now.

In the former a young lover is alighting from a carriage to call upon his fiancée. He starts across a velvety sweep of lawn shaded by magnificent elm trees. On beyond rises in dignity the massive brick mansion. With gallant yet humble decorum he advances to speak to those who have come out to greet him—the modest and fluffily dainty young woman, her mother and father of gracious but stately bearing, and the keen-eyed grandmother, zealous guardian of the name and traditions of the family. In the modern scene, a nervy young fellow, incessantly active, starts the honks of his Ford horn echoing insistently down the solidly paved canyon of a street above which rises the spectacular façade of a massive apartment house. He cranes his neck up toward an open window on the third floor out from which leans a girl smoking a cigarette. Her expression seems to indicate that she "knows all the answers" already. She gesticulates her answer to him. There need be never a thought of a moment's delay for bidding adieu to her elders, because her parents are already gone to their country club and her stranger-grandmother is keeping a late appointment for a facial and a permanent in preparation for tomorrow's departure on the next lap of her perpetual and restless gadding about. Such a family means little beyond some practical arrangements possibly of advantage to the individuals involved. There are no deep roots. The sense of the family is tenuous, unstable, and all but powerless.

Far from desirable would it be for the modern family to try to establish rootage in the same way in which the earlier family did. It could not do so if it tried. Rootage it must have, but it must be established in the soil of going interests and experiments in living carried on amidst the realities of the culture of today rather than in the soil of long-possessed place and things and of a closely knit geographical neighborhood. Because, generally, the modern family has but shallow rootage, it has not yet come into self-consciousness in terms of its place in modern culture. This means that it does not grasp the nature and extent of its distinctive significance. Hence it can hardly be expected that other preoccupied organizations will have done so. All the more, then, the family becomes the prey of groups turned by the profit motive into wolves most scientifically dressed in lambs' skins tested against sales-resistance.

In these days, the outcries from the family for protection and salvation are largely the pained pleas of individuals who find themselves caught in specific difficulties. There is as yet no general feeling of outrage against the basic violation which is being done the family as a major cultural unit, and which, consequently, is being done to our whole culture. There is still a blinding masculine prejudice which regards the family as nice and fine, as necessary of course, and as being all the rest that makes it a suitable realm for the activity of our dear women, but as having hardly a serious claim upon our attention in the midst of issues held to be of much more profound importance. Hence, there is not the crucially urgent drive toward the necessary type of social planning which shall adequately provide for the rights and functions of the family as an indispensable cultural unit.

The problem of the family is of profound and cardinal import. It is an integral part of the total problem of social organization which is giving us grave concern today through its many ramifications, economic, political, and international. Civilization has reached that complexity of interdependence where the rights, functions, and problems of any one area of social interest cannot be considered and treated without considering and treating every other major area. This is why the situation of the family unit in our national organization is more defenseless than that of a small autonomous nation in the international organization. Only partially is it an autonomous organization and it is not self-contained economically or culturally. Its members depend critically upon their interfunctioning with other organizations of the community, with industrial ones for their means of continuance, and with cultural ones for their means of growth and effectiveness. The family no longer *can* have any existence at all except in so far as its rights and functions are provided for in the total social plan.

"The family no longer can have any existence. . . ." What is it that comes into existence in society when a family forms? What is it that carries enough meaning and value for human beings so that it continues to struggle on against terrific odds? There are many small groupings which pass by the name of *family* which are not truly so, just as there are many individuals on a college campus that pass by the name of *student* but who would be astounded were they plunged into genuine student experience! What are the distinguishing features which mark a group as being a family?

The family is that fellowship of parents and children, created and promoted through the sharing of vital interests, which initiates and individualizes growth of personality and a concomitant development of culture [1] in the community.

The family is a fellowship. The world has little concern for fellowships these days—they do not produce marketable goods. The family is a special kind of fellowship where vital interests are shared, no interest too trivial nor too imposing if it is vital to any one of the members. But society does not hesitate to set fashions, institute practices, and make demands which disparage, obstruct, or exploit the sentiments and personal investment which support this sharing fellowship. Every material, every activity, every personal element which goes into the making of a family is scrutinized by many calculating eyes to discover possibilities for commercial exploitation with no appreciative concern for possibilities of injury to the intangible but real values that inhere in the genuine family. It is little wonder then that the family process "which initiates and individualizes growth of personality" in its members "and a concomitant development of culture in the community" is breaking down at many points and in many instances. Always the family has had and will have problems, but

[1] *Culture* here does not refer to the conglomerate accumulation of everything which society has produced, intentionally or not. It is recognized that this is the common use of the term in the social sciences, which makes it almost synonymous with civilization. We need a new term to designate those social developments which have furthered the integration of all worthy social interests, enriching them through the constant inclusion of new interests and rendering them creative in promoting human fulfillment. Perhaps *progressive cultural consummation* expresses these integrating and fulfilling developments of society which we wish to indicate by the term *culture*. We use the term in this normative sense rather than in the descriptive sense throughout this writing.

its most disruptive problems today are induced by current social organization and trends.

Basically speaking, the situations which are commonly called "social problems of the family" are not problems. Here are a number of them: increase in sexual promiscuity among unmarried young people in their twenties; general extension of the conventional vices (drinking, smoking, lewdness, and carousing); increase in divorce; growing irresponsibility toward one's job and toward other people's property; greater number of itinerant individuals and families; multiplication of extreme and spectacular forms of amusement; extension of the casualness of attitude in parents toward their jobs; and decrease in birth rate among the more intelligent. These are symptoms, not problems. They are symptoms that the family *cannot* function effectively in the social organization of today.

Again, there are other sorts of signs: increase in taxes to meet the rising tide of delinquency and crime; fierce strikes for a living wage; intense struggles for insurance protecting periods of unemployment and old age, for more "free" essentials to human living in the way that the school, playgrounds, postal service, and library are free; dogged efforts for pure-food laws and similar decent regulations; astounding increase in the amount of dishonesty among students and employees; and the prodigious and mounting national debt for family relief to be reckoned eventually into exorbitant, small-home-confiscating public taxation. Once more, essentially, these are not problems, but are symptoms of the tense predicaments being suffered by homes that are overstraining or breaking because of the present impossible conditions of living. Both aspects are evident: the family growing lax, sinking, breaking, disintegrating; the family struggling spasmodically, haphazardly, fearfully, yet desperately, for the essentials of human fulfillment.

The family is going through a long and perilous crisis. Nobody noticed just when it started; nobody can say just how long it will last; nobody knows what the outcome for the family will be. However, some of the activating factors of this crisis are distinguishable. Since they are integral to the whole situation they challenge attention.

VULNERABILITY THROUGH CHANGE IN MOTIVATION

Biologically, as we all know, the family is founded upon the conditions and activities instigated by the sex drive, and industry upon those instigated by the drive for self-preservation. Socially, however, other motivations have entered in. During many centuries, the dominant motivation in instituting marriage and family life has been moving in a diametrically opposite direction from the dominant motivation underlying the organization and activity in industry and in the other less intimate social institutions.

Long ago, the family was a mighty clan or tribe with property and other forms of physical power, including at times armed retainers. Even in relatively recent periods, though its membership was less dramatically defined and its might more political than physical, the family looked out for the greatest advantage to itself as a substantially worthy institution. Marriages were arranged, frankly or by indirection, upon the profit motive. The disposition of the individual marrying was a consideration subordinate to that of the gain to the family through the new "connections." Remnants of this policy, not altogether rare, are evident in those modern families who count their unit-importance as somehow remarkable.

Another very frequent motivation in marriage has been economic advantage to the individuals involved—cheap labor and personal service on his own terms for the man, economic support for the woman and her children. As in the case of the motive of family-advantage, this bond of economic dependence still exists today, particularly in the case of the married woman who has small children and in the case of the unplaced or poorly placed unmarried young woman who feels that she "must get her man."

The main tendency, however, has been to place more and more importance upon the personal relationship between the two being married. Less consideration is given to the power and profit accruing to the family through their new connections or to the economic profit accruing to the individuals through their new partnership. It is only comparatively recently that "true love" has been the first requirement, at least in theory, of the betrothed and the married.

Many factors have strengthened this tendency of change in motivation. Particularly potent have been three of them: frequent shifts in population which tear at long-established family roots; the spreading of the Christian teachings about love as the basic human bond; and psychological insights into the conditions which best promote development of balanced and effective relationships in family life. Where love is the motivation, inequality, tyrannical possessiveness, parasitic individualism, and self-abnegation tend to disappear. Equality, freedom, mutuality, and cooperative reinforcement tend to take their places.

Current opinion asserts that the young couple starting their family should be permitted to build it democratically in reference both to the families from which they are presumably weaned and the family to come. But consider! They find themselves setting out to build this new, tiny, powerless democratic institution upon the love motive in the midst of a hardened, gigantic, powerful industrial civilization built and operated upon the profit motive. Further, they are dependent in cardinal ways upon this civilization; they cannot exist as an industrially independent unit. The family cannot compete with institutions dominated by the profit motive. It cannot with integrity fit into the conditions of a society so dominated. It cracks or splits up as soon it becomes individualistic and intercompetitive. The profit motive is antithetic to its character and functions as now developed. Yet the profit motive controls most of the operative environment wherein the family must work and play and study.

A corollary aspect of the destructive effect of the profit motive on family life, and an aspect equally devastating, is the relentlessness of the demands of the intricate economic system. Since increase in material production is the subgoal of economic enterprise heading toward its main goal of increase in profits, there is an utterly inhuman disregard for personal relationships. Individuals are handled as one type of necessary equipment to keep the wheels of production going. What they signify as persons among other persons is ignored. Time and opportunity for fellowship are cut below a workable minimum. The absorption of the father's time illustrates this. Whether he is a commuter and hardly sees his children except on Sunday, or whether a professional man egged on to overtime by threats of what will happen to him if he does not keep abreast, or whatever he may be, his father relation is all too often an unredeemed pledge. Energy, too, is overdrained. We now know that a surplus of physical energy is the first essential in keeping intimate relationships in good order. One's social sympathy and patience depend largely upon this ingredient. But the demands of our complex society use up so much of personal energy that it is likely to be only remnants of ourselves that gather as a family at the end of the day's work. Relationships cannot be kept in working order without intelligent and generous personal investment. The demands of present society upon the individual are prohibitive from the point of view of adequate personal investment in the family fellowship.

SOCIAL DISCREDITING OF MARRIAGE

Like the telling blows of great battering rams upon the heavy, hoary walls of a guarding fortress, one event after another has beaten against the social foundations guarding the institution of marriage. Its traditional patterns of thought and practice are exposed to appraising rebels who would tear down much of the old structure. Some of these rebels are barbarians, cohorts from the ranks of chronic social wreckers who would destroy social control wherever it proves annoying. Some of the rebels are provincially oriented individualists, possibly highly cultivated in the conventional sense, who think only of what would best suit themselves and their close cultural kindred. Some are shortsighted reformers who would adjust society in such a way as to abolish painful consequences by making legal whatever irregularity now imposes a social penalty or a strong sense of guilt: they do not see the deeper implications of such symptomatic treatment. But a number are thinkers honestly concerned for the welfare and fulfillment of human beings.

Through the varied attacks of all these rebels, whether motivated by self or social interest, the institution of marriage is up for examination and must prove its human worth. We moderns must get used to seeing social institutions put on trial. Each one of them must be evaluated periodically until such time as we become sufficiently intelligent in our communal living to provide permanent and specific means for continuous critical analysis of them, and hence for guidance in promoting more steady social growth in the midst of swift, often unpredictable changes. Noting some of the principal factors which are beating at the established foundations of marriage helps to locate points of weakness.

The leading gospel of salvation in this country—individualism—has so conditioned personality that many, many modern individuals are not capable of adjusting cooperatively in any adult social group, much less in the most intimate and difficult relation of marriage. Their experiences in living have brought them no activating convictions of the values to be found in that rich, mature love which comes only through the disciplining of the self to meet the requirements of some deep, precious fellowship. Such individuals do not expect a fishing license to guarantee that they will catch the fish skillfully, and cook and serve them delectably. But they do expect the marriage license to secure for them the satisfaction of all their "rights," the coddling indulgence of all their appetites and whims, and to render their living perpetually adventuresome, ardent, and "happy." They expect all this, too, without the inconvenience of feeling themselves bound into any "entangling alliance" beyond what yields advantage to their self-interests.

The chronic individualist, be he man or woman, is an exploiter, dangerous socially, for he himself grows increasingly unaware of the exploiting nature of most of his activities. However, his attitude is so like that of most others he meets in business and profession, in market place and general association, that he feels himself in the right most of the time. It may be only in his home that he has difficulties of adjustment and satisfaction, whereupon he is inclined to think that the trouble is with the institution and not with himself. He truly cannot see that his individualism, so successful in business, blocks and tramples upon the many delicate processes through which love grows in marriage.

For most individuals daily home-coming requires each time a complete reversal, both as to direction and style, of the patterns of social response that have dominated their day in the market places of the world. The intimate, personal nature of marital and parental relations calls for mutual appreciation and reinforcement, whereas individualism and competition are necessary to survival in the present typical world outside the home. This complete reversal of patterns of association, repeated twice daily, does violence to the personality. It puts an exorbitantly taxing strain upon the marriage relation even where this daily reversal of social demand upon the persons is clearly perceived. It becomes stupendous when, not being recognized as a continuing problem in the adjustment, it bedevils, time after time, sincere effort toward finer relationships.

The distressing and insistent nature of the evidence of dissatisfaction among husbands and wives also makes a forceful attack upon marriage. It is registered socially in many ways.

These two factors—individualism and increased marital dissatisfaction or failure—are largely responsible for another. Social rejection of marriage by an increasing number is a third factor. It appears in several forms, most common of which are free love, trial marriage, companionate marriage, and the substitution, particularly by some of the better-endowed women, of a career for marriage. While these forms of rejection exist without benefit of formal social authorization, they are sufficiently common to be more than a mere threat to marriage as traditionally instituted. They are a revolt against present conditions affecting marriage. This revolt cannot be put down until there is a reevaluation of the institution of marriage from the point of view of its adequacy in taking care of the human values entrusted to it.

The changing status of woman, the fourth factor, has so many ramifications in connection with marriage that it is impossible to consider them here. But there are involved such critical issues as the single moral standard; truer bases for man-woman relationships; home management when the woman is absentee director during the day; division of family responsibilities; and articulation between family and vocational functions on the part of the wife, on the part of the husband, and on the part of both in the area of their common obligations and fellowship.

There are other factors which are forcing us into conscious appraisal of marriage. Society's need to keep up its birth rate is no longer a major one. Consequently, producing children is no longer a source of parental prestige. Indeed, a number of factors have made the bearing and rearing of children an awesome undertaking. All this has strengthened the tendency to think of marriage as an arrangement primarily for the benefit of the two adults contracting it. This tendency has gained further impetus through those popular reactions to the Freudian doctrines which have conjured up passionate possibilities of paradise for the individual who succeeds in achieving "freedom" *from* all repression of desire and *for* all self-expression.

A further factor is the sharp decline in the power of religious sanctions to control social attitudes and standards in regard to marriage. The participation of the church in the instituting of a marriage is all too often sought for the sake of adding social or aesthetic effectiveness to a ceremony mistakenly thought to be the major matter in marriage. How much *Christian* marriage is there actually today? How many entering marriage under the auspices of the church understand, and are convincingly pledged to, Christian principles of relationship?

Then the extension both of knowledge of contraceptives and of their actual use has lessened the number of those who enter marriage to secure a legalizing of sexual relations. In addition, like any new form of power, contraception has been exploited. It has increased the amount of cheap extramarital and premarital promiscuity. There appear two results of special interest here, namely, the increased exploitation of sex as a tool for casual physical satisfaction rather than its control as a foundation for greater human fulfillment, and an increased disregard for marriage as a social institution. Contraceptives have a significant service to render society. For one thing, they can force us to search for sounder principles as support for our set of values and our standards in sexual relations. If we open ourselves to the emerging implications, we shall have to admit that fear can no longer be the chief social control in sex life. We need sounder motivation for sexual control than fear.

Psychological study has contributed much enlightenment upon human motivation, upon love, and upon the problems and possibilities of personal adjustment. This in turn has set us to evaluating what does and can happen to personalities through the marriage relation. Some of the romantic mystery and the sense of grand adventure which have stirred dreams of married happiness in those "madly in love" must now make place for such realistic factors as intelligent preparation, the pledging of loyalty to an undertaking recognized as complicated and lifelong, and a sustained openness to those factors fostering personal growth which all enduring experiences in creative sharing possess.

Lastly, it is discouragingly difficult to witness the values present in successful marriage in these days. For one thing, the more intimate, prolonged types of community association are rare because general associations are speeded up and consequently conventionalized past the point where it is easy to get really acquainted with the meanings of life others have discovered. Secondly, the movies, the press, and current fiction capitalize upon irregularities and tragedies in marriage. The negative side wins by default because of inadequate representation of the positive side. Young people have too restricted an opportunity to experience vicariously the values that can come from long-continued, sincere, richly nurtured love. Quite the contrary often happens. They are enlisted in "charm schools" and drilled for "conquest" on the presumption that it is "open season" everywhere and all the time. Many moderns have not been taught that the domain of each marriage is distinctly marked off by the contract of mutual loyalty, legal and often religious, voluntarily signed by a certain two persons. Observably, the boundaries of this domain are scantily recognized by many individuals both within and without its preserves. A point frequently overlooked is the fact that, not only the particular couple involved most closely, but *every* citizen, male and female, enters into every contract of marriage instituted according to the laws of the land. This is true because the institution of marriage legally celebrates and fosters the primacy of the personal loyalty voluntarily pledged between the husband and wife. Invasion of this domain of pledged loyalty, so long as its contract stands, is traitorous on the part of any citizen, traitorous not only to the particular marriage in case but also to his civic responsibilities of allegiance to the institutions of his land. Today such treachery is treated casually. Values found in marriage when it is intelligently fostered by the protection and allegiance of a concerned society are far greater than now prevail.

Such factors as these reveal how negative has been the social approach to marriage. They are forcing us to introduce positive attitudes, values, and methods into social dealing with this institution. Because marriage is entrusted with the care of strong human drives which implicate other persons in their functioning, what happens in it and to it are of signal importance to everyone. Yet not only are there all these complications within the institution of marriage today, but marriage is involved in the complications of other institutions. The crisis here is all too disturbing not to be apparent in manifold ways.

LACK OF UNION AMONG FAMILIES

Individual workmen for many years have experienced their helplessness against the conditions of a monopolistic industrial organization. They have formed unions—workmen's organized minorities—with which to meet the dominance of the capitalistically organized minorities. And these unions have amalgamated so that a great number of organized minorities may in emergency become a great majority. Certain evils have grown up in connection with these unions and they have not been able yet to achieve a basic plan which would result in a just and, at the same time, richly productive industrial system. But they have achieved one important step. They have made society conscious of the tragic dangers and evils of the present oppressive system, and of the need for basic reconstruction of the present plan to the end of securing for all workers the chance to work under conditions that permit living on a full human level.

Each family unit is as helpless as a single workman would be. Yet there has not been as yet any general tendency for the family to develop organized minorities with which to focus social attention upon its profound crisis and to assert and guarantee its basic needs. There are signs of the awakening of the family to a realization that it cannot stand as an independent institution in a profit-motivated society. First, all over the country there are springing up sporadically little groupings of mothers who feel the need for a nursery school or a playground or medical attention for their children: they have frequently achieved very worth-while results for their own specific neighborhood. In some localities fathers have grouped to clean up the vice spots near schools and to take care of other menacing situations as well as to cooperate with the mothers in many of their projects. Second, the National Congress of Parents and Teachers has done and is doing a tremendous job of bringing about more intelligent family-consciousness. It is achieving this principally through its program of parent education, but also through improving local conditions and in augmenting the efforts of the public schools. This organization has an enormous potential force which may be felt more profoundly as it develops. In terms of national history, it is exceedingly young.

The efforts just cited are family-instituted. In addition to these, through a variety of enterprises, forces outside the family are attempting to set up more intelligent approaches to the family situation. The whole adult-education movement bears constructively upon the issue. A number of national agencies are promoting parent education and child study, such as the National Council of Parent Education, Inc., and the Child Study Association of America. Then, social work being done both in the field of family welfare and in connection with the courts is on the whole constructive. The very fact that there now are courts of domestic relations and courts for juvenile offenders against the law is an indication of progress. Also illuminating and useful are many of the interpretations and analyses contributed by sociological research laboratories. From diverse quarters are coming findings which are making more and more clear the nature and severity of the family crisis.

Part of the crisis of the family is identical with the crisis of the industrial worker. Since the individual workman is usually co-head of a family certain menacing conditions of the family are bettered whenever his economic and industrial situation is improved. These two, the home and the economic situation of the worker, are closely related. There are, however, other basic requirements of the family that are not inextricably involved in the struggle for economic justice. But whether for dealing with its separate or its joined issues, by some process the family will have to gain the strength of an organized minority in pressing its case. Already it has the potential strength of great numbers and of providing a very large and significant part of the experience of all individuals.

THE LOOTING ATTITUDE—EACH ONE FOR HIMSELF

The family has taken little more responsibility for correcting the evils of the economic system than have the exploiting profiteers. The vast majority of families have looked upon the economic system as an area of free pickings from which they hoped to gather in a goodly booty without feeling any deep responsibility for the system or for the effect that their conduct in it had upon it. They castigate the many ways in which unscrupulous big business squeezes and drains the family while remaining utterly callous as to outcomes. But the attitude behind these acquisitive onslaughts of big business is usually no better nor worse than the average family's attitude toward the whole economic system. It goes out to get what it can and all that it can without ever pondering upon the immediate, mediate, and remote effects of its procedures. The driving purpose behind capitalistic activities is not that of degrading and destroying the family. This happens incidentally while big business is carrying out the purpose of becoming a bigger business and hence a more profitable one for those few fortunate families who were luckier or smarter or slicker in locating and gathering in the booty. It is plainly noticeable that there is nothing which moves a family from the leftist toward the rightest position so painlessly and swiftly as good financial fortune.

As a matter of fact, families, and particularly their women members, so statistics tell us, spend an enormous total amount of money, acting in the family capacity. This means that they have a tremendous potential power in influencing both production and consumption. Here, where intelligence and action, concerted at least locally, could have wielded telling power, there has been no realization of possibilities of control until recently. In consequence, there has been little effort toward control.

Rather the spending for various articles, hence the support of the conditions which produced them, has been largely under the flattering tutelage of the high-pressure salesman of big business. In other words the average family has been so intrigued over watching its boots being licked by suave salesmen that its members have walked, without lifting their eyes from their shiny boots, into the trap of buying in line with what is most profitable for big business but not according to what is wise for the consumer and the producer. The double job of supplying the market and then rushing spectacularly to the buyer's elbow in time to coach him to buy what has been supplied has been so skillfully done that it has proved very profitable—but not to the average family. The failure of the family to appreciate its function and status as large consumer and hence important determiner of production has complicated its present crisis. The sudden springing up of consumer education and of consumers' and producers' cooperatives are signs that realization of this is upon us. It is not here suggested that the united action of families can correct the evils of the economic order without being supplemented by political action. But organized families must unite with other agencies to achieve a better social order. Further, they must put their buckets down where their own well is. They have majority power as consumers—once this power is mobilized.

The obverse side of this each-one-for-himself policy presents a much more serious situation. Even though the driving purpose of current capitalism has not been to degrade and destroy the family, nevertheless this is increasingly the inevitable outcome. When the gathering up of booty by huge business organizations has succeeded so far that there are now millions who have nothing left with which to buy, and no job with which to earn the money to buy, this concentrated booty, dire results follow. The morale of the family is undercut; participation in community activities of the sort essential to development is impossible because of lack of minimum equipment required; the self-respect and confidence of the wage earner is drained away; tensions in family relationships grow taut while the physical resources essential to patience fast dwindle; preventive and presently curative health measures are out of the question; there is increased pillaging of the loot of others on both petty and vast scales; reckless or bizarre or vicious or degenerate forms of temporary escape from misery are resorted to; the hard, daredevil cynicism of disillusionment incloses like a cemented vault the humanness of spirit. Many families are now tried beyond their limit of resistance and endurance. Many, many young people long postpone or give up the thought of establishing a family, only to be faced with the corresponding problems connected with personal relationships of a fortuitous sort.

The discipline of the depression seemed for a short time to stir a realization that there must be worked out some basic approach to this crisis of the family, but this effect of the depression is fast dissolving. Enough bubbles of favors and sops and gilded hopes are being blown about to divert attention from the fact that so far we are essentially in the same place where we were before. We don't stop to realize that always in times of those socioeconomic crises which came earlier in national history there were new horizons to explore and exploit open to those families who were dissatisfied or broken, whereas today there are none such. We are now forced to handle the problem instead of moving away from it. We are faced with the task of building an order that provides for the needs, functions, rights, and fulfillment of the family on the human level.

DISREGARD FOR HUMAN LIFE

The world has gone so mad over its new tools, its new magnitudes of power, its monstrous mechanical structures, playthings, and laboratories, that it has much neglected the most important thing on earth—human life. Yet the great concern of the family, the prime medium with which it works, is this human life. In a countless myriad of ways and places we see all sorts of things reckoned as of prime importance and human life reckoned as nothing at all. An automobile factory regularly keeps its men at the acetylene torches overlong, because it dares just now so to use "labor" (human life). War is enriching to armament manufacturers or is used as a ruse by a dictator to keep the attention of his subjects off his economic failure; and the loss of "soldiers" (human life) is an incidental corollary. Many of the children at the radio laugh and thrill only when "somebody" (a human being) is killed every minute in the lurid tale being told. Certain procedures in some of our public schools are mechanistic means of more efficient "covering of the ground" without due concern to notice that it is with the fresh, keen mental eagerness and creative spirits of little children that the ground is all too often strewn when the curriculum has been completely run. There is an academic pose that regards as entirely out of caste any work that directly seeks to deal with human life in the light of human values rather than in the abstractedness of statistical tables. There are the dead bones of at least one person under the foundations of almost every institution that has sought to protect and promote human welfare, so hard is it to arouse modern support of culture-promoting agencies. Only when the controlling system of values of a nation is topped by a genuine and intelligent concern for human fulfillment rather than for self-power and individual aggrandizement, will there cease to be the violent, murderous strife and the stagnant, crawling rottenness of depressions.

The family most of all has the charge over human life. Because little children who are loved come into the home and then must eventually make their way out into the larger society, the family has a deeper concern for what that larger society is like in terms of human living than any other institution. Specialization marks the aims and activities of all other institutions—educational, scientific, economic, "cultural," political, and religious. Specializations are in constant danger of getting lost in fixed prejudices or vain abstractions or tangential skyrocketing. There must be some perpetual touchstone to which each specializing interest regularly resorts for testing its soundness in terms of human living. There must be some validated system of checks which restores balance, growth, integrity. Fundamentally, this touchstone is the evaluating means or agency that clarifies the relation which these specializations have with sound growth of personality and of group culture.

The family, most of all, should insistently push the use of such touchstones. Right now it is failing to do so in any telling degree, for it is lost in the swift transition that is going on. The old combination of conditions under which the homes more directly guarded and fostered human values has passed away. New, complicated, exceedingly difficult conditions exist today. The crisis shows here in the confusion of the family over how it is to meet its trust, or in discouragement in the effort, or in rationalized escape into an economic race or into a social whirl, or in a *laissez-faire* attitude functioning under a new label, "emancipation" of the individual. There are signs of new constructions by the family in this regard, but it has a colossal task in lifting concern for human fulfillment to the first place in the national system of controlling attitudes and in keeping it there. Fortunately the family has not only help but eminent leadership already at work on this task.

It is imperative to bear in mind, unceasingly, that the principal and prized medium of the family's work, human life, is not the principal and prized medium of most of the other institutions today. Each institution thinks its own medium of most significance and invests heavily in it. Then, because concern for their desired values so seldom includes concern for human life, there is a dangerous lack of recognition of the work of the family. This shows in the failure to give to homemaking the status of a business and a profession. Both parents and other business and professional groups so fail. In consequence, there is a general lack of an active sense of social responsibility in the matters of planning for, and of treating, the family as a basic cultural unit.

THE ALTERING MOTHER-FATHER RELATIONSHIP

As Benjamin Kidd,[2] John Macmurray,[3] and others have clearly pointed out, there has been for ages an impeding differentiation of function between the mother and father in family life. Typically, the father has gone out into the market place to sell his services, or has developed a business of his own, or otherwise taken up the economic support and connections for his family. In all but the most menial types of labor, this has meant an increasing specialization on his part, with a consequent opportunity

[2] *Science of Power*, Chap. VIII.
[3] *Reason and Emotion*, pp. 117-144.

for some degree of individual development, expression, and recognition. Further, men have learned that, as a result of their economic activities, they can acquire and keep control over many of the activities of society. Exploiting to their own best advantage this opportunity, men have developed largely a man-made society which not only restricts first-rate opportunity and recognition pretty largely to masculine types of strength and specialization, but even bars women from those activities where there is strong reason to believe that their contribution would be superior to that of men in certain important respects. One hundred or more years hence when our descendants look back at those men of today who are trying to keep the world under arbitrary masculine control, they will chuckle and say, "My, but they took themselves seriously!" And it will be as funny as looking back now to the time when certain earlier men classified women with idiots, Chinese, and minors in the matter of political enfranchisement. But it's not so funny now. Incidentally, it is strange that the professions connected with the two areas where one would expect most enlightenment and human justice, higher education and religion, are among the worst in this matter of self-interested masculine arbitrariness of control. Practically, then, when we look to see just what kind of a man-made world has developed for human beings to live in, we know that something is terribly wrong.

The mother until recently has occupied herself with the family and with those community interests that were most intimately allied. She has been regarded as the custodian, for the family and to some extent for the community, of the moral and spiritual values of human living. Her own living has had to be generalized rather than specialized, for she has had to carry on simultaneously a great diversity of vocations in order to officiate in her function as mother. Consequently the average mother has not been able to develop specialized distinction of person and so express herself in ways that would bring recognition. She has been at the service of her family. Her efforts have been scattered widely to meet the demands of a woman's workday which has never been delimited as to hours or types of service. In earlier days this meant the running of a rather complex industrial organization on the home place, whereas today it is more likely to mean meeting the demands made upon her through her responsibility for preparing her family for their various outside activities. By the school, by the clubs, by the church, by music teachers, by dentists, everywhere she is told what is expected of her. A great many mothers think no farther than to try to live up to these external orders, or even snobbishly or childishly to compete with other mothers in the pace.

Now, however, there are an increasing number of women who are refusing both to dissipate their energies by trying to meet the disjointed requirements of a generalized existence, and to carry for all mankind the interests and activities included in what is sometimes called "the finer things of life." They feel that they are persons no less than men. They have come to realize that much of the arbitrariness of men over the opportunities open to women is slavery, less spectacular but more widespread and inescapable than was slavery of the Negro in the South. They are insisting that they be freed from these artificial and arbitrary restrictions, and that they have the equal right both to develop and express their distinctiveness and to receive recognition for their achievements. They see that the slavery of women has disrupted even their marital relations frequently. They have found out that family life, where there is this marked specialization in the functions of father and mother, results all too often in a widening gap in the personal relations of husband and wife. In the early days of marriage, because of newness of the relationship, they *do* share little, and later, because of diverging specialization of functions and hence of interests, they *can* share very little. The sense of equality and of deepening fellowship cannot then grow.

To be sure, large numbers of these women have failed to be very intelligent in their rebellion: many a one sets out to see how much of a man she can be. The majority do not yet realize that the task awaiting is to explore experimentally for a sounder basis for the sharing of function between father and mother on one hand, and for a sounder fellowship between husband and wife on the other. So, when we look at many of the woman-made homes we live in, we feel just as we felt when we looked at the man-made world we live in, that something is terribly wrong.

Here are serious materials in the crisis. Women are refusing to be shoved into a corner, however lovingly. No longer will they remain cooped up there to carry on the generalized activities of the race while being belittled repeatedly by the chanticleers of the world. They have heard so much loud crowing about women's failure in specialized achievement that many of them have at last taken heed of it. Some have taken heed as *women*, accepting the derogatory masculine judgment as a personal challenge to specialize and succeed. Others have taken heed as *homemakers*, feeling free to treat as relatively inconsequential this discredited business of homemaking, and consequently free to spend their energies on individualistic interests or various popular forms of mental chewing gum.

If women refuse to bear alone any longer this ancient responsibility of guiding the emotional development and of protecting the refinement of personality, how can it be done? Men and women together must do the work. On the one hand, both must act in the light of the requirement that the specialized activities of the world be so organized and operated that they serve ultimately to help actualize the possibilities of human living. This posits participation of both men and women in these *specializations of culture* on the basis of organic (though not identical) equality. On the other hand, both must act in the light of the requirement that the family be so organized and operated that it fosters the highest possible development and integration of the personality of *every one* of its members. This implies participation of both fathers and mothers in the *generalized activities inevitable in family nurture*, on the basis of organic (though not identical) equality. All men and women, whether within or outside the family, must recognize that only in the highest development of the family can any culture find its deepest roots and its finest fruits.

At present men must work under such deadening tension in building their man-made economic and political world that they get far away from the vital centers of life. Their building does not fulfill the cultural requirement of producing universally abundant life. Further, they themselves are cut off from revitalizing and equilibrating experiences. Reciprocally, all the intimate community associations need men members as much as women members. A child needs a father fully as much as a mother. Again, children bring up their parents just as really as parents bring up their children, and fathers need bringing up as much as do mothers. The father's rights and development in this *vital* respect need attention.

Similarly, if the mother is to be able to have rich and challenging fellowship with her husband and children, she will have to have some freedom for her own distinctive development. As a person she must have the experience of equality in status, power, and opportunity. Also, she needs keen functional interrelations with the world that is changing so necessarily fast for the sake of her family as well as herself. The mother's rights and development need greater attention in these matters of an *organizational* type.

This complex world needs the presence of both men and women in every type of interest and activity. Not in every capacity nor not on the present sex-competitive basis should such universal cosexual cooperation be established. The basis must be deep organic equality where consideration is given to all present and probable values involved in the various human aspects of this problem—the capacities, development, functions, relationships, status, and contributions of both men and women. It is too soon to point to current happenings as validated indices upon which to work out a plan. What we see now are only symptoms that realization is growing that the present status cannot continue. Current happenings are largely confused, random thrusts toward something not yet thought through to the point where it can be clarified into tentative plans of cosexual cooperation on the basis of organic (though not identical) equality.

OTHER ACTIVATING FACTORS IN THE CRISIS

Consideration of the foregoing conditions brings with it the necessity of facing more and yet more factors in the present crisis of the family. No less important than the items already discussed are such matters as the unpredictable shifts in social interest with the consequent avalanche of shifts in population, in vocational education, and other tangible outcomes; the greatly increased tempo in all branches of associational living; the fiercely weaponed coercion of minority-group pressures; and the many changed, and hence hardly distinguished functions of the family. Nor are these all. From whatever angle one approaches the family circle, different factors become evident, but enough have been cited to indicate the nature of the emergency in which the family finds itself.

UNWIELDINESS OF THE PROBLEM

The stresses within the family and the strains from without are shaking it to its very foundations. However, it is an institution which has been a-building for thousands of years. It has custody in the most effective way yet discovered over the essential human satisfactions as well as over many important acquired ones. Such an institution does not die easily nor quickly. The modern family has serious faults and still more serious handicaps. It needs critical analysis and reorganization in a number of aspects. At present it would seem that most of the forces impinging upon the family are centrifugal ones which, gathering force and speed, are causing such a suction against its inner bonds as threatens to explode it into bits. But also there are centripetal forces already in action, and more which can be rallied to the work of reconstruction.

It is painful to think how long this reconstruction of the family may take when one realizes that it depends in substantial part upon a reorganization of the present industrial system. This system has wrecked and will wreck countless families through strain of unhealthy conditions of work, unemployment, overtaut nerves, untreated disease, poverty, insecurity, and other forms of disaster due to the irresponsibility of the system for its effect upon the individual and the family. Ghastly and dangerous features of this economic aspect of the family crisis are far from over.

The other cultural problems involved in this crisis, which we have been considering, also embody widespreading, deeply penetrating social ramifications. They call for changes in our attitudes and objectives, our training and our procedures, our ideas and

our systems of value, which in turn require complicated, under-
girding social processes. A myriad of daily incidents is causing
thoughtful persons to view the crisis of the family with deepening concern. They see that the crisis of the family is both cause
and effect of a great cultural crisis involving our whole civilization.

This is the pattern of intricately interrelated problems which
the church must take into account when it attempts to serve the
family. Discouragingly ineffectual must be the few sporadic attempts made by the church to serve the specific difficulties of
specific families unless it envisages this cultural setting in which
the problems arise.

Chapter II

LONG-TERM PROBLEMS OF THE FAMILY

THE forces producing acute cultural transition ravage society as a storm plays havoc with a great river, lashing its surface into unnavigable roughness topped with debris, scum, and foam, and rendering it turgid through erosion of the banks which formerly had set its confines. Yet at the same time, other forces long responsible for producing the currents which give the river its particular characteristics are continuing. Even these are disturbed unquestionably by the storm: nevertheless they hold their general course. Because this is a particularly long, painful, and dangerous transitional period for our society the American family is primarily conscious of suffering a severe crisis, a number of aspects of which we have been discussing along with their devastating effects upon the home. But another group of forces, like the changing yet perpetual currents of the river, continue to shape the family and affect its character. This latter group of forces are those which determine the prevalent cultural level of American life. Certain of the problems and obstacles with which individual families are now dealing are not due primarily to the current crisis, but rather are outcomes of the nature and level of general cultural standards attained and maintained by our country.

This cultural level functions in daily life as mental set and emotional set. Individuals born into a certain cultural level develop the sets that characterize it without knowing it. They assume that "this is just the way life goes," unless by some chance or under some leadership they experience some cultural contrast which cracks the set. Just as plant and animal structures became fossils in a bed of gravel and ooze, so these sets tend to fossilize in the various traditions, precedents, organizations, arrangements, classifications, manufactured equipment, customs, ordinances, and rituals by which society flows around and fits itself to the sets.

Certain areas of our prevalent culture have attached to them a number of mental and emotional sets which materially affect family life. Citing a few of these areas will illustrate: the relative importance of individual contentment as over against responsibility for voluntarily assumed parental contract; the national status of child life; the status of homemaking among other vocations; conditions and control of city planning and of housing; the status of women; public appropriation for education as over against that for vice and crime; and legal effort to reduce the handicaps and hazards of the family. There are always vested interests that spare no pains to keep the sets solid. Besides this factor, there is one even more deadening: indifference. Added to these are other hindrances to development—procrastination, inertia sometimes known as social laziness, and shrinking fear of change. Despite all this, the cultural current does keep moving, though like that odd river in Victoria, it may flow toward the ocean now, and away from it again.

Since society is changing continuously, each institution must be ever changing, also. This must mean a continuous reevaluation and reformulation of the underlying concepts, the governing attitudes, the functions, the standards, and the techniques of these institutions. This process must issue in fresh examination and ordering of the provisions for educational preparation of those who carry out the functions of these institutions.

The chief long-term handicap under which most of us are suffering is due to a lag in educational preparation for participation in a society where the one thing that can be counted upon is change. Our handicap consists in living under a controlling attitude which is a hang-over from days before we were born. This attitude sets us to striving "to get things going smoothly" as the sure prerequisite for reaching the acme of satisfaction and success in living. We have a mental and emotional set against interruptions, problems, and reason-controlled social experimentation. This is fossilizing. In place of this old, persisting attitude heading up into its paralyzing ideal of perfectionism, we must develop a newer and truer controlling attitude—"to get things growing meaningfully." Once this newer attitude begins to function, we shall stop wasting time in deploring changes that bestir us. We shall cease harking back to times when things went pretty well without all these modern performances and notions. No longer shall we feel somewhat indignant because confusion and problems mark our days in spite of our sincere "good intentions," our proper efforts in living.

Certainly we shall still suffer and yearn, but we shall understand that continuous change must mean continuous readjustment, and this readjustment must be more than mere accommodation or compromise if it is to yield finer meanings in living. In turn, continuous readjustment involves frequent confusion, for confusion is the first symptom of the immanence of a problematical situation. This new controlling attitude of expecting growth and of readiness in providing the conditions that foster it involves then also the attitude of expecting problems—the more growth, the more problems and the more of resilience and creativeness in dealing with these problems. It is really the attitude of going out gallantly and adventurously to meet life, knowing that it will be full of change and hence full of challenge.

The lack of this controlling attitude—i.e., expectation of continuous change, hence of numerous problems, hence of opportunity for growth, hence of emergence of new meanings—is a chief present cause of the failure of the family to meet the difficulties of its time and place. The members of the family take it for granted that there are certain mystical yet infallible patterns which, automatically, will shape all their experiences so that they will "come out all right," or "live happily ever after," or "settle down and have things run smoothly." This is on a parallel with the faith of many an American citizen that there is a United States government hovering somehow over Washington which will run according to the Constitution and his individual ideas of the best standards while he gives his attention to his own private business. "It was all fixed once, now why can't it go?"

But there aren't any mystical, yet dependable, patterns that invisibly shape the family toward success and effectiveness. Each couple who marry are setting up an entirely unique combination, the exact like of which has never existed before. Further they are setting it up in a locale and a habitat that are also different in some degree from those of any other marriage. It is the responsibility of all appropriate social agents to teach the uniqueness of living and to foster and strengthen in the family a controlling attitude that seeks the growing edge in every problem and difficulty.

Patently there are a greater number of specific, long-term obstacles to the effectiveness of the family than can be here presented. Below are cited some of the more outstanding ones which have been brought to light through a long period of psychological work dealing with problems of family adjustment and with projects in parent education.

SOME SPECIFIC PROBLEMS

Camouflaged Initiation of Marriage

Our young people enter the marriage relationship with many illusions, delusions, and confusions regarding marriage and homebuilding. Society throws up a showy screen composed of wedding bells and bouquets, showers, smart doings, and other superficial externalities which keep the minds of the young people diverted from the real issues involved. After a few artificial, conventional gestures, the average couple enter the most difficult of human relationships. No one seems disturbed over their ignorance concerning the requirements and significance of their new life. Many parents will spend from fifty to five thousand dollars on the wedding fete, but not one penny on appropriate education for marriage. The fact that the couple love each other is supposed to provide sufficient equipment and technique to insure success. Their early experiences in adjustment more times than not are marked by unnecessary difficulty, misunderstanding, and suffering. Most counselors assert that the experiences of the first few months of married life tend to condition all the years that follow.

Now necessarily, since each couple is a unique combination, there will have to be a period of adjustment early in marriage where many efforts will not be marked by instant or even partial success. But if the young people know what factors are involved, and, even more important, if they realize that it is the rightful expectation that adjustment in marriage is not a happening but an achievement, they can experiment with more judgment and composure of spirit. They need to realize that all new human relationships that have any intimacy of fellowship require an experimental and a creative approach. Where such preparation of expectations prevails their attention is engaged in discovering the conditions and procedures for their mutual experiment in finding the richest approaches to their common life rather than calculating the individual satisfactions each is getting out of marriage.

Then, too, if the young people have learned that, fortunately, there is no such thing as a perfect mating, they can take a more constructive attitude toward their communal enterprise. It is the very differences in each that provide one great source of diversity and richness in interests, skills, ideas, appreciations, and ideals which square or cube the values possible in the common life. Where the greatest returns from marriage are sought, the aim is not to agree in everything but to make the differences yield value. Because this is not widely understood, many a member in a family feels deeply hurt whenever another who he thought loved him disagrees with him. If there were such a thing as a perfect mating, then adjustment would be quick and easy and there would be nothing left to do all the rest of married life but just jog along together, half-dead and wholly bored. Five minutes' effort at conversation with a jogging couple that "never had a disagreement in their whole married life" is enough to cure any desire for this form of doubled stupidity.

Our customs and our fiction tend to represent the process of becoming engaged as the more thrilling and adventurous part of the mating experience, with the marriage ceremony as the grand finale. This is topsy-turvy. The process of getting engaged, when undertaken with a somewhat adequate realization of the possibilities marriage holds for either a veritable heaven or hell, must be regarded as a highly interesting, yet very difficult and responsible, preparatory period only. It is preliminary to the real adventure, initiated through marriage, of building experimentally and creatively a meaningful common life in the cultural unit called the family. If neither one loses the way, there's incalculable thrill and joy—yes, and strain and sorrow—in this partnership when undertaken as experiment and growth.

Chasing the Will-o'-the-Wisp, Happiness

The majority of married couples still consider individual happiness to be the paramount criterion of success in marriage and family life. Through, lo, these thousands of years, men upon proposing to women have promised to make them happy. Women tend still to believe this, though it is a promise that has never been kept and never can be. Times without count, this promise has been resurrected to taunt a lonely bitterness or to bring to white heat an angry retort. No one can *make* anyone else happy. It is true that other persons can do things which provide conditions that help or hinder the securing of happiness, but happiness is an individual and inner *achievement*.

A most frequent plaint with which a consultant opens his case of marital maladjustment runs like this, "But I'm not happy!" Now when he is asked what he set out to achieve in marriage, he looks blank. "Achieve? Why, nothing special. Just to be happy, you know. I have a right to expect that, haven't I?" In most instances it turns out that what the individual really wanted was not true happiness but a passive, blissful state where all his expectations were regularly met, even though many times he himself could not tell without the help of probing questions what these were. In other words, he did not want ever to be disappointed in anything. He was still a spoiled baby.

Now marriage and homemaking are the most unpromising relationships to go into if one is looking for the passive bliss of never being disappointed, disregarded, or depreciated. And all emotional infants who are seeking this form of blissful coma should be told so. Happiness is quite a different experience from indulged contentment. Happiness comes in just one way. It comes when one, having chosen an objective which he feels is of worth, discovers that he is making progress toward that objective. Of course where a couple or a family have chosen a common goal and do make progress toward it, each individual experiences happiness not only for himself but through sensing his unity in happiness with others. Thus happiness is attainable by every family, happiness in different degrees and quality, to be sure, depending upon the richness of their objectives, but happiness nevertheless.

Blundering Relationships

Marriage and family life produce a battery of diverse and difficult tests for proving the individual in the matter of his ability to associate with others. How meaningfully, how creatively, how joyously can he participate in the communal life? It takes only a glance at the characteristic combinations of persons in the family to stimulate the memory to recall instance after instance of such testings within one's own circle. Husband-wife, parent-child, child-child, father-daughter, mother-daughter, mother-son, father-son—these are but the beginning of the comprehensive list of possible combinations. What is more, each of these relationships is experienced by persons other than the principals directly involved in each combination. A child may suffer severely when he witnesses a break in relationship which involves a parent, and vice versa.

Here are a few flashing glimpses of some of the dangerous strains and blunders in family relationships furnished by the testimony of case studies:

Husband-wife combination: growing apart because of no sharing of interests that really count in life; estrangement because one persists in treating the other according to what he has conceived as the pattern of this other and so cutting off the other from freedom to be himself; miserable sex relations because they are mechanical or lustful or despised or fraught with fear, resentment, or dissatisfaction; unsuspected pose of superiority in one so that without thought he assumes advantages, tributes, and exemptions for himself while belittling or betraying his mate, often doing so subtly under the semblance of faultless devotion.

Parent-child combination: utilizing the child as a source of pride in display or of selfish emotional satisfaction or of entertainment; exploiting the affection of the child for the parent as a club of control over him so that conditions will be conformable, comfortable, and appropriate from the point of view of the parent; making the child egotistical through babying or indulging him, or through asking his opinion in matters not appropriate for him to pass upon; gullibility in the parent (often rationalized as "trust in the child") which tempts any ordinarily intelligent child to work the parent for what he wants; treating the child as a little tin god or as something rare; standing between the child and the consequences of his dispositions and deeds so that the child blames the environment entirely for his maladjustments instead of realizing his need to develop increased self-responsibility and self-discipline; using loss of parental love as a threat.

Besides these immediate family relationships, there are many intermediate ones: husband and wife with relatives-in-law; wife with men other than her husband; husband with women other than his wife; parents with neighbors; husband with his group of personal friends, and wife with her group; children with neighbors. The reverberations of creative fellowship or of serious disturbance or of break in any one of the family relationships may shake through any and all of the others, depending upon just what combinations are in association at the time. Since human beings communicate through symbols, it takes very little personal expression to affect relationships potently.

In most instances of blundering relationship in the family, there is conspicuous lack of persistent, intelligent effort either to clarify the valid bases of the trouble or to discover the most significant and satisfying forms for reconstructing the relationship. Rather there tends to be a silent (or almost silent!) amassing of disappointment or resentment or disgust over a period of time until finally some trivial, precipitating event explodes it all loose in a devastating storm. Then, to increase the wreckage, the participants usually fail to understand that the storm is largely the eruption of riled feelings by the person who is suffering rather than an indication of the rational bases and nature of his grievances and difficulties. Not only is much human energy so wasted, but many worth-while bonds are permanently shattered past repair though they could have been kept growing if the family had made it their business to understand the principles and processes involved in human relationships.

Confused Individuals

Today there are fewer generally established standards and sanctions by which the individual may organize his personal living. On the other hand, there are a vastly increased number of possible choices of conduct and of plan demanding his decision. In brief, he has fewer guides for his self-organization and behavior, yet a greater number and variety of situations in which he must behave. This means that the individuals who make up the modern family group tend to exhibit more types and degrees of personal disorganization than was true fifty or a hundred years ago, when the conditions of living were less swift and complicated while community sanctions were more fixed and rigorous. The more personal disorganization, the less chance there is of family effectiveness in at least two ways. First, the load of the family is increased —there are more instances of individual maladjustment with which the family must deal. Second, maladjusted individuals generate additional conflicts involving sometimes only members of the family, but sometimes outside persons.

On beyond this disparity between the increase in the choices that have to be made and the guidance available in evaluating choices, there is a still more portentous source of confusion. It is the tumultuous, tortuous jungle grown up in the unplanned, uncultivated aspects of our society, in which lurk and stalk human hogs and beasts of prey. Jungle conditions tend to frustrate the choices of those who are not mighty and swift according to its standards, or to demonstrate the futility of choosing certain courses of action known to be highly worthy. The future seems to be in jeopardy for many individuals; yet without an objective, without a destination, it is easy to become a wanderer, a derelict, an opportunist, or a rotter. A new type of slavery is growing up in our midst in this country. It is the arbitrary control of certain of the conditions essential to living on the human level by groups who have monopolized power over natural and technological re-sources. The chains and whips are invisible, but the effects of this slavery upon personalities and culture are not.

To cite just one group who are suffering from this modern version of slavery: there is an increasing mass of young persons who are forced to postpone or give up marriage and the estab-lishment of a home because of the economic shackles that are upon them. Now, the dreams and visions of future achievements based upon the more serious choices of life are chief activators of intel-ligent self-discipline in any youth. Take away these and self-discipline almost vanishes. The heartbeat of his loyalties, even his loyalty to himself, grows dangerously weak. Here and there a rare youth sees beyond his own plight and gives his loyalty to the cause of breaking up the jungle conditions which enslave many men and women, young and old. In fact, more and more young people of today are devoting themselves to this drive to-ward better social planning. All too many, however, are living messily. They are groveling in the confusion of a world that doesn't make room for the essential choices of young people.

While there are an increasing number of agencies which un-dertake to help confused individuals to organize their living, by far the bulk of this burden of readjustment must be borne by the family. Not many families, relatively speaking, have had the training either to see what the underlying problems are or to treat the individuals who are disorganized. This helplessness of the family increases the confusion, for it injects a disquieting fear for the security of family relationships. Nevertheless, in spite of all this strain, there are today, as always, family loyalties so real and so meaningful that they hold the essential unity through every disruption. In this there is a deep thrill for the heart of man.

Lack of Professional Attitude

There is little realization on the part either of homemakers or of the general public that homemaking is a tremendously big business due to the nature of the vocation itself and the many subvocations regularly involved in family life. The government, the school, and public opinion have classified homemaking as a rather casual, semiskilled occupation for which no standardized preparation is essential. Indeed, it seems to be assumed that in some magical way all the knowledge, attitudes, skills, standards, and ideals essential to success drip from the minister's fingers at the conclusion of the marriage ceremony.

There is no human relationship which requires for its fulfillment so much of art, science, character, philosophy, and religion as does the family. To presuppose that in the setting up and organizing of the family, the fellowship and inspiration of a newly fledged and uninstructed love is sufficient without administrative structure and method is to court disaster. The family, perforce, has many active interests, among them business, government, fine arts, friendly intercourse, recreation, hygiene and therapy, education, community planning, and religion. There is no one single scheme for the organization and procedures of the family which will enable it to meet the requirements of the several and differentiated functions which it must fulfill. Each of these needs to have its policies and procedures defined, its personnel organized, and its duties allocated in particularized and effective ways.

One of the first tasks which must be performed before homemaking can receive professional recognition is the formulating of the more basic norms that should guide the functioning of the family. Movement in this direction has already begun in several areas. Here are examples: working out of tables showing the ratio of expenditures for the various necessities (shelter, food, etc.) to the total income; growth charts for infants; development of tables showing minimum, balanced dietary requirements for growth; and marketing standards of several sorts.

It is natural that the first norms to be distinguished should apply to the more concrete aspects, for they are easier both to work out and to use. But there must be norms of one type or another to guide the less concrete items which include disciplining of children, social development, emotional maturing, religious conditioning, and the many other major concerns in family functions. No doubt there will have to be some new way of formulating norms in those areas where mathematical units of measurement will not serve directly, some method which will allow the norms to be relative and yet significant.

Increasingly essential in the professionalizing of homemaking is the instituting of more definite standards for licensing marriage. When one sets out to build a *house*, he very soon discovers that his community has set strict building ordinances which are rigorously enforced in regard to the use of such materials as brick, cement, lumber, conduit, and plumbing goods. But he finds no corresponding ordinances when he sets out to build a *home*, though this involves much more important and complicated material—human life. To our national discredit, anyone, be he mental defective, syphilitic, tubercular, criminal, or otherwise unfit (unless his case is so obviously serious as to require segregation) can get a license, marry, and control the lives of little children. So can others who are physically and mentally sound, but who know not one thing about the basic functions they are contracting to perform and fulfill. Every marriage of either of these sorts is a social liability.

The rise of the professional spirit in regard to marriage and family will insist upon two sets of ordinances regarding the licensing of marriage, one having to do with personal fitness, the other requiring a minimum in the way of specific educational preparation for marriage (such education to be made freely available, of course, in the system of public instruction). Unquestionably, the general public will have to be educationally prepared to appreciate these ordinances before they can be effectively instituted. This will be a case of reconditioning mental and emotional sets. It will have to be undertaken by those more intimate community institutions which are socially though not legally concerned and responsible.

Disconnectedness with Social Planning

The average family does not recognize that the great social changes now going on involve the home far more deeply than by merely reducing income and standards of living. This average family meets social change in whatever way it characteristically meets local difficulties. Commonly it takes all the vicissitudes that come as though they were a dose of bad medicine required in these times. It has no historic sense of the permanence of impression that endures through all social change.

Not being conscious of the onward sweep of social change, the family tends to follow, sheep-style, the fashions and patterns of social conduct devised by commercial interests to extort their tribute money, often congratulating themselves upon their modernity while they are being herded around despotically or milked. They mistake the shallow puddle of their faddish provincialism for the main stream of modern life. As a matter of fact, they know nothing of the deep, main current of modernity. Consequently, they neither do nor can make the contribution to the changing order which each generation of homemakers must make if the family is to maintain its required equilibrium and hold its rightful place among community institutions.

There are excitingly interesting developments to be worked out by those who know the functions to be fulfilled and have reason to care to have them fulfilled richly! Here are some areas that cry for intelligent, devoted study: new forms of housing; changes in emphases in family functions; practical floor plans for family dwelling, based upon the functions and interests of the modern home; methods of closer cooperation among community agencies concerned for family welfare; unique, appropriate solutions of the old problems of play space and privacy; the building of such forms for social participation as can be meaningful in spite of terrific pressures of time and group; greater availability of the resources of culture; balanced emphasis upon the function of the father in family living; the rescue of women from their gullible servitude to commercially generated and accelerated shifts in fashion; discriminative suggestions regarding changes in the institution of marriage; and methods of fostering the deeper currents of meaning and of strengthening the higher loyalties of life.

There is more fun and adventure in this progressive social reconstruction of family life and of the conditions affecting its operative environment than in all the home-centered industries and activities of the family of bygone days, and far, far more than in all the usual conventional activities of the much-dated, hypermobile modern woman. The family will have greater meaning and increased power when it is more validly and securely connected with the culture of which it is a part on bases that promote both its own fulfillment and its cultural contribution.

Increased Investment—Diminishing Returns

Many of those features of the average American home of fifty years ago which enhanced it in the hearts of its owners are no longer usual. Home then meant putting your roots down, having your own detached house with its garden front and back and perhaps a bit of orchard or woods. Deeper friendships grew where families were so rooted. All the family had common interests and many tasks and adventures together. Each one felt that he counted and that there was something to show for family endeavor. Those days were not halcyon, far from it. We need have no nostalgic longings. Often family and neighborhood relationships were tragically painful, frustrating, shattering. Often there were oppressive external limitations as to what the family could do and enjoy and achieve. However, many a family could see and feel itself grow rich in a hundred ways—treasured heirlooms, records, memories, rituals, celebrations, additions to their dwelling place, long-anticipated and cooperatively planned improvements, pets that survived long, favorite retreats, a host of endearing experiences.

Today one resides where his work is and in such shelter as he can afford. He doesn't know who built the particular cluster of holes in somebody's wall which serves as his apartment. If he has children, he has a hard time locating anywhere, and sometimes a harder time staying after locating! Marriage may have come late and the "nerves" of one or both parents are too taut to resist what they are called upon to stand. Moving may be frequent and the family may find it impossible to own a stick of furniture and consequently have to adapt itself to a very weird assortment. Quarters may be crowded. There may be no one with whom to leave the children to allow husband and wife opportunity for normalizing play. The children are bound "to catch something" or several somethings before they are through school. Work for both parents may be overtaxing. There's the problem of the children's higher education. Children are likely to be longer dependent upon their parents these difficult days. The future does not look secure. Perhaps the family can't trust the motives behind the advice of its own doctor or banker, grocer or lawyer. Hundreds of persons, it sometimes seems, are lurking in the shadows just out of sight, waiting to drain the pocketbook of the family should any one of them become ill, weak, or hurt, or should the plumbing get out of order, or father's suit grow shabby. On top of it all, there is an enlarging group of irresponsibles who laugh at anyone who is trying to live meaningfully in his family group in the midst of all the easy availability of diverting rackets and garishness. There's so little to tie to and there's no telling when even that little may vanish.

Where investment is high and continuous, there is bound to be expectation of reasonably comparable return. It takes real talent in a father and mother, and in the children when they are old enough, to locate and foster the values in modern family living. This is grimly true particularly among those families whose conditions of living are often totally unresponsive to their efforts, or even forbidding and destructive.

But even all this does not mean that the resources which the modern family has to invest are more limited and less desirable than those of the family of long ago. Actually, these modern resources are more difficult to get but more desirable when gotten. Naming a few of these may quicken exploration and creative imagination in this expanding territory. Open to our inventiveness and purposes are opportunities for wider, more selective fellowships for our children and youth; more self-conscious and hence better evaluated theories concerning growth of personality and processes of education; more leisure; superior books; easy transportation by automobile and streetcar for the family as a group to places of interest or play; wider acquaintance with significant social developments and events through improved public communication and transportation; greater accessibility to several forms of the fine arts and also the crafts; closer participation in the deeper issues of human living as being experienced in the larger society; less expensive yet improved tools and equipment to support the interests and projects of the family; some advance in practice as well as in theory in the democratic form of government in the small intimate group; a limitless variety of interests which may be shared; sounder conceptions regarding love, sex, obedience, sacrifice, and discipline as these enter into family relationships; and a dawning realization as to the dazzling possibilities available through our highly interdependent society once its technological facilities are assimilated and organized to promote human fulfillment instead of miscarrying into individualistic monopolies of power with their consequent depressions and oppressions.

In other words, quite new features are present in variety to enhance the modern home in the hearts of its members. Appreciative utilizing of them will require a change in the patterns of aspiration, activity, and satisfaction on the part of the family. The family must come to see that its community may liberate and equip the individual for a larger world instead of rooting him inextricably into the local group, and that it may find greater joy and reward in so doing.

The Uncoordinated Influences Shaping Youth

Because so many of the activities and relationships, toys and tools, of the young are located in scattered and unconnected centers in the community outside the home, the family feels increasingly frustrated in its efforts in social guidance. The sincere family hopes for the balanced, progressive integration and fulfillment of personality in its children. Many times this hope is evident chiefly in the form of militant eagerness to see to it that its own children receive "the best there is." Most often parents yearn to have their children "make the most of themselves." Yet as soon as the child moves into the larger community, he becomes subject to a haphazard assortment of influences which tend to break down his own distinctive self-organization and force him to meet first one and then another of divergent sets of group expectations and requirements.

Quite naturally the young person wishes to be acceptable to whatever groups hold the power to grant or withhold the satisfactions cherished at the time. When there are several groups, different in type, to which he is trying to conform, he becomes a chameleon-like multiple personality. Usually this is on a very superficial level rather than a pathological one. Even at that, the process of personal enrichment and maturing is retarded, for social conditions work against the organizing of the personality around any self-developing, self-enriching purposes. Or the pattern of the group may distort and destroy personality by calling for addiction to conventional vices, dissipation, or worse.

Year by year there are an increasing number of families who are experiencing continued anxiety, grief, and disaster in connection with this situation. Also they feel the helplessness of any one home in dealing with the problem. This must be so, for it is a group problem which must be handled in and by the groups involved. Some aspects of the problem can be met by groups of young people and their families working together, though usually the various groups of families will have to work with school, church, and other agencies. The enormous number and variety of community influences shaping youth must be cooperatively criticized, coordinated, and controlled as the major approach. Perhaps this is one of the first points where the family will enter with earnest drive into the reconstruction of society. The incentive is surely great enough—providing community conditions that promote rather than retard or destroy the progressive integration and fulfillment of youth.

A CONTINUING PROCESS

While these specific problems and others related to them are considerably intensified by the present cultural crisis, they existed long before we began to sense the crisis. Hence we may call them long-term problems. Forms, degrees, and distribution of them vary, and the list here is not complete, but the type has become sufficiently clear to disclose them as major sources of frustration, insecurity, discouragement, or failure in family life. These long-term problems are putting the family under handicaps which overtax it and frequently overpower it, yet all of them are either preventable or resolvable to some degree at the present time. They are fields where every family and every community institution can find interesting work to do which will be profoundly significant in the immediate situation and for the larger society.

As has been said, no one family unit endures for long. Families must work in groups, cooperatively. Further, these groups of families urgently need the sponsorship of one or more long-term institutions whose interests are inextricably bound up with their own to amplify the work for the betterment of the family and to give it continuity and power. One such long-term institution, so interested, already exists in the church. These needs and difficulties, with their emergent possibilities, should guide the church in shaping its policies and services in regard to family life. Its own fate as well as much that lies in the future of the American family will be worked out largely in terms of the nature and extent of the interaction between church and family in this matter of building better conditions for family life.

Chapter III

THE CULTURAL SIGNIFICANCE OF
THE FAMILY

SHOULD THE FAMILY SURVIVE?

THE question of the social worth of the family has been pressed for some years now and remains an unsettled one. The question of the social worth of marriage is closely bound up with that of the family. Whether viewed from the inside by individuals who are actual or prospective participants in the forming of a family, or from the outside by professional workers and social agencies who deal with marriage and the family, the answer to these questions is far from a convincing and whole-souled affirmation of worth. At one extreme are those who say that the family is a failure and that marriage is outmoded. At the other extreme are those who sentimentalize because of idealized memories of their own past experience. In the middle ground are the individuals and agencies who are thoughtfully pondering these questions.

The family is substantially responsible for many human ills, from fixated personalities to criminal delinquents, from dull living to vast cultural waste. We have indications to show that society is the poorer for the lack of contribution of countless individuals who have been rendered mute or slavish by family mismanagement. It may even be that the home should be blamed for the behavior, which is not yet humanly adult, of *some* of our community and government officials! All of us who deal professionally with the personal problems of adults have learned how frequently the family influences of childhood have played their part in present difficulties.

But however impressive are the testimonies and social costs of

49

family failings, they must not bring us to any final conviction until certain other elements that must affect the answer are given consideration.

First of all, we must strike out the testimonies of those who are unqualified to judge marriage and homemaking. Notable among these is that growing number of individuals who are wary of *any* situation which characteristically demands the assumption of responsibility. They are so skittish at the least sign of a requirement of increased self-control for social cause that they fail to look for the possibilities of greater value which always grow out of such control. Their revolt against marriage and homemaking is actually a revolt against any institutional control that limits their infantile type of "freedom." To be included, also, among those disqualified from bearing testimony are the thousands upon thousands who believe that marriage and the family are what they aren't, and go through life without ever learning what they truly are. They interpret under two severe handicaps: first, their expectations, being false, are repeatedly and severely disappointed; second, they fail to experience the indigenous values, for they do not know how these grow nor how to recognize them should they appear. There are others whose testimony is unintentionally but markedly false.

A second element which needs consideration is the type of institution with which we are dealing. The family is a social institution primarily, not an instrumental one. Its overarching function is the provision of the conditions for human well-being and fulfillment. This means primarily the conditions for the growth of culture in the most intimate social groups, not the instituting and running of the businesses which, when true to their fundamental function, provide the economic basis for this growth of culture. Being educational rather than technological or industrial, its measure of achievement must be in terms of *progress* in development, not *products* as end results. The chief material with which the institutions of marriage and family work is unique and developing human nature—no two individuals alike and no one individual alike twice; no two families alike and no one family alike twice. No other profession or industry has as its chief medium a material so plastic while still so self-initiating, so un-

predictable and unstandardized while yet so capable of constructive, meaningful, and enriching interaction with society. It is true,
of course, that some other professions and industries work with
human nature directly, but where they do, they limit the scope
of their work by restricting their dealings to certain ages, conditions, or interests of individuals: the family *cannot* so arbitrarily
restrict its jurisdiction and remain true to function. Add to this
the fact that the social web into which the members of the family
are constantly weaving is itself in a state of continuous change,
and the enormous intricacy and variability of the material with
which the family works begins to be appreciated. It becomes
obvious that the propensity for a modicum of problems and failings is inherent in family living. While decrease in the incidence
of these should be radical wherever all resources for helping the
family to help itself are made available, yet the nature of marriage and the family preclude any standard approaching infalli-
bility or frictionless, conflict-free tranquillity.

Thirdly, just appraisal must take note of the fact that family
influences are the prime foundation for innumerable present
worths in personal organization and social contribution. Even in
cases of maladjustment, there may be more indications of constructive family influence than of destructive, though these are
frequently overlooked because of the concentration of attention
upon the few acute aspects responsible for the immediate problem. The very fact that worthful work with human nature is the
normal expectation of the family is itself profound testimony to
the question. Because worthful work is expected of it, the family
is seldom cited for recognition or selected for statistical study of
its positively creative contributions. Great persons, great literature, and great art sound the truth here more often than a particular social worker or teacher rendered temporarily spot-blind by
the immediate behavior of some individual which rips across the
pattern of the social fabric.

The fourth element to be considered, before too much can be
said about the failings of the home, is the present cultural status
of marriage and the family. Several aspects of its status are particularly pertinent to our inquiry. To begin with, if an examination of our community institutions other than the family were

conducted solely through a study of their failings, would any one of them fare notably better than the family? City government, police protection, the public school, and social-welfare agencies are a few among the great number that could ill afford to have their social worth rated solely by such a study. We must see the family as a piece of the whole social fabric, much of which is not "ready for visitors." Further, we need to do for marriage and the family what some of the other institutions have done for themselves—assemble sound data on the successful accomplishments and constructive developments.

Another aspect of the cultural status of the family needs pondering. There is as yet no central organization of family life, which, from era to era, constantly watches over developments in the family, evaluates these, and fosters and conserves the best. What did the medical profession amount to before it developed its living nucleus? Certainly, it is true that there are still all sorts of physicians from mighty benefactors to criminals, from remarkable geniuses to greedy schemers. Even yet there are still an appalling number of failings. Do you hear cadavers groaning and skeletons rattling? And do you see certain medical groups selfishly imposing shamefully dishonest constraints upon new therapeutic techniques developing outside their craft? But on the whole there is not the least question but that the medical profession is a worthy social investment. Regardless of all the individual physicians who come and go, the living nucleus of the profession endures and steadily shoves the profession with relative efficiency ever a little farther on. Its conserving, fostering nucleus now includes standardized training schools, a body of recognized literature, research laboratories, some means of critical analysis of findings, professional requirements for admission, a body of ethics, and other carriers of its discoveries, theories, and practices. The family has not yet developed such a living nucleus, though its profession is far more complicated and requires, in the total, far more knowledge, skill, and art *in the fully effective fulfillment of its functions* than does the profession of medicine.

Another comment concerning the cultural status of the family has been made before in another connection. It is that the family is still a scattered, unorganized total of tiny cultural units, defenseless against the utilization, exploitation, disruption, and despoiling committed by irresponsible organizations and unscrupulous individuals—business, professional, and otherwise. There are among these irresponsible organizations even those who go so far as to use force to keep the truth from being taught in our educational institutions and to control legislation in their own interests and at the expense of human health and progress. Since the family, to exist, must interact with all these, and must do so many times without having any way of knowing what is being framed against it until after some irreparable damage has been done, it can at least be said that there are not two, but several, locations involved in this matter of placing blame for the failings of the family.

One last word on this aspect; at least half the time, judging by rough estimates based on many observations, the manifestations interpreted as failings of the family are really the failings of particular individuals and not those of the family. They are failings due to certain limitations or eccentricities or other abnormalities which were characteristic of the individual before he became a member in the family, or were developed outside the family group and are in no way due to his family membership. Demonstrably, some of these individual characteristics go back to his own childhood home and so still are failings of the family, his earlier family. But leaving these aside for the time, there are even then many failings due to abnormalities of the individual such as would get him into difficulty wherever he went among whatever persons. Two examples of these the young people describe as "football head" and "dementia peacocks." The family happens to be the particular grouping where these maladjustments come into disrupting evidence. Every organized group has its overfull quota of those personally unready for its requirements of association. The more intimate and constant the fellowship, the more serious are the forms in which the disruptions appear. Such cases of disruption must be clearly discerned as due to abnormalities or difficulties in the individual as an individual and not as a member of the family. Hence they are a problem of the family rather than a failure in it. The trail of the failing leads out somewhere else in society, to some other time and group.

All these considerations testify that this matt
the failings of the family, like all other vital issue
one. The activity of the family weaves a part oi
fabric as does all the rest of our group living, t
that the family's load of responsibility in the gro
sobering. Even with all the qualifying aspects
which have here been presented, it is not easy to
a wholehearted affirmative answer to the question as to the social
worth of the family by analyzing its social failings as over against
its achievements.

THE NATURE OF THE FAMILY

However, there is another approach to this question as to
whether the family should survive. It lies not in figuring the
balance sheet as to what have been the failings and successes of
the family in the past. As we have noted, even if we could get all
the data necessary to do this and could strike the balance, it would
not be conclusive, for along with these findings would have to go
a consideration of many other factors inseparable from them.
All analysis of areas of failure is illuminating and specifically helpful in developing working plans for corrective procedures, but it
is not the main consideration in accounting the cultural worth of
the family.

The real heart of the matter lies in ascertaining the essential
and distinctive functions of the family as a unit of modern culture. At any one time the family may be failing in its characteristic functions. But this is not so important to know as is the answer
to two questions: "Are these functions indispensable to the maintenance and growth of the finest aspects of our culture?" and
"Would these functions be either lost or seriously impaired if
they were not fulfilled by that particular social group, the family?" The best answer to these questions can be found through
a consideration of some of the major characteristic functions of
the modern family. In preparation for this examination, we shall
need to review the definition of family in order to bring clearly
to mind the nature of the family and to discover therefrom how
a family grows.

The family is that fellowship of parents and children, created and promoted through the sharing of vital interests, which initiates and individualizes growth of personality and a concomitant development of culture in the community.

Since the family is the *fellowship*, once it has come into existence, it abides always. No matter where its members happen to be geographically, they are culturally present in the fellowship. Too, the fellowship of the family is always in action, even at those times when there is no direct communication. Indeed, the fellowship *is* the interaction between and upon the members. Its form and content are always changing as interaction involves first one combination of persons and then another, and as it centers first in this situation and then in a quite different one. It must be appreciated that *all the members are changing all the time*, if in no other way than in growing older. Every change in any one member gets caught up into the interrelationships, sometimes directly, sometimes in ways so subtle as to be sensed rather than noted. It must be further recognized that *all family situations are changing continuously*, because society is perpetually changing. Every change leaves its mark upon the family fellowship, beneficial or detrimental. Yet through it all each true family carries its identity—the developed forms and qualities which distinguish its distinctive fellowship.

How Does the Family Grow?

The relationship within the family is not a thing, a definitely and finally established bond, but is a process which goes on continuously among persons. This process is the sharing of interests both on a voluntary and on a coercive basis. Ideally this sharing of interests expresses itself in such creative activities as tend to maintain, enrich, and promote the growth of meanings of life for *all* the members and for the environing community of which they are a part. When the interests shared are many and vigorous and significant, the relationship waxes warm and secure and precious. When the interests shared are few or weak or trivial the relationship wanes, gets thin and illusory, becomes mechanized. When no new interests emerge, the relationship stiffens into conventionalized routine. New interests shared bring zest and the sense of adventure and possible achievings, for they stimulate new combinations in relationship and hence new sensitivities within each party to it: they tap the energies of different abilities and drives: they demand fresh organization and forms of interaction.

Meaning grows for the individual and for the group only when new connections are discovered which are appreciated. Whatever I see which holds deep meaning for me does so through virtue of the connections which it has with interests already treasured within me. Two boys see a man a block away: one cries in alarm, "A cop!" and turns and runs back; the other cries in delight, "Dad!" and runs ahead. Both were correct in their recognitions, but each had a different set of connections tied in with this particular figure of a man, and the total of his own personal connections gave the figure its meaning for each.

When a family shares many and significant interests over a long period of time, there grows up a great interweaving of countless connections within each one and between them all. It reaches the place where the sight or sound of some one slight thing—a picture of a gnarled tree, a peculiar cough, the whistling of the wind—has in it the power to set going a whole pageant of activities that made up some nebula of shared interests in earlier family life. The warmth of the emotional concomitants of such experiences years after personal separation demonstrates how much potential had been generated by these meaningful connections that got built up slowly in family fellowship. Every family that is effectively functioning is continuously discovering new sorts of connectedness in the various activities of life. When many of these are discovered and appreciated in common, they become a strong bond as well as strong potential in motivation.

As the range of interests which engage the family extends in ever widening circles, its requirements become more and more interwoven with those of the community in which it lives. Then the same sort of thing begins to happen between the members of the family and the community that is happening within the family. However, the richness of meaning in the connections with the community is seldom so great, for the associations are usually not nearly so constant nor intimate. On the other hand, though, it frequently comes about that something that had treasured meaning for the family group will be appreciated in an entirely different light when it is caught into the wider and more complicated connections of the larger community. Values formerly implicit may become explicit and revelatory.

It must be understood that the sharing of interests does not mean that literally everyone in the family is always working or playing or studying together in the family group whenever any interest is being fostered. There are times when the sharing means exactly this, being in the same spot and doing the same thing together. But it can also mean that each one so organizes his own time, resources, and energy that his activities are reinforcing to one or more of these shared interests. When Ted is enthusiastically careful of his trousers that are getting a little weak in the knees but must go until the first of the month, he is sharing an interest to which all pledged themselves at last family council when the family budget was discussed. When Jane digs into her algebra day after day and finishes her work by the time the school year is over, she is sharing with the family their interest in an early summer, all-family camping trip. Or it may be that it is with her teacher that she is sharing a common interest as she works. Or again it may be with both family and teacher.

One thing more about this fundamental process of sharing interests. If the activities are vital and creative, this will mean that new elements will be appearing, strange factors, or unexpected difficulties. In other words, problems will be frequent in such a relationship. But they will be welcome when the group comes to realize that new elements, even in the form of problems, carry possibilities of greater and richer meaning in life. Something new is emerging which must be understood, must be worked with, and must be integrated into the whole. To say that problems will be welcome does not mean that always they will be enjoyed. Often they will involve disappointments, discouragement, or serious trouble. But "welcome" means only that the problems will arouse alert anticipation of opportunities for exploring for greater values. Each unexpected, difficult, or thwarting problem will be taken as a signal that new factors or combinations have been overlooked or are on the point of emerging. Experience will develop the insight that problems are announcements that there is pressing need of closer cooperation, keener group analysis, freshened sensitivities and appreciations, and loyal devotion. Problems are always challanges to hunt for truth, to discover new, richer connections.

The Mark of a Genuine Family

The family is in essence, then, a fellowship which, acting through a great variety of combinations and modes of sharing significant interests, fosters growth and fulfillment in every member and yields meanings, increasingly diversified and rich, for all its members and for their larger community.

How much of a genuine family any one small group actually is will depend then, if these considerations are sound, upon how much of this type of fellowship is operative within that group. Going through the form of getting married and the ordeal of having a baby does not automatically make a family. It provides the essential persons, but they must achieve the fellowship distinctive of a family before they are a family in spirit and in truth. A man may have in his possession every large and tiny portion of a great tree that has been chopped down and sawed into pieces, so that every piece may be fitted together again into the form of a tree. But what the man has is only wood, whatever it may look like. To be a tree all those large and tiny parts would have to be in *interacting* relation with one another and with their operative environment. So it is with the family. It isn't a family until the personal factors, the three or more members, are in interacting fellowship with one another and with their operative environment.

After the relationship has been truly established, even absence or death cannot stop entirely the fellowship with the one removed, for his membership is still active in the group in many ways. His participations in the family fellowship take place through such representations as these: his image in the sense of what he himself was really like; various symbols of the part he had come to have in the family; such tools and articles as he had made; and some of his standards, preferences, and points of view.

There are many ways in which this fellowship characteristic of the family can be perverted and rendered void. Wherever there exist great possibilities, they are possibilities for both evil and good. In this relationship called the family there are unlimited possibilities. This territory of human relationship is only beginning to be scientifically charted, though great literature has many accounts of rich experiences here.

ESSENTIAL FUNCTIONS OF THE FAMILY

It would be presumptuous for any individual to formulate a Magna Charta for the family based upon his private views of the rights and duties of the family. For one thing, there cannot be any complete and final formulation of the functions, because the family and its social environment are changing all the while. Secondly, the area of family life involves so many factors that the combined contributions of many approaches are required to secure a balanced view of it. In the last analysis, the essential functions are *discovered*, not set up, and search for these, to be valid, requires long study of the actual workings of the interacting fellowship which is the family in all the varied processes and interests that go to make up the home. Every sincere effort to distinguish the functions as clearly as possible is profitable, however, for it prepares the way for the discovery of the norms needed for guiding and appraising the behavior of the family. Like the functions, the norms are *discovered* not invented. They are discovered in the functions by ascertaining what is required for the fulfilling of the functions. The exploration of the functions of the family for the purpose of discovering the norms is one of the most intriguing fields beckoning to modern social explorers.

There is, of course, no walled-off territory wherein each function is in process of fulfillment. Each function in some degree involves or posits the others. Each is a group of processes which make up the whole process. Out of many possible ways of expressing and grouping the functions, the following scheme has been developed because it emphasizes the nature and the progressive growth of the interacting fellowship which is the essence of the family. The thirteen functions presented show the gradual concentric enlargement of group consciousness in the family from the first, tiny, close group of three to the mature, world-interlocked group whose vision of the human universe extends far beyond physical sight. These thirteen functions are distributed into three groups according to the focus of their prime concern.

Group A. Three Functions Centered in the Welfare of the Child

1. *Regulated Transmission of Social Heritage*

The family launches the socializing process of each new member, and selectively extends it for those already initiated. The family conserves and makes available the more intimate and particularized features in this heritage, and so tends to keep it richer in diversity of interests and expression.

Usually this is done wholesomely through (1) unself-conscious sharing of what is meaningful to the parents rather than by the deliberate setting of example, and (2) regulating the availability of the various features of the social heritage according to the developmental level of the child. When successful, this socializing process makes the child more than an individual. He progressively becomes a person. Most of the attitudes and ideals of his later life are rooted in these earliest years of living with adults who tend to weight his experiences according to their own convictions regarding the meanings and values of life.

The family also provides the meeting place of the conservative social element, adulthood, and the radical social element, youth. Unless the resulting tension is arbitrarily repressed, this issues in a frequent reappraisal of the possibilities and limitations available in the social heritage. Such enforced analysis fosters better regulated social growth in both the younger radical and the older conservative elements.

Chief dangers are (1) false or provincially prejudiced transmission; (2) incomplete of impoverished transmission; (3) inappropriate or ill-conducted transmission.

2. *Responsible Control of the Conditions of Growth*

Because they love the child, the parents are sensitive to the relation between the conditions all about him and his development. For them it becomes necessary to examine and test all the operative conditions and to become informed and skillful in fostering the right conditions. There are two chief avenues for this endeavor. One is the actual building up of the indispensable conditions in the home. The other is the selection of the right conditions from among all those already provided by forces outside the home and the building of connection between these and their own children. In the rural home the former avenue of effort is likely to predominate; in the urban home, the latter.

Chief dangers are (1) oversolicitude, too much parental direction; (2) relationship based upon domination and subjection; (3) control over the child instead of over the conditions affecting his growth; (4) blind acceptance of conditions traditionally or fashionably held to be "good."

3. *Equipping the Child with the Tools Indispensable for Modern, Complex Living*

Some of these indispensable tools are the following: techniques of problem-solving; the habit of success (closely related to the previous); a sound self-estimate; high sensitivity to order (in the sense of perceiving germane and essential interrelationships); educated social good will; masterly proficiency in at least two skills, one vocational, one avocational; a reasonably adequate scale of values for making choices; self-built foundations for a valid, working philosophy of life.

There must be two sets of cultural tools in every youth's kit: one set containing all those generally needed by everyone living in this milieu; a second set, supplementary to the first, containing all those particularly needed by himself. This latter set is made necessary by the unique combination of characteristics, both aptitudes and limitations of the individual child. All the institutions for nurture will help in equipping children with the first set, but the family has the chief responsibility for the second.

Only the family can know sufficiently well the child in his uniqueness. In addition to this, the family has a distinct function in regard to the first set of tools, for while everyone needs these same tools, the set of any one person must be particularized to his individual use if it is to serve him efficiently.

All these tools are acquired by the young person quite gradually and ideally without deliberate awareness of what he is doing until self-consciousness in this field begins to emerge after early adolescence.

Chief dangers here are (1) making the child overserious or introspective; (2) making the child think the world too conclusively and completely a harsh or difficult or wicked or hostile place; (3) self-righteous elevation of tools to the status of ends in themselves instead of regarding them as a matter-of-fact means for securing more important things.

Group B. Four Functions Centered in the Welfare of All Members of the Family

4. Initiating and Individualizing Growth of Personality

There are four avowedly personality-fostering units in the community: the family, the school, the church, and the character-developing agencies (Scouts, Y.W. and Y.M.C.A., children's departments in the public library, Camp Fire groups, and others). All of these except the family work with groups far more than with single individuals, and have particularized aims upon which their programs are built. Their chief interest in the child is as a potential member of society or of their own organization. For the family, though, the child is a bundle of characteristics and possibilities interesting in his own right. The parents care for the child for what he is and what he may become as a personality. However little he may seem to outside units to merit their attention, within his own family generally he is cherished. There he feels that he counts. There it is that he stands distinctive, is not treated merely as one unit of a group. It is the family, also, that is the one institution that runs the full course in serving growth of personality throughout the whole period of immaturity and, ideally, gives continuity, consistency, and balance to it.

What is said here about the opportunity of the family to cherish and to develop the distinctiveness and versatility of personality of the child applies also, though in lesser measure, to the adults of the family. The very process by which the family is bringing the personality of the child to maturity is also fostering the continued growth of the adults. The parents bring up their children; the children bring up their parents; and the two parents force growth in each other, if the conditions are right.

The fact needs impressing today that this fourth function of the family requires a type of marriage in which there is no tentativeness. The family cannot bring personality to maturity unless it is a relatively permanent institution. Where it is avowedly tentative, it stimulates the egoistical and individualistic propensities because each member of this venture in fellowship is watching to see if his own interests are being sufficiently served to warrant carrying on. Such intensification of the egoistic interest prevents maturing of personality. Neither throws himself wholeheartedly into the enterprise and forgets his own individualistic advantage.

Chief dangers connected with the fourth function are (1) trying to mold or build personality according to one's own ideals or defeated yearnings instead of providing the conditions necessary for the distinctive development of the other; (2) possessiveness toward another; (3) regimentation instead of cooperative evaluation and planning; (4) disruptive coercion by pressures from groups representing popular or conventional patterns; (5) fostering of individualism instead of individualizing the educational procedures; (6) coddling, indulgence, or idolatrous worship of the one loved.

5. Interpreting Life

In former days this function would have been grouped with the section which is centered in the welfare of the child. Now, however, adults need the interpretation of life as it is being experienced by their children as much as the children need the interpretations of their parents. Changes come so swiftly today that there is bound to be a gulf too wide to permit real communication between youth and adults unless there is constant and mutual interpreting of life by each of the two generations to the other.

In its effective forms interpretation is a constant process accompanying genuine experience. The most impressive interpretations of all are the uncalculated reactions of adults to the many matters that stir their sensitivities and predispositions.

Chief dangers are (1) interpreting as a final authority rather than as a student of life making a report of progress-to-date on the specific matter in question; (2) being too preoccupied to interpret more than superficially when sensitive attention would have indicated that more is being called for; (3) side-stepping an issue brought to one's attention by another through lack of courage to come to terms with this particular issue oneself; (4) failure to admit ignorance and error when guilty of these.

6. Equilibrating the Individual

So many aspects of present living are unstable, unpredictable, upsetting, exciting, strange, that the various members of the family are frequently thrown out of equilibrium. Whether these disturbances are valuable unrecognized openings to new ventures, or are frustrations from meeting seemingly unsolvable problems, or are personal experiences involving deep inner conflict or disorganizing emotional repercussions, one of the pressing daily needs of members of a modern family is that of restoration of emotional equipoise. Only those who are close to the disturbed individual will be trusted regularly with his confidence. Only such can be frank with him, and sometimes even they cannot. Only from his familiars will he take easing ministrations.

Both through hardly realized ministrations in slight disturbances and through thoughtfully loyal devotion in more serious disruptions, the effort of the competent family goes on to help the individual to locate his real and his whole self, to come again to his best. In some matters, such, for instance, as the building up of a sense of security for the future, the process may be long-drawn out and may be only partially successful. But always one force of equilibration is possible, the sense of comfort and support in knowing that there is someone who cares and shares.

Chief dangers are (1) encouraging undue dependency; (2) overloading the more generous with all the burdens, without return of effort to equilibrate him; (3) equilibrating on too low a level so that larger values found through more extensive problem-solving are excluded; (4) bringing to status of equipoise an individual who needs to have his present personal organization broken past restoring, that is, overprotecting from all real shock and so retarding growth.

7. *Establishing the Direction of Growth of the Family toward the Most Worthy Values Discoverable*

This is one of the prime functions of the family, this fostering of admiration and worship of the greatest, and of devotion to it, however this greatest may be conceived. It gives the family areas of reference outside itself toward which to strive, by which to appraise and criticize its activities, and through which to seek daily renewal of life. It helps to preserve perspective and hence encourage a more dauntless sense of humor in daily interactions. In time, it modifies individualism and tense rivalry. When this loyalty to this greatest becomes religious devotion to God, all life takes on new and enriched meaning. The reason for this is that devotion to God is interpreted in terms of sensitive devotion to the most vital realities of daily family living.

Chief dangers are (1) adults may try to harness the child's loyalty to their own dogmatic convictions which remain meaningless to him; (2) adults may be so fearful lest the child ultimately miss God that they will induce the child to imitate their theological jargon and gestures, still meaningless to the child, and teach him to call this religion; (3) inconsistency between what is held highest in periods of worship and what is held highest in everyday unintentional behavior; (4) unsound theory of value by which to measure the greatest.

Group C. Six Functions Centered in Communal Life as a Whole

8. *Specific Channel for Regulated Racial Continuance*

In the family, production, protection, and the rearing of new racial stock are carried on by a group who are investing so much of themselves that they care about the outcome. This deep concern opens the way for society to furnish to the solicitous family some degree of guidance and regulation; where the guidance is sound, it redounds to the good of the race.

Chief dangers are (1) decrease in birth rate among those of better stock or superior cultural privilege; (2) injury of fellowship through ill-advised regulation of mating; (3) propagation by those unfit or those indifferent to racial and family welfare.

9. *Generation of Different Types of Social Energy*

Obviously the care of health by the family is a prime determining factor in the provision of physical energy for social enterprises. The family is also of first importance in providing mental, social, and emotional types of energy required in the undertakings of other institutions. The long years of training in sensitivities and responsiveness of all the members of any particular family make them effective in certain situations, and ineffective in others. When the offspring emerge from the family, they evidence certain mental and emotional sets. Their motivation and their openness to appeal are intricately conditioned by their family life. Hence, where the family functions effectively, there is a tremendous increase in the sources of the various types of social energy.

Chief dangers are (1) social exploitation of these energies; (2) poor stewardship of human energies on the part of the family through shiftlessness, indulgence, prejudice, or ignorance; (3) family discouragement through finding no *meaningful* call upon their energies, or possibly no recognition of them of any sort; (4) inculcation of unsocial or antisocial policies in the matter of investment of energies.

10. Throwing Up Danger Signals When the Larger Social Trends, Particularly Those of Specialization and Monopoly, Threaten the Vital Interests of Human Living

The great interest of the family is in human fulfillment and hence in social conditions which foster this. It must cry out in fear and warning when trends begin to crush humanity.

Chief dangers are (1) powerless feebleness of the voice of the family, defenseless except when organized in a highly organized industrial and political world; (2) calling attention only when immediate want must be relieved and not seeing that the troubles go deeper, hence allowing the wearing down of the social strength of the family and the keeping of growth retarded; (3) deluding notions as to which are the most vital interests of human living.

11. Fostering the Attitudes of Trust and Love in Human Relations

Human relationships are popularly spoken of as being either of a business or of a personal nature. The business relationships are assumed to be utilitarian, implying that one had better keep his eyes open and his mouth and pocketbook shut most of the time when in the midst of these. Personal relationships are assumed to be friendly, implying that one can trust himself and his interests to his personal associates. However, because we have so little opportunity to know our associates for what they really are, and because competition has become so aggressively keen almost everywhere in society, more and more we find that we cannot trust ourselves to any but a rare few relationships, whether called business or personal. When trust goes, diplomacy, conventionalization, hardness, suspicion, hostility, and offensive approach are likely to take its place. Society cannot remain on the human level when person cannot trust person. Thousands upon thousands of modern individuals are lonely, walled-in, and isolated because they live too continuously in the midst of a surging, untrusted multitude of near-strangers. Today, individuals "make contacts" instead of building fellowships.

The fellowships within the family are the most deeply marked by love and trust of any regularly occurring relationships. It is in the family that the individual undergoes first-hand experiences in what happens to two or more human beings who are loyal and devoted each to the interests of the other. The outcome is of even richer, deeper significance when the family group gives its devotion to some cause which is greater than its fellowship.

Love is the bond which holds persons in communion more inextricably even than memories bind together the mental life. When men learn directly through experience the power of self-disseminating love to promote the good of mankind, they begin to seek to extend it to more and more human connections. Although not nearly every family has truly worthy love, there is very little opportunity outside the family for such direct learning of the work of this kind of love. A great responsibility rests upon the family in this function of fostering the growth of such love and trust among mankind in these times when one man's success typically means another man's loss or failure. The family must continue as the germinating center of this self-disseminating love so that men may have convincing daily experiences of it, and so be aroused to promote meaningful and potent fellowships in a widening radius of communal activities.

Chief dangers are (1) family interests may take an undue portion of devotion as over against other interests; (2) provincialism; (3) excluding certain activities from the government of self-disseminating love; (4) God will be too exclusively identified with this kind of love.

12. Community-building

When the children go out into the community, the family becomes interested and solicitous about the conditions which there prevail. This interest may extend all the way from material conditions, such as sanitary provisions and type of countryside, through social ones, such as sorts of teachers, movies, hobbies, and group standards present, through legislative measures which either protect or betray the family and its interests, to spiritual and religious conditions. When the family is on the job there is an insistence upon conditions promotive of decency, safety, enjoyment, and culture within the community.

Two further ways the family has of community-building. The first is by keeping all the new developments appearing in group life assimilated in the understanding, attitudes, and habits of the family, so that they can be intelligently cooperative or resistive in their community relationships. The second is by contributing back into the community life whatever the parents have learned through their family experiences, after their own children have gone from home.

Chief dangers are (1) family members may seek to participate in community-building before well informed or trained; or (2) they may be overinfluenced in their participation by certain aggressive groups so that they become pawns; (3) partisanship in promoting the selfish interests of one's own group; (4) failure to discern the larger values and aspects of the community through serving zealously in specific cases of need.

13. Fostering a Sense of Unity and Community in the Human World

Because the family can exist only if it is a unity and a community, it is bound to have to experiment in forms and techniques of fellowship. Present society allows no one set of forms or techniques to remain adequate long. For example, individuals must learn how to live with others in the small house or apartment. Individual members must learn how to settle disagreements, how to work out common plans, how to allocate resources, how to develop responsibility, how to set up an administering plan for carrying out some project, and many other processes. Criteria for the use of power and authority in the family, and the formulation of its working definitions of property, love, order, work, and other vital matters are factors of importance in building the sense of a creative community.

One of the chief aspects of this function of fostering a sense of unity is the demonstration of the attractiveness of marriage and family life when sincerely and intelligently lived. The world needs this demonstration over and over again, so long as young people keep coming on. Such a demonstration is not a mere matter of setting a good example, but rather of devoting the self to a deeper experience for its own sake.

Chief dangers are (1) self-sufficiency within the family group; (2) isolation of the family community from the larger one through unwillingness to persist in trying to work out a basis for interacting especially when the community represents more often the extremely competitive types of groupings; (3) perverted attitudes in regard to communal ideas and developments.

While this list of thirteen functions is not, by any means, the record of achievements of any one family or of the great majority of families, it is not, on the other hand, a mere set of ideals. These functions are those which in some degree every genuine family is serving well or ill. Because the family is as yet untrained professionally, its functions are not clearly formulated by a majority of its members and its procedures remain largely makeshift ones. It is necessary to help the institution to become intelligently aware of its functions and of adequate procedures for fulfilling them.

In other words, the family needs both professional education and the interacting support of allied institutions. It is in decidedly simpler circumstances than it used to be in so far as labor-saving equipment releases from backbreaking occupations the time and energy of many men and women. But on the other hand it is in much more difficult circumstances in the matter of the number and scope of intricate interests and activities it must understand and deal with. For this it lacks plan and drive. It no longer has a *patriarchal head*, a strict *code*, and supporting community *sanctions*. It must locate its new type of head, a much more difficult head to follow though markedly more interesting and promising. This *new head* is its informed sense of function. This new head must continuously define in particular terms for each family the master task to which the loyalty of that family is pledged. This task might be generally couched in these words, *To foster human fulfillment in the most meaningful ways possible through the fellowship of the family group.* A new type of code—a growing one—must be built up to guide and sustain the family in performing its task. This new code must be developed through studying the functions and the personal factors of the family: its regulative, mutual agreements will chart the way. Supporting social *sanctions* will come when the code or set of norms has been validated and then so formulated as to be a serviceable guide for the majority of families. Guiding sanctions will emerge to foster and guard what brings values to the family.

Certainly other institutions in common with the family have some responsibilities in the matter of the various functions here presented. However, they approach them from an opposite direction, from the point of view of a society concerned with a mission to execute. This is useful, but it makes the contribution of their work in distinguishing functions and norms quite different from that of the family which is primarily concerned with the conservation and creative growth of the more intimate, rich, unique, and delicate meanings in human life. The family is the true guardian of the living human heart.

THE FAMILY AS AN INDISPENSABLE INSTITUTION

We have stated the functions which the family is constituted to fulfill. The question, "Is the family indispensable to society?" cannot be answered merely by showing that the family might be coached to serve these functions. Rather the indispensable worth of the family can be defended only if it is the sole possible way by which these certain essential needs of growth of personality and of culture can be met. If there is any other institution or grouping which conceivably can serve these functions as well as can the family, then we can dispense with one or the other institution.

There are, however, certain biological [1] facts which demonstrate that no other possible grouping of individuals can do the work of the family. The thirteen cultural concerns which we have described all require a nurturing group which can focus the sensitivities of each member upon the peculiar needs and potentialities of every other member.

Mass handling and mechanized techniques cannot provide these

---

[1] See also Chapter VII, p. 128ff.

means. Individual differences and capacities require discriminative attention if human life is to be abundant and rich. These can receive sufficient continuous, particularized attention only in the home. No other institution can regularly be depended upon to provide the intimate and sensitive interpersonal interest.

There are five biological facts which make the family incomparable in the fulfilling of these functions. They are the relation between mother and child, the sexual relations between the parents, the relation between the father and child, the fact that there is usually only one infant at a time calling upon parental attention, and finally, the prolonged dependence of the infant upon the intimate cooperation and mutual understanding between the parents. Each of these biological facts needs but a few words of explanation to disclose the basis of its coercive power.

To begin with, the biological relation between the mother and child is established at conception. From then until the end of lactation, the sensitivities of the mother are focused upon the child by physiological necessity. No other institution or group can bring such coercive forces to direct the devoted attention of one person upon the developing personality of another.

Second, between the two parents the deep sensitivity and responsiveness of each to the unique personality of the other is sustained by sexual interest. All literature is full of portrayals showing the power of this bond to focus attentive concern. We do not need to elaborate the coercive action of this biological drive.

Third, the father has two forces weaving him into this intimate fellowship. One is his sexual interest in the mother which draws him into the relationship between her and the child. The other is his direct interest in the child because of his blood relation to it. Here again we have a physiological coerciveness, not found elsewhere, which engenders acute personal interest.

Fourth, ordinarily there is only one infant in the family at one time. Thus he can be the recipient of needed attention from the whole group. No other institution can launch human life with such great possibilities of appropriately adjusted personal interaction. Many different ages and interests are represented in the persons who form the family environment of the new-born in-

† See also Chapter VII, p. 124f.

fant. Thus we have as the medium of culture within the family, a small, intimate, but highly diversified group of individuals, intricately sensitized to each other. This sensitivity, also, is based upon coercive physiological propulsions.

Finally, the helplessness of the human infant demands conditions requisite to survival, chief of which is keen sensitivity to his unique needs. This helplessness continues for so long a time that an organization of group life is developed to meet its requirements of such a sort that all the individuals who cooperate in this organization have established the attitude of personal concern for one another by the time the infant is physically independent.

After these five forms of physiological propulsion have coercively held the personal attention of each of the individuals upon one another for a period of time, another factor, a deeply ingrained psychological drive, has become potent. Each person has invested time, energy, and resources in promoting the welfare of the others. Hence, by the time the physiological propulsions begin to weaken, this personal investment of each in the other has become coercive in directing the attentive consciousness into steadfast and usually loving concern. That into which one puts his muscle becomes his in the only way by which he can ever truly possess anything. One who has spent his very self upon others can never tear his attention from those others because they have become a part of him and he of them. So it comes about that the family will do all sorts of things for its members, things that society could not hire or train anyone else to do with equally sensitive and dauntless devotion. It does all this without financial recompense.

All the functions here presented are expressions of the peculiar degree and quality of personal interest found in the family. No other institution has or can have such powerful forces back of personal interest in members of the group for which it is responsible. This profound concern for one another, whereby personality is initiated and individualized, is indispensable to the growth of culture. To be sure, this invested fellowship has miscarried or otherwise failed in countless individual cases of family life, but that does not void its indispensable nature. There is no other possible way outside the fellowship of the family by which growth of personality and of culture can be as richly attained. The indispensability of the family despite its failings is beyond question. The values to be found in its fellowship are worthy of the highest type of individual and group promotion and devotion.

Part II

THE CHURCH AND ITS RELATION TO THE FAMILY

church and family.

Introduction

UNTIL recently it has been the way of society to give first and
keenest attention to the spectacular battlegrounds of the world
where men have fought for great human principles and where
the achievements could be counted in number killed, property
destroyed, and territory gained. But we are beginning to realize
that these devastating spectacles are barbaric, stupid ways of dealing with the festering symptoms of social ills. We are beginning
to see that we must be more radical in our treatment. We must go
back to the areas of human living wherein the vital issues are
rooted. We must act upon the insight that the quality and progress which mark a society where civilization serves culture are
dependent more upon the quality and progress of the family than
upon any other one factor. The home is the real though nonspectacular battleground of culture. Achievements here are
harder to count, for they appear in the forms of personal and cultural growth. The integrity of the nation can be measured by the
integrity of its homes. Yet the family today cannot be self-
fostering nor autonomous.

Now the church is substantially interested in the integrity of
the nation. It has organized its ideals into a philosophy of human
living which it holds will promote the highest fulfillment of individuals and the most noble organization of group interests. It
seeks to imbue all living with the supreme values it serves and
worships. It cannot achieve such purposes except through the
family. No two institutions are so culturally close as are church
and family, and no two need each other so fundamentally. Neglect by the church to deal with the vital issues of family life in
terms of the present time and place has brought the crisis for the

church which is discussed in Chapter IV. The cultural significance of the church is presented in Chapter V. Then, in Chapter
VI, the profound importance of the communion of the family in
connection with the growth of religion is indicated. Chapter VII
seeks to make explicit the mutuality in functioning between
church and family.

Chapter IV

THE CRISIS FOR THE CHURCH

THE church today stands before a great opportunity. But it cannot seize that opportunity until it undergoes extensive transformation. This opportunity lies in the fact that men today, perhaps more widely and fervidly than ever before, are seeking for something worth living for. In many cases, however, they would not say that it is a "faith" or a "religion" which they need and seek, because these and all other churchly labels have fallen into disrepute among a vast number of people. What they crave and explore for is much more vital to them than anything which the conventional symbols of religion connote to their minds. In fact, right here in these statements, we see at once the nature of the desperate plight of the modern individual, the great opportunity of the church, and the inability of the church to serve that opportunity.

Our endeavor in this chapter will be to analyze some of the major causes of this ineptitude of the church in the hour of its great opportunity and the world's great need.

POPULAR APATHY TOWARD RELIGIOUS VALUES

One outstanding cause of the crisis of the church lies in the fact that most modern individuals are insensible to, even insusceptible to, the values which the church offers in the name of religion. This is not entirely the fault of the church.

For one thing, the values promoted by the church are implicit rather than explicit in human living. Also, they are only securable high on the ascent of self-control. Further, they are hard to define. On the other hand, those which our commercial civilization offers are explicitly on display, immediately attainable, glamorous, and concrete. Furthermore, a highly organized and richly financed system of advertising has progressively conditioned the modern mind to heed only those tangible and sensuous goods which industry can produce, and to ignore those more subtle and growth-creating goods developed by family and church. The values which the church cherishes are difficult to vivify truly, even by those who seek them most sincerely. They seem nebulous in comparison with those of economic success, literary eminence, or membership on a championship team. They promise nothing which the individual can with pride exhibit before his fellows whose practice it is to accord personal status by evidences of material possession. The appearance on the market of new commercial goods is marked by such insistence and prodigality that there is a protective dulling of the senses. Religious goods, difficult to sense, are rendered less palpable by senses so dulled.

Values that are not sensed remain unknown. Men will always turn their attention where they believe values lie. If the values seem great enough, nothing can stop their onrush. The hardships of Alaska did not stop the gold rush, nor ignorance and inexperience the stock-market rush, nor common sense and mathematics the Townsend rush. Possibility of value excites men. It activates them. But the opposite is equally true. Where they sense no value, they keep their distance and invest no energy. Even where they feel that there may be value of a sort but do not discern any connection between it and their own needs, they pass it by. Now the values of genuine religion remain ever the same, and they are vast and deep at their best. They grow, however, only under certain conditions. More important still in this connection, they can be distinguished only by those whose nurture has fittingly sensitized their appreciation. There is much standardized church training these days, but not enough genuine religious education either in church or family to provide the conditions of this nurture.

Again, religious values require a long-term loyalty for their realization. But the modern temper is impatient with other than a "quick turnover," whether the investment is of cash or energy.

This contrast shows, for example, in the differences in the terms of fellowship in religious and unreligious groups. The religious standards for developing fellow feeling call for self-disciplined, loyal, creative interaction of the best that one has and can become. These requirements appear very exacting over against the easy, impulsive terms of camaraderie of the usual social crowd. In the first instance, barriers and restraints are progressively overcome by struggling into the upper reaches of greater truth, beauty, and goodness. In the second instance, they are often instantaneously dissolved in alcohol so that there need be no controlled effort since all are reduced to the congeniality of common animal nature. Assuredly, the friendship growing out of religiously inspirited fellowship has a richness of quality which spoils the taste for any other sort in all those who have experienced it. But it must be earned before it can be tasted, and it is earned only by large investment of the total self. On these accounts, many do not undertake the disciplines it requires. In fact, not many churches have intelligently prepared themselves for guidance of such creative interaction.

Other elements enter in. Individuals live in such close association that they tend to take the opinions of their "crowd" in regard to most things claiming to be valuable, and the crowd is moved by intensity, immediacy, and frequency of appeal coupled with the prompt, tangible nature of the yield. The unthinking "crowd," commercially baited, is caught by an endless succession of fads. True religion cannot spread as a fashion or a craze. Then the conspicuous discord among the churches as to what the great values are is unsettling to such laymen as do try to think through the place of religion in life. Further, the urgency of the practical aspects of living is intense, and the associated attractions and perplexities leave no free margin of time or energy which would provide natural opportunity for contemplation of the supreme objective. Again the church is a beggar institution depending upon the voluntary contributions of its communicants, and hence subservient to the will and mercy of the large contributors.

For a time, the church acted upon the hope that all that was necessary to win response to the values it offers was to capture attention, to keep a place for itself in the forefront of community interests. Costly buildings, catchy advertising, silver-tongued or flattering pastors, impressive choirs, elaborate ritual, club life with dancing, sports, and recognition of class distinctions, movies, drama, indeed almost all the attractions which seemed to be alluring in the case of other community enterprises were tried as magnets. But those individuals who were enticed by such appeals continued to want just these same things after they were received into membership. They counted upon just these things from the church. By this false stratagem the church now includes many who are not primarily interested in religious living. It has weakened itself thereby. And too many ministers have discovered themselves managing a very active, and sometimes very smart, social club. Religion in such a case becomes a perfunctory matter like reverence for great heroes long dead. The church can never succeed by using attractions which do not pertain to its distinctive functions.

The real crux of the problem lies deep under these more obvious difficulties. Today, the thrust of growth, genuinely religious, must take place against a terrifically strong offensive—the coercive pressure of overweening organized selfishness. This is the same problem which is baffling the family. Briefly put, the values with their corollary standards which distinguish religious from both unreligious and irreligious living are diametrically opposed to those which motivate the dominant economic, political, and general associational interests of current living.

This condition would be perilous enough if the existent church stood united in the matter of dominant motivation. But the situation is brought to a desperate crisis by the fact that the membership of the church-at-large includes a notable number of individuals who are supported and enriched directly or indirectly by graft, profiteering, exploiting, and enslavement of the defenseless. Characteristically, the more affluent among these individuals tend to find place as members of boards of control within the church. In any case they are usually the larger contributors. In many churches, they can oust the minister, cripple the educational program, and dictate the policies of the church toward social action. They can do so, and they have done so. Furthermore, since they are members of the church, they have rights as members to speak and participate according to their convictions. They can modify or shackle church motivation until it bears little resemblance to religious motivation. It has gone so far that there are now churches activated by the profit motive in much of their program. Thus, to the indifference to, and negation of, religious motives which the church finds outside its walls must be added vitiation of motives within its membership.

No one local church, any more than one single family, can be true to its functions and, at the same time, survive as an independent, unfettered institution in these days of voracious, competitive preying of the power-hungry upon the defenseless. Those churches which have vigorous, well-established central organizations are in a better position to meet these trampling, subjugating forces than are the churches of loose national organization. On the other hand, there always exists the danger that the central organization may be bought off, vitiated, or lost to the control of self-interested forces. The church as a material institution is likely to loom up so large in the eyes of its own vested interests that it becomes the main issue and religion is forgotten.

The helplessness of the church then, in holding high its values in all human undertakings, is not a temporary disability which judicious nursing will overcome. There is utter disparity between the values and motives which the church as an institution is supposed to be fostering and the dominant values and motives of the present civilization in the midst of which religion and the church must function. Since the dominant forces of civilization control the materials and means essential to existence both of individuals and institutions, they have the upper hand, particularly during and following a long period of want.

Another aspect of this appears. At present these forces have made the establishing of the connections necessary for mere existence such a struggle for millions of persons that there is no possible surplus of energy or time, and consequently no aspiration, to reach out toward other connections which could bring plus values into living. In fact, for these millions, existence has become so grim or security so threatened that there is much cynicism, pessimism, and hard despair regarding possibilities of more abundant living.

What the average church of today has to offer seems to a great number of people to be artificial or inconsequential, sentimental or hopelessly futile in the face of the stark realism of our actual world. Whatever one's place or part, he cannot but know that we now live in a society where property and profits are of more value than human life; where the proud palaces of business look down upon disease-ridden, crime-haunted slums; where many husky men idle on yachts or play golf for hours or days while many women slave and many little children sweat at suicidal labor; where the ingenious instruments of war may at any moment begin to shriek ravenously for the strong, promising bodies of our sons in order that might (not right) shall prevail; and where government is constantly hammered into a tool for shoveling the fuel of special privilege into the firing boxes of the production plants of powerful organized minorities.

The values which the church characteristically has to offer are far below par on today's market. Yet the fact remains that never more than in these present days has mankind needed to connect with the values which the church is designed to offer. The majority of individuals do not experience this need explicitly, but they are disturbingly aware that the sustaining sources of meaningful and abundant living have somehow dried up. They are conscious of a severe drouth of human kindness, a famine of goodness, beauty, truth, and fellow feeling. A list of the consequent reactions becomes a list of the common mechanisms of escape from the meaningless and the intolerable: keep too busy to think; act the cynic; turn to the securities of "the good old days" by reading the classics or becoming a fundamentalist under some modern label; sell yourself to an ambition or a career; go excitement-mad; paralyze the judgment with alcohol; find a simple, clear conviction and become a fanatic; build yourself an ivory tower; commit suicide.

It is not only the downtrodden multitude milling about the extreme left end of our abnormally skewed curve of economic distribution who feel the need of escapes. The powerful, fortunate few at the extreme right-hand end of the curve feel at odds with life, also. Even after all their gains of acquisition, they sense that they are missing something vital, the abounding heart of life not inherent in possessions and position. Case-study records of the grounds upon which many of the more fortunate seek professional counsel plainly bear testimony to this fact.

At the bottom, then, the crisis of the church presents this paradox. The values and the motivation of religion which the church officially seeks to promote are desperately needed by modern people, yet they cannot work in the same situation as the values and motivation dominating present civilization. The two can neither cooperate nor compromise. They are antithetic, and the latter, being dominant, have the power to crush the former. They have the power, yes, but, on the other hand they have demonstrated that they cannot be trusted with power over human living. Their use of power makes human fulfillment impossible. Devotion to God alone can have the power to redeem them from their exploitive enterprises. Only as the demands of this devotion continuously criticize and direct the economic and political values and motives can these latter be kept in their correct place. This place is to serve as instrumentalities of human life and growth. Here, then, in the present social crisis is contained both the critical predicament and the critical opportunity of the church.

But the church as a whole is not ready for this double crisis. Like the individual family, the individual church is occupied with concern for its own survival. The church-at-large hears social prophets estimate how long it can remain in existence. It is wracked by strains from without and stresses within. It suddenly finds the demands upon it tremendously increased at a time when its resources of all sorts are seriously decreased. It is fumbling for a sound, adequate philosophy of religion and a system of values, clarified and serviceable for this age. It does not see its way. It is not ready.

CONDITIONS WHICH RETARD READINESS

Inability to Act as a Cultural Unit

The most conspicuous mark of the unreadiness of the church-at-large is its present incapacity to act as a cultural unit in a cultural crisis. It has been said that there are two things which will bring close unity among the many divisions of a group: (1) a clearly conceived common cause, and (2) a threatening common enemy. All too well does the world know that there are many major divisions of the church-at-large; the Jews, the Roman Catholics, the Christian Protestants, the Mormons, and others. Just as well do we know that some of these major divisions have their denominational divisions, the Christian Protestants having more than two hundred. Further, there has been developing for some years now, a new demarcation which cuts crosswise through all established denominational lines. It is an increasingly clear cleavage between the conservative and the liberal or progressive elements in all groupings. Indeed, it seems to be coming about that there is more likemindedness between the progressive elements of all the major divisions of the church-at-large than between the conservative elements within any one denomination.

Though nominally all the major divisions of the church-at-large have always had a common cause as heirs of the Christian tradition, yet actually they have not been able to come to any unanimity in the matter of pledging their dominant loyalties. In fact, the more they have talked about the Great Object of their loyalties, the more divisions there have arisen. Many of the seceding groups have been so bitter or so bigoted that they have gloated over their separatedness. There has been far more churchianity than there has been Christianity, far more dogmatic preaching than gathering together in His name. This has weakened the church in both the material and the religious sense. It has been cheapened in the eyes of men.

Nothing short of a vivid sense of the greatness of God and the worth of His cause is sufficiently potent to bring the churches into functional unity. It remains first for the churches to be converted. Where is the leadership that will essay to convert the churches? It is not to any one existing creed that all should be converted. Rather it is to the love of God and the way of Christian love that they must be converted. Both the Christian Bible and human experience bear witness to this.

It remains also for the churches to act upon the knowledge that love is not primarily a feeling, but an interacting relationship based upon the sharing of interests in organic equality and in mutual freedom and reinforcement. Love eventuates in a way of living marked by certain characteristic forms of behavior and relationship. The *feeling* of love is but the emotional concomitant of this particular way of living. The churches must learn how to establish this relationship amidst their own institutional diversity before they can establish it amidst the antithetic drives of society. Otherwise, as a house divided against itself, the church will fall. The church-at-large still has its choice between (1) *voluntary* submission to such a degree of *inner* disorganization and reorganization as shall be an adequate preliminary to a more Christian unity and hence a more culturally effective organization, and (2) *involuntary* disorganization and destruction of its present form by various *outside* conditions and forces, some indifferent and some antagonistic.

The church-at-large should know, for so it preaches, that it will be destroyed if it has reached the point where its multiplicity of wills toward sustaining divisiveness is held superior to God's will toward building a unity of functioning.

Interestingly enough, it is common enemies rather than a common cause which is now drawing many of the divisions closer. They have found themselves facing the same threatening conditions: the drawing away of the young people by more exciting, competitive community interests; the undermining of seemingly foundational beliefs by scientific pronouncements; the loss of prestige by the church; the threat of fascism; the increase of violence against defenseless persons, families and nations; mechanization of human relations; wholesale poverty; treachery in community offices; and unscrupulous coercion by organized minority groups. This has resulted in an increasing amount of conferring. There has already been some pooling of resources for the sake of research, and some publishing together of needed materials. Opportunities for vitalized study have been developed for groups of leaders irrespective of church affiliation.

This tendency toward unity induced by common dangers has been strengthened astoundingly in the last few years by the crucial issues that are before us as a nation. In quick succession the meetings of various representatives of major divisions of the church are being scheduled for the purpose of working together on one or more of these conspicuous social issues: world peace, economic justice, human fulfillment, the Cooperative Movement, the hostile or blank future before the majority of young people, interracial adjustment—these and more.

Finding themselves drawn together by being cooperatively set against certain oppressive or degrading conditions, these major divisions of the church-at-large are forced to see that the hypothetical, argument-drawn lines between them are too faint to be noticed when compared with the actual, blood-smeared lines between their total group and the forces making for unhuman conditions in the nation and the world. They are compelled to discern that they have common ground sufficiently solid and broad to hold them all on the same side of the major issues involving social justice. Further, they are discovering that they can work as a homogeneous group in developing methods. Chiefly, the present differences agitating the progressive elements concern such matters as the details of plans, procedures, financing, and timing. This is forcing a closer cooperative study and preparation in anticipation of specific planning and action.

Of course, this federating of Jew and Gentile, of Roman Catholic and of Quaker, of Mormon and of all the other divisions is yet far from general. It is still largely a matter of the voluntary leaguing of their more progressive leaders, lately augmented signally by the organizing of youth under these leaders. Nevertheless it is a sound beginning for the development of a widening church unity preparing to deal with basic social evils.

As soon as the church-at-large can mobilize into one all its divisions so that it can act as a significant cultural unit in conditions of emergency or of purposive endeavor, it will grow very powerful and be nearly ready for its opportunity. Just as states can be fused into a nation, or a number of nations into an alliance, when occasion calls for it, without loss of identity, so the divisions of the church, minor and major, must be capable of confederacy. Large group problems must be met by the church through large, organized group pressures if the problems are to have the benefit of direction by the system of religious values.

Perhaps, too, the enormity of the crisis will force the various individual churches to cooperate in distinguishing their particular cultural functions and in working out an interpenetrative program for participation as constituent organized, cultural units. Differences are all to the good if they can be treated creatively. The disastrous fact is not that there are differences among the churches, but that their differences are the masters of the situation and of them. The churches have allowed these differences to become shackles instead of using them, first, as the creative basis for diversity of contribution, and, second, as signals indicating that no one group has yet discovered all of truth and therefore greater truth must be sought. The individual churches need to explore their common ground and hence their common functions.

Uncertainty as to Its Social Task

In the church-at-large inability to affect unity when this is indispensable to effective functioning is the most conspicuous mark of lack of readiness for the double crisis. Nevertheless, there is a much more fundamental condition underlying this one. It is that the church has not yet been able to interpret its distinctive values, functions, and objectives in terms of the vital issues of the time with sufficient confidence in its interpretations to result in a reasonably clear program of responsibilities and procedures. Such terms as "social gospel" and "social action" are rather widely current, and the majority of church people feel that something must be done by the church to better social conditions. But opinions as to what should be done vary all the way from those who hold that God will work it all out for us if only we close our eyes in prayer and "have faith" to those who feel that the church should enter directly into group conflict even though this be carried to the point where it involves planned violence.

Again, there are still far too many who believe that by saving individuals we shall save all. Their questions remain these: "How can I be saved?" and "How can I save my brother?" They do not seem to realize that this ego-centered individualism in religion is the profit motive just as surely as is the ego-centered individualism in the world of industry. The problem of salvation is no longer the former, comparatively easy one of "making the individual right with his God." It has become the very difficult and involved one of progressively building a society where men *can* live together as the sons of God through making conditions right for all men regardless of social status, though justly considerate of essential individual differences and capacities.

Building such equality is not a mere matter of distributing identical responsibilities and opportunities, resources and advantages, status and relationships for all. Such a mechanistic idea of "equality" is unjust, wasteful, and cheap. Since no two human individuals are identical, none will have identical conditions of living. It is an organic type of equality which must be built. The human organism provides a parallel. The eye, the stomach, and the hand are not identical members of the body and do not have identical functions and needs, and hence are not identically served by the rest of the organism. Yet every organ, every part, is equally well served in relation to its nature, needs, and functions. Organic equality among all persons is the modern way of expressing the "brotherhood of man."

No longer, therefore, can the church remain either remote or neutral in relation to the major social problems of the day. Its cause and its constituency, indeed its own existence, are inextricably involved. Its policies, program, and procedures must increasingly reflect the awareness of the church to its particular responsibility in social reconstruction. Two clear clues for the doing of this present themselves: (1) inasmuch as the church is neither an economic nor political institution, its responsibilities here cannot be defined in the same terms as those of these latter institutions; (2) since the church includes persons of all interests and types, and of every status, it must attack social problems on the *vital* rather than the partisan level. Even then, this is a tremendous problem—to locate the distinctive function and projects of the church in progressive social reconstruction. Until this has been done with reasonable clarity and validity, the church will not be ready.

Creeping Paralysis within the Conservative Groups

There are sufficient reasons why the church tends always to become ossified and senile. It fosters single-eyed, dominant loyalty to the One Supremely Worthful as at the time conceived. It is difficult to lose oneself wholly in devotion to what one believes to be the Supreme Value yet keep his sensitivities keen to emerging insights revealing higher possibilities of value.

The average individual craves a rounded-out system of belief and a precisely defined objective. His living is made up of specific objectives rather than of a progression of loyalties that reach toward the incomprehended Sovereign God of God. He serves a definite ideal rather than develops a progressive loyalty wherein each greatest known objective is treated as a symbol of a greater to come. As a result, religious living tends to be controlled by the petrified thinking of ages gone by. The theologically conservative forget that the very creeds they stiffen to conserve were once innovations in the formulation of beliefs. Devotees need to be true to the spirit not the letter of the earlier creed-builders they serve.

Not only do religious loyalties tend to get set into inflexible forms, but the organization of its representative institution is usually such that the church gets stiff in the joints. There is a preponderance of old men in positions of administrative and executive importance, both in the local churches and on the national church boards. Often these individuals have vested interests in the church. As such, sometimes by intention, sometimes unwittingly, they tend to develop ulterior motives for holding the church in the status quo. The degree to which "politics" in the vulgar sense enters into some official gatherings called in the name of the church would bring the tongue of the Tammany Tiger into his cheek. Until the church provides some permanent means for keeping its boards of directors vitalized and growing, it will find its gait too stiff and halt to allow it to function as the official agent of a living religion in a speeded-up civilization.

In one direction alone, this creeping paralysis of the church is sufficiently evident to be alarming. Today the cultural gulf between the adults who are parents and the maturing generation of youth is greater than it has ever been before in this country, and it is widening. But the older men on the ruling boards of the churches are not even of the parental generation. They are two, three, or four cultural generations away from the young people coming on to take such places as they can find in the social order. The majority of these young people are not in the organized church. They feel that there is no possibility of joining forces with an institution whose ruling body has become ossified on some level of past systematization. There are ominous, current indications of this yawning breach. To the extent that this is occurring, the church is committing suicide by self-fostered anemia, for it needs the constant transfusion of new blood to keep its vitality at a sufficiently high point for effective functioning.

Another indication of the masculine senility of attitude within sections of the church is the absence of women representatives on all those boards where the activity and interests of women and children are in any way involved. It would be chucklingly funny, if it were not so serious, to note the completely complacent air with which men take unto themselves the task of exclusive control of almost all social interests which seem important to them, as though this were predestined. The democratic idea of fair representation of all elements in the constituency on all governing bodies is not sufficiently recent to explain this rigidity of the church in failing to take into proportionate account the youth and the women among its membership.

The church needs on its boards the representatives of youth to give it constantly some irritating prodding to growth and some dynamic coercion to test ever anew its beliefs and findings. On the other hand, youth needs to be kept in better balance through fellowship within a far-flung community and by the leavening influence of the noble concepts of the church. So, also, the church needs constantly the concerned tuggings of women to keep its interests centered in the vital issues of life. Because of the nature of their family activities, women's interests tend to center closer to the vital heart of human living than do men's. The noblest fulfillment of human life rather than material or institutional values must be given first place. Jesus Christ frequently warned the church against the tendency of organized religion to become preoccupied with matters remote from the vital issues of life.

Because of this tendency to ossify, the church has too often refused to recognize and honestly appraise the discoveries and the developments taking place outside the field of religion. It has not assimilated the emerging cultural products which nourish and give character to general cultural growth, and so it has kept itself a retarded cultural agency.

Vagueness of Basic Concepts among the Liberal Groups

While the orthodox sections of the church are suffering the creeping paralysis just discussed, the more liberal elements are threatened with a form of aphasia. They are having difficulties in orientation regarding religious interests. They feel the vaporous condition of an institution which has no definite creed and nothing to take its place. They are put to it to discover that true distinction of function which will allow the liberal church to rise impressively with structural soundness from the flatness of its present plane of accommodating itself to every subversive community pressure. The liberal groups cannot define the bases for their religious community except in humanistic terms which seem to convert them into ethical rather than religious institutions. They are not "persuaded." The objectives of their loyalties are nebulous. Consequently, they are not convincing and challenging.

The growing church must act upon the knowledge that creeds are only tools for closer discovery of God, and that no tools are perfect. All tools must be appraised and modified and, in time, replaced at least in part. The indispensable need of the growing church of today is a sound and adequate philosophy of religion. When this has been reasonably achieved and vitally apprehended, a cultus will evolve such as will provide both for concreteness in functioning and for confident direction in growth.

Between the paralysis due to the ossified, retarded orthodox sects in the church and the lack of significant coordination and adequate objective among the as yet unformed, undeveloped liberal elements, the situation is critical from the point of view of effective functioning in the culture of the day.

Neglect of the Democratic Spirit in Church Government

While democratic government is essential where cultural growth is to occur, it necessarily involves a slowness and clumsiness of functioning not found in a well-organized hierarchy. In the long run, the human and cultural developments in a democratic society are much superior to those in an authoritarian one, provided democracy is tried intelligently and persistently. But if it becomes mere *laissez faire,* or is put to too great a test before it has developed its modes and techniques, it faces severe difficulties, perhaps breakdown. Then, too, even a well-organized democracy finds it necessary to set up arrangements for a more authoritarian control during periods of real emergency when there is not time to educate the constituency before specific action must be taken.

It must be noted also that the more tangible and immediate are the values which any particular organization promotes, the more ready its members are to submit to authoritarian control in a crisis. Now the values which the Protestant churches promote do not seem as tangible and immediate to their great constituencies as do personal property, national rights, and territorial possession to the citizens of the nation. Hence these churches have not felt impelled to provide for that sort of close unity which would give them power in a crisis, as has the nation for time of war, for instance.

Democratic church government is still too young to have developed its own basis and techniques of unity with its implicit strength and creative possibilities. Primarily, among many other matters, it involves the education of the will of the church members, that is, *the education of their loyalties.* Religious education of the finest sort is an absolute prerequisite for the growth of such a church unity with such interchurch and intersect connections as inevitably must follow. We are only at the beginning of the development of an adequate plan for religious education. Indeed, at the moment, religious education is under a cloud because it is being appraised as though it had been tried thoroughly and creatively, yet found wanting. Judging by the length of time that secular education is taking to locate a reasonably adequate plan of education, there is no justification for such discouragement. Especially true is this in the light of the superiority of the practical advantages enjoyed by the secular schools. A democratic unity develops slowly. It requires constant, skillful fostering. Furthermore, it will never be complete, but always growing.

The Increasing Social Load of the Church

Not the least condition which retards readiness of the church for the present cultural crisis is the extension of both the social expectations and the social complications with which it must deal. In consequence, some of the major divisions of the church have begun a businesslike elaboration of their total program. The Roman Catholic Church furnishes an example of this. The pastors of many churches have stated that their jobs are twice as hard to fill as they were ten years ago. This involves not one but many items for consideration. A sampling of a few of these greater expectations and complications will illustrate the diversification of the load of the church.

The competition which the church must meet as a source of the renewal of life.

There are health cults; leisurely activities at country clubs; adventure through excursions, auto rambles, detective stories, movies, and other avenues; release through hobbies, dancing, carousing, change of scene or work; and every sort of "philosophy" and "psychology" and "art" and "science" concocted to feed the vanity, inferiority feelings, the desire for exoneration or for encouragement and inspiration, which the frailties of man could crave.

The church used to be one of the great continuous sources for outside excitement, fellowship, and renewal. It was the "meeting house" of the community. Its life-and-death messages, revival meetings, annual conferences, concern for the welfare and doings of its members and heated doctrinal controversies made it dominant. Now attention is given to other resources which are more exciting, carry no responsibility, and do not tax the participant in any way that disturbs him, even to the extent of having to think.

The different quality and solidarity in professional leadership against which the church must compete, particularly through the pastor.

Not so long ago the minister was one of the outstanding capable scholars of the community. This gave the church a superior authority. Now a wide variety of conditions reduce this position: the presence of highly schooled teachers in local schools; frequent appearance of all sorts of lecturers, experts in drama, music, science, and exponents of other religions; prevalence of the scientific method as a basis for authority rather than rationalized revelation; and superior professional services for scientifically diagnosed maladies no longer theologically explained or treated.

The demand for able counseling service in connection with individual and group living, though with no sense of obligation for the support of such on the part of those being served.

The assumption that the church will cooperate actively in all community undertakings in which the cause is considered "good," with no consideration as to the limitations of staff and resources.

The expectation among many of the church constituency that the church will provide some sort of program for the redeeming of our present social disorder, and along with it ample leadership capable and strong enough to set it into action. This expectation is based on a misunderstanding of the distinctive functions of the church and of its responsibilities and resources, both personal and institutional.

Conspicuously, this expectation includes a proviso that this redemption of society be done in such a way that no individual and no class interest suffer inconvenience, embarrassment, or loss.

The shifting by the general membership upon the few regular workers in the church of the responsibility of building and maintaining a program which will be interesting enough "to hold" the people, particularly the young people, and this usually with inadequate equipment and resources.

There is a "spectator" attitude prevalent, expressed frequently in two ways: "I don't see that the church has anything to offer me"; "I don't get anything out of going to church."

Inadequacy as to Leadership

The training of the leaders of the church is still too largely pedantic and culturally remote, occupied overmuch with old routine material and tricks that do not apply tellingly to anything but the requirements for graduation from seminary. Then, since their system of training tends to unfit religious leaders for virile, effective work in the modern world, the vocation of religious leadership does not attract as preponderant a number of the remarkably endowed as the character of the functions requires. As a result the majority of brilliant thinkers are found outside the church. Consequently the church is not in a prominent, much less frontal, position to participate creatively in cultural developments or to use to full advantage scientifically improved principles and practices. Even at this, or better be it said, because of all this, there is a widening chasm between the leadership of the church and the lay members in matters where intellectual inquiry has been at all active. The religious leaders do not know how to work with their constituencies in cooperative discovery of sounder insights and of more meaningful practices. In consequence, the loyalties of church members exhibit a damp fogginess not conducive to dauntless courage nor impressive achievement.

Swift Infusion of Differing Cultures

Just as the nation has not yet been able to assimilate constructively the various peoples who have entered its ports during the period when the country was freely open to their entry, so the church has not been able to adjust itself to, nor to assimilate, the various religious cultures with which these immigrants have been conditioned. This has weakened the church in two directions. First, those immigrants of differing beliefs and practices who remained ardent religiously have manifested how widespread is the confusion regarding religious authority. This has been felt especially by children among their playmates. Second, those immigrants who were or became unreligious have increased materially the number of individuals who have no interest in religion. In fact, on the foreign-mission field as well as at home, each major church division has tended to feel complacent about the ultimate triumph of its own faith without bending perseveringly and open-mindedly to the study of just what was happening during the transfusion of cultures, and just what cultural elements and values were involved. Hence there are whole groups of persons of whom the church is hardly aware; yet these people deal with religion positively or negatively.

Failure to Foresee Man's Sudden Increase of Power

Certainly one of the most operative factors that retard the readiness of the church is its unpreparedness for the suddenness with which mankind has developed power to control many of the conditions and materials of human living. Added to this power to control there has come marvelously increased power to explain and understand the things and processes that go to make up human environment. This has markedly amplified man's confidence in himself as his own guide, builder, and savior. This confidence has grown so strong that it is now expressed in the formulated conviction that man can conceive and develop "the good life" without giving his loyalty to any sort of God.

While all the research, inventions, and construction which furnished grounds for this humanistic conviction were in process, the church was so busy with its own internal duties, ambitions, and dissensions that it did not see the handwriting of warning on its own walls. It did not realize that a stupendous change in dominant human conviction was coming for which it would have to prepare itself and educate its constituency if it would avoid a catastrophic flood of doubt and atheism. If the church had comprehended, man's swift advance in control of his world could have been paralleled by the church's swift advance in rigorous critical reevaluation of its premises and formulations. Then the church might have discovered under the debris of outmoded, man-made creeds that Reality which does endure, and about which men may experience a basic conviction. Further, it might have helped men to use modern patterns for experiencing this ancient Reality.

Because of its self-isolation during the development of this startlingly significant increase in man's power of control over his world, the church cannot now lead power-drunk men to the dynamic conviction that God is more present and more needed in the complex modern world than ever before. It cannot do so because for years it has resisted the impetus to keep itself oriented toward changing concepts. If it had learned how to let go of convictional forms become empty of meaning, it might now be holding fast only to such truth as could stand the tests of validation which a scientifically trained generation can respect. However, the church did not strengthen its faith sufficiently to act on the fact that genuine truth need fear no test.

As a consequence of this cultural lag of the church, the majority of individuals today have no adequate forms or patterns for experiencing religious conviction. This present generation during every day and almost every hour has vivid experiences which yield a conviction of the power of man in forms with which it is acquainted and so can recognize and appreciate. But it has no such sure patterns by which it can recognize and become acquainted with the power of God and so develop a rousing conviction of His reality and work. It cannot discern the difference between how the power of man and how the power of God works. Therefore, regardless of what it professes to believe, it *acts* on its conviction that the power of man is sufficient unto the day, and unto human fulfillment, even the highest.

As a result we have, on the one hand, the inquiring minds of the time usually absorbed in unreligious interests and, on the other hand, the more zealous religious devotees lured to cults offering high emotional ecstasies or heavenly concessions. Further, we find not only religious, unreligious, and irreligious church members, but also religious and unreligious atheists. For certainly, the atheist who holds himself open to the possible discovery of God, and who will not substitute wishful thinking for tested conviction in so important a matter, is more religious than the church member who claims to be religious but clutches at a confused crackling battery of queer feelings as a basis for an evanescent, self-interested conviction.

There is a further group of individuals who weaken the church, those who feel that they must apologize for any connection with the church as though such contact might be interpreted as a symptom of personal weakness, particularly intellectual weakness.

For the majority of modern individuals, then, there is no vivid conviction of the presence and work of God. The church has not developed reformed concepts and fresh patterns understandable to the modern individual, and so has not been able to educate him toward conviction. The general constituency of the church remains lukewarm. As a spectator it criticizes what is being passed out rather than as a participant is stirred to the will to create cooperatively the conditions that favor the work of God. The present generation awaits the experience of vivid conviction in forms appropriate to its milieu.

SAVING THE CHURCH

Today there are groups of the more radical ministers and of those young people more conversant with the vital issues of the day who are debating withdrawal from the established church. They are contemplating the instituting of new organizations, religious in name or in quality, which will be neither shackled by the dead chains of the past nor made impotent by denominational stubbornness of will. And such new developments may have to be, as are new hybrid plants, typical yet different from the now dead parent stock. However, such secessions would involve regrettable waste. There is much of great value in the church and much that would be facilitating and protective against error in new religious ventures. Looking at the church as it stands, the task of saving it may appear overwhelming, but looking at it in the long light of history there seems full justification for earnest effort and courage.

Certainly it is true that if the church would save itself it must lose itself in the causes that are immediate present-day representatives of the Great Eternal Cause the church is instituted to serve. It has spent too long a time in preserving and magnifying itself and has thereby lost itself. Just as an individual who is suffering disorganization in his personal life cannot find his full self again until, having carried through the necessary introspection and self-appraising, he has thrown himself wholeheartedly into attaining the objective which he feels is of great worth, so it must be with the church. Undoubtedly, with the individual and the institution both, there must be a preparatory period of critical analysis and of discriminative decision as a foundation for reorganizing the self into a unity ready for action. Until the church has distinguished and clarified genuine religious values worth serving, it cannot call the attention of men to the overarching values to be sought through the guidance of the church. Nevertheless, salvation, integration, and the testing of new values do not begin until creative action begins. It is in such action that there are discovered the guiding insights for further evaluation and action.

Chapter V

THE DISTINCTIVE CONTRIBUTION OF THE CHRISTIAN CHURCH

"Is NOT the church outmoded?" "Is not the church breathing its last?" "Is it not practically dead except for the protracted burying of the remains?" These are questions we hear directed to the church, as other similar ones have been applied to the family.

But these questions overlook a fact of major importance. It is not difficult to imagine the death of particular local churches. They often do perish. But the fellowship of people who have a common devotion to what they hold to be supremely important for all human living will never perish from the earth. Ideas of what this supremely worthful reality may be will change. Consequently the manner of this fellowship and the institution which embodies it will change. But the fellowship which has this devotion for its central motivation will not disappear. Then, also, the church is a kind of fellowship which has given an indelible character to the personalities of many people. The traditional fellowship of the Christian church will not pass away as long as there are these personalities who have been, and are being, so shaped by it that they cannot live without it, and there are many such. Furthermore, this fellowship of the church overarches the generations. In it the living join with those long dead and those yet to be born in the central quest of man for the Highest.

Not only is the church a fellowship between human beings. It is the institutional agent to support and direct man's relationship to God. God, however diversely conceived, and however named or unnamed, will always be a primary concern in human living. To mankind, God is always the most important reality and therefore interest in Him will always have such significance that an institution of some sort to support this interest will be indispensable. In Russia, for example, where God and churches are being killed by neglect, there is rapidly forming an institutional method for cultivating man's devotion to what the communists think is the supreme concern for human living.

In this twofold sense, then, as an indispensable kind of fellowship and as an institutional way of fostering the highest loyalty of men, the church is indestructible. Particular individual churches may die by the score; and the traditional form of the church may blunder and fail and pass away. But the church as the institutional agent for an essential function in human living will always rise from the dead, whenever any outworn form of it does die.

ASCERTAINING THE CONTRIBUTION OF THE CHURCH

The church is like the family in this respect: it stands for an interest which cannot be rooted out. Also, as in the case of the family, when it comes to the question as to whether it can and should go on, the matter is not settled by citing the failures and weaknesses of the prevailing institutions. The question may well be asked: "Will the present accepted form of the church endure?" If, however, one asks not about any *given form* of the church, but about the endurance of the institution in *some form*, one must go deeper for the answer. One must go on to a consideration of the distinctive functions which the institution represents and the significance of these for the welfare and growth of human beings. If these distinctive functions are no longer of sufficient cultural worth to warrant the social investment required, or if other institutions can fulfill these functions more effectively or with less waste and error, then the church should wind up its affairs and go. Did such a condition ever truly come to pass, the churches would be closed by society, anyway, after a period of miserable social starvation. On the other hand, if the distinctive functions of the church are now, as previously, of vital significance to cultural welfare and progress, and if no other institution can fulfill these functions as effectively and efficiently as the church, then, even though the church of the day shows a discouraging social balance, the church as an institution and a fellowship should survive. Further, it should become an active interest of society to foster its rehabilitation.

In truth, society now carries a large debt to the church for what it has conserved and contributed culturally down through the centuries. Today is a good time to remember all this. The effect of the coming of a church upon pioneer morals and "justice"; the conservation by the church of cultural treasures of literature, art, music, and the like; the influence of a church upon the morale of a neighborhood; the renewal of lives that have been confused, degraded, and shattered—these only start the list of types of social credit the church has built up. There are figures in red, also, for the church as for every other human institution. They are the figures that record waste, error, weakness, failure, and even crime.

It is revealing to study this social ledger of credit-debit, but the balance as calculated does not pronounce the church a failure. A just conclusion recognizes also the great achievements and possibilities of the church in view of the fluctuating nature of the consideration and support accorded it by other cultural units. Just as a tracing through of most cases of misbehavior in children ends at the door of some adult, so perhaps the faulty functioning of the church may point to basic social neglect. Indeed, our country has been so preoccupied for era upon era with material developments that, until recently, all its higher cultural interests have been left to grow up as must children on a rugged and half-conquered frontier. Our public-school system, our arts, philosophy, and science shared for long this neglect due to materialistic preoccupation. Science sooner than the others has experienced the favoritism of cultural support, for utilitarian reasons. But our associational activities are still characterized by the frontier attitude. "We must wrest from nature the best living possible. Other matters, highly worthy but not literally essential to existence, will have to wait." For example, this has been a controlling attitude of many businessmen who focused upon making a living up to an ever-postponed time of retirement when they dreamed that they would begin to live—really. In our present civilization, the acquisitive interests of men are lustily aggressive; they do not need fostering, though they do need perpetual critical guidance. However, the interests engaged in the nurture of personality and culture always need fostering as well as guidance. These interests work through the more intimate community institutions. The sustenance and cultivation of them is an urgent present problem in social administration.

In order, then, to seek answer to the question as to the cultural significance of the church, it becomes pertinent to note its distinctive functions. At the same time, it must be borne in mind that the failure of any church or group of churches to fulfill these functions does not make the functions any the less real or necessary or valuable. Rather such failure puts a responsibility upon society to help provide the conditions which will aid the church in finding itself again and in beginning to function with more cultural effectiveness. If society is not ready at this time to appreciate and cherish the distinctive functions of the church, or if the church will not leave its comparatively trivial obsessions and divisive preoccupations and set out to fulfill its major functions, then there is an *impasse*. In this extremity, unless the church-at-large is aroused to the point where it will rise to the task of pressing the reeducating of a befuddled society, its own present organizations will dwindle. The task is not that of setting to rights any one institution. It is not so simple as this. However sleazy or tattered the whole social fabric may be in various parts, it is all of one piece. The degree of interdependence is exceedingly high. When any one necessary social institution falters, it produces a large group problem. The point of inquiry, then, will not consist in asking what churches are carrying out these functions, but in evaluating the significance and distinctiveness of these functions for present-day culture.

THE SIGNIFICANCE OF THE CHRISTIAN CHURCH

Viewing three different aspects of the functioning of the church will yield a more complete understanding. The first view sweeps across the pages of history, interested in distinguishing the long-term functions. This aspect might be named the church-at-large, for differences in detail are lost in the range of the perspective. The second view considers the influence exerted upon a community by its churches, treating all churches in any one community as a functional unit. This aspect might be named the church-as-a-community-unit. The third view is an interior one and examines the church as seen through particular churches at work among their own constituencies. This aspect might be called the local church. Through these three aspects of its functioning we shall now consider the significance of the church.

The Church-at-Large

Looking at the church-at-large must necessarily involve retrospection. It is a vast, complex institution and its functioning can be observed and understood only when considered over a considerable period of time. So viewed, the church is a history-shaping cultural force. It shapes history because it holds that the values it serves are the supreme values for all living, and because it zealously seeks to have these values incorporated into the controlling attitudes and plans of its time. Therefore we find many traces of the influence of the church-at-large upon historical events. Officers of the church have conferred with sovereigns and ruling bodies in an endeavor to educate points of view or bring insistently to mind forgotten or ignored issues. They have acted as mediating agents for countless persons and in various sorts of enterprises, and have gone as reconciliating messengers between nations. The missionary work of the church has had appreciable effect upon nations of the world. Then there have been causes which the church-at-large has felt loyalty-bound to serve in such ways as it could, and its influence has been signal in some instances. Now, for example, it is working in behalf of world peace, of fair interracial relations, and of economic justice. The proclamations of the church in their various forms of petitions, encyclicals, pledges, and resolutions have often had telling weight. They have served as clarifying statements concerning plans of social action. They have revealed issues that were hidden by illusory, or self-seeking motives. True, the church-at-large has sometimes besmirched its name by the manner in which it has attempted to shape history, but on the whole it has sought to have incorporated in current living higher than current values.

Ideally the church is the supreme institution for shaping history, for it has no national boundaries in the scope of its loyalties, no geographical limits of its location, no temporal period confining its existence. The nation is its nearest rival in the work of shaping history. But the nation is acutely conscious of its national boundaries wherever it is in actual or potential competition with other nations. True, sectionalism within the church has voided much of its potency in this function today. The church of the Middle Ages had astonishing strength in this function, though, as intimated before, not always wise strength. Mankind is so nearsighted, culturally, that he needs a long-established institution which will constantly urge upon him the larger values which only vision of longer range can discern and appreciate continuously.

The church-at-large conserves the great insights of the past which have to do with good and abundant living. These are handed down to the present and on into the future as records of ideas and as records of the lives of persons. The church has been too prone to superimpose these records upon the present generation as fixed molds for development and conduct. But when they are used as crystals through which the present generation, as it reflects upon living, can look upon its own experiences and see them illumined and clarified, they become invaluable.

Not only does the church conserve its own peculiar part of the heritage of the past, but it makes this heritage live in the hearts of modern persons by vitalizing and dramatizing it in modern terms. How easy it is to illustrate this. There are Moses, Ruth, little Samuel, the boy David, Jeremiah, the Marys, and St. Paul, among persons. There are the courtship of Rachel, the sojourn in Egypt, the friendships of Jesus, the announcing of the beatitudes, and the symbolic Lord's Supper among events. Through art, story, and comparative discussion all these become significant carriers of the meaning of life and are made to live in the present. They get built into modern character in so far as the modern local church makes use of these products of the functioning of the venerable church-at-large.

The Church-as-a-community-unit

Every institution in a community is the sponsor for certain values, the worth of which it attempts to demonstrate. But the church is the only institution which avowedly undertakes to point to the highest values man can know. Its purpose is to keep these supreme values ever in the active attention of the whole community. It seeks to keep men living on the peaks of the culture of their time, and to criticize all the processes of human living from the standpoint of these peaks. This does not mean that it is the function of the church to ignore and scorn the values of these other institutions, but rather that it seeks to lead them to set the values of the specializing institutions into sound relationship with the highest values discoverable. The relating of these specialized values to God should bring an exaltation of them rather than a subordination.

The church-as-a-community-unit leavens the community. It exposes the community to the social contagion of its loyalties. These loyalties are given to causes which are the immediate forms through which the church serves the Highest. Through its symbolic reminders, its bulletin board and other announcements, its songs and discussions as they are carried from lip to lip, its choice of community projects into which it invests itself, and in many other ways, the community feels where the weight of the church is placed. In a community where there is a strong church, there is also a consciousness among the people of the presence of backing for standards and endeavors which they feel are worthy even though they may not be accepted by many groups socially important.

The provisions of religious resources for use by the community is another function of the church. Its doors stand open for those who would enter for quiet and worship. Its several sorts of services are announced where all may take note of them. Its staff often serves those who are not members in a number of ways—information, interpretation, counseling, comfort, and aid. It administers the sacraments to nonmembers in many instances, as through inviting those who are sincere participants to share in Communion, and in performing the marriage ceremony. It would take only a short stay in a church office to realize how many outside calls are made upon the religious resources furnished by the church.

A large share of responsibility for the morals of the communal life as a whole is expected of the church and usually assumed by it. It stands as critic and protector of the community. When acute problems of a moral nature arise, whether these concern recreation or education or vice or other matter, the church is counted on to take its stand and to participate in the needed reforms. Just as the state has its function in interfering in pernicious practices involving the various utilities essential to its citizens, so the church makes itself felt whenever there are pernicious influences upon the communal relations.

Further, the church-as-a-community-unit supplements the work of other community institutions. It is expected to render a sort of reserve service, entering any breach left unfilled by the other standard institutions. Where there is a real need not being met, it undertakes through its leadership, or through lectures and forums, or through sharing its building and other resources, or in some other way to meet the emergency. That it shall supplement and help sustain balance in building the good life in the community is an expectation growing out of its position as the institution which cares what happens to people and to society.

The Local Church

So large a part of the contact between individuals is mechanical and conventionalized that much personal expression is cramped and fellowship often lacks or loses meaning. An important function of the local church is to sponsor the type of fellowship which will bring persons into more profound and creative interaction one with another. Many other community institutions bring individuals together, often in huge masses, often again in smaller groups for specialized kinds of participation. But most institutions want to *use* the individuals so collected or to train them for social use. They have purposes to carry out. In these circumstances the relationships between the individuals are based upon their particular abilities or functions,[1] and not upon the desire to share their personal interests. The church can provide that type of fellowship where personalities do not have to act within the mold set by utilitarian, specialized interests. Such molds are necessary and proper in social enterprises organized to realize a specific aim. But individuals need additional fellowship on a personal basis in proportion to the extent to which they are required to give time and energy to utilitarian association. Since the church is concerned with the greater and deeper issues of life, there is tremendous opportunity here for fostering such meaningful fellowship that interaction tends to issue in creative developments worked out cooperatively. It is not a restricted, dutiful fellowship so much as a free and devoted one.

Because of the peculiar quality of the fellowship possible within the church, it becomes one of the important personality-fostering institutions. The sharing of deep loyalties to what is held as of highest worth sets up those voluntary self-disciplines which result in growth of culture. There is no means for promoting progressive integration of personality so strong and so rewarding as a progression of loyalties. This takes place through devotion ever to the Greatest known while ever sensing a Greater beyond. Such a process prevents complacency or other form of stunting of personality. Communion is in terms of what is vital and meaningful.

There is a corrective side to this function of fostering personality. It involves the care of the sick, the suffering, and needy. It is interesting to note an announcement of the Mormon Church in this regard. The Mormons gave themselves until October 1, 1936, to work out a program which would leave no Mormon on relief rolls or in serious need. Most churches have their individual, official arrangements for this aspect of their work.

[1] Cf. Macmurray, John: *Reason and Emotion*, pp. 94-106.

Since the church welcomes the family into its membership as a unit, it has a greater opportunity for serving little children than has any other institution except the family. Very early it can condition the young of the race with those aspects of the social heritage of which it is the carrier. Some churches continue the conditioning into the years of childhood and adolescence through parochial schools of their own instituting. There can be no question as to the contribution involved in arousing in the child loyalty to the Highest. The difficulty comes in making sure that this process does not become the equivalent of indoctrinating him with prejudices, untested traditional beliefs, and other stereotypes.

The church develops channels and patterns for the expression of enthusiasms, aspirations, loyalties—the strongest emotions. Sometimes this is a process of sublimation. But at its best it is a process of linking strong drives to an immediate objective which is a worthy representative of the basic object of loyalty, or of providing relevant tasks or ceremonial patterns which symbolically carry into overt expression powerful propulsions. This is a service which tends to keep the individual in equilibrium and to give him a sense of function and achievement.

Individualism characterizes much of the conduct of business, politics, and our general community association. The Christian religion goes to the opposite extreme and urges the necessity of a community of all mankind. The church, in so far as it is the agent of this tenet, draws the attention of men away from their self-centered preoccupations to become aware of other individuals in the world. It objectifies their interests, increases the circle of their social consciousness, and in time, with opportunity, builds a sense of brotherhood. The church needs to develop in its cultus appropriate and potent symbols for this function.

A venerable function of the local church, and one which needs further development these days is the sacramentalizing of the great crises of life. Some of its present sacraments have been long established: marriage, baptism of infants, and burial. There needs to be recognition of the other types of experience, such as appropriate celebration of events of great communal significance. Fitting commemoration helps people to discover the holy in notable human events. It imbues these crises with rich meanings. Further, the rituals used tend to provide patterns for the reactions of the persons undergoing the crises or strongly touched by them. Thus the emotional experience is somewhat objectified and given relevancy. This prevents that short-circuiting of the individual wherein his emotions strike back into himself at a time when he is illy prepared to suffer it. It is amazing to learn what Hitler has done in the way of sacramentalizing among the German youth those occasions and ceremonies which celebrate the reprehensible values he wants them to serve. It is doubtful if he could have held their loyalty to so great an extent otherwise.

The most particularized function of the local church is the development and provision of symbols by which men can become more conscious of God. Each church has its own rituals, music, tenets of belief, group practices, selections from literature, and other materials which promote this purpose. Also each has its methods for doing so, a very conspicuous one being a system of education of the young. Some other methods are revival meetings, religious counseling, retreats, study and discussion, and guided experiments. One of the chief failures in function today is in this particular. The old symbols are no longer potent enough. A new cultus must be fostered.[2]

In a society where the pull of most of the activities is toward oppressive individualism, toward disregard of personality, and toward materialistic values, there can be no doubt of the value of functions such as these which are distinctive of the church in one or all of its three aspects. Crowning all these other functions, stands the major function of the church, the fostering of religious loyalty to God. This it is which leads the church into such forms of service as are here suggested. Such service is indispensable to society always, but most crucially so when the system of values which dominates society is one which tramples the meanings out of life for millions, and then often goes still farther and shatters human life itself.

[2] Wieman, H. N., and Wieman, R. W.: *Normative Psychology of Religion*, pp. 90-107.

Now in the light of these significant functions of the Christian church, how can the church of today make its distinctive contribution? What are the ways in which the modern church must go about fulfilling these functions?

THE DISTINCTIVE TASK OF THE MODERN CHURCH

In its undertaking to guide the loyalties of men through search, worship, and service to the Supremely Worthful, there seem to be four main aspects of this task of the church which require attention. These four directions of effort are always the essentials in any one immediate period. The specific forms and objectives vary from period to period, as does the emphasis, but the main drives are the same because the practical objective of the church is always basically the same, i.e. to furnish the strongest, wisest, and highest guidance possible in the area of man's devotion to what he holds to be of greatest value. In such guidance are involved these tasks:

1. Develop such forms of those supreme values which the church promotes as will make them intelligible even to the meanest capacity and render them discernible in contemporary interests and problems.
2. Implement these values in terms of the day.
3. Provide opportunity for individuals and groups to have convincing experiences of these high values.
4. Critically evaluate contemporary processes in the light of these values and in the range of long-term perspective.

Developing Discernible Forms of High Value

The first aspect of the task involves the development of the forms by which God can be discerned and served in the modern world. If God cannot be found in the actual world in which people live, no matter how terrible is its condition in certain respects, then vital religion is impossible. People need to be helped to perceive the work of God in their ongoing activities, in the development of little children, in the economic system, in the cooperative efforts of state boards of relief, and in all the other processes closely connected with human living and fulfillment.[3]

When the Christian church can keep developing contemporary forms that are adequate to a pervading, deep, and vivid discerning of the nature of God, religion will be dynamically supercharged. The motivation from such a discerning of God will not be insecurely dependent upon individual or current convictions concerning immortality, nor upon the galvanic potency of particularly graphic portrayals of heaven and hell. Nor will it be conditioned upon the support of the theology of any one time or group. It will spring from a vivid sensing of the reality of God repeatedly experienced. People will always invest their loyalties in what they believe is of first value. There is no problem here. The task comes in developing the forms necessary to enable them to see that God is that First Value. Of themselves, the making of fiats and much vehement exhorting cannot accomplish the task. It is a matter of the effective guidance of the interests of human living and of the accompanying efforts at evaluation. Of course, before the church can render this guidance, it must have developed its own sound philosophy of religion.

Rendering Supreme Value Specific

The second aspect of the task is to enlist the loyalties of men in the rearing of those specific conditions required for the more abundant working of God in the midst of human activities. If we set out to list the areas of human interest where there is crucial need for the building of such conditions, we would be naming all the critical problems of our own time. We need conditions which will support deeper and more meaningful community between person and person, between persons and nature, and between persons and the technical implements now available. We need conditions which will foster an extension of the "we-feeling" out beyond intimate groups to the point where we can make effective and delightful the vast network of social interconnectedness. We need conditions that will give to all

---

[3] Wieman, Henry N.: "Man's Work and God's Work," *Christian Century*, April 8, 1936, pp. 531-533.

workers free access to the means of production to the extent that they are equipped to learn to deal with these and use them for the common good. We need the conditions of living that will decentralize our congested centers of population and so deflate those artificial prices upon real estate now responsible for many of the unhealthy conditions in human environment.

Some of these things could be done at once, relatively speaking. For instance our congested areas grew up out of the need to concentrate workers at locations where steam power was available, a power not transportable nor divisible. But now we have electric power which is both transportable and divisible, and which, furthermore, is cheaper in proportion to increase in the amount used. Other conditions will take longer to build, for they cannot be erected until many people are so educated that they can cooperate in carrying the present order through a series of breakdowns until the obstinately individualistic forces are overcome. The church itself can neither specify for its members, nor itself champion, the specific immediate objectives calling for crusaders in basic social reconstruction, but it can render a much greater service. It can unremittingly arouse and foster a progression of loyalties, leaving the individuals to decide in what particular form of social action these loyalties shall be expressed.

Promoting Convincing Experiences of Value

Once in Paris while an American woman was waiting for a conference with Mme. Curie, she noticed a slight, drably dressed, unassuming person skurrying through the room a number of times as though on an important and pressing errand. This person spent no glance upon anything outside her immediate business. The visitor took this person to be some worker assisting at the Institute. Her surprise was great when Mme. Curie entered and introduced herself at just the moment set for the conference. Mme. Curie and the unknown woman at whom she had been looking for some little time were one and the same person. The visitor had been seeing Mme. Curie without seeing her, for she had had no pattern by which she could discern her.

So it is in many matters, particularly the more profound ones. We are not always able to distinguish, to interpret, to comprehend the experiences which are ours. The third aspect of the task of the church is to help individuals and groups to know what is happening to them, to make sure that they taste convincingly the values which are of great worth and that they know how to interpret their tastings. Much that goes on in personal and community life uncovers or produces values that need penetrating interpretation.

As an example, when an employer sets up some sort of cooperative organization between himself and his employees whereby they are recognized as persons and recognize him as a person also, he feels his pulse quickened by the joy of deepening meanings coming into his living. He may come to think that this joy is entirely due to a very clever scheme of his for bettering his organization. Later he may begin to utilize it as a subtle means of increasing his own power over labor. If so, in the end, the joy and the meaning will be replaced by ugly tensions and conflict. But if he can gain the insight that he has fostered something of great significance both for the persons involved and for all of society, if he can be led to see that what is growing is of far more worth than any increased percentage of financial profit to himself, he will probably apply himself more assiduously than ever to the task of bettering the conditions for this growing order of value. Thus he will learn to distinguish the superior quality in the taste of power *with*, as compared to power *over*, others.

Again, when shameful conditions in the community are cleaned up, or some better form of association is instituted, or there emerges some new degree of plenitude through creative cooperation, there should be impressive recognition of the deeper meanings being fostered. Perpetrators of evil have their communal ways of celebrating their successes. All the more does the community need to have celebrated the many specific achievements that add meaning to the communal life. A little praise of the fostering of growth of good has more power as motivation than much haranguing about evil-doing. The church needs to bear in mind that evil-doing often glitters with the lure of adventure and other thrills: the community, particularly its youth, needs acquaintance with the more abounding adventure and thrill in creative promotion of growth of good in all its limitless variety. Since evil is the breaking down of what has been built up, while good is growth of value, it takes more able organization and more intelligent self-disciplines to promote growth of good than to perpetrate evil. For these reasons, continuous cultural training is required to lead individuals to understand and experience the satisfactions that come in the growth of value.

Criticizing Human Undertakings in Their Deepest Connections

The fourth aspect of the task of the modern church is that of studying out and demonstrating to present-day society the deep and ramifying interconnections among the diverse interests of life. These interconnections are first of all between the major interests of our immediate social period. Then there are the further important interconnections between these and the major interests both of the past and the future in so far as these can be discerned. The church can help give perspective.

Enthusiasms, aspiration, and loyalties, once thoroughly aroused, are likely to drive ahead with a zealous single-mindedness which precludes any appreciation of the relationship between the chosen enterprise and the rest of human living. Loyalties can be misdirected, can miscarry, can become fanatical, can lead into blind alleys, can involve the devotees in destructive conflicts, unless the values they conceive and serve are repeatedly scrutinized in their effective connections with other interests. An objective which seems worthy in itself may be discovered pernicious when viewed in relation to a wider social reference. A number of laws passed by governmental bodies provide examples of this. Such laws are instituted in an attempt to correct one evil or promote one good whereas it turns out that they have startlingly different effects, good or evil, upon matters and in ways not calculated.

This task of keeping the world ever informed and sensitized to the interconnections of all the diverse interests of human living is a colossally great one, but it is thrilling. The church is one major means of doing it. Jesus Christ used the figure of the vine and the branches to express the organic unity of all human living. There is no spot to which one can point and say, "There, the vine goes thus far and ends, and this branch goes thus far and there stops." Organic interconnectedness, as illustrated in the figure of the vine and its branches, is a connectedness of *functioning*, not of mere structure. Our need is desperate for continued, well-oriented, disinterested criticism of interfunctioning in terms of human investment and devotion. The church as the institution which promotes highest values must institute some means for providing this critical evaluation based upon a sound, enlarged perspective which comprehends the interconnections among all interests. Specialized institutions, because of their particularized interests, cannot furnish it.

Viewed in the large, the distinctive task of the modern church is centered upon continuously and progressively righting of the value-sense of society. On what grounds can the church be supported as it sets itself to this task of directing the reconstruction of the systems of values which dominate our society? Primarily on three premises: (1) that the present, dominant system of values called into practice and dominated by the ruling value, the profit motive, is destroying the meanings of life and, to an astounding extent, life itself; (2) that the church is the one institution which avowedly discerns and serves those values or meanings which are the highest as yet conceived, and which are comprehended in the value supreme over all, God; (3) that the function of the church overspanning all other functions is that of promoting religious living, and religious living requires a society directed by a system of values which recognizes the love of fellow men as the primary force setting into action and controlling all its varied currents of human interaction between persons, nature, things, and processes. The religious working system of values which makes love the controlling motive cannot function where the ruling system of values is dominated by the profit motive.

To work with the many particularized ills and evils resulting from society's present greed for individualistic profit is treating symptoms only. Radical treatment requires the reforming of the value-habits and value-ideals of mankind, a radical change in the ruling value in society's working system of values. Everywhere there is always devotion to what is believed to be of great value. The cardinal problem is that of determining the nature and relative magnitude of the value to which devotion is given. This is primarily a religious problem, hence a chief concern for the church.

THE STRATEGIC POSITION OF THE CHURCH

When Lincoln Steffens in his autobiography [4] reports what he learns from "Jake Riis," Dr. Parkhurst, and Richard Croker of Tammany Hall, he says in effect: When you strike at one group for the evils it is causing, you find out that this group is what it is because other groups are what they are: the evil practices and social malfunctioning of each group are inextricably involved in the nature of their connections with other groups: to solve social problems you have to go down deeper: just striking at one group will not work.

So it is when one tries to see clearly the position of the modern church in relation to its cultural functions. It must be viewed in the complex network of the total culture of which it is a part. On the one hand, there are at once obvious a discouraging number of handicaps, too real to make light of. The church has lost much of its erstwhile prestige. Its emaciating divisiveness has rendered futile much of its total investment of energy in promoting religious education, in lifting moral standards, in furthering racial and other forms of social justice, in dealing with its own conflicts with prevailing culture, in working for world peace, in socializing religion, and in otherwise trying to do its part. Indeed, it has largely lost adequate sense of its own function and hence of its own worth. In many cases its financial support is far from adequate for minimum effectiveness. Having grown up with the profit motive, it has become entangled in the antithetic interests of capitalism and has shared in the vaunting of individualism characteristic of this age of materialistic industrialism. In panic rather than in sound deliberation it has made compromising concessions

[4] Steffens, Lincoln: *Autobiography*, Chap. X-XIV.

of doctrine, policies, practices, and religious disciplines. To date it has built up no effective, universally helpful and respected source of appraisal and renewal for itself as a guiding institution, no well-supported agency of research and criticism free of coercive influence to deal with religious and institutional problems larger than the transitory ones of the moment. There are other faults and difficulties, described in the previous chapter, which handicap the church.

On the other hand, the church has a number of notable advantages of position. It is not intrinsically connected with any of the special interests—politics, organized industry, class distinctions—and hence *need* never suffer the involvement of its distinctive loyalties in their conflicts. Indeed, the practice of the church in financing its support through voluntary contributions, however crippling this may be in the direction of adequacy and of control of local programs, is nevertheless freeing in the direction of its larger policies and interests. It need not be under the jurisdiction of any other organized group.

The church is one of the two major institutions which may teach freely and openly the values which religion exalts. Next to the family and the church in this regard comes the school, though its teachings in this area must as yet be accomplished through quality of guidance rather than through open communication. The consensus of opinion still accords the church the distinction of being the one institution which avowedly and professionally stands for the highest values yet discerned. Such consensus is demonstrated both by the sharpness of the criticism of any existing church which fails in this function, and by frequency of the calls made upon the church for participation whenever good and evil are doing battle in the community.

Two further advantages accrue from this one: (1) many parents still send their children of formative age to the church school in the hope that they will be conditioned by superior influences, even when they themselves do not attend; (2) the influence of the church, when expressed with any reasonable degree of soundness, does have weight in community policies and practices.

A considerable asset of the church consists of those strong human sentiments attached to the church-at-large. This asset provides the local church with a clearer road of approach to individuals and groups when it seeks to enlist their cooperation for some cause. Because of the place it holds in public sentiment, the church is regarded as trustworthy, free from tendency toward public bribery or the criminal serving of ulterior ends. One type of evidence for this is the public shock when socially reprehensible acts are traced to officials of the church.

Perhaps the greatest practical advantage of the church arises from the fact that it has the family as its unit of membership in all but a comparatively few communities. This gives the church an opportunity to work on individual and racial beginnings of cultural development. The extraordinary potency of this element in the strategic position of the church is only coming to be appreciated.

Although the church is still guilty of discreditable maintenance of inequality in the man-woman relationship, it does have, potentially, great influence in bettering this condition of inequality. It affords normally two sorts of unusual opportunity: (1) a relatively nonexclusive group of men and women meet and work regularly together on a personal rather than on a man-woman basis; (2) both women and girls on the one hand and men and boys on the other are exposed to the *same* challenges to think in larger terms, and to share profoundly vital experiences.

The church provides opportunities, limited in variety and scope yet used by many women, for the meaningful investment of their talents and energies. In this aspect it has, at least potentially, influence over the attitudes and objectives of women as citizens, workers, mothers, and wives. This area, also, has not received the intelligent treatment its importance merits. The possibilities are of importance to all society.

Not the least advantage of the church is the reputation it has established as a recourse or a haven for those who are in some way troubled, whether by sense of isolation, or guilty conscience, or illness, or deprivation, or anguish, or devastating loss, or anxiety, or inner conflict, or deep perplexity, or whatever has broken the organization of their lives. At such times individuals are more open to learning better values, better ways of living, than when things are going along smoothly. Thus the church has the strategic opportunity of dealing with many individuals "at the psychological moment." Increasingly, groups as groups also are turning to the church when disturbed. Conspicuous among these are the family and the young people.

But there is a still higher point in its strategic position. The church possesses a perspective which, when used, enables it to evaluate issues above the bounds and the bias of class, race, nation, or other specific cultural division. The church is thus possessed of a great tradition, a slowly and painfully accumulating record of human experience, and an historical approach by means of which it can provide a wiser type of social guidance than can any one specialized institution in so far as the church holds true to the spirit rather than to the form of its heritage of vision. To the extent that the church avails itself humbly, comprehendingly, and efficiently of this enlarged and enriched perspective its counsel will be sought by mankind.

The two larger aspects of the church, the church-at-large and the church-as-a-community-unit, still continue to have certain unusual advantages of strategic position in this country in relation to cultural developments. It is the local church which is in much specific difficulty. This is to be expected, for the local church is the field of action whereon the prevalent culture and the Christian tradition must fight out their specific differences. This is less true of those churches which have strong national or international organizations. But it is true even of them, for while their head offices can control the local churches to some extent, they cannot control the community forces which act upon these churches. Both the Mormon and the Roman Catholic churches with their international unity of organization have recently felt the consequences of this fact and have renewed their zeal in building up reenforcements with which to meet more effectively the cultural impacts outside their control.

Perhaps the predicament of the local church will compel the divisions of the church-at-large to build up more assiduously and universally a new advantage, now appearing in its tentative beginnings. This is the unifying of all religious forces for functional purposes and projects. Since it is essential to the survival of the church, there is greater chance that it will be done and that relatively early in future history. Mention of this possible advantage has right of place here in this discussion of the strategic position of the church, for it is now not only a possibility but has beginnings which make it an emerging reality. The international conference of churchmen in Oxford in the summer of 1937 is a case in point.

If the churches truly believe in the supremacy of God, they will subordinate details of difference between cults and major divisions in this terrifying chaos, just as individual interests are forgotten when some valued community interest is tragically imperiled. How otherwise can the church as an institution make its values felt? How otherwise than in this uniting of great loyalties (not necessarily of creeds) can the church develop a sufficiently strategic position to deal effectively with the other major interests already organized to preserve lesser values? The resultant unity of loyalties would give the church enough power to be heard above the raucous bids on the market place, the burdensome groans in factory and field, the gloating laughter in high offices, and the shattering outcries of those for whom hope has gone.

Certainly unless all the divisions of the Christian church care more about God than they do about their own organizations and so set His cause above their several individualistic wills-to-power, they can ill expect the world at large to know enough or to care enough about God to seek His values first. All the divisions of the church know at least two things in common about God, that God is love and that His great commandment ordains that love shall govern the relations of mankind, including the relations of the churches. This provides sufficient dynamic and enough territory for all of them for stupendous common endeavor. In this potentiality lies the crux of the difference in power between the church-at-large and current culture. The achievement of functional unity under the commandment of God for the purpose of promoting the cause and the work of God would constitute the incomparable and invincible strategy.

Chapter VI

THE FOUNDATION OF RELIGION IN THE FAMILY

THE family is capable of achieving the deepest community. If particular families do not bear out this statement, it is because they have not realized the possibilities. The modern family has more with which to contend yet less inherent and social propulsion to functional unity than the family of the last century. The functions of the home have become involved in the functions of other social institutions in such inextricable ways that the home cannot now keep its social distance in reserved seclusion. No longer is there hot debate over the slogan "Woman's place is in the home," for the home extends as far as the interests of its members. Whereas in the old days the members found their toys, tools, much of their occupation and education, their favorite haunts and retreats, and most of their fellowship within the family, these are found now largely in the community. If the children go far to school or the employed members a distance to work, this community of the family spreads into a very extensive one.

The fellowship of the earlier family was implemented and actualized through countless possessions and undertakings shared by all its members. It was compact geographically and functionally. Also it had a much more centralized autocratic organization. Consequently, the strengthening of bonds and the guidance of choices and conduct were relatively simple matters. Everyone and everything was quite constantly, often painfully, under the paternal eye. Now that so many of the materials and processes of living are strewn all over the community far beyond the direct observation of the family, the functions of fellowship and guidance are complicated beyond measure. When almost every choice, relationship, and other reaction of every member involves one or more connections with outside factors, administering the family life becomes an undertaking of vast magnitude. Parenthood has become a distinctly public as well as a private office.

This change in the scope of family administration must be recognized. Increasingly the family must have its commensurate share in control wherever its major interests and investments are seriously involved. Therefore it must be educated for exercising its due part in this control. As its power for shaping society is enlarged in proportion to its extended responsibilities, and as the corresponding training is regularly established, the family can begin to take its place as a cultural unit with a sounder sense of its own importance and strength.

THE MODERN NEED OF FAMILY COMMUNITY

It is obvious that, in our day, deep community is much more difficult to achieve within the family. But it is equally true that there is more need for it than ever before. To begin with, individual need of it is greater. When population is not dense and industrialization has not mechanized and speeded up operations, there can be vital bonds of fellowship not only within the family group but also between neighbor and neighbor, between employer and employee, and among all the members of particular organizations. Whenever face-to-face contacts prevail, individuals can sense themselves and others as persons and as social agents. They can be conscious of the currents of mutual stimulation and response flowing between them. They can discern growth in themselves and others. They feel the sustaining and shaping nurture of their culture. But when the members of a family are caught into the gears of a conventionalized, routinized, specialized, impersonalized system as soon as they step from their doorways, they experience little nurture or community outside the home. Many current expressions reveal this: "Find out just what I'm up against." "It's tough sledding." "Got to stand up and take it these days." "It's a fight however you go at it."

Whether in business or in large schools or in various organizations, the individualistic aspects of expression are to the fore. Members of the family find little personal reinforcement unless these are present in the home. Any deep sense of kind, of kin, of human *kind*-ness, is generally lacking in modern society. Very little of our associational activity enriches personality or promotes community. Rather there is much to depersonalize every individual. Now, depersonalized individuals become a burden to themselves and their associates: they soon become a liability or a hazard to society. They have lost the drive toward higher values and the sense of joy in creative interaction with their fellows. They become dead weights. Their breaking may show first in their physical health, with mental, social, or religious disorganization following, or any one of these latter may be the forerunner of personal breakdown. Sharing of life is indispensable to the health of human personality.

We have seen how deep community of life in the home is needed by the individual. For the larger society, also, it is urgently important that the family renew its interest in fostering the rich community characteristic of it. The mechanization and standardization of most of the processes carried on today both by particular and by general group association tend more and more to break down all patterns and practice of personal communion. There may come certain basic changes in the social structure which will correct this tendency. If so, the close bonds of interdependence which have developed may then provide for a deeper life of personal enrichment. At present, however, the method of producing and distributing goods prevents the development of this life of sharing. Hence the tendency is now in the opposite direction. This fact calls for the equally constant building up of the forms and practice of communion by those institutions which are most concerned about the vital issues of life. Of these the family is the chief.

Individuals may be hungry for a quality of human-*kind*-ness in social intercourse, yet not know what it is they crave. Such hunger is a basic cause for much of the despondency, cynicism, and hard doubt of everything and everybody, which characterize many of our contemporaries, including some of the more eminent thinkers, writers, and artists. Unless growing individuals have had a convincing experience of the peculiarly rich, deep, and significant community possible within the family life, they will not as adults strive unceasingly to promote such community in all organizations. Such an experience gives them not only the taste and the appetite for this superb and essential value, but it trains them in some of the forms and practices by which it is developed and expressed. So equipped, they may help to develop and deepen human community in the larger society.

In truth there are present spirited examples which demonstrate this. Some business firms are experimenting in communal forms. Individual plants, however, cannot single-handed long maintain this fellowship of interests between workers and employers once they get caught into a grinding system of competitive struggle between industries. Certain schools have succeeded in building each teacher-class unit into a reinforcing and creative community. The small college is perhaps the most frequent example in this country of deep community in a group which quite literally shares diverse interests and aspirations. This life of community in the small college has been developed unconsciously for the most part, just as it has been in the home, through essential sharing of personal interests. It is a tragedy to see these small colleges [1] which were making a distinctive contribution (as can be proved by tracing through their alumni lists) lose their sense of function and their unique worth through trying to see how much of a university they can be. Not a few of the units of the various national youth movements have exhibited an ardent and powerful community. In some quarters the Cooperative Movement is a basis for a dynamic type of fellowship which claims wholehearted loyalty in its members.

All these examples presumably are indications of what may come. But the family will always remain the germinal source for such community, since the individual must be equipped with two things before he can seek or participate in such life of mutual enrichment. He must have developed that kind of personality

[1] The kind of training given by small colleges is not the kind which equips the individuals for the prizes offered by a competitive, individualistic social system. What it can and often does provide are the attitudes and patterns of true cultural enrichment and achievement.

which qualifies him for such association, and he must have a strong sense of the forms and values of such communion. These two requirements are developed normally in family fellowship.

It is clear that the present economic and political orders will have to undergo some change before this community essential to human living can become general. A number of leaders both within and without these orders are already voicing this need in one or another manner. In the interim, the family must bear a greater share of the responsibility for fostering and promoting the community within its intimate group and its closely related groups so that it continues as a developing and radiating center of supply for this cardinal social value.

Since this contribution of the home is increasingly both difficult and imperative at present, the family has need of every possible resource in sustaining this function. If the church is able to recognize this community of the family as the working of God, and is keenly wise enough to throw its strength to the service of this way of living in the home, it will meet a great emergency of our time. It will become a leader in great social transformation.

THE QUALITY OF LOVE IN THE FAMILY

The community, characteristic of the effective family, is one which furnishes conditions of freedom, of equality, and of mutual reinforcement commensurate with the development levels of its members. Because of these fostering conditions, the spontaneity of personality is released. Other institutions [2] must either constrain the individual in conformity to their duties and purposes (as an officer or employee in business), or release him in isolation (as the research worker).

Four factors typically undergird this possibility of family community: (1) its association is based fundamentally upon biological propensities which make its members peculiarly and essentially interdependent; (2) the interests of all members progressively become deeply and intricately bound together by the neces-

---

[2] Certainly friendship also releases the spontaneity of personality, but it is not an institution.

sity and the joy of sharing them; (3) it is relatively small and so can be intimate, flexible and experimentally creative; (4) the family seeks above all else to make life as meaningful as possible for all its members.

It is difficult to compress all these considerations into a working definition, but perhaps this one will carry the essentials from the point of view of present interest.

The family adjusted to its functions is that relationship of husband, wife and children, which tends to promote the greatest mutual appreciation, expression, reinforcement, and generation of personality.

This definition is really a description of love at work, for only when the family is bound by love can such promotion take place. It is in the family that interpersonal love reaches its highest development. The primary fact of love is the *disposition of acute sensitivity and responsiveness* toward another person. The *feeling* of love, in the sense of the glow or thrill, is secondary to the functioning of this type of relationship. When this functioning of the disposition becomes mutually conscious, then there is communion.

To set these statements into the form of definitions may serve to point more clearly to the essentials in family relationship.

Personal love, wherever experienced, is that disposition of sensitivity and responsiveness in one person toward some other person which requires for his fulfillment that the two carry on life together in the areas of shared interest.

Love may be experienced by one but not reciprocated by the other. It may be conscious or unconscious. It is always earned, never just happens, though it may appear to do so at times. It is always generated by the sharing of interests, though not all sharing of interests generates love. Changes in the character and degree of love are caused by changes in the character and degree of the sharing of interests.

Mutually conscious love is the communion, generated by the sharing of interests, between persons who take delight in each other and who mutually reinforce each other.

Communion is only a brief way of describing the process of manifesting this disposition of the one toward the other.

Personal communion is the mutual expression, appreciation, and reinforcement of personality. It requires the disposition of acute sensitivity and responsiveness between the persons involved.

Love, then, is a way of living.. Through the sharing of interests, mutual sensitivity and responsiveness are developed. This is not mere feeling about which one may wonder whether or no he has it, but a way of interacting. To be sure, such interacting is stirring, sometimes to the point of self-transformation or exalted achievement, and it may be thrilling to the point of deep felicity or of ardent ecstasy. But the feeling is a concomitant not the primary process. When the sensitivities and responsiveness between two persons become acute, it means that their sharing of interests has become so thorough that a break between them of any sort will mean a serious break in living. The two "have become one" in the sense that they are peculiarly interdependent. Each is trustee for the other of the most precious values of his life. Hence each is equipped either to promote the highest fulfillment of all the possibilities of the other, or to shackle and shatter him. Each senses that it takes the functioning of the other combined with his own to make up a wholeness in living. Each senses that he is not his full self without the other.

A brief digression is relevant at this point to call attention to the fact that there are a number of forms of extreme selfishness which sometimes masquerade under the facsimile of "love." Possessiveness, paternalistic and maternalistic domination, self-identification, lust, jealousy, sudden infatuation, oversolicitude, idolizing, babying, subtle hypocritical exploitation, spoiling, and "self-sacrificing" martyrdom are among these. They are in reality aspects of self-love, not of love in the true sense of sensitive and reinforcing communion with another. The confusion of these very different qualities of relationship with love is increased tremendously because it is constantly authorized by the ordinary movie, short story, and novel. Since many individuals sincerely believe that these counterfeits are love, they grow indignant or bitter when the values inherent in the love relationship are not forthcoming from these falsely labeled forms of selfishness. But these cannot yield the values of love, for they are diametrically different from love. They even destroy the conditions necessary to the growth of love. The focus of attention in these other relationships is upon the advantage or pleasure of the self instead of upon the sharing of interests with the other, however cunningly the selfish motive may be rationalized.

Love grows great only through interacting. The more diverse and all-comprehending the sharing of interests and the more significant the interests shared, the more complete is the love. Whenever one of the persons in the love relation has certain areas of interest which he believes he cannot share with the other, there is a barrier which is bound to make itself felt. This is true whether the reason for the shielding of one or more areas is shame, or fear of outcome, or distrust that the other will treat his protected interests with injustice or sacrilege. *Complete love* can come only when there are no factors to limit complete loyalty and trust. Complete love is, of course, not a matter of chance but a development which takes time and devotion.

GOD IN FAMILY LIFE

No man can say unto himself, "Now I am going to fall in love." Love starts before the persons concerned can know it, for it arises in the spontaneous interweaving of personal interests. It cannot be made by man, nor developed where and when and as he would.

This does not excuse man from looseness in the love relation, for while he cannot make love grow or stop its growth directly, he can regulate the conditions of its growth. Knowing the conditions and how basically to control them makes the love-life of a person subject to his responsible concern. This holds both for the growth of love where the individual has already pledged his interests and loyalties, and also for the prevention of love in contacts where a deepening in the sharing of interests is illegitimate to the business at hand and is violating to other relationships.

Love grows under the same conditions that govern all significant growth. There are two requirements, one concerning the materials, the other concerning the process. These as particularized in regard to interpersonal love must be formulated. (1) The persons must each represent such an organization of interests, actualized or potential, as shall make the sharing of interests mutually helpful and meaningful. (2) The conditions must be provided for an enriching and progressively comprehensive sharing of these interests. When these two requirements have been met by persons, the rest is the work of God. It must be understood, however, that the fostering of these conditions requires constant attention and frequent reestablishment by the parties concerned.

It is abundantly apparent that the family is the institution which is incomparably organized to provide these conditions. It is not therefore surprising that poets and philosophers, novelists, and even sociologists recognize that love develops as an essential characteristic of any home at all adjusted to its functions. The family more than any other institution brings together persons whose interests can be shared, indeed must be, and then provides the conditions for sharing in such a way that mutual expression, appreciation, and reinforcement of personality take place.

Now this is only another way of saying that the family is the situation most open to the presence and the work of God. God *is* love. God is the interweaving of the interests of men into larger wholes which increase the abundance and meaning of all living. Out of the unity which comes of such interweaving, great values are realized, and they emerge through the work of God even though the persons concerned may not recognize God in them. It is through family nurture that the individual becomes aware of this unifying process by which he is interwoven into the fabric of the whole.

This interweaving creates human personality out of the vegetative organism of the infant. It transforms the self-centered personalities of the young man and woman about to marry into first

a family-centered and then a community-centered expression of
their personalities. This interweaving of interests and activities
is the generator of all the meanings and growth of culture, such
as language and art, science and industry. It transforms man from
an animal that struggles merely to exist into a human being that
struggles for an ever-better way of living. This superhuman,
transforming, and value-making power is God at work in human
life. It is constantly manifest in the typically functioning family
as the communion which organizes and unifies their interests.
"The Kingdom of God is within you." It is open to the experience of every member of the family.

THE FAMILY AS A SOURCE OF CULTURE

Principles of social psychology and historical fact both show
that the family is the situation in which take place all the developments just cited and more. This social situation which appears in
the family is not a mere aggregation of individuals but is a bond-
building interaction generated by the intimate and long-continued
interdependence and cooperation which occurs characteristically
in the family. The mechanisms by which this interdependence and
cooperation produce the development of the great values of life
may be briefly sketched.

The beginnings of family life marked the beginnings of a new
necessity in human living. The long-continuing helplessness of
the infant and the occupation of the mother in the care of the
baby instituted a prolonged, intimate, and complex interdependence and cooperation within the family group. Out of the
interstimulation thus engendered, forms and symbols of communication arose by which meanings were generated, discovered,
expressed, and built together. Each symbol, whether vocal or
visible, was a convenient receptacle for holding and dealing with
their common experiences in various areas of their activities. The
use of these symbols enlarged tremendously the scope of their
living. As soon as symbols emerged in their fellowship, the family
began to organize cooperatively their shared interests. Whereupon the order for mere preservation of life gave way to the
order which promotes the abundant life. It could do so because

the use of symbols facilitated its dealings with many of the aspects of life.

When this stage was reached, the critical point had been gained, for then plans of action, i.e., ideas, could be lifted out of the immediate situation and dealt with in the abstract. The significant symbol, and it alone, made this possible. With this practice of dealing with ideas in the abstract, the life of aspiration and of enlargement of meaning originated. The individual and the group began to strive for ideal possibilities. Living was no longer like the stringing of beads, but more like the growth of a tree. Each activity was connected with others into a growing system of interdependence, cooperation, and meaning which opened out into unexplored possibilities. When human life thus aspires and strives for ideal possibilities, personality and culture develop. The family, because of the necessities imposed by its essential functions, has developed the use of those symbols by which significant communication and abstract thinking become possible in each maturing person. Therefore it has been the originative source of the life of aspiration toward unrealized possibilities.

In primitive conditions the family was practically the sole source of cultural growth. Today there are many agencies and institutions that aim to promote it in specialized forms. But the family remains the only place where the most vital interests of culture are selected and synthesized for the development of personality. It is as true of the modern family as it was of the primitive that close-knit cooperation and complex interdependence make for community of interest. Family life both fosters and finds inevitable the communication and development of meanings among its members. The coercion of biological dependence is as great as ever before, perhaps greater from the point of view of the prolonged preparation now required for independent economic existence. Then to this profound biologically coercive force are added propulsions toward community in the form of modern intensifications of certain other human demands. Two of the most driving of these propulsions are the need of emotional satisfaction of a balanced and releasing sort and the need of special areas in living where individual differences and aptitudes receive understanding attention. Both of these needs have become acutely intensified through the modern massing of individuals together in work, study, and sports in ways that result in the treatment of the individual as a functional unit. When so treated, the individual must act within the external limits which have been set up, rather than as a person free to interact creatively, or at least reciprocally. These and other demands which cannot receive adequate satisfaction except in the intimate relations of the family life amplify enormously the coercion set up by biological need toward deepening communion within the family.

Every augmentation of the need for communion increases communication, and communication involves a sharing of meanings with the concomitant development of the symbols which carry these meanings. The family makes use of the accumulated symbols from the past, but, in addition, develops new symbols. The husband and wife, as adult social agents, introduce into their communications a more or less generous selection of the cultural symbols which make up their social inheritance. As these are used in the family, they are enriched by new meanings which they silently gather. Then, because each family is a unique institution composed of unique personalities and developing a unique communion, it develops new symbols through which to conserve and use its own common experiences. From the rich accumulations of symbols into which the members have rolled up their past experiences and are carrying them about with them, they can project themselves and their interests farther and more clearly into the future. Ideals begin to take form, for ideals are only projected ideas toward which persons feel a strong drive of interest.

Now as soon as a person has built his own access to the realm of possibilities, his life of aspiration with its expanding meanings begins. The person under the compulsion of his aspirations, begins to discipline himself, seeks to organize his personality with discrimination in reference to these possibilities. His activities are guided and pervaded with the meanings he conceives as immanent or possibly now emerging. In brief, culture is growing.

In contrast to this, when the individual tries to sustain merely his own existence amid plentiful supplies, each object is dealt with directly rather than through symbols, accepted or rejected in accord with its serviceableness to the tastes and needs of the organism. There is little opportunity for the development of meanings which connect his activities into a system. Life in such conditions tends to be like the string of beads just referred to—one detached activity and one separate day after another. The more individualistically men have lived the more tendency there has been to remain subject to this external type of control of their individual interests. Indeed, it may well be questioned whether important community *can* be deliberately fostered where there is not already present an order of interrelated activities which press the individuals toward communication and sharing of meanings. *All important community is engendered and maintained by the coercion of interdependence.* So appears the testimony of both growing and dissolving groups. Sometimes the interests which are shared within a group are not easy to recognize, are covered under a nominal statement of aims, pledges, or by-laws. But wherever true communion exists there seems to be significant interdependence coercively fostering it.

The individualist, however, is relatively free from the unrelenting compulsion of such common interests. He is not forced to build connections which are supporting and promising between his interests and those of others, and between his present interests and the future. He not only *acts* independently, but he *passes* independent *judgment* upon his own acts. There is no reciprocating criticism and communication by which rich meanings grow. Inevitably, with his independence of action, there necessarily goes an absence for him of the support, loyalty, and creative development characteristic of mutality. That is the price he must pay for his individualism. His self-determination does not permit true freedom. Many realms of value are closed to him.

The quality of communion which the person has with his fellows conditions the quality of his growing personality. Where the interests shared are great in number, variety, and significance, communication is great and significant. Hence life also is great and significant as experienced both in the activities dealing with the realities of the everyday and in the activities reaching out toward the highest, as yet unactualized, realities in the realm of possibility. The interests of the individual persons are interwoven into the fabric of the whole, a progressively comprehensive whole.

The individual feels the unity of the whole through experiencing his unity with it. He comes to serve this unity, sensing that it is the growth of meaning in the world through which comes the highest possible fulfillment. Through this reaching out even to the highest, his life comes to be a progression of loyalties.

Now the family fosters this process in so far as it fosters the kind of community peculiar to its organization. The family may get started on the most individualistic bases, and for some time may act in selfish and divisive ways. But the moment a genuine sharing of significant interests begins, love begins, too, and love engenders increasing communion. It is a common sight to see mutual interest in the first child draw husband and wife together into a functioning unity which brings deepened meaning into their living. They sense that a new something is working in their midst. Their attitudes and plans of action are gradually transformed through their loyalty to this growing and meaningful unity. They discipline themselves and organize their interests to provide better conditions for its growth. They find that their own interests are being interwoven with an ever-widening cultural area. They find that love does not suffer from wider sharing, but rather so grows. They find themselves doing things for love's sake which are beyond their most aspiring earlier dreams. They may come to know that they do them essentially in the name of God, since God is love. When they do recognize these processes and works that deepen their communion as the work of God, and realize that what they are doing is building up the conditions for His work, their living has become religious.

RELIGIOUS EXPERIENCE IN THE FAMILY

By authority and by conviction the Christian way of living is rooted in love. It sets first the love of God as the supremely worthful object for all human devotion, and the love of one's neighbor as one's self. These are the two great Christian commandments. They have come to have a wider than avowedly Christian application, for most men sense in them principles of living fundamental to the highest human and cultural fulfillment. Except as men devote themselves to the highest Reality of which they can conceive, and then express this devotion in terms of effective loyalty to the most significant immediate realities of their diverse, everyday associations, they suffer chaotic depressions, devitalizing wars, contaminating and contagious evils of all sorts.

The constant effect of religious living when devoted to God as above described is the promotion of ever-greater unity among men through the sharing of loyalty to that which they hold as of Supreme Value. A religious group is a group marked by this high type of personal communion. This is the kind of association which is more characteristic of the family than of any other institution. So it is that the family is the fostering home of this kind of religion for the individual and the race. To repeat: it is through family nurture that the individual becomes aware of this unifying process by which he is interwoven into the fabric of the whole. If it were not for this unifying process within the true family communion, the individual would be a sort of ricocheting atom bobbing about in a mechanistic, individualistic way. This would be so because he would connect with his world only through mechanistic and external relations instead of through organic ones which could give him the creative freedom open only to those bound within the communion of shared loyalties to great and greater worths. When the individual realizes that all these values of life are generated and carried by this unifying process which operates preeminently in the family, he sees the religious significance of the family.

God is the unity-building power, the love-stirring power. In the family the individual comes into the most full and direct connection with it. The child can find God in the communion of family life as he can find Him nowhere else. Other manifestations of God are beyond his scope until he approaches maturity. But God is operatively present in the family and has to do with the direct concerns of the child. Therefore, it is of great moment to the child that the unity of his family be sustained. Even when he cannot say what is the matter, he knows it and is emotionally unstabilized when this unity is threatened or broken. God is love, which means He is the interweaving of all the diverse interests and elements into a meaningful whole. The child can feel the work of God simply and directly, and in time can himself help in providing the conditions which will supply more ample room for the presence and work of God. The child grown to full maturity will have many ideas of God, but this foundational one of God as love, as the builder of deepening communion, as the interweaving of the diverse interests of several persons into a progressively significant whole, he can experience before he can be told of it.

The essential thing is that the adults shall themselves recognize this unifying interaction in the family as God, and give their religious devotion to it accordingly. The naming of God will come as no bewildering event if members of the family have seen to it that the child has been richly introduced to the experience of God through His working of unity in the family. But the naming should not come until after there has been ample experiencing of the reality. Then the naming of God will be primarily a matter of identifying God in the very real concerns of the child. The great religious function of the family is to introduce the child to God in this way.

Parents are always asking, "How can I help the child to find God?" All the opportunity they can use is in the everyday life of the home. What unfailingly attracts the child's attention toward God are those doings of his parents which express their loyalty to this unifying interaction. The child can see for himself great things done for the sake of this growing unity. These arouse his wonder and eventually his questions.

It is interesting to note that the family of limited means is much more likely to be compelled to build up a creative and meaningful sharing of their interests than is the family which has enough so that each member may live as an individualist. A young couple who have to work together to build a common life are less likely to miss God than the couple who are not compelled to lose themselves for the sake of a valued objective in their common life. This fact, that those who are *compelled* to share interests more interdependently and cooperatively are less likely to miss God, is very significant. It means that, as a people, we have not yet come into the recognition of how God works in the intimate group and hence how we can promote His work consciously by providing the right conditions. When we do learn this, we shall see that it is necessary to make some colossal changes in conditions. Also we shall hear a great call to intensify our devotion to certain conditions now at our hands. It is unseemly that so cardinal a matter as recognition of, and cooperation with, the work of God be left to the chance compulsion of limiting, difficult circumstances.

The deep significance of two facts should be noted: (1) the association of the family is the kind of communion where the child can be most effectively introduced to God; (2) it is through this communion that God can most potently shape the living of the child. Whether this second will eventuate, will depend primarily upon the quality of the religious living of the parents. The type of interweaving of interests going on between them and the effectiveness with which they build the conditions for increasing communion within the family will determine how full and how convincing the child's experience of God will be. There is no other area of life open to the child where God is so observably and intimately dealing with persons as in the family. It is here that the child can get his first deep sensing of God working for human fulfillment. The child starts by sensing and appreciating God as manifest in the home, and this prepares the way for sensing and appreciating God in the neighborhood, in the larger society, and finally in the great perspective of history.

Not only does the child find God intimately in the home, but also husband and wife have potent experiences of God. Their relationship is ideally the deepest and closest of all interpersonal communions. Hence it is here that God is most fully manifest and most readily discerned by adults. The fact that husband and wife have freely chosen each other as the ones most signally equipped for a progressive sharing of interests provides the essential bases for establishing reinforcement and communion, equality and freedom.

The modern couple, perforce, must develop its deeper communion under many serious handicaps. Not the least of these is the illusion that love is something that can happen to come or happen to go, when in reality it is something which grows when and as it is nourished under the correct conditions. This illusion eventuates in the tendency to "settle down," or to watch inertly to see what will happen. Instead of this, the marriage should be the commencement of a conscious active devotion to the building of an ever more enriched and powerful love-life, first between the two, and later in the family and in the operative community. When the sharing of interests between husband and wife becomes so interpenetrative that they can function and create as one in consummatory moments, they have vivid and pervasive experiences of God.

This central fact, then, that God finds entry into the life of man more intimately and directly through the community of the home than anywhere else, shows the importance of mastering the difficulties which beset the family. It also demonstrates that this is the crucial point upon which the church should concentrate its powers. There is not one of the problems of a growing culture and of the work of God in the world but must be grappled in the issues of this institution, for it is a basically indispensable one. But when the church tries to deal with these problems as they occur in other institutions and organized group conflicts, it becomes compromised in serious difficulty in areas where it has not the training or functional authority to work. Its difficulty here is serious because the problems appear on a partisan and competitive level. When these problems appear in the family, however, they come in the form of vital issues of life, essentially nonpartisan and profoundly significant. It is on this level that the church can most fittingly and competently deal directly with the great social problems of the day. Dealing with these on the vital level of the family tends, also, to correct the prejudiced distortions which characterize them on the economic and political levels. The character of the community of the family clarifies and simplifies the nature of the values involved in these problems, for it reveals which are genuine and which are artificially inflated or false in terms of highest human fulfillment.

Chapter VII

THE INTERDEPENDENCE OF FAMILY AND CHURCH

ONLY now after it has become clear past any doubt that religion is essential to full family living can we be dynamically interested in the relation of church and family. The chief function of the church is to foster religious living. The family is the most propitious group for growth in religion. Only through religion can the community of the family reach its richest and most comprehensive best. Only through the fostering of genuine community in the family can such community be fostered and increased among mankind. Only through the growth of community among men can religious values prevail in human activities. The child depends upon the family for early discoveries of value and early guidance in his loyalties to the highest values discovered. In other words, he depends upon the family for his progressive discovery of the working of God. In turn the family depends upon the church for guidance of its highest loyalties, for its discovery of the working of God in the larger, more diversely interdependent, and hence more involved community.

AREAS OF COMMON INTEREST

When the church is functioning with the family as this kind of community, it is functioning with the mainspring of the growth of religion. This is so whether one thinks of the growth of religion in connection with the growth of the child or in connection with the growth of culture in the larger society. The two highest observable manifestations of God are the development of personality in the individual and the growth of culture [1] in the group. Both the family and church are personality-fostering, culture-fostering institutions in the major sense. They have the same purpose though they approach it from different angles. The family pursues its purpose out of a biologically conditioned interest in the bringing of the personality of its members to the highest fulfillment. The church pursues its purpose out of a religiously conditioned interest in the bringing of human life to highest fulfillment throughout the wider reaches. These purposes are attained only through promoting both the development of personality in the individual and the growth of culture in the group. But it is in these two processes that God is most manifest. In promoting these the family and the church are promoting the work of God. These two institutions work with the same purpose and the same material. The purpose is highest human fulfillment, and the material is human life.

God, religion, the church; these three terms have come to the fore in considering the community characteristic of the family engaged in fulfilling its functions. These are not the same, even though they are frequently confused in thought and use. Confusions hinder effectiveness in functioning. What do we mean by these terms? How do they enter into the matters of concern here? Let us try to state these distinctions between God, religion, and the church as they need to be discerned by the members of the family group endeavoring to cultivate the religious life of the home.

God is the power which interweaves the interests of the members, at first and always within their own group but later including an ever-widening community. Our century-old way of saying this is, "God is love." As we have shown, this interweaving is not a mere matter of the wish or labor of the members, but is a process acting beyond their full knowledge and direct control. The community of the family, founded as it is upon an inevitable sharing of interests, is the working place of God in the home.

[1] Culture here, as elsewhere in this writing, is used in the sense defined in foot note 1, Chap. I, p. 9.

Religion in the family is the devotion of its members to the cause of God. This centers their efforts upon the discovery and setting up of such conditions as will promote the growth of creative fellowship both within the private community of the family and gradually throughout the larger community of which it is a part.

The institution of the *church* is the reinforcing fellowship of families that widens and deepens the community in each family by making its members participants in a larger fellowship which includes the "invisible community of all the faithful" in their common devotion to God.

To consider comparatively the functions of the family and of the church is to see how many areas of interest are common to the two institutions. They have the same basic objective, highest human fulfillment. As has been pointed out, the church, religiously conditioned, seeks to realize this goal in a vast, comprehensive form. The family, biologically and psychologically conditioned, serves this objective in an intimate and specific form. Because their essential purpose is the same, both institutions find themselves interested in fostering the same conditions for individual and group living, namely, those which will best promote rich and integrated growth.

In institutions other than the four personality-fostering ones, concern for the conditions of living is incidental to their main objective. If they work directly in promoting the right conditions of living for some specific group, it is because they feel that they must do so in order to fulfill their own particularized ends. Many industrial plants have found that they have had to give such heed. It is to be hoped that this coercion exercised upon industry by the necessary requirements of its own success will eventuate in the correction of its own principles and procedures at those points where these are responsible for the evil conditions in question. Certainly, it is a right order of things when, in the long run, the mistakes and crimes of a social institution return to it like a boomerang. It may arouse foresight to take the place of hindsight. Industry would not have to arrange directly the conditions of living of its workers if it rendered a wage which would allow the family to provide the conditions necessary for living on the human level. All personality-fostering institutions are aroused when it becomes impossible for them to set up, each according to its particular share, the conditions essential for human living. The home and the church are most directly disturbed, however, for they deal intimately with the conditions basic to the development of personality.

Because the church and the family have, then, a common basic objective and a common field of effort, they experience much the same joys and sorrows. Their values and disvalues are shared. What promotes one promotes the other. What frustrates one frustrates the other. Their interests are radically enmeshed.

A cardinally significant point of union for the working of church and family is their focus upon the immature. In the main, the most effective work of each is that done with individuals in the earlier years. At this time the interests of the growing child are generalized ones. They become differentiated only gradually. Religion is the last interest to come to maturity of form and content. This keeps the work of the church much like that of the family during these earlier years. So it is that these two institutions find themselves united in serving the individual throughout the period of his immaturity. There are important differences in total plan and specific aims on the part of the parent in the home and the teacher in the church school, but these differences exist as inner purposes open only to indirect expression for some long period. During this time the objective of direct guidance for both of them must be that of helping the child to the greatest fulfillment possible to him at each period of his growth. Differentiation of economic, vocational, scientific, religious, and other interests must be an evolving process. The adults concerned must build the conditions to prepare for and promote this evolving, to be sure, but they cannot work directly with the interests which have not yet evolved, though a discouragingly large number try to do so.

They can deceive themselves into thinking they are doing so by using the vocal symbols of these interests even though their words are as yet meaningless to the child.

As the child matures, the particular work of the church and of the family in promoting his fulfillment begins to show distinctive differences. Even then, however, the two institutions are continuously and vitally concerned in his maturing. It is chiefly a difference of emphasis. During the beginning years the church must support and supplement the family, for it carries the chief responsibility. During the later years of this maturing the family must support and supplement the church in its specialized development of religion as a major interest of the young.

That these two institutions are essentially interdependent has become apparent. Each of them needs and supports the other in so far as they serve their distinctive purposes. Their mutual support can be more effectively achieved where each institution understands clearly the major grounds for the interdependence between them. What are these bases?

THE DEPENDENCE OF THE FAMILY UPON THE CHURCH

A Cultural Neighborhood

The family requires a cultural fellowship. Seldom does the geographical neighborhood any longer furnish this. The family counts upon the church for a new kind of neighborhood, a cultural neighborhood based upon a community of interests. No matter what the background of the particular home in economic, social, educational, racial, or other respect, the family is reasonably sure of finding fellowship in some church group. The need is an acute one today when most geographical neighbors are strangers.

A reinforcing fellowship in the sharing of interests that have real import for the participants not only promotes more significant communication and more diversified cooperation but also provides for mutual support of noble effort and aspiration. Most other institutions have restrictions in the form of admission charge or of standards of clothing and entertainment or of social connections which are prohibitive. But the church, normally, is concerned not with exclusiveness and display, but with building a meaningful community in which there is place for every family and every member of the family. Even many families who do not themselves participate in this fellowship realize its value. The church is the one institution which has shouldered the responsibility of instituting this meaningful fellowship in the midst of a society all too much afraid of being caught serious-minded or devoting itself to higher values. Recently, certain new developments have made some contribution here: adult education, organized groups for forum discussion, and various brotherhoods and associations united for social action. However, they seldom include the whole family; they tend to be limited in devotion, and they are instrumental rather than nurturing groups. These cultural neighborhoods provided by the church are primarily nurturing fellowships. Normally, they serve the needs of young people just as truly as they do those of adult members of the family. They are important cultural soil for the family.

The Discovery of Its Deeper Functions

The jurisdiction of the home now extends so far and involves so many factors, both accessible and inaccessible, that it is the unusual family which does not get lost, culturally speaking. For this reason, the home needs the cooperation of other institutions constantly. The public school gives certain forms of assistance, but thus far its prevalent attitude has initiated the policy of keeping the parent in his place, with the understanding that his place is not in the school except on announced occasions. The Visiting Teacher Movement, the Parent-Teacher Association, and parent-education classes are evidences of growing school-family relationship. There must be more of this cooperation, for the family requires it. But when the school has done all that it can, the fact will remain that it specializes in the promoting of those aspects of personality held at the moment in highest regard by society and cannot help the family in developing many of the more fundamental aspects. For one thing, the officers of the school do not yet have time to get truly acquainted with parents. Also, the family hesitates to confide its concerns, plans, and ideals to the school since the relation between a specific family and school is ordinarily a much more formal one than is the relation between a specific family and church. Further, it is a more transitory one in that the child passes from one teacher and school to another, or from one whole group of teachers to another whole group. Beyond all this, the school is very busy completing its curriculum: its focus of attention is upon the *children* it must deal with; its concern is not centered in the family life of its students except when trouble with a child compels this.

In opposition to this, the church has the strongest of reasons to care how the family, in whole and in part, grows and succeeds. Usually each local church does care. Increasingly the church is feeling its way toward meeting this need of the family for more help from the church in discovering and in performing its distinctive functions. Since to both adults in each new partnership in homemaking their project is a new and complicated one, they are all too likely to become totally involved in the specific undertakings of their workaday worlds. They need guidance if they are ever to discover that deepest good, truth, beauty, and unity of family living without which the program of activities soon becomes a type of bondage. It is a pathetic fact that many parents wear themselves down into nonentities without ever once thrillingly awakening to the personal and world importance of their distinctive functions. Nor have many of them experienced the peculiarly rich satisfactions which emerge as the family progresses in the fulfilling of these functions.

The children of such parents as have discovered their essential functions need guidance also. It is no glib task to lead them to see that their parents are setting up the principles, standards, and programs of living according neither to their own individual biases nor to the styles in the neighborhood, but upon the basis of a dominant loyalty to the Greatest Good they know. Today the average child tries to establish authority for securing what he wants by personal encounter with his parent: "Why can't I go? Mrs. Freeman *always* lets Bill go."

In these days, the Babel of authorities on the conduct of living is so irrational and discordant that the family can find neither meaning nor harmony of purposes in listening to its voices. This is a shattering misfortune for those families who do not realize that, failing a common social authority, they need to go deeper for their authority in life. Contrariwise, this situation is the fortunate opening of a life full of thrilling meaning yet of deeply challenging consecration for those who have located their ultimate authority and have discovered the functions which support and sustain the *growth* of this Greatest Good to which they have pledged their devotion. There is no aspect of educational guidance more essential or more difficult than this—helping the family, as a unit and severally, to discover and fulfill its deepest functions. There is no other institution today other than the church which has the motivation and equipment for carrying on this indispensable educational guidance.

Religious Ministry in Time of Strain

The family has long counted upon the church for religious ministry whenever the pressures of life have become oppressive. There are two general types of trouble in which the family seeks such ministry. One type includes the problems and perplexities which are involved in its efforts to adjust itself, either as a unit or through one or more of its members. The other type includes the crises of life, those so great that the present organization of life of the family or of the individual is broken temporarily or permanently, and a new organization must be built up. Examples of the former type involve such matters as domestic friction, neighborhood problems, and parent-child tension. Examples of the latter type are death, marriage, sudden, sweeping loss, and deep conviction of guilt.

Today there are other social agencies to which families may turn for help in time of trouble and many do so. This is well, for there are numerous problems of the family which the church is not equipped to treat. However, there is no agency so universally available as is the church. It is easily accessible almost anywhere and its ministry is free. But beyond these advantages there are two others of deeper significance. One of these is the peculiar appropriateness which many families sense as present when the church helps it in times of special stress. They feel that this service rightfully is connected with religion, particularly in those cases where the pastor has known the family during a long period. The other advantage is the religious way of handling the trouble. To be sure, many pastors do not know how to handle problems and crises religiously. They do it conventionally, that is to say, theologically. However, ideally administered, the religious approach is deeply effective, for it seeks to restore to wholeness. It is not satisfied with either inadequate extreme—mere preaching and exhorting, or mere reestablishing of equilibrium on the easiest level possible. Religious treatment becomes a part of the total progressive integration of the individual and of the group.

There is no question but that the church must know the limits beyond which it should not go in this field of ministry to the family in its times of trouble. However, there is no question either but that the church must increase rapidly its facilities and preparation for this type of ministry to the family. As has been pointed out, times of trouble are times when the spirit is open to learning higher levels of value. The prime work of the church is, at bottom, work with values.

Cultivation of the Extension of Its Community

Not only does the family depend upon the church for these three ministries we have been discussing, the fostering of a cultural neighborhood, guidance of its regular functions, and special help in times of trouble, but it needs the church urgently as an orienting agency.

As we have already noted, the family tends to become remote, provincial, and ingrowing. Once its unity is established, it tends to treat its home as its exclusive club, its castle, its city of refuge, its clan, and so to cut itself off from the possibility of growing. The more it takes delight in the unity it has built within itself, the more likely it is to become fixated. When this happens it loses whatever social power still remains to it. It discovers that it has not kept up a functioning relationship with the other social orders of its time and place and consequently finds itself caught in their power. There is a parallel in the relation of the human organism to the material world. It is ever renewed and sustained and strengthened so long as it reacts with air and sun, but is disintegrated by these very materials as soon as it ceases to interact with this raw energy. The only way in which the family can keep outside forces from gaining arbitrary, determinant control over it is to learn to work with these forces in increasing mutuality. This requires a progressive widening of its community. The family which resists expansion of interest and persists in complacent satisfaction within the limits of its pleasing or favoring community will eventually suffer deterioration and spiritual death. It will save itself only to lose itself. Its community must grow or die.

Forms for Interpersonal Fellowship

Interestingly enough, history indicates a great reversal in the source of the derivation of forms for interpersonal communion. As a matter of fact, it has been the family which, in the past, has provided the social context out of which the church derived for its own organization its forms of personal association. A study of the religious vocabulary of earlier days reveals this. Here are some examples: Brethren in the Lord, Sister, Fathers of the Church, Mothers in Israel, Children of God, our Church Family, our Spiritual Home. The strongly patriarchal family has been the source of these patterns for meaningful association. But this patriarchal organization of the family has now practically vanished. It will not work in our present order.

The new organization of the family, if it is to meet effectively its full situation, must be democratic, based upon organic equality. This connotes a vast change in the bases of fellowship and hence in the forms. A number of these already bear marks of what is happening. To note one instance: the former basis for sustaining the father-child fellowship in good status was implicit obedience of the father by the child. The word "Father" was pronounced respectfully, whatever the feelings of the child. Today a host of children and fathers have developed the use of the term "Dad," sensing in it an enlargement of the area of genuinely shared living and a guiding comradeship of the more mature for the less mature. Undoubtedly the term "Father" will come into its own again, but it will be with a changed connotation developed during its partial vacation from widest usage. Other terms may never regain their old significance for fellowship. The marked decrease in the size of families certainly drains the terms "Brother" and "Sister" of much of their former significance. Even in modern large families, the complexities of living seriously affect and limit the fellowship between brothers and sisters. Indeed, one author goes so far as to say that a large family living in modern conditions is almost sure to be a source of factors which contribute to the delinquency of one or more of its members. This seems an extreme point of view, but it recognizes vividly the changes in the conditions and bases of fellowship.

Some terms other than obedience which bring to attention the areas of family living where transformations are pervading the bases and forms of interpersonal fellowship are the following: independence, interdependence, possessiveness, reinforcement, monotony as an aspect of mature relationship, confusion as an aspect of growth, the will to create, birth control, the emancipation of women, balance in living, competition, sensitive loyalty, creative harmony, and social responsibility. In the main, the bases and the forms for fellowship charged with genuine democratic spirit are yet to be clearly developed.

Thus it is that the family, now itself in flux, cannot provide the social context from which new forms can be developed. Extensively, it has lost its patterns for building communion and along with these consciousness of the distinctiveness of itself and of its functions. Its unity is so constantly threatened because of inner stress and so strenuously attacked by outer strain that its frantic efforts at self-preservation keep it embroiled in extraneous or desperate or humiliating enterprises. It cannot get that sense of its own individuality which can come only in experiencing contrast between characteristic self-behavior and the characteristic functioning of other associated groups. This power to identify itself as a distinctive institution is a condition essential to the growth of forms of interpersonal communion in the family. Vice versa, the growth of forms of interpersonal communion is an essential condition for the maintaining of this sense of its own identity.

New bases for association out of which the forms for interpersonal communion can grow are much more difficult to locate today than when the family had its own relatively permanent estate and status. Its own fabric is too sleazy to carry the weaving of the required new patterns. The fabric of the larger society is too complex and tangled to indicate to the average family clear possibilities for these new patterns, though actually it contains many such. Since the family, in most instances, can neither provide the context out of which the necessary new forms of fellowship can be derived, nor of itself locate the possibilities in the involved and often contradictory context of the larger community, it rests with the church to take the leadership here if this requirement for family growth is to be met at all. Of course, before the church can fill this need of the family it will have to give up its own obsolete and strangling associational forms, with their discriminations as to age and sex, based upon the ancient pattern of the despotic, patriarchal family.

A Working Philosophy of Religion

Particularly during this present uncharted period of social transition and interfusing cultures, the family must have guidance in building a working philosophy of life apexed with its working philosophy of religion. To be sure, the family always has had need of such education as leads to reasonable comprehension of what life itself is all about, what place persons have in the grand scheme of things, what value is and how it can be recognized, how meanings grow, and how meanings can best be built into life. But during these years when living is so disjointed and knowledge so relative, there is little that seems dependable enough to count upon. Hence it becomes crucial for the community of the family to have a reasonably sound and adequate foundation for its operations. For this the family looks to the leadership of the church. No other institution regularly takes care of this great essential.

Further, it is very easy for the modern family to become confused, panicky, or exploited if it does not understand current developments and events. The family requires continuous interpretation of what is going on in the world in the light of the highest values mankind knows. Only such deep and inclusive orientation will enable the family to discover and set up some sound scale of values and some effective plan by which to chart its way. Sensing that the church is the one institution which seeks and worships supreme value, the family rightly depends upon it for fulfillment of this paramount necessity.

THE DEPENDENCE OF THE CHURCH UPON THE FAMILY

Its Constituency

Almost in its entirety, the constituency of the church is made up of families. Observably, in churches located in the downtown districts and in communities of specialized interests, the majority of members are unmarried students, or industrial workers, or lone individuals temporarily separated from their homes. Special types of church ministry must be worked out for these institutions. It is informing to note that these churches ministering to specialized interests are usually supported, at least in part, by fostering churches of the family sort. On the whole and normally, however, the church is a fellowship of families. This is true of no other of the major institutions. In a peculiarly responsible way, therefore, the church has the family in its keeping. It cannot evade guidance of the family and service to its needs and to its sustained integrity without being guilty of neglect. Further, it cannot do so without self-injury. Families are the primary social medium in which the church works. The existence of the church depends upon the existence of families who seek and appreciate its services.

Its Support

The plan for the financial support and for much of the personal support of the church is that of voluntary offerings. This is wise from the point of view of the genuineness of the expression of religious devotion by the devotees. But it is precarious from the point of view of dependably adequate support of a program commensurate with the distinctive functions of the church. No matter what individuals think about the existing government and its yield of value to them, they have to pay their taxes or be penalized by loss of property. Further, much of whatever yield of values the administration of the tax-supported government does bring is in observable form—better roads, flood control, free schooling, and other such. Lastly, citizens have learned that these values are distributed over the country, that no one section can expect continuous satisfaction of all its wants and needs.

On the other hand, the contributions of members to the church may be cut off at any time because of either some misfortune or some displeasure among its members, and these members usually suffer no impressive penalizing. Again, much of the yield of values which the church brings is not in observable or immediately satisfying form. These values are harder to appreciate by the individual who pauses to appraise. Lastly, many church members expect, as their right, continuous satisfaction of their own wants and needs, and give trouble when dissatisfied. They are inoculated by that strong spirit of individualism within the church which has been generated largely by the emphasis placed upon the importance to each member of his own individual salvation.

The members give to the church only as they appreciate its values. The church is thus dependent for its support upon the attitudes of the family toward value. This means that the church is dependent upon the developments occurring in family living which influence its scale of values.

Its Functional Foothold

The church is having a difficult time discovering how to make itself an essential part of social living. It has been troubled with a severe case of farsightedness, else it would have long since realized that the family is the one approach most open to it and most promising of effectiveness. Every sort of cultural background is represented in its family constituency, not in any one local church often, but in the church as an institution. There are Republicans, Democrats, Socialists, and "reds"; rich and poor; highly schooled and illiterate; religious conservative and radical; old and young; those of illustrious family connections and the "self-made"; provincials and cosmopolitans; intellectuals and day laborers; mean-minded and magnanimous; practical-minded and romantic. Further, innumerable social interests are represented among the members. When the members evidencing all these cultural backgrounds and interests come together in the church, they do so with attention on their common loyalties rather than on their differences as to interests. They come for something beyond themselves. No other institution has this opportunity to work with such a widely representative cultural sampling of adult population over a long period of time.

Since most of them come into the church as members of the family, already they are actively concerned for the matter of human fulfillment, even though with the majority it is on the restricted level of concern for their own. In any case, there *is* dynamic concern for human fulfillment present. It needs enlarging and evaluating and implementing. There could not be a stronger foundation for building participating interest in the vital issues of the larger society and for training in sound social evaluation on an ever-higher level than the interest that families have in the welfare of their own. In some degree, they appreciate, also, that this welfare lies partly in the keeping of the larger society. "A little child shall lead them" through parental concern for his welfare out beyond their shallow, provincial, ingrowing, divisive interests, into the deeper problems and hopes of a highly interdependent society trying to realize itself.

The church cannot affiliate itself intimately with any other one of the major institutions as a general policy. It cannot join forces with particular political parties or minority movements. But it can and must form an alliance with the home. Here it has the peculiar opportunity it needs of dealing with the vital issues of the larger society as problems in value, rather than in their festering forms as partisan measures. Through this approach the church need not feel itself called upon to contribute directly to the reform of political or economic theory and structure, which it cannot do anyway, but rather summoned to keep ever before the eyes of mankind those values which make a frame of reference of greater significance by which to appraise the immediate values toward which men are struggling. It is in the family that these complicated social issues become resolved into problems of essential values. The church has a strategic position here because of the vital and intimate nature of the services which it renders to the family. In the family it finds the problems of the community, the nation, and the world. Through working with the family, the church builds up the strongest fulcrum possible to give leverage for its work for human fulfillment on the vast scale.

The approach to the larger issues of the day, when undertaken through work with the family, does not restrict or belittle the scope of church influence upon society, but rather focuses its dealing with these issues lower down toward the roots where they appear not as specific divisive struggles between groups, but as mistakes or crimes in social evaluation. With this approach the church is not drawn into partisan battles and faced with the fatal undertaking of choosing sides in matters out of its trained understanding and jurisdiction. Yet with this approach the church need never fear lest it go too deeply toward the roots of issues. In this sense it cannot become too radical. It is not a matter of confining action to pussy-footing on neutral ground. Often the church will have harsh words and deeds to perform in being thus radical, but it will not be done from the position of a partisan participant in a specific group struggle, but from the position of the institution most concerned that mankind shall find their way toward Supreme Value through their daily struggle to secure more value in the present issues of their living.

Its Future Membership

There is little chance that the church can sustain its present membership, much less increase it in the future, unless the generations coming on are religiously conditioned in their family living. For one thing, statistics show that there are not so many little children coming along. For another thing, there are an appalling number and variety of conspicuous and insistent devices for catching and holding the attention of the youth of the land today. Most of these have been worked out with skillful consideration of what will appeal most immediately to the age groups commercial promoters wish to inveigle. The prime concern of these promoters is to present attractions which will entice youth to spend their money and hours where it will bring financial profit to commercial interests.

In view of this, the church must meet tremendous competition as it seeks to develop the religious interest of the young. It is a matter not only of amount of competition, but of kind also. The commercial promoters think largely in terms of how much glitter, glamour, "kick," and carefree allure they can introduce into their offerings, with little concern for what happens to their young customers short of scandal that would bring investigation. The church, in the nature of the case, uses a set of criteria in working out its program for the young which is in keeping with its scale of values. These criteria are so far beyond the appreciation of uncultivated young people that the program of the church at its best seems dull and strange to such. In all too many cases the program is dull and strange, to be sure, but even an excellent one is likely to seem so to the young person whose total cultural nurture has consisted in tutelage in locating the farthest limits society will allow in the way of indulgence of whims and of license of appetites.

But how can the church hope to reach the attention of young people whose lives are crowded full of diversions, who know nothing about the adventure, allure, achievement, and deepened meanings that come in the developing of genuine interests? From the outside, any complex interest looks poky and laborious. The religious interest, being the most complex and intangible, as well as the slowest in maturing, tends to look most unreal to those whom it has never stirred. If the religious interest is to be developed in the young along with other interests, it will require increasingly the nurturing of the family group under the guidance of the church. The church is dependent upon the family for this religious nurture of the young, and hence for its future membership.

Provision of the Culture Which Fosters Religion

The kind of association typical of the family which is fulfilling its functions, has been discussed at length,[2] together with its connection with growth of religion. It remains here to emphasize the fact that family communion produces religion.

For one thing, the family can furnish the freedom, equality, cooperative endeavor and mutuality through which the spontaneity of personality can be released and love can grow. Secondly, the family tends to correct individualism through the sharing of interests and resources. Every member of the family learns that all his living is reinforced and meaningful in proportion as he does his part in promoting the bonds of fellowship within the group.

Further, the love for the little child which includes prudential concern for his welfare becomes the genitor of a social interest which tends to expand toward world brotherhood.

Again, the intimate association within the family tends to locate and develop modes and patterns to guide associational life within the home. Later these are spread to other relationships outside the home. Effective, tested patterns facilitate the spread of fellowship.

Lastly, the family can provide that selected, somewhat segregated, and fostering environment required for the religious development of the young. Since interest in religion does not become differentiated from other developing interests very early in life, it is all the more difficult to provide the cultural conditions which will insure the foundations and the actual emergence of this interest. The church, meeting as it does only at scheduled times, cannot provide sufficiently that deep sort of interpersonal communion which is the fostering culture for religion. It can, however, promote it in the family, and must do so. Individuals who have matured in such a culture will have tasted the values of the religious way of living. They will be ready to fight to

[2] Chapter VI, pp. 128-141.

open a way for it in society. They will know that worthy religion grows only in a certain type of human association and they will seek to spread understanding and patterns of this Christian type of fellowship.

Continuous Revitalizing

Not only must the church depend in most part upon the family for the fostering culture in which religion develops, but it must depend upon it also for compulsion toward continuous revitalizing. The church is an enduring institution with its property, its almost permanent boards, and its long-established loyalties. It is always in danger of living for its vested interests and on that account ignoring vital issues. Without knowing it, the church can lay deposit after deposit of impediments closely about itself under the illusion that it is growing stronger through thickening the protection of its status quo. Then, when social change makes itself felt, such a church finds itself not protected but incased. It is shut off both from God and from man.

It is much more difficult, in the family, to incrust living to the extent that the reality of God is shut out. Here it is hardly possible to cover over those disturbing conflicts which arise when God's way is not undertaken or to conceal those rich experiences which emerge when living is loyally devoted. The reality of God is continuously face-to-face with the members who are promoting the growth of meaning through the building of their family fellowship. It is inescapably present. It can be much more readily perceived in the home during experiences either of anguish and frustration or of increased abundance and fulfillment.

Of course, even in the family the reality of God may not be recognized. None of the members may know that there is such a being. But if the members are able to recognize God, He is more readily discerned and dealt with there than in the church. The church tends to congeal into a static order and so form a glissade over which men's thought and feeling can slide too smoothly to detect vital reality. There are a number of factors which lower the temperature of the church toward the congealing point. Some of these are: the infrequency of meeting; the increasing difficulty of building intimate, meaningful fellowship; the fact that the members come together on their best behavior and hence are "not all there"; the large number of members in many church fellowships; the concern for vested interests; the automatic celebration of special occasions; and the mechanization of official functions.

In the everyday activities and relationships of the loyal family, there can be no congealing. The urges of the organism, the disturbances of intimate relations, and the drives of society take care that there is no static state, no vacuum. Therefore, when the churchly form of religion becomes unreal, the interests and problems of family life tend to bring it back to reality. Thus, religion as shaped by the church, is constantly put to the test for its genuineness, its truth, and its effectiveness for human fulfillment in the family. If the church does not open itself to this opportunity of developing ever-truer insights concerning vital religious living, it is likely to find itself a semiestranged institution. Without continuous revitalizing from dealing with the actual problems of life, particularly as found in the intimate communion of the family, all that will remain to the church will be the conventional loyalty of individuals who still have a traditional basis for their allegiance. To yield best results, this must be a cooperative task, for the family must become increasingly aware of its part in the revitalizing of the church.

THE RESHAPING OF FUNCTIONAL RELATIONSHIPS

It has become clear that the family and the church are each dependent upon the other for conditions and services indispensable to their effective functioning. Also it is evident that each can supply the other with an objective of loyalty so great as to keep it from growing self-centered.

In studying the crises which the family and the church are undergoing it became apparent that many problems in each must be met cooperatively by the two. In recent years neither one has done its building with sufficient consideration of the transformed conditions of living. There has been too much drifting in compliance with the pressure of outside forces not interested in keeping these institutions true to their essential functions. Individualism has marred and broken both in a number of instances. The weakness of each is demonstrated daily in all too many ways.

Yet these institutions carry on with the firm expectation that they will endure. Encouragingly, there are healthy signs appearing. For one thing there is increase of the inquiring attitude. This has developed far enough in many instances to result in the launching of long-term experimentings to discover necessary data regarding the functions of family and church, and their conjunction in the service of life. This would seem to be the direction of promise—intelligent and cooperative experimentation started at points where there is promise of emerging insights to guide working principles and plans.

Further, there is increasing conviction that this inquiring attitude will have to become permanent. The realization is growing that we are not getting our world ready so that we may settle down after a while, but so that we may continue to grow in the understanding and skills needed for this fulfilling of functions. We are beginning to sense that we must accept change as the unchanging factor. It is no simple problem. More than the church and the family are involved, since they are interdependent institutions in a universally and increasingly interdependent society.

Participation in reconstruction is going to mean that most of the time most of us must be hard at work down where all sorts of definite problems are disturbing the existing order of things. But it is wise for us to rise occasionally above this level of tangles within tangles in order to try to discern what may be working through it all. We are being forced, in spite of ourselves and in spite of the proud orders we built only yesterday, to see how limited has been our outlook and how trivial have been many of the values lately held dear. In other words, we are being forced into wider connections. This, in turn, requires an adjustment of our scale of values. If we can meet the new demands now upon us, it may eventuate that we shall find ourselves in a world of deepened, richer meanings. Before this can come in any marked degree, each institution will have had to toil to build its share in a more inclusive community. Certainly one present meaning is clear: each institution is being *forced* to care what happens to every other, since each is bound up in some way with all the others. Particularly true is this of the family and the church, for each of whom the most immediate source of strength and of renewal of life is in the keeping of the other.

Part III

THE CHURCH AT WORK WITH THE FAMILY

Introduction

WHILE distinguishing its indispensable and peculiar functions is a tremendously important undertaking for the modern church, when this has been accomplished there remains an equally essential work to be done. This is the interpretation of its large objectives into processes, programs, and methods of work. Since this this can be done only in terms of the specific persons and conditions with which the church is to work, this second undertaking increases the load of the district and local divisions of the church. The headquarters of the church can collect, select, and present all sorts of raw materials, but the various localities must develop these into appropriate and adequate plans for the work of each church with the family.

However, there are strong threads of common human experience which hold together the work of all the churches. In regard to these there can be much profitable cooperation. This can take two chief forms: (1) the interchange of ideas, resources, and instrumentalities; (2) the federation of all in the effort to universalize needed developments. No matter how well one church does its work, it is handicapped disproportionately until other churches of the locality meet the standard. This is because people cannot be segregated by congregations in everyday living. The great, common experiences of human beings loom so large in their living that comparisons are always going on, though not always on a valid basis.

This part of the book treats of the work of the church in those common areas of interest connected with family life. Chapter VIII discusses the work of the church in launching the family through attention to marriage. Chapter IX presents some of the major aspects of work with parents. The next two chapters deal with work with the immature: Chapter X, with the little children; Chapter XI, with the young people. The last chapter of this part, XII, contains suggestions for dealing with the family as a group.

Chapter VIII

THE CHURCH DEALING WITH MARRIAGE

THE first direct step in a positive approach to work with the family is constructive attention to the inauguration of each new family. Soundness in the establishing of marriage is the most telling factor in promoting normality in the family. For all the major social institutions except three, marriage is an incident, but for the home, the church, and the state it is a significant undertaking with far-reaching implications.

The home sees marriage primarily as the opening to greatest opportunity for personal fulfillment. The church sees it first of all as the germinal center of an intimate group which by nature *must* be interested in promoting growth of the highest values discovered by them, presumably apexed by religious values. The state sees it principally as the event initiating the founding of one more of those social units fundamentally occupied with the production, rearing, and support of future citizens. All three institutions tend to be satisfied to deal with what they see as the central aspect of marriage on a superficial level. Personal fulfillment through marriage, in the eyes of the average family, has all too often been interpreted to mean good fortune, ease, gayety, security, a minimum of responsibility, or being idolized. Many churches have emphasized the quest for highest values almost solely in terms of extent of loyal support to some particular denomination or sect of the church. The state has been satisfied to leave to the man and woman contemplating marriage all responsibility for considering the sort of future citizens their union may produce.

In other words, the three institutions whose interests are most deeply at stake whenever a marriage takes place have not yet made it a major part of their business to see to it that it is instituted under the most propitious conditions culturally possible. Much less have these three gotten together for cooperative approach to the improvement of marriage. Many efforts are being made these days to improve marriage, but most of them are expended by outside, remedial organizations [1] which have been aroused by what they have witnessed of human waste and suffering due to inadequate conditions connected with marriage. These organizations are trying to prod the three institutions who should be most concerned into wiser, more constructive treatment of marriage.

The three institutions are not on a par when it comes to allocating responsibility for improving marriage. Since any one family is short-lived compared with the church and the state, these two latter institutions will have to carry not only the share of the responsibility which is peculiarly theirs by virtue of their distinctive functions, but they will also have to hold themselves responsible for educating continuously the oncoming families in respect to their functions. The educational guidance of the home by state and church will be differentiated in accordance with their distinctive purposes and ideals. But the two processes should be articulated sufficiently to result in a total program which is consistent and mutually reinforcing. Upon the national headquarters of church and state devolves this problem of articulation of their educational program.

Not only has the church heavier responsibility than other community agencies in the matter of improving marriage, but it has also a more strategic position for carrying out the responsibility. Because its membership is typically by families, and because these families remain in the same church organization over a period of time, the church can know its constituent families much more intimately than can the school and state. This is of prime import, because it is through the more intimate, continuous type of fellowship that the most deeply penetrating education is accomplished. Underlying these observable reasons for the responsible position of the church, there exists a deep-seated foundation. The

[1] Conspicuously and admirably represented by the American Social Hygiene Association.

church and the family are the two great institutions whose prime concern is the fostering and strengthening of fellowship, of love. The Christian church stands for a way of life based on such a fellowship. This is exactly what the family supremely symbolizes. Hence the family finds the church peculiarly congenial in spirit and purpose, and turns to it for support and advice.

The church can be a bulwark to the home as the home cannot be to the church, because the church is not subject to the precarious possibilities of sudden damage which threaten loss or destruction to the home whose chief reliance for continuity and maintenance must rest upon two mortal individuals. On the other hand, that fellowship which is the church cannot continue except as it is nurtured and vitalized by the fellowships established in marriage and developed in the family. So it is that the church to continue importantly must appreciate the deeper levels which underly its relationship to marriage and the home and meet its responsibilities accordingly.

AVENUES OF APPROACH FOR THE CHURCH

When the state sets out to improve marriage, it can distinguish what it thinks are the minimum requirements and, after preparing the ground, pass laws and ordinances, armed with penalties, which incorporate these requirements. The school as an instrument of the state presents facts and illustrative material in such a way that the child feels behind these the pressure of the very real society at hand and of the awesome, though still vague, society at large. Under the conditions in which he receives the teachings of the school, the child tends to accept them without question as keys to the most satisfactory social policy.

The modern church, however, can use neither the power of legislation nor the pressures of established social policies in its efforts to disseminate its values among men. The method of approach which is open to it is a much more difficult one but vastly more potent when successful. Having no way of bringing such organized social pressure as would force the individual through fear of legal or social penalties to follow its teachings, it must depend upon the captivating power of the values it fosters and supports. The influence of the church cannot rest permanently upon its own dominating power, for of such it has none except what is temporarily usurped. That is, its approach must be positive through the *appeal of enduring values*, not negative through the restraining fear of imminent penalties. This requires greater skill than any other type of education.

There are a number of opportunities open to the church for this positive, distinctive approach to its responsibilities. Unceasingly, its main interest must be focused upon vivifying the values which are to be discovered in the fellowship of love and upon guiding its members in their loyalties to such community of lives. The first step of this process is wise fostering of the inauguration of new families through marriage. Such fostering may take several forms.

AVENUES OF CHURCH GUIDANCE

Doctrinal Conditioning in the Principle of Relationship

The whole cultus of the Christian church, if it is to be true to the principle of love upon which it was founded, must interpret and celebrate this principle of relationship. Such a cultus must develop in any group whose aspiration and expression are shaped by their loyalty to that kind of interaction between persons which Jesus Christ said would promote highest human fulfillment. It is not so much the deliberate exhorting about the fellowship of love which indelibly conditions the members, as it is the thousand indirect ways in which the principle of love vitalizes and shapes all that is done by those that serve it. The church must help youth to appreciate both in family and in church life the workings of meaningful communion. When the adults live so zestfully a life of loyalty to this doctrinal principle that it becomes second nature to them, they are educating youth in the doctrine by the most potent method. Such indirect doctrinal conditioning, acting through several years upon the youth of the church before the time of marriage, will train them in the disciplines essential to every fellowship of love. Further, it will make such disciplines acceptable by providing substantial tastings of the highly desirable values to be attained through such fellowship. In late adolescence, these actual experiences as a participant in meaningful communion may be interpreted theologically to youth.

So trained, youth will not be as subject to skin-deep infatuations nor headlong precipitation into marriage as he is when his concept of love is built upon popular hearsay which makes it an unpredictable, uncontrollable, but exuberantly gratifying occurrence. Quite early he will have learned that love grows only through a sharing of significant interests, and that genuine sharing requires self-investment. Then later his theological training will have revealed to him that he can find God in the right kind of love relationship more readily than anywhere else, and so he cannot regard his coming relationship individualistically. Consummating it on the richest, highest level possible will be an expression of his religious loyalty.

Group Fellowship and Sanction

Both before and after marriage, there is need of a supporting fellowship. As young people near marriageable age, they become quite sensitive to the standards and attitudes of the married members of the church. There is much sharing among the young people of their opinions and reports about what is going on among the married. It is a wise church which recognizes its liabilities and assets here and takes the lead in turning this situation into a constructive one. By encouraging the more interesting, attractive, yet sincere married couples to share the findings of their own experiences with small groups of the young people, and by training them for this delicate yet invaluable service, the church institutes a very effective type of education in the fellowship of love. If these opportunities are utilized for moralizing or sentimental testifying, they will be worse than wasted. But if they are honest, natural experiences in cooperative evaluation of criteria for successful marriage and of the dreams that quicken readiness for it, they make accessible to the younger people of the church the soundest sanctions of the sanest married couples within the church fellowship.

This is a peculiarly potent avenue for vivifying the values of the right sort of fellowship, for the young people realize that they are sharing with those who know. Besides, friendly connections of this sort made before marriage are likely to form the basis for further connection after marriage. The couple endeavoring to chart their way will quite naturally turn for counsel to the older couples who have shared their findings with them earlier. Such relations are particularly steadying during the first few real disturbances of married life when the way, at times, seems to be rather hard going.

In addition to the building up of sound sanctions through promoting specific fellowship between married couples and unmarried young people, the whole adult membership should be led to realize their responsibility for shaping the prevailing attitudes on marriage not only within their particular church but in the community. Associated with the otherwise glowing, earnest memories of my own early experience in marriage is a deep, ugly scar. It was made by the shock I received when I began to attend meetings of the women's organizations of the church and heard many of the members comparing notes and gossiping openly and cheaply about experiences of a most private, intimate nature. I endeavored to find some constructive purpose in all this, but found only treachery to the husband-wife relationship, seemingly due to a thirst for individual recognition. Since then, I have known many organizations of married women, in and out of the church, who carried on no such trafficking. On the other hand, many young married women are still reporting experiences similar to mine which occur in both church and other community groups. Many young men have cited equivalent experiences in their contact with men's groups. Certainly the most influential way for the adult membership to build up sound prevailing attitudes on marriage is to forget about being examples and concentrate upon making a success, each of his own marriage. It amounts to this: *so live* that the attractiveness of marriage, when undertaken intelligently and creatively, may become manifest to those who are considering it.

After marriage has taken place, there is a particularized need of fostering group fellowship and sanctions. An overwhelming number of young married people are realizing that it is very difficult for them to locate a congenial group—a good-time group —whose social standards and practices are such that they can participate wholeheartedly and still keep their own self-respect and their marital loyalty. The young husband is frequently thrown in with older men in business who take drinking and other disorganizing habits as a matter of course. Indeed, many businessmen make it painfully difficult for young men to associate with them both in and out of business hours without conforming to their personal vices. The test of social ridicule directed against the nonconformer is a more severe test than many men have the caliber to pass, particularly when there is no other congenial social group open to them. The young wife frequently has the same type of experience as she begins to participate in the group life of the community.

Whatever the local church can do to foster the forming of congenial, reinforcing social groups among young married people will serve to improve marriage. Most probably such fostering will include the provision of an attractive clubroom with kitchen facilities, open to these young people at all times, where they may gather informally or arrange for discussion meetings and merry good times. Such a clubroom may be in the church or in a community building. A private home whose children have become independent can scarcely find a more culturally profitable use for a portion of its domain than to make it a club center for young married people. With such provisions the young people can build up their own code, free of the coercion of groups carrying on loose practices.

Recognition Given to Marriage

Growing out of the quality of the sanctions concerning marriage built up by the adults of the church will come the character of the recognition given to marriage by the church. The nature of such recognition will affect the attitudes of the maturing young people. Marriage is frequently recognized as a social *event* involving church members and hence important to the church. In such a case the preparations and ritual involve largely the conventional going through of certain forms, with perhaps a brief period of conferring about marriage between the pastor and the young people.

On the other hand, marriage should be regarded as the instituting of a new cultural unit of profound importance to religion and hence to the church. Then, ideally the ceremony itself will be a joyous ritual [2] (1) of recognition that the two being married have sufficiently prepared themselves in every way for the launching of their communal enterprise, and (2) of pledging their loyalties to the greatest values discoverable through their community of interests. No two rituals will be alike in every respect, for no two couples are alike. The ritual for any one couple will be worked out in terms that best convey to them the meanings and purposes and loyalties involved. It may be wholly or only partially their own formulation, but it will be their selection. They will have developed their ritual through the months preceding marriage, during their periods of reflection and discussion when they seek to distinguish the values, responsibilities, opportunities, and controlling purposes which should characterize their communal living. Usually, their pastor or counselor will have participated in some of their discussions and in the formulating of the ritual. The evaluating necessary in the development of the ritual is bound to affect present ideas and activities as well as attitudes and plans for the future. Thus the young people will have begun living in the terms of the values and purposes being built into their ritual during some long period before the marriage itself. The evaluating will never be complete. Each couple will be acutely interested in the developed rituals of other couples, and such interest will lead to deeper examination of their own.

Education for Marriage

Premarital education includes both general preparation of all young people and specific preparation of each couple contemplating bethrothal and marriage. The former part, ideally, is shared by all community agencies, for all these influence the

---

[2] It is interesting to note among thoughtful young people the increase of this practice of working out their own ritual, at least in part.

ideas, attitudes, and practices in marriage. The chief responsibility for the second part rests upon the family and the church, though either of these institutions may call upon professional assistance in the fulfilling of its responsibilities. Among the growing number of counselors, physicians, leaders of youth, clinics, institutes, and educational associations there are now certain ones who are prepared to contribute valuably in this area.

Premarital education, where wisely administered, is not merely a course or curriculum worked out by adults and superimposed upon the young people. Rather it is the process of guiding the fulfilling of the natural interests of the young people, whose ripeness for such education is shown by their questions and by their social activities. In meeting their needs, the finest and richest selection of social findings, resources of various kinds, should be made available to them in the amount, order, and form best suited to the particular group in question. And it should be education, not mere information, i.e., the young people should be guided to try out and incorporate into their present policies, attitudes, and codes whatever ideas they develop which seem sound and appropriate for their present activities and relationships. This education of present habits and ideals will become the foundation for the specific premarital education that will come later. This will help the young people to develop criteria both for the period before engagement and for deciding as to whether a particular relationship justifies mutual promise of marriage.

The Sacrament of Betrothal

More important even than the sacrament of marriage is the sacrament of betrothal. By the time a couple have come to the point of marriage, there is little that can be done at the moment in the way of correcting or enlarging their ideas. They are set. Their attention is fixed. But the time of betrothal offers much greater educational opportunity. The young persons have been, and still are, questioning many matters. Providing, of course, they are sincere in what they are doing, they are in the midst of organizing their ideas and so are in the best condition for learning.

Ideally the sacrament of betrothal should be the consummation of a long period of premarital preparation, at first indirect and later deliberate. It should be the outward sign that the two young people are inwardly ready and eager to pledge their loyalties to each other with the idea of continuing on together into the co-operative building of their home. The ritual for this ceremony, as in the case of marriage, should be worked out by the young people with such counseling as they need. That is, it should incorporate not only the responsibilities and ideas generally held to characterize this relationship of loyalty, but also and notably those which are unique or important for their own particular relationship. It should be specific as to those standards and purposes and values which they are desirous of promoting together.

Some couples may feel that this building of a ritual together following their discovery of their common desire to become engaged would take all the romance and spontaneous joy out of the experience for the participating couple. Undoubtedly this belief would be justified if the relationship were based on lust or other self-centered motive, for then the interest of one or both is upon his own gratification and the securing of such at the least possible cost to himself. But if there is genuine love present, growing out of the sharing of significant interests and including sexual attraction, they will be eager to do all that they can to make their relationship fine, effective, and mutually reinforcing. Genuine love always wants to find something to *do* for the one beloved, and the presence of something eminently appropriate and worth doing for their coming marriage provides a channel which tends to keep the relationship wholesomely worked out into expression. It is certainly no compliment to a lover to feel or say that the effort to build the right conditions for the deepening and enriching of friendship is boredom or drudgery. A love that wants incessant stimulating to fever heat through increasing mutual absorption, each in the other, is a sick love. It cannot endure because only a part of the self is involved; in time the rest of the self will wake up to make demands that cannot be filled through this type of relationship.

As a matter of fact, all sincere young couples do work out a code for their relationship and activities, but usually this is done step by step, unwittingly, as one difficulty after another forces intelligent planning of the association. It is better done with the eager zest stirred by the desire for a beautiful type of friendship than by anxiety over this or that episode which threatens to break up the friendship. In this way, many areas of potential disagreement are threshed out ahead of time and much more objectively when there is no issue at stake. This saves unprofitable injuries and scars later on. In addition, the couple begin to learn how to disagree creatively.

The ceremony of betrothal should be impressive, marked by fitting, natural, and symbolic beauty. Emphatically, it should be private, including only those very few who are closest to the young people, perhaps their own family and their two or three most intimate friends. There should be no *display* of any sort— fine clothes or decorations or what not. If the young people have been adequately prepared for it, they will find the real significance of the occasion in the terms through which they pledge their loyalties. Their attention should have been focused here during the weeks of preparation ahead of time, and it should be kept here during the ceremony. Many young people may wish to observe the ritual without any others present, feeling that they are not yet desirous of making their plans known to the world.

It will be a real calamity if this sacrament of betrothal is instituted by the church and then allowed to become the flashy, material-minded travesty that many church weddings are. A number of churches are now incorporating tiny chapels in their buildings, places of meditation or of prayer, for individuals or very small groups. Such a place would serve well for the observing of the sacrament of betrothal. So, too, would the home of one of the participants, providing the mother in it could realize that the meanings built into the ritual are vastly more important than the trappings of the occasion. The setting should not distract attention to superficial aspects, but rather build up a supporting background.

Preparing young people for the sacrament of betrothal would undoubtedly, in some instances, result in the discovery that they are not really suited to each other. But this is a markedly good outcome. Much better that they find it out before their lives have become so intimately involved in each other that parting, however voluntary, causes cruel suffering.

One certain outcome of such preparation for marriage will be a change in the bases for appraisal of personality or character among the young people. The training in the disciplines, values, and ideals which a sincere, close friendship involves will make them review their estimates of what makes an interesting and worth-while friend. As a result there will be a fostering of character through the social interests of the young people.

It is very important that this education of young people who are considering becoming engaged should be done by one well trained to work with youth in the several aspects of living involved—physical, mental, social, emotional, and religious. Since the work with any one couple involves a number of meetings, it is hardly possible for the average pastor of a large congregation to undertake it. A very good plan can be developed by a group of churches which combine to engage the right sort of an expert to give full time to the youth of their several congregations. This counselor would then work with both the particular church and the family involved as closely as the nature and needs of any one case indicated.

Developing a Responsible Attitude toward Marriage

There are a number of groups who need to have defined for them more correctly their responsibility toward marriage. Only three of these will be cited here.

Parents need to ponder upon the changing conditions under which the young people of their family must select a mate and plan for marriage in the present social order. The sort of positions open to those young people who do not go far in their schooling is often such that they cannot marry on the wages received. The length of time required in vocational preparation of those who do go far in school involves both a heavy financial load for schooling and a postponement of marriage. This would seem to require two responses on the part of parent to the marriage of those hampered young people: (1) some arrangement, where at all possible, for economic assistance of the young peo-

ple who are ready to launch their married life; (2) some concerted drive to bring about a change in the social conditions
which put these young persons under undue strain.

Subsidizing marriage at the appropriate time may take the
form of a financial gift or loan, of assistance in working out some
cooperative plan whereby the financial cost is reduced for the
young people, or of some adjustment of the property of the family such as to facilitate the marriage. There are two dangers to
be avoided: (1) allowing the conditions of the young people
wanting to be married to become so very difficult that they re-
sort to undesirable practices in an effort to reach some tolerable
adjustment; (2) giving assistance to them in a way or to a degree
which undermines their self-reliance and aspiration. This subsidizing of marriage should be regarded as a temporary measure
during this period of social disorder. But it will not be temporary
unless parents go far enough in their plans to unite to bring pressure for the building of different conditions for all young people
approaching maturity.

The second group who need educating in their responsibility
toward marriage is composed of those individuals who have it
within their power to modify the conditions under which the
work of the world is done, and, therefore, the vocational opportunities and conditions of the young people. To rob the youth of
the nation of their future is a grave form of stealing, however indirectly it is done. This group of business executives needs arousing to its responsibility to confer and act as interestedly in this
matter of *organizing industry for the coming generation* as it
does in organizing it for selfish monopoly of power. This group
has demonstrated its power to organize effectively toward any
end it chooses. It needs a tremendous challenge to consider a new
and less-primitive end than grabbing all it can reach. A number of
individuals in this group are moving in this direction, but it will
have to be an organized group undertaking. A few individuals
cannot accomplish it alone, though they may act as the irritating
nucleus for stimulating responsibility.

The third group who need to have their responsibility to marriage defined are those men and women, unmarried and married,
who seem to feel that it is perfectly fair for them to try to break

up a marriage if they take a fancy to someone already married. They do not seem to appreciate that there is a civil loyalty to all state-instituted marriages required of the public as well as a personal loyalty required of the married couple. Nor do they realize that, in violating a legal relationship they are exhibiting symptoms of personal deficiency. In the breaking of their civil loyalty, in coercing the one courted to break his or her personal loyalty, these civil traitors are clearly demonstrating their own incapacity to achieve a mature and deep level of loyalty with anyone.

Marriage is a difficult relationship, which means that true marriage is an achievement progressively furthered both by problems and by fulfilling experiences. Honor requires that every man and woman thrown into contact with another who has already pledged his loyalty in marriage should feel responsible to see to it that contact with him or with her does not undermine in any way the loyalty of this other. A number of recent articles written by covetous, unscrupulous, or provincial-minded office girls, opportunist writers, and others, seek to justify the right of individuals to make conquest where and when they can. Such expressions are indications of the need of education of the public in its responsibility toward marriage. Unless the principals themselves have indicated beyond doubt a break in their pledged loyalty, it is illegal and ignoble of outsiders to try to despoil the relationship. This is a form of education for marriage that is overlooked. The church with its concern for highest human fulfillment cannot afford to overlook it.

Guidance of the Growing Relationship after Marriage

For this later part of the program of the church as well as for the earlier educating of the unmarried young people in the fellowship of love, the staff of the church will need a corps of well-married church members to assist them. Also, cooperation with various community agencies will result in more adequate guidance of newly instituted marriages. Out of the many aspects of the growing relationship which may need fostering, a few are here cited to illustrate.

Guidance during the material instituting of the home so that it will include in its setting and program a fair representation of things of deeper significance. These will include the observing of its own uniquely developed rituals, the cherishing of symbols of experience of rich meaning, sharing with others, and the like.

Encouragement of a professional attitude toward their new undertaking. This will involve study and the cooperative development of techniques and of an objective attitude.

Assistance in distinguishing the norms of wholesome married living and in formulating these in terms of their own interests and activities.

Preparing the newly married for the later period when necessary business and other serious matters begin to encroach upon their intimacy, when they begin to feel the limits of the actualities of life, when they begin to see each other with less romance, and other such searching experiences.

Keeping the new, tiny circle from closing in on the two within it, by drawing them into a larger circle of group participation and into some service to the community.

Making available sources of information and counsel in the areas where they are most likely to need these.

Planning some sort of follow-up which expresses the fellowship and interest on the part of the church in their newly developing community. This follow-up should be rather close during the first year or two.

Maintaining the Established Marriages

This is no small task in these days when community sanctions are low, required investment high, and storm areas frequent. The call of material values is so insistently strident that it is hard for the church to make its call to the cultural values of human living impressive. Yet never has there been more needed this work of the church of centering and recentering the attention of the husband and wife upon the building of conditions for fostering that kind of communion in which greater cultural values grow in the world. Some of the forms which this work may take are briefly indicated here.

Stimulating both husband and wife to keep growing, i.e., developing widening interests, and to regard growth with its changes, its possibilities, and its problems as the normal expectation.

Helping them to distinguish the values that are developing and emerging in their relationship, however these may differ from those anticipated; teaching them to watch for progress not products.

Guiding them in special preparation for unusual events and experiences, such as the coming of children, temporary separations from each other, and the like.

Education in keeping the married relationship interesting, sound, and deep, when there is danger that concern or love for the children may distract interest from the married relation itself.

Guidance in the reformulation of their norms to meet reforming situations.

Instruction in how to deal with their intimate and family problems so as to avoid unnecessary strains in relationship.

Guidance in keeping them from getting lost in outside activities which bring individual recognition and success much more easily and flatteringly than does loyal devotion to marriage.

Making available information as to helpful resources of all sorts, as well as the pertinent findings of leaders working in this field.

Working with Unstable and Broken Marriages

There are three general approaches in this work with tottering marriages, two indirect and one direct. The church which sees a marriage shaking on its foundations can keep this in mind when developing its program of forums, bulletin materials, and other means of adult education in the church. In this first type of indirect approach the church will assist through putting the couple into a better position to help itself.

The direct approach is through counseling [3] with the couple involved either to the extent of working with them on their problem or of helping them to make contact with some suitable professional counselor or community agency who can do so.

[3] See Chapter XII.

The third approach is through drawing the couple into a small group whose program of activities is such that there is fair expectation of therapeutic effect. Improvement may be brought about through change in some obstructing viewpoint, through the widening of perspective, or through gaining insight into some personal or other complication of the troublesome situation. Such guided group participation is one form of group therapy. Such therapy is a sounder and more effective method of treatment than is individual counseling where it is appropriate and well directed. This is so because the problem receives natural treatment in the form of group participation, which is more active and wholesome than isolated, conspicuous individual treatment.

Improving the Institution of Marriage

Most of the service of the church to the institution of marriage will be done through its service to the marriages taking place in its own constituency and neighborhood. But its work here will render it increasingly capable of making a larger contribution. If the local work is done reasonably well, the findings will become significant. There are many aspects of marriage about which much more reliable data are needed. For instance, these matters need further exposition: present causes of difficulty in marriage and the instigating conditions; constructive approaches to the aforementioned conditions; current man-woman attitudes and their bearing upon marriage; women's status, work, social activities, and careers as these pertain to marriage; and possible changes in the conditions which obtain in plans for marriage of young people.

Already there are simple beginnings of such service to the institution of marriage. Some churches are gathering data. The Federal Council of Churches is active in some areas. But national headquarters [4] of the major church divisions have not yet built adequate programs for this work. Certainly most of the data to be used will have to be secured from those institutions which are specifically equipped for such study. The national headquarters

[4] A worth-while example of denominational effort in this field is Spaulding, C. A., ed.: *Twenty-four Views of Marriage.*

or, better still, a national research bureau in religion should assemble all useful and needed data for the use of the local churches. The data gathered in the local churches may be of such a sort that it can be used in building up the program of the work of the church. A more telling use of it, however, is the furnishing to the national office of information and clues as to what the church most needs in its efforts to improve marriage.

One persistent effort of the church toward the improvement of marriage has been its austere, and in some cases forbidding, position in regard to divorce. No doubt this has had some effect upon the number of divorces. How much it has done to improve marriage is hard to say. So long as marriages are carelessly and ignorantly and lustfully contracted, attack upon divorce is symptomatic treatment. The best attack upon divorce is the constructive treatment of the premarriage period.

PRACTICAL PROCEDURES FOR THE WORK WITH MARRIAGE

Each church must use such means as are possible to it in its own unique situation, of course. The resources of some churches may seem, at first, to be restricted in almost every way. The specific items listed here are not a set of requirements against which a church should check itself but rather a summary of suggestions of possibilities which may assist in locating resources. The use of any of these will vary from church to church, for each institution must adapt each suggestion to its own requirements, facilities, and purposes.

Selected loaning library of books dealing with marriage.

Short lists of reference books to guide reading, preferably annotated.

Bulletin boards carrying pertinent material, perhaps kept posted with fresh, interesting items by the members.

Study groups on important aspects, either regularly organized or called into session for a special series; discussion will be an important activity here.[5]

Forums of the several varieties possible.

[5] Syracuse University has developed an interesting outline for a course on marriage which opened in February, 1936.

Series of lectures or sermons, perhaps scheduled annually.

A column of material appearing on a certain day in the local newspaper.

A portion of pertinent material regularly appearing in the church calendar.

Building up a research group of the more mature that will help locate findings and formulate general norms, also make available valuable information. Idle, educated persons may be enlisted here.

Program of counseling.

Program of guided group activities for the purpose of correcting certain undesirable situations—group therapy.

Corps of married members particularly selected and trained to assist in certain aspects of the work.

Social organization of members of similar interests who would find growth and reinforcement through fellowship.

Specific connections with other community agencies who have similar purposes and problems, or the means to meet these.

Issuing of special bulletins dealing with particular interests, for distribution to all members concerned.

THE CULTURAL EMPHASES OF THE CHURCH IN DEALING WITH MARRIAGE

First, there is the arousal of those entering marriage to consciousness of the peculiar and precious nature of the community that may grow in marriage, and the relation of this community to the growth of personality in the individual and of culture in the group.

Then there is the ceaseless centering of the attention of the participants upon the greatest religious values which the church fosters, and the relation of these to their own growing community. The church challenges the participants to a continuous reevaluation of what they hold to be worthy.

Third, the church seeks to connect the pledges of loyalty given in marriage with the deepest commitments of the persons pledging, including their religious loyalties. It would thus make marriage not an event but an integrative achievement.

Finally, through guiding the attention of the participants to something outside themselves which is greater than they are, to something that is worthy of their highest devotion, the church objectifies the interests and purposes of the participants. Then, not only are they somewhat fortified against introversion, ingrowing interests, discouragement, boredom, and disillusionment, but they are rightly oriented in their quest for value toward high and ever-higher causes. Further, their quest, thus oriented, leads them to a progressive widening of their intimate fellowship to form an ever-enlarging human community.

Chapter IX

WORKING WITH PARENTS

For the church, the focus of work with parents is the promotion of family communion. It is in this that all the members of the family most readily find God and experience Him. No amount of talking about God or exhortation to loyalty toward Him can equal in potency this direct experiencing of Him.

Much of the present work of the church with parents is an effort to serve the ends of the church. This selfishness of the church reacts upon itself in two ways. The adult subjects of such propaganda sense the institutional self-interest behind the program offered in the name of the family, and resent and mistrust efforts so motivated. Further, the church does not grow substantially for the reason that it is activated by concern primarily for its own continuance and power rather than for stirring in the human spirit the sense of the unparalleled significance of the Supreme Value which crowns its hierarchy of values.

The church that labors to bring the family into loyal support of itself as an institution will have a very different atmosphere of fellowship and a markedly different program from the church that seeks to engage the loyalties of the family in devotion to the God for which it exists. In the first case, the attention is centered upon the importance of the church: statistics of attendance, size and type of membership, and financial status are far the most conspicuous interests. In the second case, attention is centered in the great common Cause and the common interests to be served in His name: institutional concerns are secondary to these and are given consideration in due order. Loyalty is intensified by the greatness of the work to be done and by the meanings that pervade all functioning and emerge from it. The former sort of church is a *social* organization principally, endeavoring to promote a community institution. The response of its members is dutiful in quality. The latter sort of church is social, to be sure, but it is primarily *religious*, endeavoring to promote the cause of God: the response of its members is consecrated in quality. It is in this promoting of the cause of God that the family and the church find common ground for their fellowship of loyalty to something beyond them both, and infinitely greater.

There has been some feeling that it may be very good but it is hardly religious for the church, and particularly the minister, to become occupied with the interests and practical aspects of family living. There is much talk still about "keeping attention on the higher things." The lesson that needs to be learned is that those things are higher at any one time which most promote the growth of the kingdom of God. Sometimes keeping attention on the higher things will involve thought-provoking, loyalty-stirring discourse on the concept of God. At other times it will mean introduction of parents to the practical techniques whereby the communion of the family is so strengthened and deepened that every member develops a more vital connection with God.

There is no authentic, permanent, established list which ranks in final order the higher or more holy interests of the church. One function is highest and holiest at one time, another at another time, depending upon the nature of the requirements for the growth of good at the time. What makes a specific function religious is its particular, present relation to the promotion of God's order among mankind. When the parents need it more than anything else, then the pointing out of the specific practical conditions that promote its communion is the holiest of holy services.

So it comes about, therefore, that whatever either the church or the family does to foster and reinforce the other, it does because of the essential importance of this other institution as an agency in building the kingdom of God among men. The effort is directed toward discovering and strengthening those aspects of each institution which most worthily contribute to such building. In the family, it is the peculiar nature of its fellowship which provides the conditions for the presence of God and the growth of religion.

The church, then, is not put to it to scheme cunningly to find an answer to the question, "What will bring them?" Rather it must focus upon understanding deeply the essential nature and requirements of the family, and working meaningfully to promote these. Certain portions of such work involve entering the home; others do not. The church is working with the family when it is endeavoring to improve those social conditions that vitally affect its life. The needs of the family are rooted deeply into the social matrix in the form of property interests, community influences upon the child, law as it affects the family, prevailing economic conditions, availability of supplies for its needs as a consumer, opportunities and patterns for social fellowship, and other operative cultural forces. These needs and conditions drive the interest of the family beyond its own four walls. In consequence, they build the system of connections through which the family may naturally and wholesomely be approached by the church.

It must be recognized, however, that there are certain conditions in modern life which oppose or hamper the approach of the church to the family. To speak specifically, it is often hard, for one thing, to get at the family geographically. Its members are away from their residences a great deal, or the church membership extends over territory impossible to cover frequently, or they live in apartments which act as fortresses on occasions when a church visitor comes at an inconvenient hour: then the speaking tube makes it easy and impersonal to give excuses for not receiving him. Again, countless parents avow good intentions, but they are hard-pressed to "keep up" and to "keep going." Others are confused or skeptical religiously. An increasing number associate with those with whom "religion" is unpopular because of some personal disappointment or disgust experienced in connection with some particular manifestation of it. Further, there are many, many parents who do not know how to promote religious living in their families and feel that the church as they see it today cannot help them learn to do so.

For these and other reasons it is an enormous undertaking for the church to endeavor to bring parents to the place where they seek actively and earnestly to incorporate religious values and practices as essential elements in the daily living of the families. It will never be achieved by a cut-and-dried "program" blocked out by church leaders working by themselves. The church must learn how and when and where to work with the family by studying its nature and needs, and by distinguishing the conditions which must be set up *for the sake of the growing love-life of the family* and not for its own advantage.

In a recent informal discussion, Professor Radhakamal Mukerjee of India shared with some of his American friends his interpretation of the spiritual guidance of the educated family in his own country. Each family selects its own *guru* or spiritual adviser, most families choosing one of orthodox beliefs but some seeking one remarkable for insight. The mother in each family is charged with the special responsibility for the guidance of the spiritual development of the entire family. Then she and the *guru* take counsel together in regard to the religious needs of each individual. Prof. Mukerjee recounted that, in his own family, there was a daily season of precious fellowship in meditation and worship after the evening meal, led by the mother: often she read passages from literature that opened up deeper resources: symbols and rituals, long agrowing, enriched their devotions. Also each day, according to long established practices, every member conducted private meditation and worship, preferably in the hour of quiet before breakfast. Spiritual disciplines formed a prominent part of this devotional hour: each member had his own course worked out for him by the *guru* after counsel with the mother. A number of these disciplines were directed toward promoting fairness, beauty and appreciation in the intimate life of the family and were deeply potent factors. When a marriage occurs, our informer says, the couple come to live with the man's family for several months or even longer. This is a period of education for both. The bride is initiated into the ethos of her husband's family as well as into the business of homemaking. But even more important, husband and wife separately are guided in their private meditations and disciplines through courses specifically arranged by the *guru* which lead them both to see the larger and the religious significance of their marriage, including their sexual relations, and to prepare themselves for their life together. In this process of religious guidance there is a spirit and some suggestions for the church which would serve the growth of the love-life of the family rather than itself.

This certainly does not mean to imply either that the church will not receive benefit and prosper by its interacting with the family, nor that it must ask nothing of the parents with whom it works. But what the church may ask the parents to do should be determined by the requirements of the cause which church and parents together are trying to promote. Demands on the parents should not be shaped by the arbitrary, church-centered decision of the ruling board of the church. It is the God-centered appeal of the meaningfulness of the cause which the parents must feel. The first requirement of the church wanting to make a strong appeal, then, is that its representative cause at any one time shall be sufficiently meaningful to arouse and engage the parents. Its concern is not to discover "what to bring to the people," but how to build up a fellowship of families, sharing interests, co-operating, and learning together. This is fundamentally a matter of parent education. There are a number of forms and directions which such education may take. Four of the more important of these will be presented here, and in as practical a form as is possible within limited space.

SOME URGENT AREAS IN PARENT EDUCATION

Pointing Out the Conditions Which Affect Family Communion

The main work for the church in this connection is not to set parents all aglow with entrancing pictures of the value and glory issuing from the growth of the love-life of the family. Many parents have been wafted to the heights in the iridescent bubble of the minister's effervescence, only to suffer complete and humiliating collapse when they returned home into the normal growth-confusion or the abnormal chaotic disruption not uncommon in the course of ordinary family living. But the really important thing is to educate parents to the point where they have a working understanding of the nature and possibilities of the interacting fellowship which is the family, and of the conditions necessary to promote it. This equips them for their profession, gives them tools with handles by which to get at their situations, and fosters the attitude of expecting growth together with the problems and experiences which accompany it. Here is one possible formulation of these conditions prerequisite to the growth of communion in the family.

The necessary resources: personal, material, financial, spatial, cultural, and all the others. It must be realized that the quantity required is always *relative* to the functions and the present status of family life. When a truly essential resource is lacking, attention must then be focused upon its supply and other higher values and purposes neglected.

A worthy objective: a dominant purpose determines organization, methods, order, and programs for activities. It develops unity and love, through necessitating a working together for something which all hold as good. It makes progress and hence happiness possible.

Appreciation: of persons, things and conditions, so that the best and most in each is encouraged, enheartened, into participation, and hence so that communion will be facilitated and grow ever more meaningful. A sense of responsibility and other cardinal virtues of relationship root out of specific experiences of appreciation.

Cooperation: the supplementing and amplifying of the work of every member and of the group as a whole, by every member and by the whole. Investing the self for others inevitably develops concern and love for these others.

Mutual reinforcement: a sensitive understanding in each of the interests of all the others, so that each can promote the other toward worthy fulfillment. This creative interaction locates and develops values beyond expectation which enrich the fellowship.

Organic equality: a pattern of relationship in which each has equal opportunity and responsibility concordant with his qualifications and his particular functions. No one has need to compete against others, or to work them or deceive them, nor need he develop will-to-power or inferiority awareness.

Every member finds all available resources and privileges open to him as soon as he has demonstrated his own readiness to deal with these. He knows that he belongs and that he counts.

Freedom: that condition where the bond of love, intelligently developed, makes each individual want to be so true to himself, to the other members, and to whatever the group hold dear that he finds himself more and more trusted, more and more free to work toward his own plans, and with fewer obstacles in his relations with the others and in the conditions of his living.

Perforce, it is in suggestive rather than comprehensive form that the conditions essential in promoting the fellowship of the family have been here presented. But however condensed the formulation, it is a natural and rightful expectation to look for *love* at the head of the list. Though seemingly omitted, it is there. All of this is love. All of this is love at work. The church performs a great service for the parents when it draws their attention away from thinking about love in vague or confused or sentimental terms and focuses it upon setting up the conditions in which love can grow and function. When parents know that there is something they can do about the growth of love, they feel more secure in their love for each other and hence in life itself. Further, they begin to sense themselves as a part of a larger, growing unity, for they soon find that these conditions for the growth of communion can be promoted in circles widening out from the family.

The conditions which tend to break down community need to be studied also, particularly those which tend to grow up silently and inconspicuously. Dealing understandingly with disorganizing conditions protects the communion of the family. Citing some common ones will start the list.

Continued, concentrated preoccupation of some one member of the family with matters extraneous to the group.

Lack of a surplus of physical energy in some one member, particularly if this continues over a period of time.

Individualistic ambition or regime as a pattern for living.

Exclusive relationship between some certain two of the group.

Loss of interest in some other member or in the whole group by some one member.

Disruption in the husband-wife relationship.

The habitual seeking of those satisfactions, by one or more members, which are on a lower level than is the developed standard of the group.

It is just as important for the family to recognize that there are certain irremediable conditions beyond their power to change as it is to be able to construct ingenious ways of meeting an obstinate yet remediable one. Conspicuous failure, disastrous loss, death, involuntary unemployment, permanent handicap, growing old—these and many like them are not uncommon experiences in any neighborhood of families. Any one of them could entirely disrupt the fellowship of the family if it had not learned to see the deeply underlying, essential values which still endure even though some of the treasured forms in which these have been present are lost or destroyed.

Guiding the Improvement of Working Patterns

One of the first things that the average family does when it moves into a new locality is to find out just what the acceptable family in this environment is like. Usually, then, it adopts the patterns that distinguish the acceptable family as the pattern for its way of life while resident in this neighborhood. Not often does it stop to examine and appraise these working patterns in terms of the varied effects they will have upon the family. Conforming to local patterns has become so common a custom that any family which does not try to sense the prevailing patterns and conform to them is likely to become the object of coercive pressures exerted by those who do.

These stereotyped patterns of the acceptable family, however, are seldom of a sort to promote the growth of unity and of meaning within family life. Usually they have grown up without being evaluated. Also important to note, they are most vigorously defended by individuals of the lower cultural level, however high their local social or financial position may be. Finally, most of them at bottom are promoted by commercial interests, intent on increased sales of every sort of goods, not upon improvement of family function. Examples of disruptive working patterns are the habitual timing of social functions at hours when attendance means neglect of essential family interests; manias for golf, bridge, or community offices; standards of living that mortgage the future of the family or declass those who are honest toward life; condoning looseness toward extramarital affairs by those whose loyalties are already pledged in marriage; and indulgent over-equipping of children. If the patterns for family living are unevaluated, low-minded, individualizing ones, they are degrading and destructive of the fellowship which is the family. Further, in many localities, these unevaluated stereotypes cut the family off more and more from those other community connections which tend to keep it sensitive to what is happening to it, which keep it aroused to its functions, and which keep it searching for genuine and worthy values.

The patterns which tradition has handed down to the family are of no more value, until appraised, than are the current stereotypes. They grew up for other persons, time, and places. However sacred they may truly be on account of their remembered connections with revered persons of the past, they may have a diabolic quality when adopted without evaluation as patterns for the living of present persons, time, and places. Instances are all too obvious: the lustily healthy woman whose load has been decreased by labor-saving devices but who increases her husband's load in order to "keep up appearance"; the husband who is too proud to allow his well-schooled wife to take a job, yet is not disturbed by the long, hard hours she puts into washing, darning, or scrubbing; the woman who is expected to do all the housework even though she has a full-time job outside the home and contributes all her earnings; the man who is expected to do all of the disciplining of the children which is of a disagreeable sort.

The church must educate the family to see that it runs too great a risk of disruption or failure when it adopts stereotyped patterns for its functioning, whether traditionally or locally formed. The family must be led to realize that the only valid and increasingly satisfying patterns are those that are progressively built up within the present, interacting family fellowship as its guides in the fulfillment of its nature, its needs, and its functions.

Experience with many groups of parents has demonstrated that, after the first daring break from the stereotyped patterns of their neighborhoods or of their family traditions, thinking parents find it thrilling to begin to develop truly appropriate working patterns of their own. This does not mean, of course, that they have no regard for existing patterns, but rather that they accept none of these automatically: they appraise and then reject or adapt or accept them. Nor does this imply that new patterns are easily and quickly developed, for they are not. But the process of improving the patterns is rewarding from the start because all family activities and relationships begin to be more meaningful and hence enriching.

Clues for this improving of patterns must be sought through study, observation, and experiment. Certain modern developments have valuable contributions to make. One of these appears in man's effort toward democratic cooperation. It is the *permanent council* in which all members of an organized group are actively represented and actively share. Meeting regularly at a mutually convenient time, it provides a specific occasion when the members share the interests and events of the group, when they undertake to build conditions which will correct undesirable factors in the group life, and when they plan projects together with the programs for realizing these. Also it is a clearing house for complaints, criticisms, suggestions, and resources. Such a working pattern tends to forestall many difficulties, decrease tension, facilitate constructive endeavor, and deepen bonds of understanding and love. A permanent *family council*, or its equivalent, is an essential.

A second clue comes from the laboratories of research workers. It is the procedure adopted by scientists interested in the same field who find themselves in substantial disagreement. They welcome such disagreement because of the leads they get out of it for renewing their search for truth. Disagreements must be frequent in an intelligent, achieving family. Following the pattern of the scientists, husband and wife, or parent and child, when

they find themselves in disagreement, can undertake the roles of
fellow students eager to locate in their disagreements the leads
that will enable them to understand. To succeed, they must keep
their attention upon their search for new truth. That is what is
meant by being objective. They will fail as soon as either becomes intent upon proving that he or his way is right. This pattern is particularly important in husband-wife and parent-ado-
lescent conflicts. It might be called *cooperative exploration and
experimentation of disagreements.*

A third clue comes from both medical practice and the nursery school, as well as from government experimental stations.
In each of these locations, the standards or norms for the guidance of growth are discovered by long careful observation of the
actual functioning of many, many living creatures. Indeed, the
fact that the experimental stations have long given the farmer
validated norms for raising pigs, corn, and cotton has already
aroused the farmer's wife to demand at least as carefully distinguished norms for guidance in raising children. No longer
can we believe it beneficial or right to pass judgment upon a
child's behavior by parental or neighborhood ideals or styles. We
need this new pattern of *long, actual observation of behavior
and growth to discover norms* for righting our expectations of
human growth in order to decrease tensions in relationships and
warping of personalities.

A fourth clue comes from the courts, notably the court of domestic relations and the juvenile court. Here the judge and the
investigators do not put themselves into the impossible position
of deciding exactly what happened and who is to blame in troubles which they did not witness. Their chief interest is to get the
parties involved to face squarely the factors making up their situation, so that they may see them truly and see them whole.
Chief effort is expended in helping the parties to develop a consistent account of their case by discovering the bases for such
inconsistencies as appear. Parents particularly, but also husband
and wife, tend to judge "what went on" in instances where the
one judging was not present. Sometimes these judgments are
poured out in vitriolic words, sometimes repressed where their
spontaneous combustion starts smoldering, destructive burnings.

But here is a working pattern that offers aid: *refusing to assume the burden of passing judgment, but instead, imposing the burden of establishing consistency upon the parties involved.*

Certainly no one can look into the future and discover what all the new working patterns of the family will be. The suggestions noted here are already being adapted and tried with real success. They give some idea of what may be involved in this improvement of family patterns.

Most families will require leadership in this experimental and complicated task. Some of such leadership will come from child and welfare centers, government educational enterprises, and other special agencies. The church will need to keep the family in touch with whatever cultural developments offer patterns which will improve the communion of the family, and will itself have to develop those which are particularly within its area of interest. Significantly, the family can learn a great deal from a church which is improving its own patterns intelligently and continuously.

Some areas of family fellowship where new working patterns are needed are these: types of housing and equipment most effective for family functioning during the different stages of family growth, i.e., for the newly married couple, for the family with very young children, for the family with late adolescent children, and others; arrangements for meeting and sharing the responsibilities and opportunities of home life when both husband and wife work outside the house; programs for family living which generously provide for individual differences while building enriching unity; adjustment of various important interests which clash; constructive expression of appreciations and of adverse criticisms; and the place of the family in relationships between any one of its members and outside persons.

Empowering Parents for Their Work

It is hard for a modern parent to keep himself oriented toward one great loyalty, yet without this life tends to lack substance, continuity, meaning, and progressive achievement. Without achievement, too, there is no happiness. The usual parent is subject to an inordinate number of calls which scatter his efforts and sentiments. Often his work is so highly specialized or routinized or fatiguing that he suffers from cultural nearsightedness: he cannot sense the challenge of a life-size task. Or he may be of the number of the voluntarily idle parasites who think that life is good in proportion to the number of diversions which yield thrills. One of the most dangerous difficulties is individualism or specialization in the father and absorption in a career or in social life in the mother, either of which yields individualizing drive but not integrating force. Another crucial disintegrating factor is the disillusionment, the crashing of ideals, bound to occur repeatedly in modern economic, social, and political activities, in so far as early schooling continues to be otherworldly. Whatever may be the cause, many parents find no way of connecting all the details which make up their days and years into any sort of redeeming and meaningful whole. They feel frustrated and inconsequential themselves and see life as an enigma, a grim ordeal, a great bog or chaos. Unintegrated and disintegrated parents are restless with many dissatisfactions and disappointments: they lack meaningful direction. Not having found themselves, socially and spiritually, they cannot guide others.

Religion is the most potent integrating power in the world. Parents need to be led by the church to see this great power in religion and to understand how they can connect with this power and yet live in this modern world. Such leading is a matter, primarily, of continuous guidance of growth, not of occasional pressing sudden conviction. The necessary initiating questions are already in the minds of the parents in suppressed or vague or open or disrupting form. The first step is to get these perplexities into the open. "What's life all about anyhow?" "What's the use in it all?" "What are we bringing children into?" "What *is* most worth while in life?" "I don't mind keeping going day after day, only I wonder *where* it gets you." "Well, today seems to be pretty much all right, but where do we go from here?" "What has this everlasting dishwashing (or slaving over a desk or a shovel or a machine) to do with real living?" These questions may sound unpromising at times. There may be a measure of bitterness or barrenness or desperation in the expression of them.

But they are reassuring indications that the questioner has not yet let go to drift with the tides.

Through unhurried guidance, made specific and vivid by much illustration from daily living and by directed experimentation, parents can find some object of personal loyalty that will connect such of their diverse interests and occupations as merit it, and give these meaning. When this stage is reached, all the detailed activities of living will begin to arrange themselves about this objective and become imbued with its significance. Following this, the parents will grow toward a higher object of personal loyalty, a higher and then a higher one still. Gradually, this will become progressively clear loyalty to the growth of good, of God in all the world. This supreme loyalty surcharges all lesser but related interests with light, warmth, and meaning. Of course, the parents do not of themselves make these connections between all their related interests: these for the family existed to some degree all the time. But they can have no meaning for the family until the parents themselves have come to appreciate them, and these connections cannot function effectively until the parents thoughtfully foster them. When this comes to pass, the change in family living seems a miracle to the onlooker.

Training the Parents to Recognize God in Their Growing Community

There are two major aspects of developing this ability to recognize God in the midst of the family. First and always the parents must have been educated in a rational understanding of what God in the family is—the *growth* of community pervasively and abundantly fulfilling the life about them all the time. Then, second, they must themselves have had some experiences stirringly deep both of God's presence and of His remoteness in order to know the feeling of what they already rationally understand. It is the part of the church, first, to instruct parents as to what God is, and, second, to point out that what the more unusual experiences of everyday living bring so beautifully or devastatingly to consciousness is the presence or the absence of that which they are experiencing all the time. Any rich fulfillment or any sudden loss in the *growth* of their community will make them vividly aware of this communion and its significance. They can come to see that such growth is the basis of life. They become convinced that all the meaningful values of life are found in this growth of connections of mutual enrichment between activities which they appreciate. This provides the grounds upon which they render a more profound loyalty to the growth of the love-life of the family.

When the parents have learned how God appears and works in the family, and how their work provides the conditions for His work, they then must be guided to cultivate the sense of the presence of God in family living. The chief agency for it is the developing cultus with its symbols which will bring vividly to consciousness the reality of this presence. These symbols cannot be manufactured, cannot even be planned. They have to grow. Many of the old symbols have lost their meaning. In some instances a rational understanding of these and of the nature and needs of the family may eventuate in a new significance in the use of them again. For instance, stereotyped blessing at table and the custom of a period of family prayer after dinner or at bedtime would be nothing but form without spirit in many modern families. But, where the conditions in the family are right, there may be meaningful meditation often including prayer before each meal, guided by first one member of the family and then another. For the younger child, such family meditation will be meaningful only when it recognizes the needs of the community of his own family in the matter of the promotion of its growth, or the joy of the family in some mark of its growth. As the child gets older, he will reflect the wider growth of connections with their augmentation of meanings.

One promising direction for the development of symbols is the sharing with the family community whatever of greatness the various members have discovered or experienced during the day. This easily becomes an informal ritual and can be carried out at whatever time is appropriate, perhaps before dinner when the family naturally gathers into a closer group, or after dinner, or at bedtime. The form of it will vary according to the nature of the community of the particular family who develop it.

A second area of living which would seem to foster the growth of symbols is the growing interest of the family group in other groups in the world at large. One father and mother gather their brood of five sons around them after dinner every evening and together they ponder about world community. The half-hour of weighing the values and disvalues involved in current doings of mankind may or may not include prayer, but those parents are promoting the growth of community among mankind. Good is growing in that group. Certain objects and practices have come to be signs of the process. Certain words and ideas have become carriers of a great wealth of mutually shared meaning. Those boys will never forget the periods spent in connecting with the larger community, not only because significant symbols have built meanings which can be modified though not eradicated, but because they themselves have become identified with the larger community through worshipful family devotion to it.

A number of families have set apart some quiet, small room or corner of the house which is kept strictly private, at least during the daytime, to the one who happens to be using it. It is arranged simply and beautifully. Always there is some new lovely thing on the table near the big, comfortable chair that is the center of the arrangement. It may be a spray of flowers, or a lovely bit of moss, or a tiny statue. Also, there may be a book or a little folio holding some bit of poetry or other quotation. Some families have a small, beautiful altar against the wall in some secluded part of the house. To such a place anyone may go who feels that he wants to get better hold on himself or to pray or to think something through, or just get quiet inside. Also, the children are sent here when their behavior puts them out of adjustment with the group in order to recover as much as possible by themselves before an adult undertakes to guide them. This retreat is endeared to the hearts of the family members because of its service in safeguarding against many a threatened break in relations and in suggestive offerings of new resources and power for the building of more creative living together.

Besides these and other regular practices connected with the recognition and appreciation of God, there are many *special occasions* in family living which will be better initiated when done in a worshipful way. These will illustrate: the lighting and dedicating of a new hearth, going to school for the first time, the first voting of a young person, and becoming betrothed.

Certain activities particularly need the worshipful approach, such as self-reorganization,[1] problem-solving, and the organization of new, important family plans and projects. The outreaching of the family toward the Greater-than-I will result in drawing these activities to a richer level for solution and expression.

The church must encourage and guide in this recognition of God in the growing communion of the family. It must do so not only through the work which it does with the family in the home, but also through the development of the appropriate symbols in the fellowship of the church. When the parents come to see that scrubbing, repairing the plumbing, cleaning dirty little noses, and others among the more unpleasant or menial tasks which they do are performed for the sake of the growing communion of the family, they will come to see also that these are really altar service in their devotion to God. Then all parts of their activity, however near to drudgery these are of themselves, will be imbued with the meanings which go to make up the most precious aspects of their communion. They will come to see this only when they appreciate that the work of God is the growth of meaningful connections, and that all activities or interests vitally connected with a great loyalty share its richest meaning and its most splendid glory, though remaining menial and laborious.

POSSIBLE PROCEDURES OF THE CHURCH

To ponder upon all these matters that are involved when the church is at work with parents increases rather than diminishes the sense of the vastness of the responsibility and the opportunity of the church. It would be overwhelming if it appeared that all these should be added to a full program already required by the essential functions of the church. But these matters are actually the vital heart of the true program of the church. Whatever is here presented is only an exposition of the type and quality of the task which in essence has always been within the work of the

[1] Wieman, H. N.: *Methods of Private Religious Living*, Chap. IX.

church, whether or not it has been accomplished. All these needs of parents are both ancient and modern, ancient as to basic requirements, but modern in the emphases and forms of service involved. There are many procedures through which such service to the modern parents can be rendered. Citing a number of these will vivify the type and quality of the practical work that is to be done.

1. A study of the constituent families of each particular church will give clues as to what type and timing of the program of the church will best promote effectiveness in functioning in both church and family life. Also it will lead to a fairer schedule of appeals for the enlistment of personal and financial support.

To be sure, the large congregational meetings quite frequently include persons of varying backgrounds, situations, and resources. Plans for these can be less plastic, and the church renders one important service to the family as well as the community in its regularity of timing its larger congregational gatherings. Nevertheless, it is now being recognized by many churches that there can be increased plasticity in type of program combined with increase in the true spirit and practice of worship even in these inclusive assemblages. However, the major change will come in the increase of work with small groups of parents or of families, each group representative of some certain interest. Usually these small groups will not be formally nor permanently organized, and one person or one family may participate in more than one group at any one time, depending upon what interest is occupying the particular groups.

We are learning that the spirit of democracy, of organic equality, fails unless each constituent has the opportunity and encouragement both to become conversant with pertinent vital issues and to speak his own mind without let or hindrance. To work *with* rather than *on* a group requires much small-group participation. From this it is apparent that the program of the church for its work *with* the family must be built by its constituent families under the leadership of the church, and that it must emphasize work with small groups drawn together by a common interest and need.

The appeals for support, particularly in the form of personal service, fall peculiarly hard upon the family which is struggling to establish itself economically and is strenuously occupied with small or adolescent children. Overloading at this period when sensibilities or pride are more readily stirred is likely to result in a hardening of attitude later. This possibility illustrates the need of an *intelligent program of appeals* to the family. The church must not betray its trust in this particular, else its families will be the worse for overoccupied or overtaxed fathers and mothers. There are times when the church may well urge a parent to stay home or to go somewhere else to study or to rest, as well as times to urge service within the church.

Certainly, the church in these days will have to work with other community agencies in building its program both as to time and type. In some places this has resulted in a fairly community-wide recognition of one night in the week as "church night," the high school particularly not scheduling any activities at that time. But other forms of cooperation are needed so that the family will not be hectically pulled about by divisive interests, nor the church discouraged by a diversity of competitions.

2. Regularly scheduled study classes for parents are one of the most important and permanent parts of the necessary program of the church. They should provide an opportunity for father and mother to study child behavior together. After the work has proceeded for a year or so, graded courses will be necessary to accommodate parents of different preparation and of different-aged children.

There are several ways in which these classes may proceed. They may use a well-selected book as a point of departure for their discussion. They may report pertinent material on some selected subject of study from their reading at large. They may select one subject or problem and delve into it for a period of weeks. Best of all, they may have a trained leader who will guide the activities and growth of the group as it undertakes the discussion and the working out of its problems. One cooperative plan used in several institutions to initiate parent classes circulates a trained leader among the institutions. Once every month the leader visits each group to bring the work of the past month to a practical and sound focus, and to outline the work for the month to come. Local class leaders or teachers under the guidance of this trained leader carry on the rest of the time. In this way four churches, not able separately to finance adequate leadership, are enabled to share the services and the costs of one trained leader among them.

To be most effective, courses for parents should be of the laboratory type, requiring guided observation, experiments, and projects in connection with children. Unless the chasm between theory and practice is thus bridged over, most parents cannot make the jump and will be superficially "knowing" or disheartened. They need to go far enough to get techniques. But these cannot be given: they must be developed.

The chief warning in regard to parent education is this: the attention of the group should not lose sight of the forest through its interest in a few trees, that is, it should not fail to see the larger aspects of family situations and the cultural connections of parenthood through overabsorption in the specific problems bothering particular parents.

3. Open or restricted forums on characteristic or pressing problems that touch family life closely may be regularly scheduled as a means of bringing confusions or discouragements, or unwarranted complacency, or other destructive factors into the open. Such prospecting and clarifying may not only lead many parents to sounder analysis but may make known to them available resources.

The Junior High School in South Pasadena, California, furnishes a good example of this procedure. Two of their most profitable units for forum discussion were on Home Study and on Social Activities. In connection with each unit, several forums were held. Findings were organized and put into available form. In one Congregational Church, the Men's Club financed and sponsored a group of six forums under a recognized leader.

4. Frequent short bulletins on aspects and problems of family life may be regularly distributed to the families of the church. If these are gotten out in such a way that they may be filed conveniently they become reference material valuable for use over a long period of time. At least a part of the bulletin may well consist of contributions turned in by various parents setting forth

ideas or plans or techniques that they have discovered which have proved helpful to them. Reference lists, helpful quotations from books and periodicals, and other pertinent matters may be included. The main portion of such bulletins could well be cooperatively produced by a number of churches in a community or section having communal interests.

Beyond the service of these regularly published bulletins in helping the parents with more definite instructions in the general field of homemaking and in keeping them posted in regard to all sorts of developments here, there is a particularly urgent service to be rendered. It is the specific guidance of the parents in the matter of the religious education of the children in the home. This includes far more than theological instruction, as has been pointed out. It is a matter, primarily, of providing the conditions which will promote distinctively religious growth and experience. Of course, a series of bulletins cannot provide anything like full guidance for a full education, but it can call attention to the major principles and processes, and make known where further guidance can be had. These bulletins should deal for the most part with the nonspectacular aspects of child growth, for these are likely to be the cardinal ones. This statement does not exclude, of course, such deeply significant though ideally nonspectacular developments as the manifestations of sex attraction in early adolescence, the coming of a new baby, and moving the home into a new house.

Bulletin service is an effective way to make known to nonattendants the interest of the church in family life. If neither the local church nor the church-as-a-community-unit can finance such bulletins, it is probable that a section in the community newspaper may be regularly assigned to the church for this purpose.

5. A social task which calls urgently for attention is the signalizing of family achievement. The world at large has found diverse ways of recognizing achievement and success in practically all other human undertakings except this very important one of homemaking. Standards are set up for many vocations and even for many of the individual processes entering into larger fields of work which enable workers to sense progress. Until

recently, homemakers have been considered unskilled workers unworthy of social recognition professionally. The church can do much toward correcting this false social attitude and appraisal. The institution can keep itself on the alert for every possible occasion which provides opportunity to signalize family achievement. Further, it can keep in touch with such research as is beginning to give us norms for family living.

So long as society imposes penalties of social handicap rather than gives advantage of social recognition to those whose time and energy are devoted primarily to homemaking processes, there will be a drift of interest and devotion away from family upbuilding toward activities that give satisfaction through receiving quicker or greater social reward or recognition. We all tend to invest ourselves where we succeed. Russia is giving some attention now to the matter of signalizing intelligent family devotion, and of celebrating family achievement.

6. A closer cooperation between teachers and parents needs to be built both for the good of the family and the good of the church. The better private schools and most nursery schools will not accept child students for registration unless the parents agree to attend a certain number of group meetings and to come to the school for individual conferences as scheduled by the school.[2] This makes the work of the school much more effective because of more understanding and cooperation in the family. Particularly in the months before children's promotion into a higher department does there need to be a parents' training class to prepare the parents for the developments immanent in their children. Some classes in the secular schools have started parents' clubs which take a very active part in working with each class, particularly in support of special interests, educative excursions, gathering of creative materials, and the like. More and more parents actually assist during school hours in ways in which they are qualified, particularly at the nursery-school level.

There are a greater number of ways in which parents may assist in the church school than in the day school. They can enter

[2] For an account of a most fruitful development at University High School, Oakland, California, see *University High School Journal*, Vol. 13, Dec. 1934.

more directly into the development of a program of sound religious education. Indeed, they must if there is to be any, for most of it must be ministered in the home. Certainly a specific schedule of parent participation and cooperation is an important factor, both in the religious development of the child and in the dynamic functioning of the church.

7. The provision of sound counseling service [3] for parents is of prime importance. Many parents lose first courage then interest in their vocations when they have problems which they cannot understand nor treat successfully. Often they tend to drift into a whirl of business or social activities where they feel themselves making progress or at any rate functioning acceptably. As soon as parents realize that their problems will be treated in confidence and that there will be practical help for them, they begin to take a more professional attitude toward their job of parenthood.

8. The church can make educative materials available to the family. First, books may be accumulated which deal with the various phases of family life. These may range all the way from very simple ones to those which discuss problems from a more technical point of view. One sort of material should be included, stories, novels, and other accounts of "good" successful families, that is, of families fulfilling their functions with fun, adventure, intelligence, and devotion.

Several churches may club together and buy a carefully selected library, circulating it by sections. Again, each parent may be asked to contribute a book a year to the family library at the church, making all the books available to all the parents.

There are a number of magazines [4] which would add to the value of such a library. A file of the resources of the community open to, and helpful to, parents is an invaluable addition to these educative materials.

Another practical form of educative material is a collection of folios containing helpful materials either collected or worked out by the parents themselves. All the various clippings, bulletins, and reports pertinent to the subject are filed into these folios. One large group of parents divided itself into smaller groups for

[3] See Chap. XII.
[4] See p. 385.

the purpose of making folios helpful in planning for the recreational activities of children and young people of various ages. A great number of parents who are beginning to study will find the folios an easy approach in preparing themselves for the more technical books in the library.

9. No other institution seeks entire families for membership as does the church: the encouragement of good times or projects in which the *family as a whole* participates is another avenue of service in counteracting family disorganization. Literally speaking, we cannot share thinking with others nor feeling with others. But we can share doing, and such sharing builds up bonds of fellowship, common interests, and mutual admiration. Further, the group association of a number of families provides mirrors of contrast in which parents can more clearly see themselves and their ways.

Then it is a fine thing for both parents and children to witness the social recognition accorded the other members of their own family by "outsiders." Previously unsuspected skills and abilities are sometimes revealed, and, just as fortunately though less happily, unsuspected maladjustments and limitations. This is particularly true where the children and young people take their turns preparing programs, suppers, and other activities, or participate *as persons* with adults in doing so. Too many times do parents think they must "put on" most affairs. Let them try making way for the young people to put on a dinner for the parents. There is overmuch assumption on the part of the parents that young people lack the necessary capacity and maturity.

Furthermore, since effective human relationships are the basis of genuine religious expression, such fellowship among families as units becomes a continuing experiment in religious living. Gradually, working codes for association and cooperation develop in line with the real principles which the membership hold. As these codes emerge, they should be evaluated and formulated. These self-developed codes governing the church fellowship of families provide support for greater equality, trust, and freedom in group relations. They also both relieve separate families of the necessity of dissenting from harmful practices and provide large group support for wholesome practices.

10. A cooperative bureau within the membership of the church may be instituted to take care of problems of relief and emergency. One church has succeeded in building up such a program which includes every member. Those that have vacant land lend it, unemployed persons work it, and so on through. Every such plan will show up faults one after another which must be progressively handled. However, such efforts, intelligently corrected and guided, may yield the seeds of insistent desire for better basic economic structures.

11. The fostering of small worship groups composed of persons who at the time have common interests or problems is an essential service to be rendered by the church in many communities in these days. Ideally, these worship groups meet in the homes of the members. Such a procedure is a practical means for carrying worship into the family or of guiding further development in worship. To function, such a gathering cannot be treated as just one more "cottage prayer meeting": it must be thoughtfully and richly prepared for.

Sometimes these groups may share their deeper experiences and findings. Sometimes they may work worshipfully on troublesome community problems together. Sometimes they may try to help each other locate resources for their interests and difficulties. Sometimes they may deepen their sensitivities through a service of appreciation of some one among "whatsoever things are good, whatsoever things are lovely." Each time they come together it is with some specific, recognized purpose. But they may vary their activity and procedures from time to time as the nature and needs of the situation indicate.

12. Besides all these procedures with the specific families in the church, there must be built up simultaneously the larger aspects of the program of the church for the family. Some of these aspects are suggested in other parts of this volume; they include the fostering of a significant religious cultus which comprehends the nature and functions of the family, the promoting of community cooperation, and interest in national conservation of the family. It is in this building of the larger program that interchurch and interdenominational fellowship is indispensable.

PROMOTING THE CULTURAL EFFECTIVENESS OF THE FAMILY

A discouraged, disorganized family has no eyes to see nor ears to hear anything outside its own struggling; and no hands to help in any human project. The family which is restored to status and reasonably qualified for its distinctive functions has more cultural influence and significance than anything else of the same size in all the world. What the family nurtures, the world most needs. What the family teaches to the children, the world later must reckon with. Could there be any undertaking of greater moment for the church than this—its work with the parents in promoting human fulfillment in individual homes and in organizing groups of families for intelligent devotion to developing fellowship in wider reaches of the human community? Of a surety, in view of the great objectives of the church, there is no other field as fertile nor as promising of universally significant harvest as is this one of fostering communion in family life.

Chapter X

APPROACHES IN THE GUIDANCE OF CHILDREN

THE family wants more than anything else to make sure that each child shall get the most out of life. The church professes to know the best way by which this can be accomplished, for its function is to promote loyalty to that which is supremely worthful for all mankind. Here spreads the ground for the common endeavor of family and church in guiding the child toward highest fulfillment. The family, we have said, sees human fulfillment primarily in terms of its own members, but this normally leads into concern for human fulfillment in the large. The church sees human fulfillment principally in its widest reaches, but this must lead to concern in terms of human individuals, particularly of the young. The problem of value is the heart of the problem of the church as it works with children.

There are two major aspects of the educational interest of the church in the child. One focuses upon guiding the child's quest for value, the other upon fostering effective loyalty to highest value as at any one time conceived by the child. Fortunate it is that neither family nor church can pass over to the child its own established scale of values, nor can either of them control directly and fully the child's expression of his loyalties. The child can build into himself a dependable system of values only by his own personal search for value. He can give his loyalty only to those values with which he himself is vitally acquainted. Many selfish and shortsighted parents and teachers would rather see and hear the child conform to their convictions and practices even though these are not the issues of his own mind and heart. They do not seem to realize that the child is not thereby serving their values, but rather *serving them as persons* through concessions in the form of external agreement in order to hold their affection or avoid their disapproval and disappointment. That is, they are training him to be subject to the approval and disapproval of persons rather than subject to the challenges and disciplines of something he had found which is greater than he.

Implicit in this coercive control of the child's loyalties to value is a dangerous hazard. He thereby learns to build himself into unity with other persons through conforming to their demands and pleasing them. This is the lowest level on which interpersonal unity can be maintained, for it interferes devastatingly with the growth of personality. A child so coerced to live according to established stereotypes is not equipped to participate in that finer type of unity which issues in forms of interaction constantly generating unsuspected possibilities of value. This greater level of unity is (1) founded upon the sharing of interests (2) in a relationship of organic equality (3) which involves constructive cooperation rather than conformity. It makes creative use of differences instead of driving them into hiding. It does not seek to set up a smoothly running, complacent, agreeable atmosphere, but to promote maximum growth of meaning in living.

It is not at all hard to understand the eagerness of parent and pastor that the child, with all his discovering of values, shall discover the Supreme Value. But eagerness without intelligent understanding is a liability in the guidance of the child. It tries to force convictions of value upon the child before he has had the indispensable experiences with values and disvalues which would initiate and support such convictions. He may adopt the stereotyped convictions of his cultural group of the time, but the first experience which calls these seriously into question will start to dislodge them. They are not his. He has no reason for the faith that is within him beyond that of pleasing certain adults. Adopted values seldom take root.

Many parents today point to the method of indoctrinating current in their youth and its permanent results in their own living. First of all, they should note the fact that those individuals with whom the imposed convictions of value did remain permanently are in the minority. But more important still, they should realize that, in those cases where the convictions held, it was because the individuals remained in close connection with the cultural group living by such convictions. The adopted convictions were not put to a test in any critical fashion until they had become stereotypes for the child now become adult. But today, fortunately, it is almost impossible to keep a child within a homogeneous cultural grouping until the stereotypes of the group get set. Many factors make this true, among them the complex interfusion of cultures, the amplified facilities for communication, and the increase in variety and number of personal contacts. Consequently we can no longer rely upon permanent conditioning by a somewhat segregated, homogeneous cultural group. We are forced to discover the laws of growth and to guide the child's quest for value and his loyalty to the highest value by such laws, amidst the cultural diversities of our time. The only values to which persons can hold fast in modern living are those which have been self-tested deeply enough to make the persons sensitive and predisposed in the presence of such values, no matter in what forms they may appear.

The program of religious nurture, then, is one of guiding growth, not of coercing conformity. It is accomplished by inoculating the child through actual experiences of value. It cannot be done by indoctrination through discourse about value. In these early years, inoculation versus indoctrination is the issue. Three double requirements must be met by parent, teacher, and pastor in this program of inoculation: (1) adequate understanding of both the laws of growth and of the soundest system of values yet conceived; (2) discovery of the conditions prerequisite for growth and for encountering worthy values, and unfaltering devotion in setting these up; and (3) faith enough to let the laws of growth and the lure of worthy values work in the child while the adult hands keep off and the adult tongue keeps still once all the prerequisite conditions have been met. "Take no thought for the morrow" if the provision of essential conditions has been effectively cared for today.

THE PROCESS OF GUIDING THE CHILD

The educative process in religious growth means the process by which the child is guided in his quest for value and in his loyalties to greatest discovered values. All workers of whatever faith or field can come to working agreement on the processes of guidance, because they are based upon laws of growth which can be validated. In the light of some recent happenings, perhaps it should rather be said that all workers can come to a working agreement except those who are so self-willed that they will not learn what God's will is by studying the laws by which growth actually takes place in the human being.

Man does not make the laws of learning, he only discovers them. They are not different for those of different faiths or social levels. Therefore it is that workers in this new day *can* agree on the *processes* of guidance sufficiently to work together. Where they undoubtedly must still disagree is upon the *content* in guidance. This latter depends upon the characteristics of each particular situation. It is determined in the first place by the nature and needs of the individuals to be guided; in the second place by nature and needs of the particular cultural group doing the guiding; and lastly upon the resources of all kinds which are available in the particular situation. To try to discuss content here would mean to discuss it separately for each cultural division involved, an impossibility anyway unless there were specific knowledge of each situation in case. It would be very profitable if disparate conventions of workers of disparate faiths would restrict their discussions to the matter of process, leaving content for their smaller, culturally homogeneous conferences. In working out the processes of guidance there can be very rewarding sharing of interests and a type of cooperation which would yield gratifying amplified power in the work.

What are the major processes in guiding the child in (1) his quest for value, and (2) his loyalty to the highest value *he* has yet discovered?

Preparing the Conditions of Growth

A working list [1] of the indispensable conditions of growth has already been presented. The application at that point was made to the family unit. It needs to be extended to the church and to

[1] Chapter IX, pp. 194-195.

other community situations frequented by the child. As has just been said, determining the content required in meeting each of these conditions must be the task of those responsible for each specific situation. For example, inquiring as to precisely what organization of the family will provide the indispensable condition described as *organic equality* will require a very different answer in a family having three children under seven years of age, employing no help, and residing far from the father's work, from the answer in a family with three children over fourteen years of age, one of whom is seriously handicapped, and with a well-to-do father who must travel about a great deal. So with the other indispensable conditions.

One of the hardest tasks in providing the conditions for growth is that of keeping a balance between all the essential conditions. This would be difficult enough if, for instance, it simply meant seeing to it that the providing of adequate *resources for growth* did not usurp too much attention and energy from distinguishing progressively *an objective worthy of the loyalty* from the family. But it is far more complicated than that. What is balance of conditions for toddlers is not balance for adolescents in many respects, yet both are present at the same time in many homes. The discernment and delicacy of adjustment involved in balancing the conditions of growth in a family of varying ages constitutes a great enough challenge upon ability to fire the spirit of any interested parent.

On many occasions the preparation of the conditions of growth centers upon the selection, direction, or cooperative evaluation of outside stimuli impinging upon the child rather than the actual setting up of specific family conditions. This is strikingly true in those neighborhoods where the child is much away from his own residence. Also to be included in consideration here are the radio, various periodicals, public library service, and other elements that make their way into the house.

The unity of the home is probably the single condition of growth most important to children. This is equally true whether unity of family refers to the pervading spirit of the group from day to day or to the continuance of all the members in the membership of the group. Particularly, loss of a parent from the family group, for whatever reason, is shattering. The parent's face is the child's book of life. What he hears said to him may or may not be disturbing, but when he sees repeatedly the indications of strained relationship or deprivation of love in the face of a parent, his sense of his own security is undermined. Life is held in more or less suspense until he senses unity again.

In this process of preparing the conditions of growth, one caution is necessary at the outset. This caution is against the assumption that we *know* certainly and infallibly what the correct conditions are. Always, of course, we are setting conditions for the growth of our own and other children, and this usually without knowing it. In a society organized to promote human fulfillment we would not have to know it specifically. In our present society we must know it and set the most promotive conditions possible. But we must do with an ever-continuing sensitivity and a willingness to learn more than we know now.

It is a great step when we stop trying to deal with the child himself and cease asking that horrible question, "What would you do with a child who . . . ?" But we must go a step farther, a step into the background wherein we locate the conditions affecting the child. When the church, school, and club thus look into the background of a child's behavior, they learn a great deal about his family and his conditions of living. All who work with the immature must focus major attention upon setting up and adjusting the conditions of growth and must do so with the utmost sensitivity and plasticity engendered by the profound realization that we, too, are undergoing the growth process.

If we stop to realize what a tremendously difficult matter we are undertaking in shaping the conditions which are to guide a personality in its outreach toward God, the resultant humility, the alert sensitivity, and the industrious, intelligent devotion necessary to such a trust may keep us fairly safe factors among the other factors which go to make up the conditions operative upon the child.

Developing Discriminating Tastes

This is a matter of working with both the feelings and sources of satisfaction and dissatisfaction which make up the child's meaningful experience. When his satisfactions are aligned with tested values and his dissatisfactions with proven disvalues, these will be strengthened through appropriate repetition. When they are not so aligned, the experiences deviating from the norms must be corrected by a reweighting of satisfactions and dissatisfactions. Fortunately, there are usually a number of sorts of both satisfactions and dissatisfactions present in each experience. The child ordinarily sees only one of these out of the whole constellation, namely, the one he has most vividly met before. He needs guidance in discovering whatever others pertain vitally to his situation.

There are several ways of changing the emphasis in the satisfactions and dissatisfactions of the child. One of the strongest ones, particularly during the earlier years, is the natural sharing with him of adult enthusiasm for certain forms of satisfaction. The child figures to himself, "If Daddy likes it as much as that, there must be a lot to it." Another helpful way is to sustain or repeat some particular situation in which he is experiencing new values until he has had a convincing taste of them. For instance, sharing toys must start not as social sharing but as the taking of turns and the spontaneous expressing of appreciation when one's turn comes. This continues until gradually the fun (taste of value) of relinquishing to another-who-appreciates prompts the first genuine sharing. Probably this sharing will be done for the sake of the personal notice resulting, but it is a first step, based upon a first convincing taste: more altruistic sharing must develop taste by taste. So with joy in work and all other indirect values. Again, the child must be allowed to face the consequences of his choices of value or disvalue, except where this might incur permanent injury. Consistency in adults is an indispensable condition for the developing of sound tastes in the child; they cannot preach one thing and practice another; nor, without fully valid grounds for doing so, can they grant avowed disvalues (such as staying up late) as special privileges on occasion, nor punish through imposing an extra measure of avowed values (extra study after regular school hours). Cooperative evaluation is essential to this process of developing discriminating tastes as soon as the child can use language with reasonable skill.

The paramount object in this process is that of building activating predispositions toward sound values and conclusive aversions toward proven disvalues, so that the child is well launched in his building for himself that most important part of his cultural equipment, an adequate system of values. The second object, hardly less important than the first, is to launch and foster the progression of loyalties. This involves, to repeat again, guiding him to devote himself wholeheartedly to whatever he feels at any one time is worth the most above anything else in his world, and at the same time preparing him for a progression in loyalty when a still more worthy object emerges to take the crowning place in his world of values.

One of the most difficult things for the adult is to have a genuine and adequate regard for the objectives of loyalty chosen by the small child. His objectives are bound to seem trivial and transitory compared with those which we in our almost infinite wisdom would advocate! Notwithstanding how distant his objective seems from Supreme Reality, it is necessary for us to see that he is on his way. He is progressing from "glory unto glory." So long as the objective to which he is devoted in this present is of greater worth *in his eyes* than the one which previously claimed his loyalty, he is progressing.

It is precariously easy for an adult to crush the tender outthrusting of a new loyalty in a child. All it may take is one unmistakable evidence of amused superiority, impatient disdain, bored tolerance, disparagement, ridicule, or sarcasm to wither it forever. On the other hand, it requires equally little, many times, to provide the salubrious climate for the germinating and sprouting of a genuine, if seemingly small, growth in loyalties. The child is not able to stride from value unto value: his steps are short and meandering. It is his forward facing and the general trend of his achieved succession of loyalties which count.

Interpretation of the Unfamiliar

There are many things which bewilder the child. He senses elements in the world-within-his-reach which are strange, fascinating, inconsistent, evil, glamorous, confusing, enticing, threatening, awesome, seemingly unconquerable. Since he is so new in a world that is always both very old and very new, it is not surprising that he is frequently puzzled, sometimes ecstatic, or again somewhat frightened. Many adults feel flattered when a child clings to the familiar. Yet if he is to achieve rich fulfillment of life, he will have to learn how to deal with the unfamiliar, how to assay with reasonable soundness for values and disvalues, how to make the desirable portions his own, how to deal with the proven disvalues, and how to discern in all this experience the important connections which lead into further exploration of the unfamiliar.

This is primarily the problem of guiding the child to a creative treatment of fear. Without fear, he can never grow wise, for fear is the consciousness of elements in his operative situation, which, on the one hand, have some hold upon him, some power over him, yet, on the other hand, are unfamiliar and consequently uncontrollable, unconquered and hence threatening. He stands there defenseless before *Possibilities*, unpredictable because unexplored, yet inevitably bearing down upon him. In high spirits and valiantly he must storm the situation and make it his own. He must explore, learn, conquer the unknown. This is the positive approach in fear. Fear expresses itself positively when it grasps at the fringe which is known in that which is unfamiliar, and then from this point of vantage begins to approach the unknown courageously but studiously. Fear expresses itself negatively when it stares at the unknowns until daunted, panic-stricken, and paralyzed. Fear positively expressed is equivalent to courage of spirit based upon rational analysis of the pertinent factors in the situation.

Interpretation of the unfamiliar in any one specific experience involves, then, helping the child to locate what elements in this situation are known to him and then how to approach the unknown elements from these knowns. It is a matter of making him a keen and skilled explorer in the realm of values. Such he must be if his progression of loyalties is to bring him eventually into rich connection with Supreme Value. This indicates that interpretation should be a process of guiding his exploration rather than of passing to him ahead of time the completed charts of other explorers, though often these should be available to him for purposes of comparison.

Excursions into new places and new books, contact with new persons and social situations, dealing with new materials and undertaking new projects, seeking new approaches in situations where there has been disappointment or failure, and studying different points of view—these are situations where fear may be guided into constructive expression. The child must be led to regard the unfamiliar as an unexplored realm of possibilities of value. The attitude of those about him toward the unfamiliar affects the child markedly, both when the experience of strangeness comes to all in common and when it comes to the child only. God is the greatest unfamiliar which the child will encounter. It is paramount that his training with the lesser unfamiliars shall have prepared him for a positive approach to God.

Cooperative Experimentation

In the world where the established patterns for activities and association are frequently outmoded, and where there are constantly appearing new possibilities, the process of cooperative experimentation becomes increasingly important in the guidance of children. This is true for the home, the church, and the school almost equally, though in somewhat different areas. It is one of the soundest approaches in the treatment of problems of adjustment.

Three factors are essential to this process: (1) an hypothesis or proposition which the child deems worthy of trying out or proving; (2) the setting up of the conditions necessary to make the experiment valid; and (3) the criteria by which to appraise developments and findings. Ordinarily, these three factors are not formally set up, but are cared for in a natural way. Even with little children, this method is important. It is possibly the best approach in such a case, for instance, as recurrent trouble between a child and his neighbor. Here, after an analysis of the difficult situation has revealed what looks to be an activating factor, a simple appropriate experiment is set up involving this factor. For example, a child may discover that he has a habit of finding fault or expressing dissatisfaction on every new occasion. Accordingly the carrying on of his experiment involves thinking out a better attitude or approach in dealing with his neighbor, and then trying this, not once, but several times. In the end he evaluates the outcomes. If his experiment is successful, he has a deep satisfaction of social craftsmanship, which is far more convincing to him than volumes of talk. He actually learns something directly about how the community grows, by first being an agent in setting up the conditions that promote its growth, and then by tasting the values which emerge when the right conditions have been rightly set up.

Guiding the Child's Grasp of Meanings

Unless this is recognized as a process necessarily continuous, guidance here will be inadequate. Too many times the adult confines it to those occasions either of a scheduled "lesson" assigned to the child or of a deliberate question wherein the child himself seeks clarification of some meaning which actually blocks him. Typically, this is an occasion when the area where his mind is at work is one of interest to the adult. Consequently the adult is likely to feel stirred with joy or pride or zeal or concern at finding the child exploring meanings here. In such a case he overdoes his guidance. When this happens, the child may decide that turning to the adult for help in grasping at meanings floods him with too big a bargain in the way of guidance. Or he may discover that seeking adult help in certain areas gives him leverage upon the adult and so he makes his asking for guidance a tool by which to warm up the adult preliminary to working him. This happens all too often in home, school, and college. Guidance of grasp of meanings when so undertaken is too occasional and hence too conspicuous.

As a matter of fact, the healthy child is always grasping at meanings. The adult must keep himself sensitive to the many ways in which this is evidenced, such as incoherent efforts "to get at" something he half senses, reactions which are inappropriate but not deliberately so, a persistent series of questions seemingly inconsequential to the adult, struggle to find the correct wording, inexplicable attitudes, and manifestation of shock as a result of some revelation of the contrary or "wrong" meaning held by someone else.

If one observes a child in a situation whose meaning is not clear to him, one can often watch the progress of the breaking of the light of meaning over his whole body, resolving finally into some overt interaction within the situation through which he begins testing the validity of the dawning meaning. A little child will so study the meaning of the strange man Father has brought into the house with him, a new food on his plate, a pile of creative material unused by him (such perhaps as clay or sand), the arrangement of the schoolroom on his first day at school, a new object in a familiar setting, and a combination of words, inflections, and expressions that make up the behavior addressed to him by some adult or other child.

The process of guiding the child's grasp of meanings is one of assisting the child, *when he needs it*, in identifying, clarifying and formulating what happens to him in his various stirring experiences to the point where he understands them enough to be able to use them. It consists in guiding the child's own growing inductions so that he increasingly comprehends the significance of his experiences. It is not a matter of introspection as to how he feels when he reacts, but of the *objective discovery of the connections between all the operative elements in the configuration involved in a fertile experience*. It is the process through which, progressively, he comes to recognize in his own experience all the important meanings of life, including time, property, cleanliness, kindness, order, love, and God.

Patience and inconspicuous watchfulness are required in the adults interested in growth of meaning in the child's life. They must be sensitive to his reactions during his experiences, discerning when he should be let alone and when he should have guidance.

There is one aspect of this process crucially important for these overcharged days of scheduled play after school, "practicing" or errands later, home study, crowded family living, movie upon radio and radio upon reading, and all the pressing host of other activities packed to overlapping in a child's week. It is that there must be unscheduled intervals during and between telling activities. The child must have free time in order to digest and clarify his meanings. Many vacation periods planned by the family and summer conferences planned by the church are so packed with activities that they are no more than monkey living.

In considering what may be meaningful to the child, it is necessary to make an important distinction between what is deliberately presented by adults to the child "for his own good" and what is used by the adults for their own good in the child's presence. The richer becomes the child's environment with the objects, practices, and activities unself-consciously and meaningfully used by adults in their own living, the more educative it is in a deeper sense. The serious damage is done when the adult deliberately tries to obtrude the objects, practices, and symbols carrying his own meanings into the world of the child when these can be only meaningless to the latter. Adults who feel the most strongly that the meanings which they have discovered and developed are too precious to be lost by the child had best reveal these to him in the psychologically effectual way. This is by going about their own business as it concerns itself with serving these values and with promoting the growth of good. They should have about them all the things and practices that are needed *by them* in their devotion to recognized values, but they should not force these deliberately upon the attention of the child. Then these things and practices will be a very real part of the life which the child is living. He will be immersed in the spirit of them in proportion as the adults forget trying to demonstrate them for his benefit and lose themselves enthusiastically and devotedly in living for them. He will let the adults know in no uncertain ways when he is ready for deliberate presentation. He will even let them know, if they listen, how much explanation he is ready for. He will do this through the questions which he asks when by their sincere, unself-conscious living he has been moved to wonder about what it all means.

Making Available the Resources of His Social Heritage

Our social heritage has grown rich in tools, records, procedures, and practices, in knowledge, skills, attitudes, symbols, concepts, and other materials of culture. Much of the experience of mankind has gotten compressed into these social resources. These provide means by which the individual may sense, interpret, and respond to much in his world without having to work out entirely through trial and error his own meanings, formulas, and techniques. They are an invaluable form of individual and social power.

This power, however, may be so used as to either facilitate or forever stunt human fulfillment. If the individual accepts these means and uses them as ready-made channels along which his experiences must run, if he utilizes them as forms into which his interests and activities are poured and set, he becomes a cultural mummy. There are many such. If he neglects them as fully as possible, he becomes an individualist incapable of the deepest sort of community with his fellows and hence incapable either of greatest fulfillment or of most signal contribution. But if he uses these cultural materials as a magnificently rich source to which to turn when, in the midst of an experience, he feels that he has earned the right to share in them, he advances signally on account of them. Having invested himself in some particular interest to the point where he has developed some means of his own for dealing with this interest, he turns to the inherited means for *suggestion, comparison* with its resulting criticism, *interpretation* or refinement of *method, equipment* or *technique.* He lives his life in terms of the experiences of his own time and place, but it is vastly implemented and enriched by drawing upon cultural materials when his own experience has made him ready. If both he and his teachers are wise, he does not take his social heritage in arbitrarily apportioned doses, selected upon the basis that "someday he may need this," or that "someday when he is in need of this, he will remember it and it will save him."

There are five lessons which educational psychology has taught us about the child's use of his social heritage: (1) whatever part of it is deliberately forced upon him before it can have any meaning for him is largely lost, either literally shed off like water from marble or accepted in distorted or false forms and so adding complexity to future adjustment and education; (2) there are a few elementary skills (reading, writing, and arithmetic) which he will use almost continuously and automatically as tools, but even these should not be offered *formally* until the child is somatically and psychologically ready for them and needs them; (3) it is more important that he shall learn how to locate that part of his social heritage which he finds that he needs at any one time than that he shall have memorized much of it periodically passed to him under all manner of divisive subjects of study; (4) he needs to know how to make use of pertinent cultural resources in the most efficient and enriching ways; (5) he needs to know how to appraise pertinent cultural means and his own use of them.

It is in the light of these five principles that consideration must be given to questions concerning the use of the resources of our religious heritage. Questioning centers around the introduction of the Bible or other sacred literature, the practice of prayer, giving money to the church or to charity or to missions, church attendance and membership, the memorizing of passages from sacred or other great literature, and similar matters. The religious social heritage is too precious to be introduced carelessly or unintelligently or domineeringly. It is offered carelessly when adults dole it out regularly with the hope that some part of it may strike fertile soil though they do little in the way of making sure that the child's own experiences have prepared him for it. The religious social heritage is offered unintelligently when adults do not exert themselves to the utmost to discover the laws of learning and then set up the conditions necessary for learning. It is offered domineeringly when adults force the child to memorize words and gestures, institute practices, and assume attitudes because these adults are determined that the child shall accept that part of the heritage which they themselves have selected as of paramount importance.

What part of the Bible should be introduced into the guidance of little children? And when should it be introduced? When the child is having or has just completed a series of experiences connected as to meaning, and is trying to grasp this meaning, he needs access to cultural sources. At such a time, if there is anything in sacred or other great literature that is (1) pertinent and (2) appropriate to his degree of maturity, it should be made available to him. The selected passage comes then as interpretation of his experience in life, as illumination of meaning, or, to use a biblical expression, it becomes to him, "the way, the truth, the life," most literally. The Bible or other sacred literature must be used as a reference and resource, and not as a textbook, until so much of it has become surcharged with vital and stirring significance from being associated with the growing meanings in experience that the individual can turn to it as his own treasury of richest proven meanings. Such reading will not be justified to any great extent during childhood proper, though this period will richly prepare for it.

A child may build his own Bible during this time. He composes it of the passages that have come to possess stirring meaning for him and of illustrations he himself locates. This will be a *very* "short Bible," but it will grow gradually and it will be read a great deal and it will be very precious. Further, it will cause to grow a deep appreciation of the Bible itself in the child. His slow but vividly meaningful approach to it will deepen his reverence. This reverence will be further intensified by what he observes in regard to adult use of the Bible, providing this is worthy, that is, sincere and meaningful. It would not be amiss for each adult to be building his own Bible, also. Mine is very meaningful to me. It is built in sections, each section a grouping of passages searched out and arranged according to the illumination they provide regarding certain areas of experience. For the adult, this does not take the place of the Bible (actually it increases the use of the Bible itself). But it sets into relief significant and magnificent passages.

Shall we teach the child to say prayers? The wording of the question holds a large part of the answer, "teach . . . *to say*." Should it be made the "sounding brass and tinkling cymbal" of meaningless words? Certainly, the child will learn to pray. But this is a long, slow process.

First of all, the child cannot pray before he is ready. He is not ready unless he has someone to whom to pray and something which he very much wants to pray about. In other words, he cannot truly pray until *he* has built up *for himself* enough of a concept of God to understand the function of prayers to God.

Psychologists feel that this is not before eight years of age at the earliest. Long before this time he can imitate, memorize, and *say* prayers. But here we are not talking about going through the motions, we are discussing praying.

If he must have his own concept of God before he can pray, how does he build this? Out of his own experiences assisted by the cooperative interpretation and evaluation of interested adults. This is the way he builds up all his own concepts. How does he ever know what *kind*-ness is? By experience in being treated as one of their *kind* by some persons, and as not one of their *kind* by others, until he has grasped the meaning and then someone has given him the word *kind*-ness which carries all this meaning now already his. So it is that he learns what *love* is, and certain kinds of *order*, and all the rest.

Genetically, the source of prayer for the little child is the need that he has to turn to his mother when experiences demand more of him than his organism is as yet prepared to take care of. He learns to "pray" to his mother in the sense of turning to her when he has something unusually meaningful to communicate, either in elation or in difficulty. The way in which the mother, and later the father, and still later other adults handle this type of communication of the child has a profound influence upon the nature of his praying to God when he is ready for that. They can make the child a beggar, a schemer, a gold digger, a bargainer, an exploiter, a martyr, a total dependent, a self-righteous Pharisee, or a self-respecting, yet humble, sincere, and loyal communicant. For the child, there is no part of the process of learning to pray which is nearly as important as the predisposing habits of communication and supplication which he builds up with his parents before ever he prays to God. He must learn that he has to earn the right to go to others by doing all that he can himself before he goes. In other words, he does the best job he can of getting himself ready, of organizing himself, before communicating with another.

When the child has learned to commune sincerely with his parents, they can then share with him an experience of praying to God. At some time when he brings to one of them something about which the parent finds that he himself desires to communicate with God, or brings some matter involving an important difference between child and parent, the parent may tell the child in quite simple fashion that he goes to God in much the same way that the child had been coming to him. Of course, the child will have built up somewhat of a working concept of God before this introduction by the parent to prayer with God. On such an occasion the parent prays sincerely to God in the presence of the child. It is of paramount importance that the parent truly pray and not occupy himself with trying to set a pattern for the child. His prayer will not be heard for his speaking, but for his attitude toward God. The parent does not ask the child to pray, too. Most children will want to ponder their first experiences in sharing prayer for some long time, and participate with a parent in prayer a number of times, before communing directly with God themselves. Their first prayers are likely to be mere whispers when they are quite alone. They should not be pressed to pray orally. Nor should they be queried as to what they are doing in the way of prayer. They do not know God very well; communication is not their forte, anyway; they need time to feel their way into this profound experience. Fostering prayer means taking care of the conditions, not supervising the praying itself. When the conditions are right the child will pray when he is ready to commune, not by routine.

After the child has been significantly introduced to communion with God in this way, he will be quite interested in observing prayer wherever it is functioning. These early impressions when he is keenly aware of differences in attitude and response in observed adults during their praying, are of real importance. All those who pray aloud need take heed.

There are many other questions about the use of the resources of the religious heritage which must be answered by those who work with children, and they must be answered in the light of the principles which indicate how the heritage must be administered so that it may not be desecrated but rather utilized effectively and meaningfully. These two inquiries about the use of the Bible and the teaching of prayer are perhaps the ones most frequently asked. The others can be answered similarly. The inherited religious resources are for the purpose of promoting growth. The experience of the child must not be made to conform to the resources.

THE PROCEDURES OF THE CHURCH

Guiding the Child in the Home

This must be done by the church through two approaches principally: (1) educating the parents for their task of guidance; and (2) religious education of the child in the church school. This aspect of parent education may take many forms—study courses, guided reading, bulletins of selected material, training through working with the church-school teachers, a series of discourses or of forums, group discussions of particular problems in guidance, and individual and group counseling. The church will have to instruct parents both as to processes and content, either directly or through connecting them with other agencies in the community which carry on parent-education work. Very often a group of churches can combine and engage a qualified leader for one regular centralized class in parent education, preferably connected with a nursery school which acts as a laboratory so far as the parents are concerned.

If parent education is carried on in the public school, this is excellent. Then the church must supplement this by special training of the parents in the guidance of religious growth and any other important matters not undertaken by the public department. In almost any community, the public school is now empowered to plan some sort of a program in parent education if the other institutions are ready to cooperate to foster it. At any rate, parent education is the foundation of the whole educational program of the church. It is the foundation of its work with children, for parents can tear down what the church does directly with the children faster than it can be built up, if they do not understand or do not care. Vice versa, home and church, each, can immeasurably strengthen and supplement the guidance carried on by the other when their efforts are cooperative and well articulated.

Guiding the Child within the Church

The heart of the purpose of the church school is to arouse and strengthen the child's loyalty to God. The purpose of any institution should govern its organization, processes, and methods. Much of the church school has been copied after the public school, yet the purposes of the two institutions are different, even opposed sometimes in several matters. Due to imitation of the public school, we have, for the most part, church training on the basis of a superimposed program rather than guidance of religious growth through appropriate, progressive experiences. Yet it is this latter which is important for the child and the church.

The major educative processes involved in guiding the growth of the child have been presented earlier in the chapter. These can go on only where life is going on, where the child is doing, thinking, feeling in connection with the many things that go to make up his business of living. These educative processes are not attended to in any sort of consecutive order, but are going on all the time, the emphasis falling now here, now there. This vital, purposeful activity that is going on in the church school centers (1) in the quest for values, and (2) in expressions of loyalty to the highest values discovered. It is wholesome, outgoing, enthusiastic, and natural. If normal, it will exhibit harmonies and conflicts, triumphs and failures, opportunities and difficulties, fulfillments and obstructions. It is in the midst of these experiences that the guiding processes work. There is no opportunity here for a comprehensive, detailed picture of this whole process, but certain significant aspects will be considered.

1. The church school should be a place in which the child finds himself in situations where he solves problems in such a way as to discover values worthy of his devotion. In order to do this, there must be activity instead of passivity; true learning, not mere memorizing or busy work. The school must not put books, not even the Bible, between the child and life itself. What he learns by rote he will for the most part forget. What he builds into his order of life through actual doing, living, becomes a permanent part of himself.

What the activities will be is determined by the developmental level, the interests, the problems, and the resources of the group of children involved. As has been implied, in religious education they are of two general sorts, those that have to do with the search for values and those that have to do with his loyalty to such values as he discovered. There are innumerable activities essential and fruitful for each age and interest range.

While at the present time most teaching staffs are not adequate for the work of building up a program of true religious education, most churches could provide sufficient trained leadership available at regular intervals to direct the work of the teachers and to criticize constructively what is being done. These directors-at-large of religious education might be sent out by the district or county boards of the various churches. It would not be their business to superimpose a program, but rather to help each teacher build up those conditions in his own unique situation which would meet the unique needs of his particular group.

2. Since the rightness of relationships between persons is the keynote in Christian living, the experiences of the child in the church groups should be treated as laboratory experiments in human relations through which he learns the laws and principles of such living. Most of his problems in life will be those of social relationship. The attitudes and ideals unconsciously built up during these early years will pervade his whole life. Character education cannot be given in the large. No one can teach a child honesty or loyalty or any other "trait" by giving lessons "on it." Character education must mean the guidance of each behavior response as it occurs. This guidance must deal with both corrective and promotive aspects of education. Most of it must be indirect. This means that more work is done with the conditions operative upon the child than with the child himself.

3. Training in evaluating is one of the most important services the church can render to the child. So long as he is "given" various materials, ideas, and ideals, in the form of stereotypes which he must accept if he is to remain on good terms, he is not developing within him the principles of choice-making nor building the power to choose wisely. Whenever a child finds himself possessed of two things each of which is "good" in some way, he is forced to go through a process of evaluating in order to choose

the better. Then later this better must be compared with some other "good" which comes into his experiences and a new evaluation developed. If his choice has been wrong or mistaken, he is forced by some unhappiness or disappointment to go through the process of reevaluation during which he is bound to discover some factor or principle of value which he had not noticed in his previous choice. Every child should have a very rich and varied experience in choice-making with its consequences.

Informal exhibits of objects which children bring to the church school because *the children* have seen some value in them can be direct but unself-conscious exercises in evaluation. To these may be added objects of value which the staff select and also objects which the children have constructed. There is a great temptation to teachers to use exhibits as a display of best products or to incite competition. This use of the exhibit belongs to the adult, commercial world, not to education, most of all not to religious education.

It would be a fine thing to see the bare walls of the halls of churches and schools lined with shelves, bulletin boards, and cases in which an ever-changing exhibit of things which children and adults deemed valuable would be made available for appreciation and growing comparison of values. Here is plenty of expensive, uninteresting space as yet paying no human dividends.

4. A program of wholesome, constructive Saturday activities is a crying need of most children these days. It may be sponsored by the church, perhaps through its men's brotherhood or its women's organizations, or by some other community organization with the encouragement and cooperation of the church. The meager play and work space in the average home, the fact that the child finds no meaningful place left for him in the life interests or work of the adult world, the presence almost everywhere of questionable or vicious diversions, coupled with the alertness and activity of the boys and girls, means that leisure time must have direction. Excursions into the country or to places of historical or industrial interest, neighborhood play groups, hobby groups, or other opportunities must be provided, else the one day, Saturday, will tear down all that we can build up in many days.

This is a heavy responsibility. The church may not be able to assume or even take a leading place in promoting it. But at least it can be the instigating agency toward developing community cooperation in meeting this problem, which is at the same time a great opportunity. Indeed, the church has long sought for additional time with the children, and has tried to crowd into the school day. Here is a rare chance for those who have the talent and will to use it.

Since the movies and other commercial diversions charge an admission fee, there is no reason why the families of children who benefit by a Saturday program should not pay the costs through a reasonable monthly fee. In some cases the church can utilize its own rooms and equipment in promoting this guidance of the investment of the leisure of its children.

5. The little children of preschool age are frequently in the hands of an untrained parenthood. We know that many behavior attitudes and habits become established during these early years. We know also that innumerable parents who are sincere, but untutored, become discouraged in their job of child guidance. These little children need education in conduct. Their parents need help in understanding child behavior. Cooperative nursery schools established in the churches can render a valuable educative service to these little ones just setting out. Further, the church can win the loyalty of these children while they are very young if it truly promotes their life interests. Of course, the nursery school must be free from all attempts to indoctrinate for both psychological and religious reasons. In several places where this has been tried, young married women with kindergarten or nursery-school training have directed the project with the mothers cooperating.

6. Since loyalty of the intelligent sort is so important in the progressive development of character and so fundamental a quality in sincere religious living, the church can make a valuable contribution in promoting its growth. The recognition and encouragement of spontaneous but genuine expressions of appreciation and gratitude and the cooperative analysis of the benefits and good will that are expressed by other persons toward the chil-

dren in their everyday living are only two of the many possible ways in which this may be done.

An old proverb says that gratitude is the basis of all virtue. Certainly intelligent appreciation underlies all worthy moral standards. Sentimental, that is, unintelligent static appreciation, is worse than none. The expressions of the children should concern actual situations of their own, not vague, far away, adult-modeled matters. Particularly, they should not indulge in parrot-like expressions regarding realities beyond their comprehension, as often happens regarding God.

Appreciation engenders gratitude, and it in turn engenders loyalty. This is true, since we pledge ourselves to those things which we believe are of vital significance in our lives. It is very easy for all of us to take for granted much that is provided—the marvel of the speedy and inexpensive delivery of our letters to the right persons after our simple act of addressing, stamping, and posting them; the instant flood of light when all we have done is to push a button; the regularity with which, for most of us, good food is on our tables; and so on through a myriad of matters. There should be no exhortations to appreciation and loyalty, but rather a natural, happy study of all the planning and effort and thinking and fine spirit which have been necessary to bring these things about. Such study is most vividly successful when it consists in actual coparticipation. That is, we can help the children to find meaning in most that surrounds them by arranging conditions such as will relate them to their surroundings. It is thus that we can stir their loyalties.

7. Competition is the most frequently used form of human association in our American society, and competition of a very individualistic sort. Competition always isolates and divides persons. It is the enemy of communion in group life. The public school in many places, because of the artificial nature of its curriculum, continues to train children in this individualistic competition through its system of grades and honors.

The church school in most places has taken over, unthinkingly, the methods of the public school and uses competition as a means of furnishing drive for much of its program. Since the Christian religion in all its various divisions holds that the most fundamental and telling area of religious living is in one's relations to his fellow men, it becomes important that the church train the children to work for better forms for their association in the various activities carried on. Competition means that the success of one can come only through the relative failure of others. It should have no place in the church.

8. One of the most important opportunities which the church can afford the growing child is that of devoting himself to various projects which enlist his interest and gradually extend it to areas beyond that of his own present, little world. In the past there has been one extensive example of this, the field of missions. It is, however, a dangerous area for the child, for it is so much easier to handle it wrongly than rightly. Since the mission fields discussed are usually too remote from the child's world to seem integral with his own life, his relationship to one of them is almost sure to be artificial, held by his predisposition to please his teachers, based upon pity for the poor heathen, or an egotistical, snobbish sense of superiority or of comfortable sentimentality. It is much wiser and more sincere, at first, to enlist the devotion of children to situations much nearer to their own worlds. Close to the children are such vivid situations as the treatment received by the foreign children in their schoolrooms, the condition of little American babies in congested districts, the loneliness of shut-ins, and the burden carried by fathers who are out of work because we Americans do not know how to live together. These causes they can come to understand. Further, they can devote themselves to helping in simple, appropriate, but nonsentimental ways.

Indeed, there is one type of situation that comes up very frequently in the lives of all little children. They find certain people who are "queer," or displeasing, or different. Their unthinking response is likely to be that of spurning or ridicule. When a child's response becomes cruel, as it often does, it is barbarically so as judged by educated attitudes. How much the world of the child will be enlarged and his social understanding deepened if he can be led to see what is behind his reaction and to try to discern and understand the ways and points of view of others seemingly quite different from himself!

Through such interests his devotions become less selfish and move toward higher worths. Also, his living is pointed in the direction of Christ's teachings.

THE DIFFERENTIATION OF THE RELIGIOUS INTEREST

It takes more faith on the part of the church to work with children than with adults. The religious interest is the slowest to become differentiated from the other major interests of life, but it never will become clearly distinguished unless there has been constructed the necessary foundation for its differentiation in the early years of immaturity. Therefore, the church, without specific assurance of outcome, must invest its best in launching and strengthening, from birth until puberty, the progression of loyalties in the child to whatever the child believes is great, in order to have him ready for the differentiation of the specifically religious interest which may begin to grow distinctive and auto-cultivated at that time or soon after.

This does not mean that nothing can be done directly for the religious development of the child before puberty. All these early guiding processes are direct religious guidance, even though there is little mention of the symbols used by the mature religious person. Getting the soil ready and planting seed is floriculture just as much as is watering and spraying and thinning buds after the plants have grown to the place where they are distinguishable from other growth about them. But it takes more faith to invest the best in preparing the soil and burying the seeds than it does in tending plants, because there is nothing at the beginning to show what the returns of the investment may be. It does no good to work directly with the tender sprouting plant, trying to prod it on. All the plant can do is to grow according to the laws that bring it to its own fulfillment. This is all that the child can do. To try to force him to differentiate the religious interest before this is possible is to retard his growth, probably permanently, in this area. For while he is trying to please adults by putting himself into the forms and through the motions the self-willed adult presses upon him or to become like the mature pattern held before him, he himself is not developing. He is being trained, not educated.

The most telling approach the church has with the child is through guiding the parents in their functions, particularly those connected with the slow growth of the religious interest.

While approaching the children through work with their parents is the most potent, nevertheless the direct approach within the church is of inestimable value. Not only does this supplement and augment materially the guidance of the family, but it adds new elements not possible there. Most conspicuous among these is the fellowship with those of his own age or near it in common loyalties that are worth while. Secondly he sees that the religious devotion of his parents is not a thing unto itself, but a part of an enormous community of devoted persons, the limits of which stretch beyond his own land and time. Then he comes to distinguish the social attitudes of the truly religious persons from those of individuals avowedly contemptuous of religion: he finds out that true religion makes a difference in people. Also, he comes into direct contact gradually with the symbols and practices which have grown up in the church and in his own church, and is stirred to discover what the devotees find in these which makes them more reverent and less self-willed. He finds out that the church is the one institution in the community which openly pledges itself to seek, serve, and worship the highest values discoverable, and which endeavors to hold these values ever before the eyes of the world. He discovers that the community has enough faith in the values which the church promotes to turn to it for assistance when the interests either of individuals or of the community are threatened. He learns that there are numberless individuals who ridicule the church and its attendants, so that it requires caliber to be an actively loyal participant in its program. Later, he comes to see that these ridiculing individuals are, for the most part, those who are unwilling to subject themselves to any higher control than that of their self-centered appetites, desires, or ambitions: they ridicule in order to protect themselves from any challenge which might disturb their complacent comfort. The child senses in the teachers and leaders of the church a warm, active concern for him-as-a-person which recognizes his achievements and assists during difficulties. He does not often find just this disinterested yet particularized interest in him in any other of the institutions outside of the family and the church. Last of all, providing the particular church is truly a religious institution, he has within its walls some significant experiences because he is a member of a group working on vital problems. These are of a deeply stirring nature; through them he makes progress in knowing God.

Chapter XI

THE PROGRAM WITH THE YOUNG PEOPLE

YOUNG people today have much power in their hands—all sorts of information, extended opportunities of schooling, spare time, spending money, use of automobiles, much healthy energy, and access to many recently developed conveniences and inventions. At an increasing rate, modern life is supplying a great diversity of interests, of demands, of goods and effects, of instrumental devices for saving menial labor and for safeguarding the future, of intercultural contacts, of media of expression, of social stratifications, and of economic and political developments. In addition, commercial interests have deliberately seen to it that there is an exhaustless supply of artificial attractions which touch thrillingly the desires of youth. Nor have they stopped there. They have maneuvered to make the more commercially remunerative of these conspicuously fashionable. It would appear to the casual observer that for young persons today life was truly abundant and free.

However, this rapid development and diversification of the ways, the means, and the interests of life has not been anywhere nearly paralleled by a rapid development and diversification of the criteria and resources for judging the relative importance of all these things. Thus it is that the average modern young person has more choices and decisions to make than the average active adult of a hundred years ago, yet has fewer respected sanctions and opportunities for adequate counsel as guides in his choice-making. As has been emphasized, the most important single item of equipment for a modern young person is a reasonably appropriate and adequate system of values. Although without this tool he may make choices that sell him into a thousand bondages, nev-

ertheless the young person of today finds it hard to secure. There
are many reasons for this.

INACCESSIBILITY OF ESSENTIAL EQUIPMENT

For one thing, most of the activities of youth are carried on
outside the family where commercial competition more than any
other one factor sets up the values. The young people have been
thrown into the community for their activities and satisfactions
largely because of the changes in family life, more especially the
changes in type of residence, in the foci of interest of father and
mother, and in the limitation of size of the family group. In turn
these changes in the family are due primarily to economic conditions in the midst of which the family has been largely helpless.
Intelligent parents see the conglomerate, undiscriminated factors
in the community which influence the value-sense of their young
people. There is the general looseness, blamed first on the war
and then on prohibition and still continuing. There is the count-
ing of "front" as more valuable than character; the casual superficial nature of relationships, even those of sex; the deification of
"emancipation"; the self-damning emphasis upon self-expression
and self-indulgence; the minor and major violations of personality and of cultural products; and the headlong, dizzy whirl from
one Lethean diversion to another. Against these are set the influence of the public school which is all too often overcrowded and
regimented toward "covering the ground," and the efforts of the
church and the character-building agencies working with pitifully restricted staffs and budgets.

Again, the mode of recent social development has deprived
young people of countless experiences which would have required
of them judgments of value had they met them. This accidental
deprivation has not been met with any planned substitution of
educative equivalent. The materials and settings and programs
for the work, play, and study of young people are all prepared
completely for them and then passed over to them ready-made
with the unjustified expectation that they will appreciate these
and be duly responsible for them. There are examples without
end—family residences that meet the local, stereotyped require-

ments of what is fine or smart; extravagant college halls replete to the last luxurious detail; set courses of study; duplicating rounds of correct social affairs; and manufactured articles proffered to fill every possible need or whim before ever it arises. The mode calls for "smooth" affairs, for not doing anything except on a grand scale, for lavish architectural structures presumably "to promote graceful and gracious living," for self-centered daily programs. This handing out to youth of ostentatious, ready-made social equipment destroys any incentive to sense out the values involved and hence renders them scot-free of social responsibility. It tends toward flabbiness, individualism, self-indulgent practices, snobbery, shiftiness, conceit, laziness, hypercritical boredom, and exploitation. Sound response to cultural values depends upon vital appreciation, and vital appreciation depends upon genuine participation. Youth cannot acquire an adequate system of values in a ready-made world; he must share in the making of the world if he is to know its values. It is interesting to note that there are at least two colleges in the United States now where the faculty and the students are literally building the institution together. A number of families are organized on the basis of significant participation of every member.

Two other factors decrease the chances of youth to acquire an adequate working system of values. First, there is the increase of means and conditions effectual in protecting the individual both from just realization of the significance of his own attitudes and acts and from suffering the consequences of his own behavior. Common among such means and conditions are the following: concentration of population so that one is lost in the crowd and hence not often subject to self-comparison and social criticism; ease of moving from one place to another when one's social situation becomes uncomfortable; widespread availability of contraceptives and other concealing devices; speed of the automobile in removing one temporarily from the situation in which he is known; the effect upon the self-estimate of men of the prodigious amount of flattery of men by women; the blinding effect upon women of their vain, personal appropriation of the flattering attentions of men; and the mode of carrying on one's business of life largely by way of intermediaries through whom one does not usually receive the reactions set going by one's own doings. It is not surprising in the face of such conditions that a host of youth are highly indignant if found out or criticized for what they do, but are not exercised particularly about the effects of their conduct upon their own fulfillment or upon the lives of others.

The last cause of the difficulty of the youth in equipping himself with a system of values is the change in youth-adult relations. In earlier days, the life of the youth as he became adult was so little different from the life of the adults of the preceding generation that he could adopt and use their system of values with no appreciable modification. It had the authority of precedent and of tested success as well. But it is more difficult for young people to observe the system of values of adults today because adults are controlled much more by established schedules and forms than were people in less routinized eras. Also, there is vastly more difference between the world of adults and the world of youth-becoming-adults than there used to be. Basically, the same system of values may be required, but the applications may be so dissimilar as to hide their identities. Further, the system of values of most adults of an earlier day was not only particularized and inflexible but also universally revered because of its source in divine authority. Questioning it was sacrilege. There is a vagueness and lack of authenticated validity in the system of values of many, many adults today. Fortunately, youth can no longer merely adopt; unfortunately, he receives very little social stimulation to build his own system of values.

Notwithstanding the obdurate complexity of the social conditions and the obstructing factors in personal development, modern young people on the whole exhibit a basic sincerity and a dauntless urge to ascertain for themselves what are those genuine values of life which merit their respect and investment.

The young person, as always, desires to become a free person. He is trying to develop personality and trying to become an effective social agent in order to validate himself in the world. If his situation is normal, he is due to feel inferior, for he is immature in the very area of life of most moment to him, the social. This sense of inferiority remains healthy so long as it acts as a moderate excitant, keeping him alert to possibilities of social growth. It is unhealthy when it acts as shackles, halting him in futility of effort amidst tantalizing dreams of self-realization. The service of this sense of inferiority is that of inciting the young person to a search for various modes of completing himself, of self-fulfillment. These he finds frequently in a close friendship, as with a chum or comradely adult; in some avenue of self-expression, particularly if enjoyed by others, such as music or sports; in reading biography or working with adults who are achieving; in undivided loyalty to team or school or club; in day-dreams; in signal achievements; and in religious outreach toward God. Each mode or object involved in his seeking self-fulfillment necessitates social interaction of several sorts and so contributes to progressive self-completion. Just as his physical organism all his life has been fulfilling itself by gathering energy from the physical environment—air, sunshine, plant and animal foods, and water—so now his developing personality is fulfilling itself by gathering energy from the social environment—friendships and social records; community institutions; family, nation, and world-wide ethos; and current interests and concepts. He was born an individual and he continued an individual for the most part throughout his childhood, but now he is becoming more than an individual. He is being born again, a person into a world of persons.

It is in this second birth of the immature individual that the church has its second great chance. The young person is highly sensitive socially, highly aware of assets and liabilities, restrictions and possibilities. He wants to get the most out of life—quite rightly. He wants to count in life somehow, to connect himself with its most alluring and worth-while values. His pulse is running high. He has no protracted responsibilities; therefore he can afford to be radical and ambitious. He has no great loves and causes; therefore he can afford to be adventuresome and daring. His spirit is resilient and buoyant; therefore he can afford to try putting it into first this and then that. He feels his incompleteness and is eager for all possible experiences of fulfillment. What more to its purpose than this could any church find?

Of course, the work of the church with modern young people is not easy. We have stated some of the major factors that enormously complicate the situation. Further, the fact that there is no organizing center in home or in community for the interests of young people is a very serious social problem. It is also a very serious religious problem. Until there is such a center there cannot be even the minimal provision for evaluating and meeting the normal needs of youth. Nor can there be adequate examination and coordination of all the influences of the community which bear upon the activities and development of the young people. For the most part, the problems of youth are problems which involve the group and these require group treatment. This emphasis of group approach to group problems cannot be overstressed. Whatever the church undertakes to do for the youth of its own constituency, it must not forget the crucial urgency of amplifying and fortifying this by furtherance of a cooperative community approach through promoting right conditions for the activities and development of all young people.

AREAS OF EXPERIENCE WHERE THE CHURCH CAN HELP YOUTH

Locating the areas of experience in the living of youth where the church can best help is a matter of studying the trends of enthusiasms, longings, dreams, and loyalties during this period from puberty to adulthood. It is during this time that the foundations are being laid for long-term loyalties. It is not overly rare to find some relatively permanent loyalties already launched by the end of the period, that is, by the time that the young person is somewhere around twenty-four years of age. More regularly, however, youth is rather a time of organizing the self and achieving some considerable orientation in the world of values. Perhaps it is more accurate to say worlds of values, for there are many open to exploration. Ordinarily, this orientation takes place through a disjointed series of experiences with no opportunity to validate, compare findings, and synthesize. It is largely an adventitious process. Guidance of youth in his orientation in values means helping him to garner richly all pertinent values, test these out, and gradually synthesize those that pass the tests. Since the prime concern of the church is to guide mankind toward highest values, it finds its most fertile field for *direct* functioning in the guidance of the progression of loyalties in youth when human nature is more plastic. There are several aspects of this large function.

Aiding Youth to Secure All Appropriate Interests

One requirement here is a program which will promote those current interests which foster and fulfill personality, and hence are bound to be enjoyed. It must be realized that a program of genuine social growth during early and middle adolescence rests most dependably upon preparatory work done before the period begins. It involves the building up of congenial social groups of boys and girls during the last years of childhood which will carry over naturally into adolescence. Then these groups should be kept segregated in most activities from the groups of older young people. Since this is the time in the public school when the young people are most likely to be moving from one school to a higher one, such preparatory groupings are very difficult to sustain. The church is the one institution which can carry them through. If this is done, the young people thus grouped will so enjoy their own activities that they will not be wanting to ape the activities of the older young people. The program of the younger people should be such as to keep boy-girl interest diffused and to provide highly diversified types of activity. Important among these activities is some type of community service appropriate to the age and genuine in its contribution.

The personal relationships of the young person is another area where he needs help in locating and appreciating values, whether relationships with his family or others. The young person near puberty is closer to his family, but beginning to declare his independence, whereas toward the end of adolescence he is closer to the one or more friends who have become very dear, yet can now appreciate and enjoy his family in new ways. One of the chief matters to be learned by the adolescent in connection with personal relationships is the control of his expectations of others. The young person, swept into impulsive enthusiasm, is likely to set someone up as a demigod and then be shattered when he finds him human. Or he expects everybody to measure up to his standards, becoming harshly critical of those who show shortcomings. Since his relationships with others will be a major aspect of life, planning for respectful guidance in this area can hardly be minimized.

Training in social practice and other techniques of community living is a basic requirement. Many queer quirks of personality and many regrettable happenings are due in large part to feelings of awkwardness or inadequacy through not knowing how to meet situations with reasonable poise. This, of course, is not a mere matter of etiquette. Manners are only the skills by which one expresses his attitudes, intentions, and interest. Basically, it is a matter of social sensitivity and social judgment.

Since group pressures are powerful to the point of being coercive among most groups of young people, it is of utmost importance that young people understand these, how they work, and how they can be redirected to bring out the best possibilities of persons and the situation. When the group influence is inordinately strong, the young person tends to accept the judgment of the group as to what is worth while and what not. He is miserable a good part of the time through being anxious to meet the arbitrary demands of the group. He does not dare explore values in which he is interested because of fear of ridicule. Since society is governed so much by organized minorities, it is paramount that young people shall learn how to deal with these in the simpler forms found in their own situations. Then they will be more ready to deal with them in the larger society. Every organized minority is fighting for some value it has set out to gain or protect. The study of group pressures is really a study of drives toward values. The young person must be educated to deal with these pressures.

These few items are intended to illustrate what can be done to aid youth to secure and enjoy the values present in his life at the time. There are many others equal in importance to these.

Promoting Growth Toward Larger Interests

Several processes are involved in this function: (1) putting the young person into touch with appropriate interests somewhat greater than those he is now devoted to; (2) keeping sufficiently in touch with him during the launching of a new interest to make sure that he is getting good tastes of the values implicit in it; (3) helping him to grasp the larger meanings of it; and then (4) encouraging him to codify the new experience for his own living in whatever way is most suitable and effective. This fourth step is indispensable.

The first process is largely a matter of sharing those enthusiasms, commitments, concepts, interests, and aspirations so important to the adult experiencing them that they are a veritable part of him. His sharing is a part of his zestful living, not a deliberate effort to stir the young to dutiful response. The second and third processes are achieved primarily by means of cooperative evaluation of the problems, discoveries, satisfactions, dissatisfactions, and achievements which go to make up the new experience of loyalty. The fourth process is that of re-forming his present habits and ideals in the light of his discoveries, seeking interpretation and enlightenment from the sources of his social heritage, and formulating such conclusions and techniques as the experience justifies. Some of the overt forms through which the young person may codify his experience are these: appropriated slogans; consciously set up standards; making a pertinent quotation from great literature his own by memorizing it and using it; discovering a symbol which is a potent carrier of the experience, such as a picture or a vivid mental image; the formulation of a definition dealing with the experience; and the formulation of a specific code of conduct in regard to this area of experience. This fourth process involves such an appreciation of the experience as will produce some means of conserving the essence of it for future living.

The young people will have to be a very real part of its regular fellowship if the church is to know their life of interests and of loyalties and hence be welcomed to participate in the process of cooperative evaluation. Unless the church recognizes the personality of the young people and honors them appropriately through their inclusion in its offices and councils, the young people will feel that the church is extraneous to their experience.

Educating Youth for Biological Maturing

The most generally recognized aspect of this phase of guidance is sex education. This involves understanding and constructive acceptance of the implications of sexual development (1) in himself, (2) in others. These are two different problems, though inextricably related. The other three groups of native appetites can be gratified by an individual acting alone, but this fourth group of appetites—sex—necessarily involves other persons and hence is far more complicated. Because it has so much to do with attitudes, conduct, activities, and relationships during adolescence, education in understanding and dealing with the sex appetite is of major importance.

Here, particularly, it is essential that there shall be coordination of community efforts, for sex education is too extensive a matter to be fully cared for by any one institution. The school is best equipped to deal with the scientific aspects, and can do a tremendous amount of educating of attitudes through the way it interprets great literature dealing with sex relations, love, and the family. The home-economics department in some institutions is contributing signally with courses for boys and girls on family life, and on behavior problems of children through laboratory work with little children and other activities. All the institutions which assemble boys and girls together in their programs should use wisely the consequent social opportunities for guidance of boy-girl relationships and concomitant attitudes. Ideally, the home has laid a stable foundation from birth in the way of sound attitudes, habits, and ideas.

Because this phase of his living is so important to the young person, the church should make sure that he is receiving adequate education in sex, and if he is not, work to provide for it within its own walls or in cooperation with some other institution. This is one part of the work of the church in sex education. For the rest, it must help youth to see the connection of his sex life with all the other interests of life, the opportunities, responsibilities, and fulfillments which sex brings when constructively dealt with, and then help him to locate the ways of dealing with it constructively. This last will involve techniques of self-control, particularly for the boys, the building of criteria for the guidance of activities and relationship where sex is a factor, and help in sublimating the sex urge through investment of the self in important and vital issues.

A second aspect of educating for biological maturing aims to arouse the young person to understand and appreciate his own organism and the powers developing therein. His organism is the chief instrument of all his living. Therefore common intelligence indicates that it should not be subjected to avoidable experiences which tend to stunt or weaken it, or which reduce the potency of any function, or which render it more subject to disease, to periods of inadequacy, or to deterioration. Guidance here does not rest upon tablets of stone containing "Thou shalt nots," but upon vivifying to youth the great things all about him and ahead of him which call for the best that is in him and more. If the church of the past had spent less time on emotionally disorganizing "decision days," and more upon dynamic organizing experiences through which youth could realize some of the deep satisfactions that come from complete commitment of the self to a great cause, there would be more genuinely religious living today. A great loyalty calls for a wholehearted dedication. This is the supreme approach in guidance directed toward the building of intelligent self-discipline. This is the approach of the normal church.

A third aspect of guidance of biological maturing deals with the delicate matter of helping the young person to accept the person he is turning out to be. In the early years, when he knows that he has yet long to grow, the boy imagines himself maturing as a combination of Dizzy Dean, the Arrow Collar man, Einstein, Rockefeller, and the head of the G-men. The girl has a similar composite of beauty, success, brilliance. The farther through adolescence they go, the more difficult is the personal competition they meet in every phase of their living, and the more unmistakable become the evidences of their limitations and abilities.

Normally, the young person should accept himself and go interestedly about locating his fitting place in study, play, and work. But if he does not accept himself for what he is becoming, all sorts of distorted and morbid outcomes may appear. He may try to overreach through impossible ideals and ambitions, or he may take for granted that the world is his, or he may feel that it is no use trying to make anything out of life. Whatever form this declining of his real self takes, he puts himself more and more out of gear with the world about him. His system of values is distorted and he has extremely eccentric or conformative loyalties.

There is no more effective way to guide this process than by fostering a diversity of meaningful activities among the young people, activities through which each will find his assets as well as his liabilities and will see that all other persons have both. His focus must be taken off of lopsided comparings and turned toward achieving in a wider area of activity. This involves the technique of group guidance where individuals having similar problems are guided through the types of activity entering into the program. It is a most wholesome form of guidance.

Guiding the Three Great Choices of Youth

During the whole period of adolescence, the young person is making his three most important choices, that of vocation, mate, and dominant loyalty. He may not reach the final decision in any of these areas during the period. The final decision is of comparatively little importance, however, for it is what he has been making of himself during the whole period which really makes the choice, including the final decision. The young person must be led to see this—that he is actually making his final choice today and tomorrow and the next day by the kind of personality he is building. In that future he dreams of, he will be sought or neglected, accepted or rejected, on the basis of this primarily.

Preparing for Intellectual Weaning

Normally, this development occurs between the ages of eighteen or nineteen and twenty-four or twenty-five, though modern young people tend to be much retarded. They are not so much weaned as dissociated from the adults concerned. The majority become stunted through superficial sophistication instead of maturing. When genuine intellectual weaning starts, the young person begins to disagree, sincerely, consistently, and fundamentally with many of his adult associates in family, college, and community. He begins to insist upon knowing the why and wherefore of much that he has already accepted and of most of what he now hears or reads. He refuses to accept unauthenticated pronouncements concerning matters in which he has any degree of interest. To be sure, he has been disagreeing for years, but it was largely on the basis of arguing in order to get the feel of his personal power: he was not primarily a seeker after the truth. During intellectual weaning he disagrees because he is not satisfied to accept ideas that affect him without validation in terms that he can respect. This is the third period of great openness of personality. Coming as it does just before maturity, it is a wonderful educative opportunity though a heavy responsibility.

Preparation for intellectual weaning necessarily involves two groups, the youth experiencing weaning and the adults who are in close association with him. Unless these adults expect and understand the process of intellectual weaning, this period will resolve itself into a fruitlessly painful one for both adults and youth. The cue for the adults must be to launch with youth into cooperative exploration, experimentation, and evaluation. To youth must be opened opportunities to get back to original sources, to study comparatively the movements and products of culture, and to discuss his problems, hypotheses, and findings in a tolerant yet forthright social environment. Deliberate indoctrination through precept or exhortation will not avail with youth who are ready for this period. It is truth and not personal persuasion which will win in the end with those who are not still infantile. Semblances and half-truths must be put over against each other, and these over against larger truths, until, fire-new, the soundest truth possible to the individual at the time emerges.

If this later period of intellectual weaning is to be rich, the periods of early and middle adolescence must have held a wealth of study of important social and religious values with extensive use of field trips, steady part-time participation in social work both developmental and corrective, investigation of current findings in the social sciences, and pointed discussion of all these experiences.

Introducing Youth to the Growth of a Wider Community

This process of guidance really takes place through all these others, but it becomes more explicit as youth gets past the earliest period of adolescence. It involves such concrete matters as keeping them in contact with significant persons and the discussion of the vital problems of the day. It centers in helping them to delve down under the overt meanings of all that is going on about them and distinguish the deeper connections and how these grow.

The most ardently loyal, religious person is the most dangerous to society if he does not know how good grows in the world. There are conferences planned for young people with the most sincere intention which go off half-cocked because of the vagueness of leaders and youth as to how the Kingdom of God grows in the here and now, how the interconnections which give us oneness of life can be fostered in one's own community. And there are worshiping groups of young people which end in a bewildering blank or in an emotional jag because they try to find God in a social vacuum.

Over and over in the teachings of Jesus Christ and his followers there is emphasized the truth that the widening of the community of fellowship, the building of more meaningful interconnections between all men, *is* the work of God, and that we are serving and worshiping Him when we are building the conditions which promote the widening of our community. Therefore, when youth are guided to discuss world peace, interracial relations, the economic disorder of the day, and other issues vital to the building of a wider communion, it should be with appreciation of their present stage of development and actual community situations. To keep their urges directed toward remote objectives and to encourage them to express specific allegiance to a nonspecific undertaking is to foster disillusionment and disgust. They need orienting in the vital issues of the time, but they also need to know what they themselves can do right where they are to begin to build the preparatory conditions which will foster the growth of the interconnections among men necessary to each further step toward the remote consummations. Here as in the preceding area of guidance, much comparative study of human efforts to locate values and move toward them will facilitate the process.

Providing for the Special Needs of Those Launching into Productive Life

Even though the previous six areas are effectively treated under the guidance of the church, this seventh area is bound to involve an enormous number and diversity of needs and opportunities. Also the age range is very wide, because of the many factors which influence the time both of the closing of the period of formal schooling and of the opening of the period of marriage and parenthood.

For one thing, when the young person takes his first job in business or as homemaker, his ideals and expectations usually suffer severe collisions with the practices and policies of the workaday world. This is a tremendously important time for sound reevaluation, for substantial encouragement, and for assistance in building effective yet worthy codes and techniques. The young person is in a period when recognitions or disparagement are likely to loom as overimportant. Indeed his self-estimate is perforce due for a disturbing overhauling, as is also his estimate of the present society in some respect or other. It is of importance to all the rest of life that these early adjustings while he is locating his place in society leave a precipitate of sound attitudes and values.

This is also a period often marked by breaks in relationship for all sorts of reasons, breaks both sad and mad. These must be treated as laboratory material in the training in fellowship. One of the hardest parts of this training is leaving, withdrawing from, appreciative established fellowships, now outgrown.

These two aspects of this area of guidance are the beginning of a very long possible list. There is one other, however, which requires increase of considerate attention in these times. It involves the situations of those young persons who for one reason or another have not followed the course of most others of their age, such as those who have passed the age of marriage current in the particular group. It is very easy for church leadership to become so absorbed in those who have followed the more usual course that the neglect of these others becomes truly distressing. They seem to be out of place with either the young people or the young married group. It would seem to be primarily a problem of enlarging the interests of appropriate age groups to include among them other interests—the interests of those persons who often are unusually well-developed personalities with a contribution to make.

Interpreting Christian Principles in Present-day Living

A question may be forming in the reader's mind. Is all this Christian? In the fundamental sense, yes. These presentations of seven important areas in the religious guidance of youth attempt to set forth dynamically Christian principles in terms of the modern day and of the enterprise at hand. Especially for the adolescent, who always insists on being contemporary, it is essential that these principles be so expressed. He can readily understand them in their original and traditional formulations *only after he has lived them first* in the modern milieu.

When adults attempt too consciously to make the procedure Christian, they distort Christianity and disgust youth. All that is required religiously of the adult leader of youth who has been nurtured in the Christian tradition is to think and live and associate vitally today according to the principles he has discovered earlier and is still discovering. He does not focus his attention nor that of youth directly upon the Christian terminology or the Christian principles except where some special turn of experience plainly and naturally calls for this. But he lives in the spontaneity of eager seeking after the first values he so ardently worships. That is, his chief presentation of Christian principles is not heard through his much loud speaking, but is manifest in everything which he does. These principles govern the *values* he sets first and the *way* he does whatever he does. If these principles make his way of doing more significant than the way of those not living in these principles, youth will know it at once and will press a flood of inquiries upon him concerning his way. A period of such questioning is one of the times when experience takes a turn which plainly and naturally calls for forthright exposition of the Christian principle under observation.

When the young person has had sufficient directed experience he will want to start synthesizing his findings. At this period, which comes normally in the last third of adolescence, he may then well undertake a systematic study of the Christian teachings. This will inevitably involve facing the issue as to the adequacy of the Christian principles for the very different life of today. Also, if the young person is of good caliber, he will want to study the principles of living set forth in other religious teachings. All this comparative study is invaluable. Through this, he will be much more likely to discover those deeper essences of Christian truth which can stand the test of time and place than he will be if he studies the Christian principles without this fertile and complex background. Out of adequate comparative study, he will develop the ability to distinguish what principles of Christianity or other religion are working in essence in Communism, Fascism, international relations, trade unions, courses of social science in public schools, national organization of church boards, local government, and other vital communal enterprises.

PRACTICAL FORMS OF CHURCH GUIDANCE

Discussion of Problems Vital to Youth

Most often, the questions discussed by young people will be of their own posing. However, guidance is needed to bring to light (1) those frustrating problems so usual that they are not felt as acute points of suffering, such as membership in a social group too enormous to facilitate genuine friendships, and (2) those which hover over life threateningly but are difficult to formulate, such as adult-adolescent tension where the nature of weaning is unknown to one or both. Further guidance is needed to see that the emphasis of time and energy invested in discussion of problems is in reasonable relation to their real importance.

These discussions should never be exploited by leaders as occasions to expound and apply religious precepts and interpretations as such, and intentional use of religious terminology should be avoided. One test as to whether or no a discussion is religious lies in ascertaining whether it proved to be a religious experience for at least one of those participating, not in the number of theological terms used or in amount of praying. If it proved to be a religious experience it would mean either that the member gained understanding of God and hence felt nearer to Him, or that he made progress in the integrating of his loyalties.

A second test consists in noting the number and quality of the minor or major experiments in personal and group living which are launched by the discussions. Their effect will be noted in the reforming of plans for activities and relationships. A third test consists in noting the vigor and soundness with which the members develop their findings into codes, written or unwritten. Evolved codes are powerful because they are built by the young people for themselves and they are instituted on an experimental basis, not as pledges.

Specific Experiences in Cooperative Evaluation

When some issue in the experience of the group, the local community, or the larger community becomes acute, it calls for conscious examination and evaluation. Such situations provide natural occasions for deliberate discussion of the conflicting theories of value, of the means for appraising values, and of techniques for the approach to problems. These timely experiences in cooperative evaluation provide an avenue for the emotional expression of the young people, train them for larger participation and help them to discover the bases of their unity with the larger community.

Informative and Interpretative Study Courses

The content of these should be determined by current interests and problems. It would gradually take shape as the analyzed precipitate of questions and demands which recur in connection with the first two processes described above.

Guided Reading

Lists of references on subjects of current interest or discussion, as well as on phases of their own living, are helpful guides to youth, particularly if they are annotated and brief. The public libraries are very generous in helping to work out lists. The most important books, however, should be on hand for immediate use.

Appropriate Social Program

This will include the grouping of the young people according to degree of maturity and the cooperative building of a program of diversified activities. The usual activities of young people do not provide for genuine friendships nor for the recognition of interesting and strong character. They are diversions rather than interests and so have not the power to promote getting really acquainted. They vaunt "front" rather than quality of personality. The program should include creative sorts of activities and meaningful social participation in the community as well as good nonsense and adventure.

Open Clubrooms

In every community, there should be at least one clubroom instituted for each period of adolescence—early, middle, and late. It should be open during the time when school or business is closed. The needs and resources of the particular community must determine the extent of accommodation and equipment. Ideally there should be a large room for activities and several small rooms or alcoves for games, conferences, conversation, projects, and the like. Ideally, too, there should be an understanding and trained leader. But not many churches will be able to set up ideal conditions at once. In any case it is advisable that the young people shall do most of the planning, equipping, organizing, and directing of their several clubrooms. One church in a community may open its rooms for the club uses of one age level, another for another age level, and so on. This would divide the responsibility and make more resources available for each age group.

Those fathers and mothers who best understand the particular age groups may act as sponsors or counselors.

Counseling

Those of us who work closely with young people these days have learned better than to tell all that we know to parents, teachers, and other adults concerning the extent to which the conduct of youth has been disorganized by the conditions of the day. Most adults will neither believe nor face the facts and so it is very difficult to arouse them to do what is necessary to correct the terrible things that society has inadvertently done to the conditions of life of these fine and plucky young people. But present social conditions make counseling opportunities particularly important to youth.

Even where parents are willing to do all that is within their power to help these young people with their problems, there are very frequently two great handicaps—the parents have not had the training to prepare them to meet the problems in effective ways; the young people, while appreciating their parents, mistrust their points of view as bases of the adjustment of modern young people to a modern world. At school, for the most part, they are amassing extraneous facts rather than learning how to live in their own time and place in the universe. They need all the help that society can bring to their problems. A notable degree of real and valuable help is available in many localities. It should be put to the service of youth. Its emphasis should be preventive and promotive rather than merely corrective.

Summer Programs

In these days when there is little or no work for young people in the long vacation period, and urban homes provide scant opportunity to the young people for participation in real work, it becomes urgent that there be some community plan of summer activity for them. There are very few churches which, alone, can take responsibility for such a plan, but the churches can be instrumental in stirring the community to action to prevent waste of our young people through meaningless or vicious drifting through the long summers. The public school, the P. T. A., the service clubs, the woman's club, and various organizations interested in problems of civic and human welfare may separately or between them provide some plan; or all the churches of a district may cooperate to this end. Again, the church board of the region may institute a project for caring for this need. If one denomination works out a plan it should not restrict participation to young people of its own membership, unless limitation of accommodations makes this necessary. The actual costs of the summer program should be met as far as possible by the moderate summer fee charged the young people who participate. And the young people should have a large part in making plans and carrying out programs. First plans may be very simple and only part-time ones, growth of program occurring as experience points the way.

One of the finest types of summer programs for the participation of the young people is the working out of a vacation plan for younger children. This project provides opportunity for the young people to work together in ways that are real and count for something. Because the activities are meaningful, they reveal the real caliber of personality and develop friendships naturally. At the same time, the participants are getting first-hand training in the understanding of human behavior and in the study of society. To be worth while such a program should be under a leader whose ability the young people can respect. The financial outlay, even at that, would be very moderate when the values to the institution and to the community are taken into consideration, since the one program would promote the interests of both young people and children, in both enjoyable and educative ways.

Joint Youth-adult Conferences

The separate programs of work with parents and youth should provide occasions for bringing the two groups together when there is common ground. Several factors may produce common ground. There may be a common problem, perhaps one connected with the social activities of the young people. There may be a common objective, such as the sponsoring of some development in the community. There may be need for better understanding, as when the adults object to the comparative study of religions by the group of young people. At any rate, in any fellowship it is important that each of the smaller groups understand the other. When they are brought together, it should be with well-arranged agenda so that the association will be as enjoyable and efficient as possible. When the two groups have learned to work together, they may desire to play occasionally, also, and to challenge each other to certain contests.

Pre-marital Education

Discussed on pages 176 to 182.

The Sacrament of Betrothal

Discussed on pages 177 to 180.

Exploratory Field Trips

These may be arranged in connection with the program of activities. Such trips will help youth to understand better what people are after in their work, their organizations, and institutions; to appraise the manias of the day; to discover the forces in the community which are shaping their lives; to become acquainted with other cultures than their own; and other experiences which will widen their outlook and sympathies. These trips also provide the occasions for the gathering and storing of many important impressions which will find their place in experiences that ensue.

Part-time Participation in Social and Religious Enterprises

There should be a wide diversity of these, so that all the major interests of young people and many of the minor ones will be served. Such participation helps them materially with their grasp of meanings besides giving them much important training. The adult members of the church can do much in the way of opening up opportunities for such participation. The young people will enter some of these enterprises for the good they themselves will get out of them, and some for the contribution they may make. In either case it will be promotive of growth providing the enterprises are worthy ones.

Contacts of Youth with Significant Causes

These causes may be of all sorts and may concern any of the various areas of life. The earlier ones will of course be very closely connected with the personal interests of the individual, but gradually his interests will become enlarged until he finds great satisfaction in the serving of relatively impersonal causes. Each cause must be of such a nature as to command the enthusiasm and energetic support of the individual. He must feel that it is his own cause. He must feel that the cause needs him in some respect. His loyalties must be bound to the cause. As an individual becomes more and more devoted to a cause, he grows somewhat to the dimensions of the cause; his own worth and sense of continuance and security reflect the substantiality of his particular cause.

The suitability of the cause with respect to the developmental level of the young person must be given particular consideration. There are causes to which it is dangerous for a youth to commit himself before he has developed reasonable maturity of judgment in the field, and before he has assembled sufficient ballast to keep him from losing his head and so doing foolish or tragic things.

PROMOTING TRUE FREEDOM FOR YOUTH

The period of youth is the period of drive toward independence and toward freedom. Young people themselves are committed to this drive. Quite often they are of the opinion that achieving it means a breaking of all bonds that are in any way restrictive. They confuse lack of restraint with presence of freedom. Like hatching chickens, they want to get out of the egg. They want to feel themselves detached from every hold upon them. What they really want is noble. They are reaching out toward the unattained fullness of life with all its unexplored possibilities. In the case of the majority of them, no one has bothered to teach them that there can be no freedom where there is no control. Most of them have not learned that in a situation that has no bonds nor restrictions, there is no thing and no person that can be counted upon, for there are no principles or agreements by which to anticipate probable situations and opportunities. Worst of all, trust between persons and groups cannot grow up. One must watch and be ready for he knows not what.

The normal process of achieving freedom from birth to maturity covers a long stretch of transitional growth. At birth, the baby is entirely under external direction, for he has no habits or ideals of his own by which to determine his conduct. By the time he is mature, he must be largely under inner direction with a reasonably adequate and appropriate system of values with which to appraise appeals made to him and judge the consequences of his reactions. There is no one time when this or that step in control is taken. It is a silent, fairly steady, augmentative process if conditions of growth are right. Voluntarily, though not necessarily without regret, he gives up one satisfaction and increases his self-control at his present level that he may freely partake of the greater value to be his on a higher level. It will be his upon condition that he surrender the lesser value and invalidate his old predispositions. It is the tastes, or intimations of taste, of the larger value on ahead which empower him to increase the rigor of his self-discipline. These make him willing to bind himself on this level, to free himself on the next. This is progressive freedom.

But today such freedom is far from easy to achieve. There are required many preparatory reactions before one can approach some of the choicest values. There are many alluring Circes along each course. Worse, there are those whose increase of wealth depends upon discouraging self-disciplines that would advance youth to levels of greater value. Because of these various deleterious conditions, the growth of many youths presents a truncated form. It usually exhibits fair success in development throughout childhood. Then not very long after puberty, manifestations make it evident that the young people are becoming more or less sophisticated, conventionalized, routinized, but without ever growing up, without truly maturing. By makeshift and artificial mimicking of the more ostentatious and racy practices of adults—those practices which seem to promise to youth's immaturity greater independence and emancipation—they gain the illusion of mature freedom. Life is easy, comfortable, glamorous, irresponsible. But the "values" that emerge are too fragile to examine and too ephemeral to hold. Besides, the values decrease as "emancipated" living proceeds because they depend largely upon physical stimulation of one sort or another and are subject to satiation or insensibility following overindulgence. This road to freedom turns out to be a blind alley, often a messy one.

Religion has a tremendous contribution to make to youth as he seeks the road to freedom. This contribution is made in two chief ways. The first way deals with the young person as an individual. It functions through capturing his enthusiastic loyalty and harnessing it to worthy causes, then progressively directing it toward that which is Supremely Worthful for all mankind. Through launching him on such a progression of interests, i.e., of loyalties, each loyalty being given to a value which will prove its worth, he is launched also in a progressive building of a sound system of values. There is no blind end to such a road to freedom. There is sure to be suffering as well as enjoyment, and difficulty as well as progress. But there is little disillusionment of the destructive sort. The bondages to old, disorganizing habits are easier to dissolve, and the new values secured are substantiated. What is more, the way is always open to greater values, world without end.

The second way is by helping him to connect with groups of persons of his own age who are organized, or can organize, to clear their road cooperatively to those values they feel worthy, whether these lie in the physical, mental, social, economic, or spiritual aspect of living. As has been said, the young person cannot build his road to freedom alone in the world as it is. Increasingly, his problems are group problems either in source or in effect. He must know the power and the techniques by which organized minorities can protect and elevate those values which are highest in modern life. The phenomenal growth of the American Youth Movement since the first American Youth Congress in 1934 to a membership of almost two million and their effectual activities well illustrate both the need and the possibility of mutual support among modern youth who have built a system of values worth working and even fighting for. Much of the effort of guiding the maturing of youth will be wasted if they must make their way as powerless, individual newcomers into the organized world. Furthermore, wise education in this first participation in group loyalties is of paramount importance. The first group organized to protect or promote specific values may well be formed in the local church. Then there may be a larger group made up of all the churches in the community or section when a larger group problem arises. This will prepare for national participation in organized group loyalty to great but not easily achieved values. It is urgent that the values fostered by the church be represented capably and cherished zealously by these growing organizations of youth, whether they are values couched in religious terms or not. Only so can the young persons nurtured by the church find in these organizations the needed facilitation in their progress toward freedom.

The church is a major and rightful sponsor of this service in the freeing of modern youth. It can educate him and can open to him the way by which he can connect himself with others in fellowships that grow ever more meaningful. It can demonstrate to him that lack of bonds does not make freedom. Rather, the more bonds, the more freedom, providing these bonds involve such connections as allow creative interaction with his fellow men and so promote growth of good and of meaning in the world. This integrated freeing of himself is no easy task for youth, for the values in such connections are not so immediately tangible and gratifying as are those of men's individualistic ambitions. They cannot be counted off on one's fingers or added in columns. It takes faith to control one's behavior and one's group loyalties in the search and service of these great invisible values. But once the young person has tasted deeply the extent and quality of the freedom which is achieved through purposeful self-discipline and through intelligent group action, he will not be willing to accept the subtle yet self-destroying bondage and monotony that result from undisciplined or "independent" living.

Chapter XII

COUNSELING IN FAMILY DIFFICULTIES

TREATMENT of the troubles of the family is first and foremost group work. The greater part of the accumulated literature that pertains to psychiatric and counseling work is concerned with the individual, not the group. Any deeply penetrative dealing with most of the problems of the individual, however, will carry the counselor over into the field of group work, for it is through connection with a group or groups that the individual most frequently both develops and discovers his difficulties. To put all of this into the terms of this book, most frequently it is a fellowship or communion of persons that must be studied and guided, not an isolated individual. Failure to appreciate this, combined with zeal for some one systematized approach to individual maladjustment, has resulted in much spectacular but superficially symptomatic treatment of human ills.

In order to make clear this characteristic of sound counseling in family difficulties, a presentation of cases will be made the major feature in this present discussion. These are summaries of actual situations in which counseling took place, though necessarily much abridged. Designedly, the cases selected are not spectacular, highly complex, exceptional, or miraculous-sounding. They present the sort of problems that are likely to appear very frequently in one or another form in the work of any leader whose program puts him into direct touch with persons or families. To the counselor who has earned his graduation out of amateurhood, such problems are of far more stirring interest than the bizarre, the sensational, or odd situations, for they are more significantly connected with life, and human life is our treasury of meanings. The technique of group treatment which

269

each case has been selected to illustrate is stated briefly after the topical designation of the case. These techniques are described in general outline in the summary of each case. Since treatment of maladjustments through group approach is still a largely uncharted field, the techniques of treatment here suggested had necessarily to be originated and developed through many years of experimenting and testing in professional work with groups. In basically their present form, they have been in use for about fifteen years with results that would seem to justify making them available to those interested in the approach.

ILLUSTRATIVE SITUATIONS

Situation A. Marital Maladjustment, Emphasizing the Technique of Developing a Program to Guide an Experiment in Group Living

Summary of situation: A physician of high standing in the Middle West telephoned early in the morning for an appointment at once, thus revealing the duress he was under. He said that he was leaving his family for good and that I had no chance of reconstructing the situation, for he was through. All he wanted was help in working out the best plans possible for the children and for meeting his other obligations.

Case history revealed that he and his wife had had an almost ideal courtship and early married life. Then five babies had come in the span of the next ten years. He was struggling to establish himself professionally, so there had not been much money for anything, certainly not for help. But they had chummed along in their venture with only healthy amounts of disagreement and disappointment.

Then the physician had received a rare chance to study one year in his specialization, receiving a scholarship almost the equal of his yearly net income from practice. Both he and his wife had approved wholeheartedly of his accepting the offer. This left her alone with the children and on a reduced budget. She threw herself loyally into carrying through her part of making the year a successful investment. She drove into the care of her household with all her might, forgetting her lonesomeness in vigorous work and enjoying her children emotionally more than she had ever done before. She had no time for the brief periods of systematic study which she had been carrying on, and little time for friends. Besides, it did not mean much to go to the affairs of their circle of married friends without her husband, and it took fewer clothes to stay home. In the meantime, her husband had a very enriching year both as to professional preparation and contacts. He worked very hard to make the most of his opportunity.

When he came home, the beginning of the rift that was to grow was already present, but neither noticed it for a time. In essence, it was this. Out of both need and self-protection, the wife had become absorbed in household care and management and in her deepening affection for the children; the husband had become absorbed in new professional possibilities which might be realized with sufficient single-eyed devotion. Their conversation began to lag for want of common interests. They began to like different persons as friends. There was little time for husband-wife communion except as it was deliberately made a matter of plan, for each was carrying a different but overheavy load.

The rift in interests kept widening. Finally, by the time the last child entered high school and so required little personal care, the wife woke up to the emptiness of her hands. Without realizing that she was in a dangerously dissatisfied mood, her eyes began to rove around to discover some source of meanings for a life become routinized even in the most intimate relationship. One evening when her husband's professional organization was in long session, she went to a municipal dance as a favor to a neighbor woman. Neither husband nor wife thought anything of her going, but it led on to more separate social participations.

The husband began to take notice of her growing interest in this other social group. He exerted himself to plan to take her out socially more often. But he found that they had neglected their situation too long. He saw that she could not now mingle with his present group with poise and happiness. Even then, they did not heed the signs now quite apparent that their long-neglected relationship critically needed their intelligent and devoted attention to get it back upon an effective and enjoyable basis. In the end, the husband caught his wife in a compromising situation with a married man noted more for masterful technique with women than for cultural background. The wife claimed there had been no sexual intimacy, but the husband would not believe her. Vividly now, they realized the gulf between them. Yet here were five adolescent children needing the home more than ever before.

Summary of treatment: The physician was asked to take his vacation at this time and to go off with his three sons on a hunting trip. This plan had two ends in view, allowing him time to get a hold on himself before united work on the husband-and-wife situation began, and providing opportunity, under the least pressure of time and tension possible, to get at the wife's part in it all. By the time her husband's vacation was over, the wife was fairly ready for a reorganization of her living. He, too, had decided that it was no use to break up lightly in a few weeks a situation that had held some years of valued meaning.

In the delightful setting of his vacation and influenced by his contacts with his sons, the husband had already undergone some self-diagnosis. The counselor went thoroughly into his part of the situation. He reached the point where he was as ready as his wife for a program of reorganization. He realized that he as well as she had been responsible and, further, that fixing the blame was not the main consideration.

Both husband and wife were asked to make a list in writing of all the items which each felt must be included in any program for their future living which would carry promise of success. Each was to write his list solely from his own point of view, and was to be frank and self-interested and explicit. The working out of these lists helped the two to distinguish clearly just what their dissatisfactions and lacks were, and revealed to the counselor the more overt types of situation productive of trouble between them.

At this point in the counseling process, the counselor blocked out the first draft of a program of the reorganization of their interests based upon the materials now assembled: (1) the complete case diagnosis[1] of the counselor; (2) the two lists made by husband and wife of needs and desired values; (3) the actual possibilities and limitations presented by their situation as uncovered in the study of the case. This program was in actuality the outline of the conditions prerequisite for an experiment in living. It was an instrument of guidance to be used to initiate this experiment during the period just ahead.

This tentatively formulated program was then discussed at first with husband and wife separately. The separate discussions of it provided opportunity for clearing up all possible points of difficulty under circumstances which protected their strained relationship. Then the program, as reformulated, was presented to both husband and wife together. It was discussed frankly, together with its implications and the normal expectations. Some further changes were made, and then it was declared satisfactory as a working guide for their joint experience. Next, the span of time during which the experimental program was to be tried was determined in conference. They chose a six months' period, the minimum worth while. If less than six months is tried, it does not allow sufficient time either for the forming of new habits or for the convincing tastings of new values expected to emerge. Each was given a copy of the program, the counselor keeping one also. They went away under the challenge of trying to see what they could do with their relationship when they used the same intelligence and devotion upon it which they invested upon other matters of equal importance to them.

Follow-up work was largely a matter (1) of assisting them in keeping themselves open to emergent challenges and possibilities, (2) of cooperatively evaluating developments and findings, and (3) of making sure that they were appreciating the new values on deep enough levels to render these activating forces in their living. The program was really a cooperatively constructed instrument of guidance to values which they had missed. It was a necessary instrument until they could experience the growth of the new values with sufficient potency to transfer the guid-

[1] The counseling process as a whole is not here discussed because of limitations of space. The author has discussed it in Chapter XXII of *Normative Psychology of Religion* by Wieman and Wieman.

ing function over to the-requirements-for-this-growth. That is, the guidance of the program and of the counselor became progressively unnecessary as the values toward which the whole process was working began to emerge in sufficient potency and clarity to render these latter the activating forces and to make the requirements for the growth of these values the guide.

In this, as in all cases, there were successes and failures, but the general trend was decidedly toward success, particularly so by the fourth month when their efforts began to gather impetus from their sensing the richer possibilities in their living. At the end of the six months, husband, wife, and counselor came together as had been arranged at the start, to decide (1) whether or not both husband and wife felt that it was worth while to go on; and, if they were to go on, (2) whether or not a further program for guiding their experiment was advisable; and, if it were needed, (3) what revisions should be included. The particular couple in case felt strongly that they were now already under the compulsions of the values they had begun experiencing. They found intelligent, experimental living to be exciting and satisfying, and so went on together. Each had done a reasonably good job for the time covered in reforming those of his habits which had been obstructive and in building up certain conditions promotive of richer meaning in their common life.

Situation B. Family Maladjustment, Emphasizing the Technique of Counseling with the Whole Family as a Unit

Summary of situation: Mother of family, woman about forty years of age, came first. She had been aroused to action by some parent-education work in which she had participated. She reported that their family, totaling six, packed more strain and distress into each twenty-four hours than would seem possible. Each member of the family was interviewed. Briefly, this was their situation. They could afford no help, the school and work schedules of the various members were sufficiently different to complicate a situation already too individualistic. No one felt any interest in doing things which would improve the situation except to offer all too freely his decided opinions as to what was wrong. The house was altogether too small for the family and was not ordered as to time or space arrangements in any dependable way. Every member of the family was devoted to some aspect of church work but through activities which increased the complication of the home life.

The father was a lawyer noted for his biting sternness which he tended to carry over into his family life. Also he was somewhat embittered by trying to be honest in a society that is not organized to make honesty as advantageous in business practice as it appears in democratic theory. The mother was soft-hearted with an extreme "yes complex." She could not refuse anything asked of her that was presented in the name of the "good," nor could she resist making an exception of anything when a child beseeched her. As a consequence, she was utterly worn out before the end of each day, yet her regular responsibilities were never "caught up." By the time the family gathered at night, it took all the driving of father and mother and all the grudging labor of the whole family to get things sufficiently done to make possible the start of the next day. Husband and wife had the slightest margins of time for sharing interests of any sort.

The children were sufficiently intelligent to have located the painless method of avoiding being present as much as was possible. But the age-old miracle worked: they loved their parents and felt them "good," in spite of the numbers of occasions when they said, "They're all right, but I wish they wouldn't. . . ." They vied with each other to get the most privileges and satisfactions. They complained of not having things such as other children had in their associational groups.

No one knew where the money went, but only that it was gone too soon. The father was adamant in refusing to go into debt for anything.

Their annual vacation camping trip in the wilds was their one successful development of enjoyable family activity. Their common interest in the neighborhood Methodist Church, and their sincere attitude toward religion as there presented, formed their one basis for accord in objectives and standards for their group living. They all seemed to feel that their family was all right, but somehow just couldn't seem to get going as it should. In the meantime, all of them showed the effects of interpersonal jangling: the father and mother were worried and fatigued most of the time. This meant that they were often cross and unreasonable.

Summary of treatment: As already stated, each member of the family had been interviewed, the adults and the two older children directly, the two younger children informally through conversation. This yielded not only more facts, but also their several points of view in regard to the family situation and their individual characteristics of person and of participation.

On the basis of all this, the counselor drew up the first draft of a program for their experimental living. Then the whole family was called into counsel in their own home. The counselor was there for dinner, which was kept informal and social. Then after dinner, the family gathering took place.

The father explained that in all businesses that amount to anything, these days, there is frequent conferring of the members of the business, and that many times they call in first one expert and then another to give them the latest findings in regard to whatever matter is under discussion. In line with this current procedure in most other businesses, he and their mother had decided to call the family together to discuss family business and had invited an expert to confer with them. Then the mother told something of the way the family situation had looked to her when she first went to the counselor. She had been prompted to be careful to give full credit to the positive and loyal aspects of the family while summarizing the difficulties. Next, she invited the others in turn to add anything or suggest modifications in anything she had said. There were several brief comments from the children concerning those details in their own affairs which were most disturbed by the family situation.

Then the father called upon the counselor for comment. The counselor first showed the children a set of blueprints and specifications which had been used in the construction of her own dwelling. She explained that the house could not have amounted to much had there not been a great deal of thinking done before the men went into action in building and before the family went into action in living there. Then she showed that there

must be somewhat similar thinking, resulting in plans and specifications, for a family group living together in the same house,
using common property, and doing all sorts of things together.
She explained that the plans she wanted to show them that evening were worked out after she had listened to all of them tell
her about the interests and procedures of their own family. She
said that she had tried to work out plans for their living which
were just as distinctly for *their* family fellowship as the floor
plans had been for *her* family house. Now she was placing the
plans before them, as the architect had put the building plans
before her, so that they might discuss them and modify them
to better fit their own family.

An animated discussion followed. Some changes were definitely made, others noted for further discussion. Then the program was adopted on a trial basis as a guide for living for a
period of two weeks, each entering into it as an experiment carrying some adventure.

At the end of two weeks, there was another session of the
family with the counselor. At this time, comments and opinions
were much more specific and decided, for they had tried the program. Modifications were made after detailed discussion. Where
there was disagreement that could not be cleared, the item was
left to be decided by mother and father cooperatively. The span
of time for the experiment in family living was set at six months.
The family decided to have a council meeting each week to take
care of family business and developments, asking the counselor
to participate once every four weeks. The father impressed upon
the family the realization that when any one member failed to
live up to the conditions of the experiment, it threw the experiment off for one or more others.

The program for the whole family contained schedules of time
arrangement for each day and for the week and month, schedule of member-participation in the regular activities of the family, schedules of space arrangement, and a minimum financial
budget to be used until they had cleared up many neglected
details, such as replacement of small necessary tools and of needed
clothing. It contained also an expanded budget to be used when
they were properly equipped again. The items in this expanded

budget provided for matters not before attainable in the family and so presented a real incentive for the disciplining of themselves by the minimum budget in order to reach the expanded budget as soon as possible.

Besides the general plans for the whole family, there was a separate plan for each member, to guide him in his participation and bring better articulation between the interests and activities of all members. These were worked up in as simple, brief, and graphic a form as was possible. Later on, they were used as the basis for the reports of each member at the monthly council when the counselor was present. These individual reports were not made after the manner of a confessional. That aspect of the family business was reserved for child-parent relationship. They were rather like committee reports, only spoken out naturally as things came to each child's mind.

It was not long before the children caught the idea that the counselor was only brought in to get the family started on an interesting experiment in government and achievement. They began to realize that the family *could* run itself in such a way that it could do and have more of the things it really wanted, besides having a better time together. It was very interesting to note here, as in every other case of such counseling with the family as a unit, that the children enjoyed so keenly their participation in family living on this realistic experimental basis that they guarded the weekly family council zealously against intrusions and postponements. Further, they realized that the program was not a set of absolute laws, but the conditions for an experiment which could be changed provided there were good enough reasons.

Situation C. Neighborhood Maladjustment, Emphasizing the Technique of Collective Counseling

Summary of situation: Several families living in a "dormitory town" found the conditions for neighborhood association of their children seriously difficult. Since most of the fathers went into the city to work each day and were never sure how long they would be located in their present positions, their families had a tentative feeling about their places of residence. Fully half of them were renters. Hence, very few were interested in the cultural development of the neighborhood. The town was sufficiently large to include a number of neighborhoods affording a diverse variety of problems involving the adjustment of the child in his play neighborhood. From a cursory survey it appeared that there were disturbed parents in various sections. Enough of these parents had registered their statements of difficulty and need of help with the public schools to indicate that it was not the problem of a few disgruntled, odd families but a common problem in many types of neighborhood.

A series of meetings was announced, open to those who were interested in the problem. These meetings were arranged in connection with a project of parent education already going on in the city under a counselor trained to deal with problems of the family. Group investigation of the conditions and of the possibilities connected with the play problem began. First, the specific problems were distinguished. One of the most common, for instance, was the frequency with which one or two untrained children in a neighborhood spoiled the play for all the others by bullying or cruelty or obscenity or destructiveness or greediness or dishonesty. Next, the possible instigating conditions were analyzed, including those traceable to the parents who had reported the difficulties. This induced every member of the group to begin experimenting on her own account with more intelligent procedures and attitudes in dealing with the neighborhood situation.

At this point, the various possible plans for basic dealing with the situation were blocked out. These were found to consist of steps. The first step was that of trying to secure the active cooperation of all the mothers or parents of any one neighborhood. In some instances, they were all invited to join the group now at work on the problems; in some others, small informal neighborhood gatherings of both fathers and mothers took place; in still others, the mothers of troublesome children were visited in an entirely friendly way and asked if they would help to work out some plans for the neighborhood play of the children.

Then came the second step. In neighborhoods where it was

possible to secure cooperation from the majority of the residents, a neighborhood plan was worked out which included as an important element the securing of the participation of the children themselves in this building up of the neighborhood play plan. In neighborhoods where no appreciable cooperation could be secured, plans were made for loosely organized play groups composed of children selected from a wider area. These built-up groups played by turn at the different homes represented, the mother of the home being used at any one time acting as hostess-mother to the group. These latter groups were careful not to give the impression of being exclusive. They left the way open for the joining of others. It was interesting to see in how many cases the better-play programs of those who started the play groups attracted the attention of those other parents and children who had at first refused to bother themselves with active cooperation.

The counseling group kept on meeting during the development of the play groups for the purpose of further study of play conditions and influences, of cooperative solution of problems, and of evaluation of findings. Since all the participants in the experiment were very human beings, the developments were wholesomely faulty. But progressively, the group took the third step. The standards and programs which had been developed began to be consciously formulated, and hence more intelligently evaluated. Results showed in the marked improvements in neighborhoods which affected noticeably, within five years, the play standards and activities of the whole town. For instance, more supervised play on school grounds was introduced. Further, this supervised play included a greater variety of activities and crafts than usual because of the request of the parents, whose study had made them realize that such variety gave all children a fairer and happier opportunity.

FAMILY COUNSELING AS A RELIGIOUS PROCESS

The three cases presented above as illustrations were chosen deliberately because they had no theological labels which would classify them obviously as religious problems. They revealed aspects other than the formally religious. However, in the last analysis, they were genuine religious problems, for they all dealt with the most vital of the meanings of life and with the growth of community among mankind. Each of them could have been handled on the strictly social level. In such a case, the effort would have been focused upon helping the individual person who first came, or his group, to such level of social adjustment as promised minimum of distress and friction. Such treatment holds the possibility of some helpfulness, depending upon the appropriateness and height of the level attained.

The religious solution of problems of maladjustment differs from the social not primarily in the kind of problems it deals with, but in the principles employed in the building up of new, essential controls. Religious counseling seeks to discover and set up those conditions which will restore the individual to wholeness within himself and with others, will promote the conditions for the greatest possible fulfillment of each person involved, will foster the conditions for the deepest and most creative interpersonal community, will engage the individual in cooperative loyalty to the growth of good and meaning in the world, and will guide the eyes and devotions of all to that which is Supremely Worthful for all mankind as represented through the most worthful which the particular individuals can know at the time. It is not just a matter of restoring to equilibrium. On such terms, equilibrium is all too often the equivalent of stagnation, insulation, individualistic assertiveness or other type of personal and group retardation. It is a matter of promoting the conditions for the greatest development of personality and the growth of community possible in the particular situation at the particular time. Since these two developments are the great manifestations of God at work that man can know on this earth, the process of promoting the conditions required for such developments is a highly religious process.

To what degree the persons being counseled shall be made specifically aware of the religious and theological character of the process will depend upon their stage of personal and religious maturing. In many cases there should be no deliberate effort to stir this awareness; in other cases this should be done in simple directness and wise appropriateness. Jesus Christ, the great teacher, demonstrated this principle of being true to the developmental status of persons, over and over again, as have all great teachers.

In essence, the motivation for genuinely religious counseling is devotion to the nurturing of communion among mankind, because communion of the right sort is both the germinative center of religion and the indispensable culture for human growth. The family is the chief germinative center of this communion, as we have found. Hence the church as the organized agency of religion must be concerned to foster the growth and quality of the communion of the family. It must be concerned for family life as a group development and venture. Wherever human relationships are growing, God is. Counseling in family difficulties is counseling of family relationships and interactions. It is a group undertaking. When all this is clearly seen, the difficulties of the family, instead of seeming just one disruptive problem piling upon another, begin to fit into an actively developing unit where the connections, and hence the meanings, are more readily observable and approachable. Then the family is discerned as a weaving of patterns of meanings, sometimes sleazy and drab, sometimes substantial, rich, and glowing. Counseling the family is the process of guiding this development and weaving of patterns of meanings. Most behavior problems of children, for instance, are signs that something is going wrong in the weaving of these patterns of meaning.

Not only must the counselor keep himself keenly sensitive to the real essence of the family, its communion, but he must lead the members of the family to see that their prime devotion must be given to keeping this communion right, sound, and growing. This steady, informed regard for the communion of the family in itself is a large factor in both preventing and correcting family difficulties, for it makes for greater objectivity and organic equality in interactions.

PRACTICAL CONSIDERATIONS FOR THE CHURCH

Not only is the group approach to family difficulties more in keeping with the principles of religious living, but it is also more practical. Personal counseling makes great demands upon the energy of the counselor and great inroads on his time in proportion to the outcomes. Also, individual approach is not so wholesome as group work in the results secured. Certainly, there are numbers of cases where personal counseling is the only possible way, particularly at the start. But where the counselor's schedule is heavy, it is advisable as a general policy to eliminate the personal rather than the group situations calling for attention. When the group goes to work cooperatively on its own problems with such launching and guidance as is necessary, much can be accomplished not only for the whole group but for every individual in it.

When this idea is expanded, so that the group comes to mean a group of families meeting through their representatives, while the individual means each separate family participating, we have an extended form of counseling—collective. This brings further amplification of whatever is invested in the counseling process. A single counselor can achieve remarkable things through long-term collective counseling.

One situation where collective counseling needs developing appropriately is in short summer conferences of young people. It seems almost unbelievable that intelligent directors of these conferences should foster such a travesty as scheduling the young people for short, individual consultations with the selected counselor. Cases are not rare where this scheduling has been done on a fifteen- or thirty-minute basis for hour after hour. Returns on the investment would be far greater and sounder if a plan of collective counseling were developed on the basis of the needs and problems of the particular young people in case.

Another practical aspect of the group approach, whether private or collective, is that persons of less training can achieve relatively greater results than in personal counseling. This latter requires long, arduous, specialized training for work with all but the simplest sorts of problems. In the group approach the leader is like a consulting engineer who furnishes materials, helps to develop insight, and directs experimentation with evaluation of results, but does not delve deeply into the inner aspects of the situations of individual members. They are helped to work out their own problems in a healthy, helpful group undertaking. Collective group counseling is, of course, surer territory for the semitrained than private group counseling.

The church which is short of both staff and resources will usually be able to find a few persons within its membership who can be trained to do group counseling in a field where they have already had some experince. At first, the novice may be able to do no more than to assemble materials which throw light on the problems at hand. But continued training will develop his powers to guide the analyzing, evaluating, experimenting, and synthesizing which are involved in any one process of group counseling. It will take the novice much longer than it will a trained leader to guide a group through to a reasonably adequate solution—the better trained, the better outcomes. Training for group approach to group problems needs urgently the recognition of institutions now training leaders.

FORMS OF GROUP COUNSELING

Stress has been laid upon two forms of group counseling which hold great promise of effectiveness when appropriately developed for the groups in question. There are other forms, some of which have long been in use. After starting the list of forms with the two extensively discussed here, these others will be noted in order that the total list may be as suggestive and resourceful as possible.

Private Group Counseling

Illustrated by the first two cases.

Collective Group Counseling

Illustrated by the third case.

The Visiting Counselor.

In this instance, the function of counseling is taken into the individual family by some regular plan. The counselor may go under the title of visiting or home teacher, case worker, or counselor. He both serves the family in every way possible to his situation and seeks to bring the family into closer touch with outside groups and agencies. He is a shuttle interweaving more effective and meaningful bonds between family, church, and community. The Mormon Church has well developed this plan of lay leadership in this function.

Informal Counseling

Here the teacher, leader, or counselor makes it his important business to keep himself sensitive to the developments in individuals and groups. He introduces ("plants") what he hopes will be fostering factors wherever he sees these necessary. His follow-up of his suggestive "plantings" involves, usually, some discussion with the individual person or group concerning its use of, or reaction to, the introduced factors. This is a very satisfactory technique of counseling where the problem either is just taking shape or is slight, or where the individual concerned is keen to locate the undiscovered connections between his experiences. Some procedures useful for "planting" in such informal counseling are the asking of a vital, pertinent question; the lending of a selected book; an invitation to a lecture or discussion group; the bringing about of contact between the individual involved and some particularly influential person or fertile experience; and providing some experience involving such contrast as will arouse the analytical power of the individual.

Counseling through Teaching

This world-old form of counseling is done by all those teachers who know that the important thing in education is what happens to the person and group, and not what he produces in terms of set requirements. Such teachers are teaching human beings through their subjects, not the subjects by way of human students. In doing so, materials and methods are selected and modified to serve the greatest fulfillment of the particular students in case. This posits active participation by the students, for only thereby can the teacher discover their problems, trends, nature, and needs. It is a very potent form of counseling in those situations where one teacher is with his students over a long enough period to allow the development of fellow feeling in the group. Many biographies testify to the specific effectiveness of this process.

Counseling through Guided Analysis

This indirect form of counseling may be employed when a leader notes in an organized group evidences of gathering tension or of developing tendencies bound to result in undue friction, maladjustment, or disorganization, though these are not recognized as problems by the group. In this case, the individuals involved are brought into a group in which the discussion starts in the realm of their present thinking. It is specific regarding the certain problems being considered, but general regarding personal applications. The problem-situation is progressively demonstrated as clearly and vividly as possible, but the individuals are not led to feel victimized. They are left to make their own deductions and interpretations.

This indirect technique for making counseling available through guided analysis should include the announcement of easy and open opportunity to go on further with the reorganizing, should any members of the group desire. This should be offered but not pressed.

It is particularly important as a technique with individual persons and groups who tend to rationalize, locate alibis, devise means of escape, and otherwise avoid meeting squarely the facts, problems, and deeper implications of their situations. This technique is also valuable when two factions are gathering hostility but have not evidenced it as yet in any form making open approach feasible or necessary.

Counseling through Arranging the Conditions of Experience

It is easy for the counselor, particularly the novice, to talk too much. Then it is easy for this talking to become advice or preaching. In many cases, counseling can be done quite silently through arranging conditions to bring certain experiences into the living of the individuals in mind. In fact, this technique will often succeed when direct counseling would have no effect. Talking, perforce, makes use of symbols. If these do not have any cogent or acceptable meaning for the individuals being counseled, these persons can be reached much more successfully through guiding them into actual experiences where they will make a discovery or two for themselves.

One very simple form of such counseling is illustrated in the case of an individual or a clique who persistently spoils the spirit of some group event or project by repetitive complaints of the way it was planned. If this individual or group is put upon the committee which does the planning, with responsibility for some part that requires actual participating activity, better adjustment will come. Where the condition needing correction is more complex, the arrangement of the experiences intended to bring enlightenment to the individual person or group will also have to be more complex, and may have to cover some period of time. For instance, the development of social interest in an individualistic child is of this latter sort. In this just mentioned problem oral interchange is far from being the most effective technique.

Counseling through Intergroup Referral Service

Some of the wisest counseling done is that which puts the individual person or group into touch with other groups organized to furnish sources of help. Examples of some of these possible sources are the children's librarians, the Boy Scout executives, professional psychologists or psychiatrists, courses of study under capable leaders, social agencies in the neighborhood, persons who have undergone profound experiences analogous to the one disturbing the individual or group in case, and a chance to work with other persons or groups who have closely related interests.

Of course, where referral service is for the purpose of getting rid of the individual and his problem, it is not to be counted as counseling. But where the service is rendered expressly to put the individual into touch with facilitating, enlightening, reinforcing, or corrective agencies, it is genuine counseling. The leader who does the referring has obligations to discharge both to the individual needing help and to the source to which he sends him for this help. Often, too, such service involves intelligent and creative follow-up on the part of the counselor doing the referring. It is by no means a trivial type of service where rendered responsibly.

In the midst of giving fitting devotion to the development of the necessary arrangements for specific counseling in the church, it is well to pause at times to evaluate the actual effects of the total program and fellowship of the church upon family adjustment and growth. There is not one part nor portion of all that is present and goes on in the church that does not have its influence upon the homes of the constituency. These are some of the things that have made a difference as reported by members: bases upon which "the hand of fellowship" is extended, whether by worldly appraisals or Christian principles; type of church government—dictatorship, bureaucracy, democracy; degree to which all members are drawn into the significant enterprises of the church; objectives of the church, as revealed in its budget; the hierarchy of pastoral concerns, as evidenced by his investment of time; the policies of the church in regard to the use of its building and equipment; and the provisions of the church for reaching out to those needing specific guidance or sustenance.

Lapsing for the moment into personal comment, I know that I owe the fellowship of the church tremendous appreciation. I could relate facts on the other side also. Yet, in the total and in a wealth of detail, there was a guidance furnished not duplicated in kind in any other institution. The nature of this guidance could be made explicit through mention of specific instances of personal or group influence, of discerning leadership during the forming of my ideas and attitudes, of wisely offered opportunities for various sorts of participation, and of other processes. But it is as a whole, as a continuing, though varied experience of fellowship also, that the church provided much counseling service that had distinguishable outcomes. Doubtless my testimony is but one expression of the appreciation of many people. Others would bear emphatic contrary testimony.

Probably no other one factor in the church has greater counseling power than the actually existent, interacting fellowship of the members. To the extent that this is true, the terms and patterns of this fellowship must be examined and evaluated responsibly.

Part IV

FACING INTO THE FUTURE

CULTURAL lag is bound to be accompanied by cultural fatigue. This has become evident in some of the trends in religion today. Indeed, the very nature of religion makes it more subject to cultural lag than any other major interest. At present, there are a number of strong movements backwards, all of them cleverly rationalized but none the less reason-paralyzed. Like the convalescing child, who, told by his physician that he must walk around the block each day, returned with the report that when he had gotten halfway around he was so weary that he had turned around and come back home. The important difference between the boy and these goings-back-home in religion is that the boy knew that he had reacted weakly.

The opportunity of the church is at a zenith just now. But it will take a strengthened church to grasp it and make use of it. The new strength of the church must grow out of the revitalizing of its dedication to the Supreme Reality to be gained through wholehearted devotion to the most representative cause it can find in the realities of its own time and place. Since the development of communion among men is the most urgent present requirement for the instituting of the Kingdom of God in human living, and since the family is the chief germinative center of this communion, the most representative cause for the church is that of fostering the communion of the family, together with all the social connections integral to this.

The healthier churches are already launching their work in this field. Chapter XIII presents a summary of present trends in the work of the churches with the family as made evident by reports from church leaders. Chapter XIV attempts to enlarge the scale of the conceptions upon which a culturally adequate program for work with the family is being built. The first chapter in the book discussed the family in the life of today. This last chapter seeks to show what the family may become in the life of tomorrow if it has the fostering essential to bring it to social maturity. Part IV signalizes the mutuality of family and church both as to objective and as to possibilities of future cultural contribution.

Chapter XIII

TRENDS IN THE WORK OF THE CHURCHES

THROUGHOUT almost the entire church world in this country, there are stirrings of increased activity in the work of the church with the family. The International Council of Religious Education and many divisions of the Protestant Church gave the two years 1934 to 1936 to a program having first emphasis upon the home. The Church of Jesus Christ of Latter-Day Saints has developed a program of church education that makes education for living in the family a major element. The Roman Catholic Church has set up a national bureau of family life with a full-time trained director. The Religious Education Committee of the American Unitarian Association is considering the plan of making "The Home in Religious Education" one of its major objectives in the church year 1937–1938. The Federal Council of Churches of Christ in America is focusing a generous share of its attention in this direction. These examples from among many possible ones furnish indications of an intensifying concern for the family.

THE PRESENT INVENTORY OF TRENDS

This present report of what the various major divisions of the church are doing in their work with the family makes no pretense of being comprehensive or conclusive. The gathering of data of statistical importance was in no way an object of the work. Rather, this survey grew out of the purpose to feel out the main trends and emphases, and make information about these available for the sake of what the sharing of them may contribute to the cause. It is offered with the hope, also, that it may prove a potent factor in bringing about specific creative cooperation of all the divisions of the church in this area of common concern. Unless the churches are sufficiently Christian to be able to function as a unity in the love of God in this cardinal issue, the family will not receive the support and guidance it needs in adequate force or with sufficient promptness to meet its crisis.

This inventory has been under way for one year. It proceeded in this fashion. Contact was made, either personally or by correspondence or both, with the headquarters of five of the major church divisions in this country which derive from the Christian tradition. This included the Church of Jesus Christ of Latter-Day Saints, the Jewish congregations, the Roman Catholic Church, the Christian Science Church, and eighteen denominations of the Protestant Church. Contact was also made with seventeen other national or municipal organizations whose interests promised enlightenment, and with leaders connected with this field of interest.

To each of these institutions and persons was sent an outline of some of the possible "particular areas of interest" involved in the work of the church with the family. To those whose work was not directly connected with the church, additional questions were asked, formulated in the light of their interests. It was clearly stated that the outline was in no way a questionnaire, but only a means of suggesting and stimulating as full a report as possible.

PARTICULAR AREAS OF INTEREST

1. Chief problems which the church has with its families. Examples submitted: Attendance; indifference of parents of church-school children; lax standards of adults; scarcity of fathers in attendance; social stratification or competition; lack of cultural background upon which to work; superficial nature of their interest in religion; staggering loads or problems which the majority of families are carrying and in which they seek help, perhaps beyond the working limits of staff of church; dropping out of young people; rigid orthodoxy of adults. There are others just as important. The objective was to discover the chief problems of the churches with the families of their general constituency.

2. Chief problems which the families of the church or

within its neighborhood feel that they have in regard to the church and to religion.

Examples submitted: The church's teachings to the children; the type of program for the young people; the type of morning service; the ineffectual nature of religion as presented; no practical help with their problems; too many organizations and activities; constant demands for money or time; favoritism toward the fortunate or socially prominent; too much show; too little show; dissatisfaction with pastors or their views. The object here was to discover the major complaints, justified or not, made by families against the church and religion.

3. Types of contact which the church makes with its families; help given individual families in their problems; definite program of counseling.

4. Types of participation of families in the church programs, projects, and leadership, which the church fosters regularly.

5. Types of recognition given to family success and progress by the church; definite forms of interest taken by the church in family achievements and goals, in developments and accomplishments of children, etc.

6. Doctrines of the church which have some definite effect upon some aspect of family life—its organization, functioning, attitudes, permanency, policies, discipline, atmosphere of the home, etc. This refers both to marriage and to parenthood.

7. Amount of specific parent education carried on by the church—types of, nature of, methods in, by whom, appeal to what parent groups (young, mature, mothers, fathers), progress in, evidences of outcomes.

8. Amount of specific premarital education carried on by the church—types of, nature of, methods in, by whom, progress in, how made known to those young people who should be interested, evidences of outcomes.

9. Amount of education (direct or indirect, but of specific sort) of children toward marriage and homemaking, including sex education—when begun with the child, nature of, methods in, progress, evidences of outcomes.

10. Status of religious education within the family life of members of the church—how promoted by the church,

amount and type (if any) of preparation of parents for guiding religious development of their children.

11. Materials helpful in the above work, or that would clarify or illustrate.

12. References or recommended reading lists connected with any of the above work.

Replies (generally including materials being used) were received from every organization and individual on the list of contacts. It seems reasonable to assume that this practically unanimous and generous response of the churches evidences their alertness and readiness in this field of work with the family. All correspondents remarked the difficulty of giving definite reports at this time, because the work is at its beginning. Many spoke of handicaps in the way of lessened financial support and depleted staffs. In the majority of instances, work with the family had been undertaken in those one or two directions where some specific need forced it, but no adequate program had been built applicable to the whole local situation.

When it came time to organize all the assembled materials into a usable report, it grew evident that these were of a nature which did not at all allow tabulation and hence compression into the space available. If the reports had been reduced to a mere enumeration of the places where certain forms of work were going on, they would have had little significance, since no attempt had been made to secure a complete list of all such places. On the other hand, if all the distinctive, interesting, and valuable aspects of the work as given in each report had been presented, the material would have far overflowed this section of the book. The reports which are recorded here are based upon written statements, correspondence, books, and other literature submitted by officials of the church division under consideration.

Out of all the materials available concerning the following five major divisions of the church, such parts were selected as seemed to bear most directly on the interrelation of family and church. The programs and procedures representing the purposes and plans of the churches are proffered as submitted without estimate of the degree of success being made in fulfilling them. This pooling of present resources should provide critical contrasts and potential activators for further development.

The Roman Catholic Church

1. The Relation of Church to Family

"In the natural order, the union of husband and wife is a symbol of this intimate union of Christ and the Church in the supernatural order. There is the deepest fellowship of love and of life between them." "The primary purpose of the family is the propagation of the human race." "Parents know that they are the chosen instruments of Divine Providence for peopling the abode of the blessed . . . that they cooperate with God himself in bringing into existence beings destined to praise and enjoy Him forever in Heaven. They know that every child they receive is a gift of God." "The family's final aim—the education of children for Heaven. Above all else it is the soul of the child for which the parents will have to render a strict account on the day of judgment; and it is the religious and moral training of their children, therefore, that constitutes their paramount duty to their offspring."

The church is now exerting special effort to establish on a stronger and more universal basis the Christian ideals of marriage and family life. She holds up the Holy Family of Nazareth as the embodiment of all that is holy and wholesome in family life and as the example for the members. The church regards the father as head of the family whose first duty is "to foster home life by his example as well as by providing reasonable recreational facilities." Where disagreement does come, "then it is the duty of the wife to submit to her husband, so long as no violation of moral or religious duty is involved." However, despotic power in husband and father is condemned. So also are these condemned: unnatural limitation of family; conjugal infidelity by either husband or wife; divorce; living beyond the family means or in association with forms of pagan worldliness; and all activities of mothers, even social or political, incompatible with full performance of family duties. The church recommends home ownership, attractive homes, and closer fellowship within the family. It urges that parents command the cooperation of older children to influence the interests and activities of the younger children in the family. Bishop Edwin V. O'Hara, for instance, stated in an address: "The central issue of our time is the maintenance, economically, socially, culturally, philosophically and religiously, of the monogamic family—the school of character and virtue, the shelter of childhood—the citadel of women's characteristic qualities, the noblest responsibility of man. . . . It is the chief shame of capitalism that it has struck at the family by destroying the economic security of the home."

2. The Development of the Work

Present-day interest of the church in promoting parent education derived its initiatory impetus from the Pope's encyclical on the "Christian Education of Youth." Here he calls attention to the fact that "the parent is the educator *par excellence* and that the home is the school of schools." The Pope insists that "the first natural and necessary element in the environment (for education) . . . is the family." The specific nature of the program for parent education is evident in these words of Pope Pius XI: "And this should be done not in a merely theoretical way, but with practical and specific application to the various responsibilities of parents touching the religious, moral and civic training of their children, and with indication of the methods best adapted to make their training effective, supposing always the influence of their own exemplary lives."

In 1931, the Family Life Section of the Social Action Department of the National Catholic Welfare Conference was organized, using the major part of the time of a trained leader. Work was done through the National Council of Catholic Women by means of their Committee on the Family and Parent Education set up in 1930; other agencies were also active. This council is an integral part of the National Catholic Welfare Conference. The very apparent need for coordination of the work and for a scholarly or scientific approach to the important field of the family and parent education led to the organization in 1933 of the Catholic Conference on Family Life. Its first members were Catholic scholars interested in the family. Later, membership was extended to the mass of Catholic people. In 1934, this conference started publication of an official organ, *The Catholic Family Monthly*. This periodical discusses a wide variety of subjects of interest to families and is distributed through both individual and parish subscription. The program includes the building up of an extensive pamphlet list dealing with topics pertaining to Catholic family life.

3. Present Program of Work

Besides continuing the work cited above, study clubs are being promoted both by the national director of the Family Life Section, and by the diocesan units of the National Council of Catholic Women, and other organizations. The trained director spends much of his time answering requests from the field for information, literature, and guidance in developing local work. Pressure is being brought upon pastors to prepare themselves as expertly as possible in understanding the family and in promoting its welfare and education. Some foci of the work are here listed: betterment of housing, correction of bad moral conditions, meeting problems of unsanitary conditions, lack of play space and suitable recreational facilities, bad industrial conditions, and unjust economic conditions. Another direction of effort is the development of a popular and advanced literature on the family and parent education, including study texts and outlines. The organized promotion of suitable social life on the parish basis to foster sounder choice of friends and mate is under way, as is a movement to clean up the films and other amusement agencies.

4. Means for Carrying Out the Program

Besides the means obviously implied in the above, these are used: much symbolism regarding the Holy Family; the solemn celebration of the Feast of the Holy Family; a highly impressive marriage service; Sunday sermons; organization of children into such groups as Catholic Scout troops, and of young people into various sodality groups on a parish basis; special talks to these groups; instruction at retreats; religious courses in Catholic parish and vocational schools; provision of universities and other higher institutions of learning; maintenance of a vast staff of unmarried religiously devoted men and women who, at minimum expense and with great zeal, perform the functions of the Church; guided private reading and study at home; encouragement of specific preparation for marriage ("a good confessional," "a retreat before marriage," or a "quiet hour's reflection in the Church each afternoon for a few days before the wedding," and the Nuptial Mass as "the liturgical elaboration of the contract"); publication of banns; instruction of prospective bride and groom in rights and obligations as Christian husbands and wives when they present themselves to have banns announced; the teaching of Catholic children from their earliest years of the fundamentals of Christian marriage as set forth in the church's catechism; insistence upon, and guidance of, the home education of the young through example and instruction; training in familiarity with the articles constituting the Pope's encyclicals on "Marriage and Education of Youth"; gradual development of a "remarkable code of marriage laws" which exclude divorce; counseling by the parish priest, largely through confessional, in individual and family difficulties; research in Catholic medical schools to support stand on birth control; organization of the Maternity Guild to insure suitable maternity care to member-mothers; plan for sex education incorporated in general character training; clubrooms for group activities; recreation centers; and a program of social and recreational activities for the various age levels.

Besides these regular procedures, there are a variety of special projects. Two instances will illustrate these: "More than five thousand families in the diocese of Great Falls, Montana, are enrolled in about five hundred study groups which devote the eight weeks preceding Christmas to a study of subjects pertaining to the family and parent-child relationships. . . . One hundred of these groups are comprised of boys and girls of high school age or a little over. Some of the groups consist of men only and some of women, others are mixed. Membership has increased steadily during the four years that the program has been in operation." Each parish has a chairman of study groups with a staff of unpaid leaders selected for their ability in reference to the particular group they are to lead. The diocese includes three hundred square miles.

"The Youth Institute held at the National Catholic Social Service School, Washington, D. C., June 22–28, 1936, devoted considerable attention to preparation for marriage and family life.

The Church of Jesus Christ of Latter-Day Saints (The Mormon Church) Founded in 1830

1. The Relation of Church to Family

The family is the unit in the thinking and planning of the church. The individual is important because he is a part of the family. The principle behind the program of the church is the eternal nature of the family relationships. The church recognizes two kinds of marriage, one for time which ends at death, one for eternity which is everlasting. This doctrine of the eternal nature of family relationships gives the family great cementing power. The members are urged not to defer marriage too long, and marriage is considered a religious duty. Children are welcomed because of the belief that man is a preexistent being and that there are always hosts of spirits waiting for the privilege of coming upon earth and becoming members of clean and wholesome families. The Mormons recognize that there is sometimes occasion for divorce, but the rate is low and each case is dealt with upon its merits as far as the church has authority.

The church is trying to build up an ideology of the family which will elevate family living. It teaches, "As the family is so the church will be." It keeps vivid the virtues and achievements of the pioneer families. The family is responsible for the condition of the individual and for his social attitudes. There is no double moral standard: husband and wife must meet, equally clean; those who commit sexual sin are excommunicated; all these things are talked about freely in the family. The position of women is very high: women were given franchise from the start;

they have carried on much of the most important work of the church, such as buying and storing grain for bad years in the early period and having deep responsibility for the social conditions and problems in the wards at the present time. However, men are held to be the spokesmen, women the childbearers and trainers, the latter assumed to be too busy to undertake priestly duty. Since there is no pastor in the local church, the responsibility of the members is greatly increased; the local bishop has his outside vocation as has any member. The Mormon men take their fatherhood responsibly, for each is a priest and has high standards to maintain. The church tries to foster family life in such a way that economic, social, and emotional needs are reasonably cared for, thus freeing the parents to train the children in the arts of life for social ends, not as mere producers. There are church-wide plans for sharing between families. The church looks upon the family as the normal condition which determines true human happiness and progress. This elevation of the family by the church tends to have a restraining and guiding influence upon choice of mate and upon participation by youth and young married couples in the "destructive follies of the age."

2. Development of Specific Work with the Family

The Mormon Church was organized in 1830; the Nauvoo Relief Society, in 1842. The organization of this latter society marks the beginning of the program for the family. Because the early days were marked by pioneering and persecution, its work involved dealing with the serious social problems at hand. It centered in work with the family—housing, employment, sickness, dependency, transportation, exchange of thought and of experience, and the like. The "Necessity Committee" of this early period was the forerunner of the corps of visiting teachers of today who call upon every family once a month. Teacher's topics to be used in family visiting were first introduced in 1916 and made requirements in 1923. The teachers have much latitude in using the materials, depending upon the type of home visited. In 1928, a regular monthly training meeting for visiting teachers was instituted and is still so held.

At present there is no regular continuous work in parent education, though it is being planned for. The problem to be met is that of the preponderance of older parents who have finished a number of training courses in the same group with many younger parents and some new ones. The direction of effort has been reversed in work now going on. Instead of emphasizing the training of parents, the church is training the children and the young people in regard to their family relationships, interests, and conduct.

Two special projects have developed in work with the family which are worthy of notice. One of these projects is evidenced in the publications: *The Relief Society Magazine, The Improvement Era,* and *The Children's Friend.* These are the official organs by which the church reaches the family. The second project is evidenced in assemblies of an educative type: the annual June conference for Young people, the annual January conference for leaders, and the summer school at Brigham Young University. These schedule direct work in education for marriage and parenthood.

3. Present Program

Besides continuing the work cited in the preceding section, there is emphasis upon these matters: a recreation program full enough to leave no unsatisfied hungers; activities which bring together groups of families and promote family and group unity; development of the artistic aspect of the home life; guiding the family in maintaining adequate physical, economic, and social standards; guiding young people in social practice; training a few workers in social case work and home nursing so that these may instruct the hundreds of members who participate in this service of the church; and undertaking a church-wide project for taking all members off relief rolls and keeping them off.

4. Means for Carrying Out the Program

Besides those means quite evident in the preceding section, these are used: many social affairs for the whole family; annual father's and sons' outing over a week end; annual mother's and daughters' get-together; supplying a nutritional code, "The Word of Wisdom," to guide parents in promoting health; general radio programs from headquarters for youth, arranged to meet specific felt needs; special lectures and courses on home improvement; some use of psychological tests as well as physical examinations in understanding children; opportunities for young and old to represent their organizations by speaking at conferences, and to express themselves at the Sunday-evening meetings when they are asked to state their views; opportunities for every man and woman to teach and preach and hence enlarge group consciousness; building up a social service and scholarship fund so that students may get training in this field; arranging summer trips for the malnourished; running a storehouse for clothing and supplies that may be needed by families at any time; strict tithing system to provide for sharing; special work in social hygiene for youth from twelve to twenty; advisors for young people on college campuses where there are enough students to warrant it and the formation of Deseret Clubs where not enough; counseling carried on by bishop on informal basis; generous libraries of publications; and other such.

The church at one time had a number of academies but these have been turned over to the government. It still has its own institutions at the college and university level and also a number of seminaries for week-day instruction in religion at junior- and senior-high-school levels. One means widely and skillfully used by the church which pervades its work is the fostering of the development of new symbols and the appreciative conservation of existing symbols of a sort to be understood and cherished in the life of today; the handbooks of the various age levels provide evidences of this. An effective and long-used means for promoting unity and democracy in the family is the established custom in each church family of reserving one evening each week regularly for the fellowship within the family, when its plans and hopes, its difficulties and its problems, its purposes and its values are discussed, and when each makes an effort to contribute toward the joy of the evening.

The Church of Christ, Scientist. Founded 1879

1. The Relation of the Church to the Family

The individual is the unit in the thinking and planning of the church. The family is definitely recognized, however. Mrs. Eddy wrote: "Home is the dearest spot on earth, and it should be the centre, though not the boundary, of the affections." [1] Other writings emphasize the home as the "very core of individual and national well-being," and call attention of those concerned to their moral responsibilities. The emphasis in teaching fine living within the family takes the form of exhorting individuals to put the principles and practices of the church in control of daily living. Each member of the family is expected to develop individually principles and practices for himself under the guidance of the ever-present God, divine Love. The Lesson-Sermon for the week is used in many families, for regular daily study by the individual in the home.

"The entire education of children should be such as to form habits of obedience to the moral and spiritual law, with which the child can meet and master the belief in so-called physical laws, a belief which breeds disease." [2] Children are admitted into membership in The Mother Church at the age of twelve on the same basis as adults. In branch churches children are accepted into membership in accordance with the by-laws adopted by the individual churches.

Members are urged not to go into marriage without due consideration of its obligations, its responsibilities, and its relation to individual growth and to influence upon the lives of others. The manual requires that the ceremony of marriage of a Christian Scientist shall be performed by a legally authorized clergyman. The textbook of Christian Science gives more than one entire chapter to marriage. It describes marriage as "the legal and moral provision for generation among human kind" and states that "until the spiritual creation is discerned intact . . . marriage will continue, subject to such moral regulations as will secure increas-

[1] *Science and Health*, p. 58.
[2] *Ibid.*, p. 62.

ing virtue." Much detailed advice regarding the relations in marriage is included, such as counsel regarding fidelity, chastity, and the establishment of the equality of women. It states that "separation should never take place, and it never would if both husband and wife were genuine Christian Scientists . . . marriage should improve the human species, becoming a barrier against vice, a protection to woman, strength to man and a centre for the affections." The text deplores the neglect of "education of the higher nature" which keeps marriage from so functioning. The greatness of the responsibility for sound "propagation of the human species" is emphasized, and it is stated that "the foetus must be kept mentally pure and the period of gestation have the sanctity of virginity." [3] Specific suggestions are made in this text regarding the nurture of the higher nature of children.

2. Development of Specific Work with the Family

The work of the church is almost entirely upon an individualized basis, guiding each individual member to understand and put into practice for himself the tenets for the church. Church members are exhorted to meet adequately and in fine spirit their family responsibilities, with realization of the importance of these, and also their responsibilities as citizens of their communities, their nation, and the world. Aside from this, there is no direct work with the family as such. While the church emphasizes emphatically that God is love, the way of salvation is not through communion with the group but is an individualized process. The duty and opportunity of each member is to realize his unity with God, to recognize his real selfhood as an individual expression of God, of infinite good. Such passages as the following teach this: "A personal sense of God and of man's capabilities necessarily limits faith and hinders spiritual understanding." "Man has no Mind but God." "Man cannot be separated for an instant from God, if man reflects God." [4] The church recognizes the importance of the family as a situation making large and worthwhile requirements upon every individual seeking to be a good

[3] *Science and Health*, pp. 56, 60, 62.
[4] *Ibid.*, pp. 312, 319, 306.

Scientist. It encourages fine family living. But its official program does not deal directly with the family as a communion of direct religious significance nor as a cultural unit. The importance of the family is held to be its effect upon individual members of society whether inside or outside the home.

Certain aspects of the church have their effect upon family life. "No officer of the Christian Science Church has the authority to plan any program for Christian Scientists or their children, either in the Church or in the home, other than that which is set forth in Mrs. Eddy's writings, or in the Church Manual, of which she is the author." [5] This requirement combined with the fact that the Bible and *Science and Health with Key to the Scriptures* are the only preachers in the church conditions the type of association among the members within the church. Second, though there is a Sunday School for children, there are no official group organizations for the children and young people, though in some localities voluntary groups of the latter are growing up. Third, there is a large number of practitioners whose work is that of healing individuals. Fourth, the church publishes an international daily family newspaper encompassing a wide variety of departments. The immense power of this organ for interpreting developments and shaping attitudes can scarcely be estimated.

The Jewish Congregations, Orthodox, Conservative, and Reform

1. The Relation of Church to Family

Historically, the attitude of the Jewish Church toward the home has been of a high order. During the Middle Ages, the external world was so hostile and cruel to the Jews that, if they were to make any adjustment to life, they had to have a happy home life. Jewish families lived in a continual crisis, and hence family unity, love, and loyalties were strengthened. These family traditions have been weakened somewhat in the average home by modern forces. "The father in the home is the bread-winner, and his authority is only that which his wife permits him to wield.

[5] *Church Manual*, p. 27.

But in the Jewish home touched by the modern spirit, the organization is a democratic one, launched in a cooperative venture."

There have been no church pronouncements on marriage for hundreds of years, the last one being against polygamy.

On the whole, the Jewish churches emphasize strongly the significance of the family. This is manifest in many ways, of which the following are concrete examples: women have equal rights with men in the synagogue and in the home; girls are confirmed with the same interest and educational preparation as are boys; "habitual drunkenness is almost unknown in Jewish families"; there is no opposition to birth control on the part of the temple, and it is widely practiced.

2. The Program of Work and the Means for Promoting It

"Synagogical organizations are beginning to pay more and more attention to the problem of counteracting the centrifugal forces in modern life. . . . Up to recently, practically every Jewish festival was celebrated in the home as well as in the synagogue. The spiritual implications as well as the folk elements were stressed." This greatly strengthened family loyalties. Effort is now being made to restore these practices. Today there is fresh pressure against intermarriage. Further, among the orthodox group there is renewed concern for "stimulating the observance of the Jewish laws with reference to abstaining from intercourse during the menstrual period and a week beyond, and the ritual purification of woman at the end of the period of abstinence. They are issuing tracts on the subject, preaching from the pulpit, etc. At times, organized efforts are made to stimulate the observance of the dietary laws, the Sabbath, and the festivals."

"The principal problem that the synagogue is facing now with respect to the family is the fact that membership does not imply membership of the family as a whole. The synagogical activities do not touch each age group of the family and do not integrate the activities of these age groups. Both the conservative and the reform unions of the Jewish Church are working on this problem. Another endeavor purposes the coordination of the congregational school with the home by stressing in the school the skills and information useful to the child in participation in home observances and informing parents as to a time when their children are ready for such participation."

The two more liberal unions mentioned just above are organizing institutes on marriage and family life. Their method is to have several lecturers address themselves to various phases of the problem and so stimulate inquiry and consultation on the part of members. These areas are being discussed at conferences of Jewish young people, also.

The rabbis of the more progressive synagogues are doing a considerable amount of counseling on family problems, as well as promoting premarital education, in so far as their time allows. In the great majority of instances, this education is limited to an interview before the wedding ceremony. A few of them have a full-time professional psychologist or psychiatrist on the church staff, particularly for the work with the parents on behavior problems and guidance of growth. Some others refer those in difficulty to professional workers.

The Women's League of the United Synagogue of America has published *The Three Pillars*, as a factor in its effort to improve marriage. Occasional sermons on marriage and the family are delivered. The Central Conference of American Rabbis has recently appointed a Commission on Family and Marriage, which will prepare studies for young people's groups, and otherwise promote better living in the family.

One rabbi thus sums up his view of the needs of the Jewish Church in these matters: "The church must lead, not follow, in sex education, instruction in intelligent birth-control and sterilization, and other foundational matters. Religion must be integrated with the life people are leading and not given over to ancient history, badly taught, or archaeology and relics of a by-gone age. . . . The church has altogether too many activities manned by amateurs. It ought to concentrate on a few and do them well. All churches need not specialize on the same needs. But some human interests and needs, such as family organization and activities, premarital education, adult education, personal counseling, and parent education, all churches must take care of with increasing effectiveness."

The Protestant Churches: about 212 Denominations

With so many divisions as go to make up the Protestant Church it is inevitable that there be all sorts of variations in the quantity and quality of the work among these churches. Only the general outlines of the situation, therefore, can be indicated.

1. The Relation of Church to Family

Through long years the unit for the church has been the individual but recently there has begun a decided swing toward considering the family as the unit in the church. The sacramental celebration of the more significant events in family life has been well established in the church, but with chief emphasis upon meeting the religious standards of the church rather than upon promoting the communion of the family. Consequently these practices have become conventionalized and routinized in many instances. The concern of the local church for its own families, however, has almost always been peculiarly specific.

The church is now trying to clarify and formulate systematically its position in regard to marriage and the family. Rather, it should be said that the more progressive denominations are doing so. In this undertaking the Federal Council of Churches and the International Council of Religious Education are doing much of the leading, though some of the denominational headquarters are specifically at work here, also. In 1929, the Federal Council released its first report on "Ideals of Love and Marriage," attempting to find the sound bases for modern Christian marriage. This report supported the permanent monogamic ideal of marriage, larger freedom in marriage, better management of the business of the family, intelligent control of the sex relation, more intelligent parental attention to children, and other important matters. In 1931, the report on "Moral Aspects of Birth Control" was released, carrying qualified approval of the use of contraceptives and including pertinent counsel. The third release, made in 1932, had to do with the "Intermarriage of Members of Different Christian Communions," and advised against such marriage where either church involved imposed intolerable conditions. A brochure on "Safeguarding Marriages" appeared in 1935. It is a very practical treatment intended for pastors, bound to increase their appreciation of the profound significance of marriage and the family, and their skills in fulfilling their part in the instituting of these. Other related issues are under study. For instance, there is now a plan to study the religious interest of the college student. This is certain to rebound into further study of the family and local church.

The Protestant Church recognizes no double moral standard and expects the father as well as the mother to devote himself to his family opportunities and responsibilities. The women through their organizations have carried much of the load of the practical work of the church, particularly in promoting missions and doing relief work among families. Women have high standing in the church socially, though not officially: there is still a strongly patriarchal flavor in the organization of the church. The family is regarded as the normal form of life. Recently, the church has made beginnings of fostering the fellowship of the family in specific ways, including some interest in relieving its insecurity due to economic conditions. Most of the Protestant churches discourage divorce strongly, some going so far as to forbid marriage with a divorcee. Multiform is the attitude of the church toward work of women outside the home, the temporal or eternal nature of family bonds, the age at which the child is ready for theological instruction, participation of youth and of women in the government of the church, and many other related matters.

2. *The Development of Specific Work with the Family*

Psychological study of the child carried on in academic circles at the end of the last century and since has become reflected in the religious education movement conspicuous in Protestant churches. A movement in parent education has now developed from this fresh approach to child education. An investigation made in 1931 of what the Protestant churches were doing in the way of parent education gave very meager findings. "In four cases parent education was interpreted as an essential part of adult education, though very little staff provision was made for it. . . . Several of the larger denominational agencies had assigned this responsibility to staff committees representing the workers with children, young people and adults." [6] The investigator did not locate one specialist in any of the denominations whose major responsibility was parent education.

Certain other factors have influenced the development of parent education—the realization of teachers that their work was discounted in the cases of children whose parents did not understand and cooperate; the discovery by psychologists and psychiatrists that what parents did in regard to their children tended to affect individuals for many years; the development of an experience-centered curriculum which meant study of marriage and parenthood for parents, and study of social life and relationships, problems of approaching maturity, and marriage for the young people; and the increasingly evident maladjustment in marriage and parenthood even among church members. As these factors impinged upon the attention of church leaders, steps were taken to make education for marriage and parenthood the chief emphasis in adult education. Two organizations are contributing significantly to this work, the Federal Council of Churches and the International Council of Religious Education.

a. The Federal Council of Churches of Christ in America. The Council formally organized in January, 1927, a Committee on Marriage and the Home in connection with the Commission of the Church and Social Service. Under limiting conditions, this committee has continued its important work. The reports of this committee have been influential. Its plan of preparing reports is interesting—reading by all members of a selected list of books to secure common approach, monthly discussion of points of view, formulation of findings, and finally the criticism and revision of the report before its release to the press and the churches. At intervals one report after another has appeared.

Besides its reports, the committee has prepared two valuable

---

[6] Munro, Harry C.: "Parent Education in the Protestant Churches," *Parent Education*, June, 1934, p. 3.

bibliographies: *Bibliography of Education in Family Life, Marriage, Parenthood and Young People's Relationships* (1935) and *Bibliography on Young People's Relationships, Marriage and Family Life* (1932). It is interested in trying to work out study courses for young people and parents. It has approached the theological seminaries, offering to cooperate in the matter of developing plans for training ministers-elect so that they may go out into their profession conversant with the field of work with the family and prepared to lead their churches in this area: this training in leadership includes preparation to render at least elementary consultation service to disorganized families. Further, the committee has arranged and carried out field conferences treating of family life in several large cities, to the end of bringing marriage and family into the forefront of the thinking of the city workers. The policy of the committee has been to secure concerted action by denominational boards and social-service agencies. The committee has had the close and substantial cooperation of the American Social Hygiene Association. It has a full-time trained secretary who advises organizations, lectures, and writes certain of the needed materials.

b. The International Council of Religious Education. In 1931 this council set up a Joint Committee on Family and Parent Education to prepare materials from which curricula in the field of marriage and parenthood could be constructed. The committee consisted not only of representatives from other committees of the council which had allied interests, but also representatives from the Federal Council of Churches, the National Congress of Parents and Teachers, the National Council of Parent Education, and the Child Study Association of America.

In 1932, this committee communicated with some sixty churches reported as carrying on parent education. Their findings have been used as a basis for arousing more churches to action in the field.

In 1934, the committee issued in mimeograph form Book IV of the *International Curriculum Guide* in which there is a major section, "A Guide to Christian Education in Family Life and Parenthood." This section presents principles and objectives, materials from experience, considerations regarding leadership, and other items of direct importance to adult educators in this field. It is not a developed curriculum but a selection of resources for the building of curricula. It contains a tremendous amount of suggestive materials and formulations.

In 1934, also, the committee published a concise pamphlet, *The Church's Opportunity in Family and Parent Education*. The suggestions here made are practical and sound, and show familiarity with good educational procedure. Another pamphlet, *Home and Church Sharing in Christian Education*, published in 1935, contains further usable material. As the name implies, it deals particularly with the interaction of church and family.

In *Learning for Life Program*, a Systematic Guided Study Plan for Adults in the Church, published in 1935, there is a section on "Christian Family Life." An annotated list of study books is included.

The committee has worked cooperatively with the Committee of the Federal Council of Churches.

At the present time effort is being made to develop a United Adult Movement, one commission of which is on the Christian Home and Family Life. The Lake Geneva Conference of representatives interested in this project assembled in August, 1936. Many organizations participated. The report notes the present lack of leadership in the field and suggests areas where education is needed and the means for instigating it.

3. Means for Carrying Out the Program

These vary with the different denominations and with different local churches. Citing some types of church work with the family will suggest the existing diversity and resourcefulness.

The Baptist Church, Northern Convention, reports that a person has been in charge of parent education in the national office for eight years. Her office fosters this work in local churches and tries to keep in touch with the conditions in the field. Classes in home-building and courses in preparation for marriage and family visitation are emphasized. There is, as yet, no counseling program, and no adequate guidance of religious education in the home. No other Protestant denomination reported a national officer in parent education, though a number report this work as one aspect of the business of a national officer of education. All headquarters of denominations reporting said that they had no way of knowing how extensive or effective the work in their local churches is except through noting the ordering of supplies or through making field trips. The Episcopal and Unitarian churches are supporting unusually active programs and work closely with the Federal Council of Churches. Their work becomes evident in literature and bibliographies, in study courses, discussions, conferences, family welfare projects, and other efforts.

Training for family life is particularly strong among The Friends. They base their work upon the conviction that religious unity contributes to the unity of the family. Definite writings of the church suggest disciplines and queries for the guidance of the members. Particular emphasis is placed upon premarital education of the young people. Marriage between Quakers normally calls for the effort of the individuals involved: it takes place without a minister, the participants saying their own vows in the presence of the meeting of the church. The integrity of the family is a prime concern of the church, and their divorce rate is unusually low.

Several denominations state that a report on the condition of the families within their national membership is made at the annual meeting of the church, and that this report influences the program for the following year. Particularly significant is a practice of the United Lutheran Church in connection with its biennial meeting. It consists of a report entitled, *Matters of General Social Interest*, which briefly puts specifically before the members the present conditions of American life which undermine human welfare and fulfillment: the status of divorce, social insecurity and exploitation, gambling, vice and drunkenness, the moving pictures, indecent literature, and the discreditable aspects of the conduct of secular education particularly in institutions which train for teaching. This report is discussed at the convention and specific recommendations are developed for use in local churches. Incidentally, this denomination supports visiting secretaries who confer with authorities and students at institutions of learning where Lutheran students are enrolled.

Materials to be used in parent education and in premarital education are appearing with increasing frequency in the official publications of most denominations. Here again reference may be made to a form of this service developed by the United Lutheran Church. It consists of a packet of twelve letters to parents effectively gotten out, to be sent quarterly during the first three years of a child's life. Also, there are cards for the child for the first three birthdays. The envelope holding the packet furnishes place for a record of the use of these letters with the parents. An item reported repeatedly is a series of sermons or forums scheduled by ministers in the churches. Perhaps the most universal and significant piece of work at present is guided study in this field at the numerous conferences of young people, local and national. Most denominations reporting indicate that the younger pastors are more or less prepared to do some counseling.

In a number of the denominational year books there has appeared within the last decade some statement of the social ideals of the church, as for instance the book of 1935 published by the National Council of Congregational and Christian Churches. These statements are vigorous, forthright, and high-minded. The Congregational and Christian churches (merged in 1931) created The Council for Social Action in 1934, aiming to make the Christian gospel more effective in national and world-wide society.

Quite rightly local churches are becoming less and less of one type. This is a promising sign of growth. There is a vast difference between a certain church reporting from St. Paul, Minnesota, and another reporting from New York City, though both are Baptist. The former is located in a district which contends against terrific economic problems but has a membership which includes a wide cultural spread from the economic, the racial, the political, and the educational points of view. This church literally lives with its families. There is much cooperative activity and much counseling. The religious and social activities of the church are planned in the light of the circumstances and conditions of the communicants: the spirit is democratic, but even then poor clothing is a very real problem for many fine young people. Much use is made of other community agencies. The report sounds as though no two hours, much less days, of work in this church had ever been or could ever be the same; the work is all so very close to the vital issues of modern human living. In contrast, the New York church with its numerous offices, schools and clubrooms, its own playhouse, playground, and garden, carried an annual budget of a quarter of a million dollars for the years 1936–1937, less than one-twelfth of which, however, was allocated to religious education. A recent article by the pastor in the church paper makes a strong plea to the members for a deeper interpretation of Christian fellowship, and calls attention to the increased Christian responsibility which goes with superior equipment and better circumstances for this church. Three parent groups meet each Sunday morning. There is a cooperative nursery school charging tuition to pay costs. It has a project in parental conferences in connection with it. There is a counseling service in the church, also. Cooperation with a near-by university raises the quality of the leadership responsible for these developments.

A Christian church of Kentucky reports a definite program of counseling, a family visiting committee composed of experienced, sympathetic women, weekly dinner conferences with parents meeting in a small group, great emphasis upon the family pew, private lending library including books for parents, a project in adult education consisting of a weekly forum and supper where vital human interests are discussed, some sex education of adolescent boys and premarital interviews.

A Congregational church in Los Angeles is interested in a dynamic and socially responsible church fellowship but it must compete for participating members with all sorts of religious cults, from the large, conventional churches where one's conscience is never disturbed to the tent meetings offering soul-warming, ecstatic experiences with an otherworldly focus. But this church is trying a notable project. It seeks to lead each family in its constituency to work out its problems within its own communion primarily on two bases: (1) give-and-take discussion, and (2) genuine family worship specifically prepared for by relevant guided meditation. There are workers in the church equipped to guide parents in their efforts and simpler problems. The pastor has developed a more meaningful marriage service, reproduced in a little booklet into which are bound also excerpts from literature dealing with the sex aspect in marriage.

A large Presbyterian church in Chicago has a pastor who keeps marriage and family living in mind continuously as the plans for the church year are made, and the program shows this concern in a variety of ways of which a series of sermons, discussions, and opportunities for counseling are only the more obvious. Group fellowship is much stressed here.

One church in Denver, Colorado, shares its equipment and leadership with the community quite literally. All sorts of social organizations hold their regular meetings in its building, and have their symbols on its walls along with those of the church and the nation. These organizations include trade unions, mothers' clubs, an emergency training school for teachers of nursery school, children's clubs, and so on through a very long list. The regular services of the church are attended by an unusual group of keenly alert persons, not at all homogeneous. They are gathered there because they know that they may speak their minds and ask for enlightenment on any subject so long as they are sincere and are concerned for the social good. The church is guiding the actual processes of social living, not merely preaching about them. At any hour of the week, it is a beehive of enterprise connected with vital issues, very different from the exclusive, silent desertness of many churches.

The director of religious education of the Southern California Conference of the Methodist Episcopal Church arranges for a seminar for pastors and church workers each winter, when, for a full week's time, they study earnestly various aspects in this field or closely related ones. The annual character of the work allows for reports of progress and creative cooperation in regard to specific undertakings.

A number of churches, particularly suburban and rural ones,

report the beginnings of effort to restore the church as the center of the community life of their constituencies. The increase in unwholesome and degrading forms of associational life outside the church is one of the prime factors forcing the building within each of these churches of a closer communion, of a fellowship of families, of a cultural neighborhood.

Community churches usually show, also, more evidence of being a cultural neighborhood than does the average church. One in Columbus, Ohio, includes these items in its report: morning church service distinguished by the number of families sitting together; pre-Easter meetings, called a School of Larger Life, in which religion and the family are emphasized, and which include work in arts and crafts as important parts of the home program; use of Mother's Day as an occasion for the interpreting of the functions of parenthood; suppers for small groups of men as opportunities to gain better understanding of their children and of the social forces which play upon the family; a behavior clinic; and vocational guidance of the young people. Another community church in East Lansing, Michigan, reports the co-operation in the building of its program of the secretaries of the national boards of education of four different denominations, of representatives of the Y.M.C.A. and Y.W.C.A., and of members of the church; open door on the part of the pastor at regular hours and also of the two full-time student directors; specific effort to incorporate more members into the functioning of the church, partly through limiting the maximum time of service of officers and committeemen; the Easter family visitation when from fifty to seventy couples (husbands and wives) call upon one or two families each; and the practice of asking all, old and young, to write upon cards any subject or problem concerning which they would like to have interpretation or guidance through the program of the church.

On the whole, the statement that the Protestant churches have become family-conscious seems justified. Only a small proportion as yet have instituted specifically planned programs for their work with the family, but the leadership is very much awake and at work.

CREED-FREE FELLOWSHIPS

A number of reports indicated the contributions to family welfare being made by fellowships united in the search of sounder and higher truth for the guidance of living but unbound by traditional creeds. Freedom of thought and speech characterize these groups. They are worthily represented by the Ethical Culture Society whose program of moral education has long attracted the attention of the country. Most of these institutions are much like community churches in their programs of activity. A report from a local "Temple" of "truth-seeking people" of Cincinnati lists its "Temple College," thirty-two weeks of day and evening classes; its "Life Adjustment Clinic and Institute of Family Relations" with a staff of several trained members; a course for parents; and many timely projects. These latter are illustrated by a series of meetings on marriage and parenthood, sponsored by the Junior Temple, in which more than eight hundred one-dollar tickets were sold by young people so that experts could be engaged as leaders in the project. Under various names these creed-free fellowships seem to be developing throughout the country. In most instances they hold themselves quite ready to cooperate with all other organizations in improving local or regional conditions of human living, though a certain percentage of them are activated by the profit motive, each individual interested in benefit for himself.

COMMUNITY COOPERATION WITH THE CHURCH

It is both encouraging and significant to note the increase in quantity and quality of cooperation being extended to the church in its work with the family. Space allows for only the briefest mention of some of the more important examples.

First there is the large group of organizations which exhibit a willingness to cooperate when they are called upon in matters of leadership and materials. Among these are some of the family counseling centers (as, for instance, The Philadelphia Marriage Counsel), the Council of Social Agencies, the Coordinating Council of city or county, the Home Economics Departments of certain state universities (as in Illinois and Iowa), a number of the character-building clubs (including the Scouts and Camp Fire Girls), the National Congress of Parents and Teachers, governmentally supported departments of parent education and of adult education, and the more progressive among the seminaries and divinity schools. An example of this last is the Pastors' Institute, sponsored each summer by the leading divinity schools and seminaries, where at least a beginning is offered in training for work in the field of family-church interfunctioning. In addition to the resources made available by all these organizations, many ministers report that they have received peculiarly helpful assistance upon request from professionally trained individuals whose work is located in their communities. Most frequently cited are those specialists, university professors, and other teachers whose field is concerned with the family, psychologists, psychiatrists, physicians, and social case workers.

Besides these available resources, there are a number of organizations which have carried their willingness to cooperate far enough to have established specific services. The public-school system of Long Beach, California, through its Adult Education Department, launched in the spring of 1937 an Institute of Character Training for all persons interested, but with the local churches specifically in mind. The ministers and rabbis were responsible for publicizing the course and recruiting the teachers who needed training, the public school for developing the courses and providing the staff and setting. Seventy-five per cent of the adults enrolled (about three hundred) worked for the credential granted by the International Council of Religious Education. The heart of the work is training in modern methods of character education, which includes psychology of learning and techniques of teaching. Hendrix College, a denominational college in Conway, Arkansas, maintains on its staff a professor who spends his full time in regional parent-education work and this college also has cooperated closely with a field worker of the Southern Methodist Church who is undertaking substantial projects with culturally underprivileged families on the basis of improving the conditions of family life, not drumming up church membership.

The definite cooperation of the National Council of Parent

Education, the American Social Hygiene Association, the National Congress of Parents and Teachers, and the Child Study Association of America with the International Council of Local Religious Education has already been cited. These organizations are generous in their attitude toward church needs, also. The Institute of Family Relations in Los Angeles lists the following as its regular modes of service: furnishing to church workers speakers, information, material, and references; taking clients seeking counsel who are referred by them; putting on special conferences and seminars for them; and providing a correspondence course in the technique of counseling helpful to them. The family counseling department of the Associated Charities of Cincinnati is developing some very interesting techniques of group approach to work with the family and is making its services available to churches. In a few cities, the municipal recreation department furnishes trained leadership and guidance to supplement and coordinate the work of the local churches in their own recreation program. A number of public schools have furnished specific cooperation in adjusting their programs and facilities to accommodate local churches which plan week-day educational or other activities for children, young people, and parents.

A particularly promising type of experiment in school-family-church cooperation is being carried into its seventh year by the Merrill-Palmer School of Detroit. A brief account of the work deserves place.

Our religious education experiment has been essentially an exploration in an attempt to gain an understanding of the innumerable and sometimes intangible aspects of religious education or religious growth of young children. In conducting Church School groups of children, ranging in age from 2½ to 10 years, the approach has been a general rather than a denominational one. Emphasis has been placed upon the child's social growth, his happy associations with the church, the development of his appreciation and understanding of his own immediate world and of a larger world.

It has been asked how the work with the children is related to what is going on in the homes in the way of religious education. Through questionnaires and reports which the parents are asked to fill out, through personal interviews and home visits, as well as through parents' meetings, we have attempted to determine what the parents wished their children to gain, and what responses of a social and religious nature their children were showing. Furthermore, through letters summarizing the program and through the weekly pages which the children take home, the parents are informed concerning the present emphasis and trend in the group. In general, the parents of the children in our groups have been encouraged to feel that they are exploring with us this field of religious education, that we are studying the questions with them and do not necessarily know the answers.

We have attempted to relate our program to the church by supplying experiences which help the children to realize that they are a part of a church, or an institution, or a religious interest, which includes many people. The children have seemed to develop a feeling for the church and an increased understanding of it by such experiences as going into the church when others are not present to look around and talk about it, by listening to the organ, by going into the church when services are being conducted to observe or to participate, by having adults such as choir members and ministers whom they have seen in the church services meet with them in their own small group, in their own small room. The churches in which we are conducting our study have been very interested in it and willing to cooperate in any possible way.

These examples of what is going on in the way of community cooperation with the churches are encouraging evidences of the increase of community resources open to the churches.

SOME IMPLICATIONS FOR THE FUTURE

There can be no question of the fact that the church has launched upon a seriously purposeful program of work with the family. A number of outcomes will characterize developments. First, the total program of the church will become a more unified one, for interest in the family will require a reappraisal of the many scattered interests of the church. Then, as has been emphasized, such a program will require the development of sound philosophies of religion, of social living, and of religious education. Next, it will require an equally sound and a normative psychology of religion, together with effective psychological methods in religious work. In this is implied more efficient and appropriate instrumenting of the program, which in turn implies a plan of more adequate financing. The Church of Christ, Scientist, has met this last need in a practical way—every member of the church is assessed one dollar per year for the support of the national and international work aside from all special contributions for specific causes.

As these and related developments emerge, the church will begin to build its relations with other community institutions on the basis of greater equality of status, eventually of superiority of status, because of the universal and selfless nature of its objectives. This will not only bring more adequate support to the church, but it will increase tremendously the power of the church.

Perhaps the most important practical implication is the change in the education of the leaders of the church. Their schooling in regard to the religion and theology of the past must become not the main occupation but rather only a thorough preparation for a better understanding of religion at work in the modern world, of the germinative centers of religion, and of the methods by which growth of good and of meaning can be promoted through their field of work. This will necessitate field work in such institutions as child-welfare centers, courts of domestic relations, juvenile courts, counseling centers, institutes of family relations and nursery and other schools which are seeking to institute genuine education. They need to understand the normal functioning of the family and how its health and effectiveness can best be promoted, particularly by religious interests. The selection and training of the leaders must become a major concern of the modern church working in a modern world.

Chapter XIV

PROGRAM FOR THE CONSERVATION OF
THE FAMILY

A SOUND family spirit is the only thing that can save the family. Except as the family can develop, sustain, and perpetuate such a spirit, it cannot hold its ground in these days when individual units remain unknown and powerless. This sound spirit must be the repository and the carrier of the more enduring truth, beauty, goodness, and unity which the experiences of thousands upon thousands of families discover or create. This spirit must become expressed in animating, activating principles which shall govern the establishment, objectives, and functioning of the myriad of individual homes which are the embodiments of it. Actual families are the vehicles by which these animating, activating principles enter individual, human experience.

The spirit of the family is its life principle. It determines the character and the disposition of the family; actuates and controls its manners, customs, and achievements; affects its genius, and pervades all those expressions which constitute its ethos. The institution deteriorates when the spirit of the family becomes anemic or infected because of undue friction, folly or fraudulence, destitution, depravity or despair. When the spirit of the family no longer governs the living of a group, the family dies: it no longer has the right to the title *family*, however long the individuals may continue to occupy the same quarters and address each other by family terms.

It becomes clear, then, why it is true that only a sound family spirit can save the family. This does not lessen or void in the slightest degree the legitimacy of the call of the family for help upon other social institutions. Rather it indicates the nature of

the assistance required of them if their cooperation is to be fundamentally constructive. All counselors and physicians working
with individuals who are personally maladjusted or physically
ill know for a surety that no one of them has ever cured one single
individual. The most that the cleverest of them can do is to
better the conditions of the individual so that he is facilitated in
curing himself. The physical and psychological powers of reconstruction in the human organism are marvelous past full understanding. And so it is with a social group which is trying to
be a family. No outside person or institution can cure it of its
ills nor make it into the fellowship characteristic of the normal
family. But the conditions of the family can be so fostered and
bettered that the family becomes able to restore itself and to
grow. As in the case of the individual person, so in the individual intimate group, the organic powers of reconstruction are
marvelous past full understanding. Professional work with problems of family adjustment reveals constantly the increased actual rate of speed of recovery as over against the estimated rate
in those cases where the spirit of the family still lives.

The life principle of the family is love. As has been stated,
love is not primarily a feeling but is, instead, a way of living, a
way of personal interacting. It builds the fellowship of the family through coercive and voluntary sharing of vital interests.
The processes of mutual expression, appreciation, and reinforcement of personality through which this takes place constitute
the communion of the family. The major part of this book thus
far has sought to indicate what soundness of spirit connotes as
it governs the inner life of the family. The conditions in which
the love-life of the family grows vigorous, rich, and meaningful have been discussed, together with practical measures for
fostering these conditions—measures particularly appropriate to
the work of the church.

This has led, perforce, to some exploration as to what soundness of family spirit connotes beyond the restricted inner circle
of the family. For sound family spirit is all one thing and it is
greater than any one family, greater than any one neighborhood
of families, greater even than the aggregate of all the families
of any one era. It is right and necessary, however, to start work-

ing for soundness of family spirit with actual families, preferably with beginning families. Whether considering the family
on the one hand, or the church or other cooperating social organization on the other hand, it is the immediate, intimate situations which must be cared for first. Both types of institution
must learn what soundness of spirit connotes for the intimate
life of the family and how it is fostered there before they are
ready, or have the right, to heighten the powers of the family
spirit in preparation for larger social functioning.

However, if building the soundness of family spirit stops with
the circumference of the family circle or even with the circumference of the circle which includes the family and its face-
to-face associates, two evils appear: (1) the spirit of the family
as a whole is provincial, dwarfed, and petty-minded; (2) what
soundness of spirit has been developed within the family circle
is blighted and deteriorates as soon as it crowds against the un-
yielding confines of that circumference which limits its growth.
It is with the promotion of the wholeness of sound family spirit
together with the empowering of it for wider social functioning that this last chapter is chiefly concerned. First of all comes
the question: "What are the conditions which will provide for
such progressively increasing growth, strength, and soundness of
the family spirit as will restore the family to a status in keeping
with its indispensable, distinctive functions?"

THE GROWTH OF SOUND FAMILY SPIRIT

First of all, it needs to be said that the conditions will not be
supplied by putting the family into some castle in Spain. Speaking literally, both castles and Spain seem to have proved themselves uncomfortable places for living. Speaking figuratively, the
well-equipped housing projects of industrial concerns and the
army and naval posts of the United States Government have not
yet been cited as examples of remarkably effective family functioning. Nor has organized relief in the form of doles done other
than sicken the family spirit. The modern family cannot expect
to be treated by modern society either as a helpless infant, as a
wandering waif, or as a cherished darling. Dame Society is too

much like the Old Woman Who Lived in a Shoe, the shoe in this case being a streamlined boot of skyscraper height, laced with strings made of power lines, political wires, and knotted human ties.

Nor will the conditions be supplied by trying to build society into a utopia where once and for all an idealized scheme of living is instituted. Such couldn't be, and wouldn't work if it were instituted, as the experiments of the communists have shown.

Again, revolution is not the answer, for while it may be a necessary means, as it was in 1776 and again in 1863, for cutting away an impossible old order, it does not build the new.

Most certainly of all, we cannot go back to old patterns of family living, for however effective they were at their time they would carry the family all the faster to disaster now. They would entirely disconnect it from the other fundamental social institutions as these appear today. Despite this fact, a number of churches and welfare organizations are still working toward this end by encouraging the family to have as little to do with this naughty world as is possible. A certain sector of the socially elite also struggle to push society backward in this direction by administering artificial respiration to antiquated, personality-warping family traditions. The objects and activities which occupy this latter group and upon which they establish their snobbery of "family" are so pitifully infantile and petty as to stir deep compassion over wasted human life and suffocated family spirit.

Lastly, the problem cannot be solved by empowering the family to dictate to all of society what it shall do and be. There might seem justifiable basis for this after contemplating two significant facts: (1) the family is the chief germinative center of the finest aspect of culture—genuine fellow feeling, true communion among mankind; and (2) the chief product of family investment—enriched, matured personality—is the most precious material in all the world. Unquestionably, control of society determined by the interests of the family would not be as disastrous as is the present dictatorship by organized economic interests, nor as the now threatening dictatorship of fascism. However, the family is not constituted for dictatorship. But more crucial still, society is too complexly interdependent to remain healthy and grow if controlled under the dictatorship of any one interest. The shocking degradation which marks the family when it is subjected without representation to an external dictator has been demonstrated in Germany.

Realigning Institutional Purposes

The rightful purpose of every social institution is to bring functional adjustment among the diverse interests and activities of humanity. Usually each institution represents one of these interests and works to promote and empower that one. Today, three great faults mar the functioning of social institutions in this respect. First, each has become so absorbed in furthering its own ambitions that it has neglected to study the other institutions and to build those connections between important interests necessary to truly abundant living and to greatest human fulfillment. Second, the several types of institutions have not studied the new inventions and other developments that are changing our ways of acting, feeling, and thinking sufficiently to keep themselves continuously reshaped in the light of these. Sometimes they do not recognize developments in any of the major interests, not even in their own field of interest. This tends to be the case with some churches who are not quickened by sound developments even in the field of religion. Most of the time, however, each type of institution keeps reasonably abreast of developments in its own field, but surmises that its field is the only one that is importantly modern. An example of this is the attitude of most businessmen and scientists toward religion: their ideas of what religion is are often antiquated, totally unenlightened. An exception to this attitude is found in the relation of business and science to each other, each cognizant of the progressive modernity of the other.

The third fault of social institutions is that they have not as yet instituted (1) a sufficiently effective and comprehensive policy of, and (2) an adequate social instrument for, analyzing, evaluating, reshaping, and improving the functional connections between major social interests. In spite of the increasing seriousness of successive depressions and other indications, most citizens still feel that this reshaping of institutions must be a matter of a free-for-all scramble. In a simple, pioneer civilization where each institution has a modicum of independence and opportunity for expansion without infringing upon other institutions, this method may work for a time. But we have passed this period in our national history long ago. Every day increases our interdependence in a hundred ways and decreases the possibility of any one interest expanding independently without seriously affecting all other institutions for weal or woe. Realization of this is appearing in the form of increase in the rate of increase of organized minorities bent upon holding or clearing a way for their own ambitions or purposes as individual units. Conflict, unscrupulous and handicapping competition, and violence are the unavoidable outcomes. Organized groups that can command the power in any form are using it to their own ends. Unorganized groups that have not gained, or cannot command, power in any form are at the mercy of the chance which gives one organized group temporary power over the others.

Any group ardent in its own cause yet blind to the causes of others is a social menace. The foundations of our society can be despoiled with equal damage by either a well-schooled, power-hungry group or by an ignorant, suffering-maddened group. The processes pressing toward the interpenetration of major interests cannot be left to chance. There must be some perpetually functioning agency which will study and interconnect appropriately these major concerns of man. This is primarily the business of political institutions, enlightened by the soundest findings of philosophy and religion, of the sciences and the arts, but it is not yet attended to efficiently. This increases the responsibility of those institutions which see the need or which are suffering in the present barbaric chaos of conflict. Those which see must lead the way.

The solution must come through the coordinated and reciprocating reshaping of *all* institutions. We noted at the start the present helplessness of the family unit lost among the larger and aggressively organized social interests. No miracle can, like Samson, push away the heavy and sharp impediments with which other institutions are crushing and despiriting the family, and so free its growth and functioning. The whole process of reshaping and reconstructing the family must go on together with the processes reshaping and reconstructing society. Once instituted, this reshaping process must become an unending one. It is a slow, complicated task. However, it is not a hopeless one. Already there can be discerned promising directions in which effort can be invested with gain of effectiveness. In the particular area of the family there must be built a perpetual and perpetuating spirit, which is sound, growing, and powerful. In the earlier, less complexly interdependent years of our national history, the family quite naturally developed its own perpetual and perpetuating spirit. Today, for reasons already made clear, this spirit must be socially nurtured and empowered. Here are some of the developments involved in this cause which is calling to head, heart, and hand.

Fostering Maturity of the Family

Before the family can be urged to participate capably and responsibly in the life of the great society, it must itself become a full-fledged social institution. Few families, relatively speaking, are such. They may be social institutions of a limited type so far as their members and close neighbors are concerned, while at the same time being unsocial or antisocial from the point of view of their relations with the larger society. It is time that the American family grew up. No longer can it achieve significant fulfillment for its several members nor for the group as a whole unless continuous enlarging of social interest, participation, and devotion mark its functioning. More crucial still, unless the family achieves maturity it impedes general social reconstruction with the dead weight of its infantile helplessness.

This growth requirement of the family cannot be too strongly emphasized, for it is not yet specifically or even vaguely present in the consciousness of most families and social workers. There is a queer quirk in American thinking here. Everyone grants that the child must grow if he is to be normal and find fulfillment. Everyone grants that society must grow if it is to remain a human society at all. But the general notion regarding the family sees it as a formula for one sort of group life which does not change essentially from marriage until death except when broken into pieces. Though the child within the home and social institutions without the home are manifesting different needs and developments each day and each year, there is no expectation of continuous significant change in the family corresponding to these, much less the necessary planning for such change. It is no wonder that the present chief recourse from the monotony of life in the typical immature family takes some form of extra-marital experimentation in relationship among adults and excitement-mad diversions in youth. The challenge and thrill of participating in the growth of a family while it is achieving status as a social institution is beyond the ken of most families.

The process of socialization of the individual family resembles that of the individual person. The human infant launches into life under the control of self-interest and of hunger for bodily comfort and pleasure. A rich experience of satisfaction in these is essential to his growth. But if this were all of his experience he would become, as have many, a self-interested individualist with prime concern for the satisfaction of his private desires. Normally, however, he is educated into an awareness of the social source of his satisfactions and of the interdependence of all persons upon other persons and institutions for the conditions essential to abundant living. This eventuates in the development of social interest and of loyalty to social purposes and standards. So, essentially, is it with an infant institution. It is launched primarily under the control of interest-in-our-home and hunger for the comforts and pleasures which are involved. Here again, as has been pointed out, a rich experience of satisfaction in these is essential to growth. But here again also, there must be education into awareness of the social source and significance of these satisfactions, and of the interdependence of all groups upon other groups and institutions for the conditions essential both to abundantly meaningful living and to growth of culture. Finally, the sign by which the family manifests its advancement of status as a full-fledged social institution will be its responsible, interpenetrative, reciprocative interaction with other social institutons.

Following through the growth that is required in the sex relationship will illustrate the point. In as much as the drive and activities founded upon the sex appetite are an important part of marriage, this will be particularly rewarding. At the time of marriage, the young people have relatively few important shared interests, perhaps none that are of genuine significance in many cases. For physiological and social reasons, they are sex-hungry. The development of a mutually meaningful and satisfying sex relationship is a major interest. After a time, normally, other major human interests begin to press for attention, and sex interest, while remaining a major interest, takes its appropriate place among these others. It is potentially able to increase power, euphoria, and creativity in the pursuit of these other interests and to be enriched, integrated, and exalted to more thrilling and meaningful ecstasy through its connectedness with the great interests of life. But this can eventuate only if the sex interest, the sex hunger, is socialized, i.e., brought under integrative control with other great life interests.

Many leaders have noted that rational sex discipline is a prerequisite to highest achievement in cultural contribution. It is not a matter of willful repression, but of genuine integration. In spite of all this, the evidence today indicates that most marriages are still on the infantile, individualistic basis, where the devising of techniques for more voluptuously extravagant sexual episodes is almost an obsession and a profession, and where the ideal woman for many men is the one who can be most thoroughly and aesthetically domesticated for gratification when and as desired. Since this basis of sex satisfaction rests precariously upon physical sensitivity, and the stunting or enslavement of one of the two parties, it can be increased only by increasing the frequency and the intensity of the sensation or by further exploiting of the female, either one of which issues eventually in human impotence of one type or another.

The use of contraceptives affects the mating process in marriage. First of all, wise use releases energy (formerly expended in fear of pregnancy) for attention upon sexual adjustment as an aspect of the growing communion between husband and wife. In such service contraceptives are a very constructive factor. On the other hand, the use of them may seriously impede the maturing process. This happens when they become the means for permanent refusal of parenthood and for overindulgence in sex activity. Contraceptives are a form of power: they require control by the integrative objectives of husband and wife. If they are used as tools of unbridled license, sex attraction begins to pall: each wears the other out.

Shallow-minded consideration of the prevalence of this outcome has suggested the legalizing of abbreviated marriages, and so is encouraging the deterioration of marriage. The wedding takes only a few minutes, but marriage takes years upon years. It is not consummated until the two have developed and shared a large number of significant interests and integrated these each with the other into a life full of warmth, light, color, and rich meaning. The terms arranged for securing the satisfaction of the sex appetite can never be entirely a private matter, for this appetite is inescapably social in nature. First, it requires two persons. Second, it markedly conditions the quality and degree of social energy expended by these two. Third, it normally brings about the birth of one or more new members of society. Mutually satisfying expression is undoubtedly one standard for the sex interest, and it is a chief one during the immature beginnings of marriage. But growth through integrative control is an equally important requirement. As it takes place, marriage matures into a social institution.

Other aspects of family living which are at present quite generally in their infantile stage are numerous. These are on the long list: attitude toward the dwelling place—now treated as a play house, a doll house, a window display of wealth or position, headquarters for supply, or a life job for the wife and mother; the investment of the marginal time of the homemakers, particularly the women during the daytime and the men during evenings and week ends; the social and recreational tastes and activities of the family; the bases of the concern of the family for their neighborhood and town or city; the economic dealings of the family; and the connections of the family with sources of culture, reinforcement, and religious guidance.

The most important maturing of the family must occur in the enlarging comprehensiveness of its objective. In the infantile stage, the objective is, necessarily, the perfecting of the love and the living of its own limited circle for its own sake. This must grow gradually but surely into ardent devotion to the building of those conditions which shall promote a matured powerful fellow feeling and abundantly meaningful living for the great community. Only when this expansion of objective has occurred can the family consider itself mature. Only then can it claim full right to the title, social institution. Institutional membership is a reciprocal relationship of mutual allegiance and protection. The family cannot expect the concern of society to be powerful and creative in its behalf unless its concern for society is manifested in loyalty of the same caliber.

Locating the Necessary Impulsion

Earlier in this study the statement was made that it seemed doubtful if the genuine communion necessary to cultural maturing could be developed except where the sharing of interests was coercively induced. Accordingly, the biological and psychological coercions which force the sharing of vital interests, and hence the growth of communion among the individual members of the individual family, were located and described. Now when it has become evident also that the individual family cannot mature as an institutional unit except as it comes into genuine communion with the other institutions of the great society, the question arises, Are there any dependable, powerful coercions which compel the individual family to share the vital interests of the great community?

Search here is rewarding, also: there are at least two such coercions. They are parental ambition and fear for the children. These factors are psychological and social in nature, though inextricably and directly rooted back into the biological coercions which induce communion within the family. They are highly potent in arousing in adults unflinching solicitude concerning social conditions and progress. As soon as the child is able to go alone out of the door into the yard, from the yard into the street, from the street to the neighbors' or to school, to church or to places of recreation, just so soon do the parents begin to deepen their concern for what he will find in all of these places and what will happen to him in the finding. Each new day in his life increases the size of the child's world. It adds its unique quota to the number of contacts he must adjust to, the diverse habits and ideals of all sorts of people with which he must interact, and the possibilities of danger, injury and tragedy as well as those of greater fulfillment. The parents share not only the building of his world with the child, but they become more and more acutely aware of the relation of his world to the actual world of work and play, of good and evil, and of culture and barbarism into which the child is maturing. Ambition concerning his future success grows within them. And so does fear for his security—physical, material, mental, social and spiritual.

It is necessary to digress here long enough to point out several important facts concerning these two coercions, parental ambition and fear for the children. First, since these forces are indirectly rather than directly rooted in the biological, there is greater chance that they will miscarry or fail in their work. Therefore they require deliberate attention and nurture from society. Second, ambition and fear are only propulsions toward taking more interest in society. They carry no indicators as to how this should be undertaken, and so each of them holds the possibility of constructive, negative or destructive outcomes. Here again the need of social attention and nurture is cardinal. Fear is all too likely to be looked upon as an evil force, but this is far from the truth. It is a very necessary force in inducing parents to care what the world which their children must live in is like. Constructively directed fear is *whole*-some, literally speaking, for it forces more penetrating evaluating and creative action. Society must recognize this neglected agency of family socialization—wholesome, stimulating fear—and give it adequate and wise direction. Third, we must face the fact that the present social conditions make it impossible for any one individual family to work out a sane program of facilitation and security for its children. Society is highly complex, frustratingly unstable, and disturbingly subject to the monopolies of power by specialized interests. This tends to discourage the average family and to make its concern in the forms of ambition and fear seem futile. But with intelligent social guidance, this frustration of parental ambition and concern can become the driving force for the union of families bent upon improving the conditions of the world of their children.

The child who is loved, therefore, is the carrier of those coercions which force the individual family to become actively interested in the conditions and activities of society. Because his growth requires that he gradually enlarge his own community of interests, he thus forces an enlargement in his parents, sometimes great, sometimes small, though usually incomplete and deformed in some respect. His leadership in the maturing of the family is unfailingly powerful. He provides the impulsions leading the parents to work upon the social environment of the family in the interest of the child. In these modern days this work must take two forms: participation in the community life as a responsible member; and promotion of social reconstruction when needed.

It has become apparent that there exist dependable coercions to force the maturing of the spirit of the family. But the coercions which induce the parents to care what society is like are compelling, not evaluating forces. The leadership of the child is unconscious and immature. It provides no discriminative selection of values.

Because the leading of the child is powerful yet unoriented, another type of resource must be found. There must be some cultural force that is concerned for the soundness of the spirit of the family as well as for its socialization, a force fostering the enlargement of its objective in accord with the greatest values man can know. This force cannot be the economic interest, nor the political one, nor the one concerned with secular education, nor any other one of the special interests. Although with each of these the family must learn to interact responsibly and capably yet, as a guide, any one of these would skew the direction of the growth of the family. There are examples where each of these specialized social forces has tyrannized over the family. The guiding force must be one which rises above partisan and specialized interests, which sees the need of coordinating these so that individuals and institutions will not continue to frustrate each other, and which seeks to build those conditions which shall establish interpenetrative fellow feeling among mankind. Such a force is genuine high religion. Its social instrument is the church shaped to perform this service. This church can and must nurture the growth of the family from its first beginnings as an individual group to its maturing as a responsible and creative social institution.

This is a major work of the church. That it is no mean undertaking becomes clear as soon as it is realized that every human being is a member of some family for a part of this period of maturing, the majority remaining members during the whole period, which occupies two-thirds of the life span. Thus the church through such nurture has the opportunity to vivify and establish the values and reinforce the outthrusts of growth by which the family progressively enlarges its objective and integrates its widening interests. It is important to note that two maturing processes are going on during these two-thirds of each life span: the young individual human beings (children) are becoming persons, the young individual group (headed by the parents) is becoming a social institution. Until both processes have been consummated, human life is incomplete and unfulfilled. We noted earlier that the church and the family have the same objective—greatest human fulfillment, but that the family sought it within its own intimate circle; the church, for all mankind. Now it becomes clear that the mature family is one which has caught up with the church in the comprehensiveness of its objective and is then ready to function with the church. The two can now go forth as coworkers in bettering the order of human living by bringing it under the control of the greatest values mankind can discover. For long we have referred to this in religious terms as the establishing among mankind of the Kingdom of God.

THE RESHAPING OF THE CHURCH AS THE GUIDING INSTITUTION

The church can never build communion among men by dealing with infantile families. Such an undertaking requires the educated devotion of the matured family. The church cannot locate enough matured families except by nurturing them. It cannot nurture the maturing of the family without reshaping itself to the task.

One chief aspect of the equipped church will be a comprehensive system of religious education. Such a system must include all ages, but give first heed to the family as the germinative center of communion among men. Also, the educational system must include not only the work in the church building, but new types of extension work in the home and in the community. It is no wonder that materialistic values now largely control what little widening of family interests or objectives occur. Hence they control the communal life of the great society. Individuals have been schooled almost entirely in these values. They know little of any others. Both individual success and group status are granted by current society on the basis of these values. Human nature always seeks the best, but only those who are matured under sound nurture can know what the best is.

Before the church can set up a comprehensive system of religious education—or to speak more exactly, before it can become an institution of religious education—it will have to develop a philosophy of religious education. For the Christian church, this will require soundness in both its Christian and its social philosophy. This is made necessary by the fact that Christianity is a social religion and that Christian religious education is the nurturing of individuals for Christian living in their present social order. Only a mature church can develop these necessary philosophies. Consequently the church, like the family, must mature. In particular it must grow out of its childish, competitive divisiveness and its adolescent opinionated biases and arguings.

Further, the church must learn to work capably and responsibly with other social institutions for the growth of good in the world, even when it cannot subscribe to all the principles and policies of these other institutions. Indeed, how are these other institutions to become reshaped toward highest human fulfillment if the church holds aloof and so deprives them from educative contact with sound religion at work? For instance, the present challenge to Christians to work with communists to save the democratic spirit from being crushed by fascism may prove to be a great modern form of opportunity for religious conversion. Not that the church would use such cooperation for deliberate evangelism, but rather that the spirit and quality of its self-forgetting devotion to the cause would have a profound Christianizing influence. This particular cause certainly is great enough to call out such devotion, for the "democratic spirit" is only the modern way of saying "communion among men," communion functioning all the way from the intimate group called the family to the national and international organizations working toward better general human relations. Such a cause calls for loyal devotion on the vital rather than on the partisan level, since the church would specify the common ground wherever it takes its stand in the joint endeavor. In doing so it is lifting up before the eyes of all the participating individuals that value among the many values and disvalues present which it believes to be most worthy of celebrating and serving. The process becomes a vivid experience in religious evaluation. No doubt many of the barnacle-like members of the church will be scraped off when the mature church gets into more dynamic, nonpartisan, but devoted interaction with other social institutions. But a new type of member will more than fill the empty places, a type which sees religious commitment in terms larger than individualistic salvation or placid insulation.

As the church progressively clarifies and formulates its philosophies of religion and of education, it will be able to discern with greater surety what the will of God is for the world today. These insights will be tested and enlarged as the maturing church interacts with other institutions to make dominant in the world of men those values which are worthy of supreme loyalty. As all this process develops, the instrumentalities through which the church functions will be revealingly tested also, and proved effective or inadequate. When an institution resorts to copying other institutions or their products as the basis for choosing and setting up its own instrumentalities, it is a certain symptom that something is seriously wrong. The present local church usually copies its organization from other churches, regardless of important differences of location and constituency. Often, it copies its architecture from the products of church life of centuries ago. It copies its school system largely from the secular one which has marked differences in purpose. These examples illustrate the anemic condition of many a local church.

All the instrumentalities of a church must be selected and shaped by the functions of the particular church at work. To be sure there will be certain similarities between churches but no two can be identical if each is fully alive. The instituting of new instrumentalities will not be launched by observing what other churches have done, but by studying the work to be done. As an incident, it will then be worth while to observe developments of such others as have similar functions to fulfill. But the functions of the particular church must determine its organization, architecture, equipment, staffing, and program. If one judged the average Protestant church building on the assumption that this had been done, he would have to draw the conclusions (1) that we had made no progress in religious growth for some years, for the form of our building is the same form which expressed the spirit of ages long gone; (2) that preaching is the chief ministry of the church; and (3) that religious education is an interesting little side function of the church, hardly worth space and support sufficient to make it adequate. It would be noticed further that there is much space in the average church going to waste, and yet there is not enough room. New ways of living must bring the continuous reshaping of the instrumentalities of such churches as would work with modern individuals and institutions. Only so can the Great Reality which the church worships and serves become known and powerful in the living of the day.

Not only will the instrumentalities of the local churches be determined by its particularized purposes and functions, but this must be true of the church-at-large. At the present time, for instance, every evanescent change in fashions, funny-paper favorites, sports, and food fads is broadcast instantaneously to all the land, and in forms so predigested or vivified by dramatization or personalized expression that all can understand and make such use as he prefers of this schooling in the interests of his fellow men. Notably, this process increases communication regarding these interests because all are more or less commonly informed. But religion, although the most profound of human interests, has no such universal sounding board. Various churches have used the radio for specialized purposes and services, but there is no national continuous effort to broadcast to all people the developments and values of religion. Devotion grown intelligent seeks the most effective instrumentalities available to its spirit and purposes. No other sort of devotion is a worthy tribute to God.

This emphasis upon the reshaping of the church so that it may become a competent guide and reinforcing agency for the family does not imply that the interests of the family shall dominate the church. God is the dominating cause of the church, ever and always. But because of the indispensable relation of the communion of the family to the Christian religion, and because of the universal form in which the vital issues of human living appear in the family, the family must be the chief concern of the church in the realities of daily living. In saying this, we are understanding by *family* now, not only those specific intimate groups of beginning families but also those socially dynamic, interacting organizations, the matured families.

RELATING THE FAMILY TO OTHER MAJOR INTERESTS

Normally, the matured family and the matured church have the same universally significant objective and system of values. This distinguishes them from all other institutions, each of which has an objective and a system of values so specialized and partial that these need constant checking against the worthier objectives and values of the matured family and church. When normally connected, objectives of these other institutions must be held as subsidiary to the objective of the matured family and church, and their functions must be regarded as instrumental to the prime functions of family and church. It is essential to the development of personality and the growth of culture that this be done. Only as the matured family and church devote themselves unflinchingly to the task of keeping greatest human fulfillment as the objective of all objectives among all social interests can life become more abundant and meaningful, can fellow feeling characterize the relations of mankind. This requires constant pressure on the part of the family and the church, constant yet ever sensitive and ever effectively adjusted to the pulse beats of these instrumental interests.

In practical terms, what does this bringing of pressure require? It involves demonstrating in every appropriate, legitimate way the effects of the activities of all these instrumental interests upon human life and relationships, particularly upon the family. Such demonstration must be achieved with keenness of intelligence, fresh crispness of presentation, and integrity of purpose and of work. It will repeatedly and variously bring to the attention of society the conditions and consequences of individualistically motivated enterprises. The forms possible for such demonstration are limitless—drama, fiction, statistical studies, authentic reports, study tours, forums, graphic presentations, discussion groups, radio, and other forms of communication of facts and ideas. The matured families who undertake this building of sound connections between the family and other major interests under the guidance of the matured church, will turn to all the sources now open to them for dependable materials—government statistics, findings of scientists, sociologists, psychologists, medical schools, social workers, and others. There are resources here which have great potentiality for readjusting the damaging connections which now exist between the great human interests. But they will remain impotent until some large, zealous group provides for them a sounding board that can be heard all over the country. Industry, politics, the school system, leisure-time enterprises, and all other activities must be educated to see that their condition and success is inextricably connected with the condition and success of human life, of which the family is the chief custodian. Then they must be educated to reshape their policies and undertakings to the end of making that human life magnificently worth while.

The modern tension between all the basic social institutions growing out of increasing interdependence is not going to lessen. But tension in itself is not an evil. It has in it possibilities both of great evil in amplified destructiveness, and of great good in empowered creativeness. The object is not to get rid of inter-group tensions, but to keep these in sensitive adjustment con-tinuously so that all the interconnected institutions may make their respective contributions to the common life. When these tensions become either too taut or too lax, they issue in mutual conflict. Then the whole social process suffers for each mistake or crime occurring in the control of these tensions.

This part of the program for the conservation of the family is a stirring and substantial answer to the problem of profitable use of marginal time for all parents who have achieved adult-hood.

CHANGING THE NATIONAL DEFINITION OF SUCCESS

The belief that extraordinary amassing of material possessions is the decisive criterion of success pervades our current literature, our everyday dealings with things and individuals, our movies, and all other activities. It makes men and women strangers to their families and to their neighbors. It cheats them out of the best of their cultural heritage. It is largely responsible for the present colossal waste of woman power among the idlers of so-ciety. It is the cause of much conventional robbery, depersonaliza-tion, nervous breakdowns, and despondency among men because it requires competition between men, cutthroat competition. It is the foundation for the animalistic and materialistic emphasis found almost everywhere in associational activities. It is the arch enemy of the communion of the family.

Everyone wants to succeed, every individual and every insti-tution. This will always be so. But success does not have to con-tinue to be defined as the amassing of possessions. The defining of success takes place through the accumulating approvals and disapprovals of society. Consequently it is a social product and can be directed. No single family or church can have much effect upon the accumulated definition, but cooperation between many families and churches can change a social definition for enough people so that it is no longer the dominant one.

The program for building a new definition of success will

work positively by approving and signalizing whatever contributes to greater human fulfillment, and will work negatively by disapproving what hinders such fulfillment regardless of what else it may achieve. This program can function all the way from the simple forms of expressing approval-disapproval connected with manners, invitations, the buying of tickets, the subscribing for magazines, passing comment, and other minor recognitions, to the elaborate forms of profoundly beautiful celebrations and drastically effective criticism. It must deal not only with individual persons but also with institutions. The real heart of it lies in the incorporating of a sound measure for the worth of living into the habit patterns of individuals and the customs of society. This cannot be done by precept or preaching. It begins to function only when actual approvals and disapprovals are experienced.

This is a more crucial aspect of the program for the conservation of the family than at first might appear. Present practices, both deliberate and unintentional, as well as future possibilities must be made the subject for serious study by the mature family and church. Then, in turn, these two must seek to orient other institutions in this area, first the personality-fostering ones and then the instrumental ones.

IMPROVING THE CONDITIONS FOR FAMILY LIVING

Because the tension between the family and the other major social institutions is out of adjustment, the effort of mere physical survival is occupying the first attention of many families. Even with those better off financially, perpetuation of their customary status is the prime concern. For them this is survival. More and more families are content to secure survival, on whatever level they define it, without regard for the social circumstances that characterize their acquisitions. The family is not rotting at the core as has happened sometimes in the static social groupings where it became morbidly self-centered. Rather the cohesion within the home is loosening, member by member, due to the suction of external forces so unrelenting that they keep the attention of the family too fully occupied with external adjustments.

There is a great vacuum at the center of the living of many families, but the members do not realize the increasing impoverishment of their fellowship, because their backs are always toward it. Their faces are turned and their eyes strained outward toward the external imperious or threatening conditions. They feel that they've got to get, and keep on getting. In the more extreme instances, home is little more than a filling station, whether palatial or poor. It is no wonder that frequently the combination of the vacuum within and the suction without have finally led to explosion of family unity and left those shattered fragments called broken homes.

All this will not right itself nor pass as an episode. Nationally, locally, and individually, we are already paying exorbitantly for this basic neglect of the family and we shall pay more painfully before we are through. Relieving the symptoms through treating the consequences of major national neglect is becoming more and more unsatisfying and destructive. This is true from the point of view both of the families relieved and of all other cultural interests, including the economic one which is primarily involved. Since all institutions are interdependent, all must be participants in the program for the conservation of the family, and they must not flinch when they experience some of the putrid smells and horrific sights that characterize degraded conditions in any neglected institution.

Improving the conditions of the family involves different procedures in different localities. These must be worked out on the basis both of data and insights gathered, and of resources located and marshaled. Some of the procedures are essential within the individual family. We have discussed these at some length. Other conditions are essential in the neighborhood; in the larger communities such as town or city, state or section; in the county; in the nation; and in the world. Space does not permit a discussion of these, but listing a few will be suggestive:

Organization for mutual support among the four personality-fostering institutions.

Provision of experiences which supplement and balance family nurture.

Articulation of the social expectations of the various members of the family with actual social conditions.

Opportunities for specific education and guidance for the family.

Ordinances governing the instituting of the family.

Availability of services essential to health and growth.

A suitable plan for the generation now passing out of the productive stage.

Official representation of the interests of the family on all civic councils.

Adequate bases for security in the realms of employment, illness, old age, and personal safety.

Education of public attitudes toward marriage and the family.

Actual recognition of the substantial equality of women.

Articulation between the public and the family life of individuals, including that of employed women.

Representation of family welfare on the president's cabinet as a major national interest.

Just dealings between nations.

World peace.

It is much easier to see the essential relation between these conditions and the normal functioning of the family than it is to institute the conditions. However, once these issues are seriously and practically raised by the coworking of family and church, they will release the wills of an uncounted multitude of persons toward the improving of the present impeding or strangling conditions.

INCREASING THE SOCIAL POWER OF THE FAMILY

The voice of the family must gain strength and influence in those areas of communal living where its members and its interests and investments are. At present, many of the other institutional developments in the larger community increase dangerously the stress and strain of the family with no knowledge and intention of doing so. For instance, the public school has affected family life through the consolidation of schools, sometimes by involving the mother in many hours of chauffeuring or the young people in unsupervised residence away from home during severe weather, and usually by shortening materially the home day of the child. Again, the school sometimes increases family load and tension with its demands for costumes, equipment, and dues for fine affairs. A very serious damage done by the school results from its neglect to educate children for the acute problems of social interaction resultant from massing them together in enormously large groupings. Local governments and other community institutions have proceeded in ways that affect the family, also, without giving any thought to the outcomes. Obvious examples are the commercially devised attractions. They can secure a license to operate in a neighborhood where the parents, without adequate means of recourse, must pay heavy penalties in the form of deleterious effects upon the children. More and more, if the family is to hold its own as the primary germinal source of communion for society, it must build up avenues through which it can share in the control of communal matters in which it is vitally involved through its heavy investment in its several members.

There are three types of leadership which the church can supply to parents in this development. These are: (1) the educating of the family for such participation in social control as will protect and promote its rightful functions; (2) the actual organizing of groups of families for the clarifying and effective registering of their needs, demands, and hopes; and (3) the organizing of wider community cooperation between groups of families and other institutions for meeting communal problems. This third direction of leadership opens up an unlimited vista of fruitful fields of work: bringing groups of parents into touch with professional groups having closely related interests; enlarging family group-consciousness by an annual demonstration and exhibit of what families throughout the community or section are doing or discovering or experimenting with; the instituting of cooperative nursery schools for truly educational (not "parking") purposes; the building up of play groups and of recreational facilities for young people; and others beyond enumeration. These three types of increasing the power of the family present long-term problems of leadership. The church cannot solve them alone, but in many communities they will not get solved until the church takes the lead in assisting the family in this crucial development.

FOSTERING A LIVING NUCLEUS OF FAMILY GROWTH

In connection with the vocation of homemaking, there has been no synthesized and growing body of professional knowledge, scientifically tested and institutionally conserved in a form to be passed into the hands of new families being instituted. Nor has there been any modern substitute for the hearth in the long-established family home around which to develop the family cultures. Rented quarters, frequent movings, and rushed schedules make it difficult to cluster into a vibrant core the sentiments and symbols which carry the meanings and unique values of the family. Consequently each modern family has had to start near the point of zero in regard to the resources, equipment, information, and sentiments repeatedly developed by other founders of family. No wonder the progress of the family has been slow and erratic.

In recent years there has appeared much literature on the aspects of housekeeping, child care, and the sexual relationship, most of which is offered with the backing of the authors alone. It has not been evaluated and synthesized. Besides these, there are many other areas of family life which need appreciative treatment. Two sorts of synthesizing are called for: (1) that concerned with an integrative treatment of the physical, intellectual, social, emotional, and religious aspects; (2) that concerned with relating special findings to the total field. Private agencies and educational institutions have carried on most of this synthesizing. This work is good as far as it has gone. But there needs to be some institution whose special responsibility it is to be the bearer of a living nucleus of accumulating information, sentiments, and wisdom.

A further responsibility associated with this first is the fostering and conserving of all new developments in family life. There seem to be at least three existing institutions which are called upon to participate substantially in fulfilling this function of sustaining the growing ethos of the family. First stands the national government. The idea of having a member of the President's cabinet who shall represent the interests of the family may be startling upon first consideration. To some it may seem even fantastic. But more penetrating analysis will reverse the reaction and make it seem startling and fantastic that there is not already such an officer. We deem the present cabinet offices wholly worth while. Our nation has a Secretary of War, though war is supposed to be only an emergency which is to be avoided as much as possible and finally done away with. Also, our nation has a Secretary of Agriculture to represent the interests of growing plants and domesticated animals most of which are raised for slaughtering, and of the individuals who raise these. On the other hand, for the far more significant matter of normalizing and reinforcing the family we have no national officer. This is true in spite of the two facts that sound family spirit is the greatest national asset and that sound children are the greatest national resource. Furthermore, the future of the country is much more deeply and fundamentally involved in what is happening to its families than in any other one interest. Nationally we are moving unconsciously toward the instituting of such an office through such avenues as our Chief of the Children's Division, the increasingly numerous and valuable government publications on family interests, the work of farm bureaus and 4-H clubs, the newly organized department of social service, and other developments. But it would be of incalculable value to the family and to the nation if the instituting of a Secretary of Family Welfare could become a matter of deliberate social planning. The need is extreme. Such an office would represent the interests of the family in all situations where other interests were pushing for attention or privilege as well as in the promotion of better family life within the home and community. Further, it would bring before the nation the special difficulties of families, urban and rural; dwellers on the mountain and in the plain, native, naturalized and foreign ones; and other family groups that need national attention. For the support of a family department in the President's cabinet and a national program of education in marriage and homemaking, more than sufficient funds would become available within a few years, realized from the resultant savings over present outlay for delinquency, divorce trials, rehabilitating frustrated or prejudiced individuals, and other ills due in part to untrained parental leadership in the American family. The program needs launching. It will then more than pay for itself.

The second institution to foster the growing nucleus of the family is a type rather than a single institution. It includes a variety of training centers, such as institutes of child and of family welfare. Sometimes these are connected with universities, sometimes not. They must be responsible for much of the pioneer work in experimentation and in direct dealing with families. Also their help is needed in connection with the building up of supporting skills of homemaking, together with the understanding of how these can be taught.

The third institution with responsibility for nurturing the nucleus of the family is the church. The family needs the church to guide it in bringing these first two institutions to its support. Further, the church must take particular responsibility for sustaining on a stable and worthy level the emotional continuity of the family. Again, the church must act as wise guardian over its transitory and abiding loyalties. Particularly, the church should help the family conserve the progress it makes in the development of an appropriate and adequate system of values with its supporting culture.

Any vocation which has no means of accumulating progressively a rich system of supporting knowledge, skills, and attitudes is bound to be treated as a relatively unimportant business. Further, any large number of separate units must have a concerted voice, ear, and hand, that is, it must have means by which it can be reached, can communicate, and can interact as one whole. Individual homes cannot sustain such a nucleus. They are too short-lived and too detached, relatively speaking. Such sustenance of the ethos of the American family must be primarily the responsibility of national agencies, governmental, educational, and religious. Governmental leadership must carry chief responsibility for seeing to it that other interests reinforce rather than injure or destroy the family, and that needed resources of all sorts are at the command of the family.

When the family has developed the perpetual and perpetuating living nucleus, is will be enabled to make itself known and honored for its creative participation in cultural growth.

THE FULL CIRCLE

A program for the conservation of the family incorporating the building of some such conditions as are here suggested will be a long time growing. There will be many forces opposed to it, either because such conservation will be inimical to their individualistic interests or because they think it will cost too much in energy and money. Furthermore, it cannot happen all at once as a conscious program, not in days such as ours.

Human history has again reached a turning point. In the beginning, growth of community dominated human life entirely and all techniques were subject to it. At that time community was unconscious and unintended; men could not live otherwise, and their community tended to be clannish and stunting. Then there came increase in techniques of power and skill in disregard of all that had made life worthful, yet not destructive of this worthful because the powers of men had not grown great enough to overwhelm it. In fact, for a time the techniques were primarily instruments for the enhancement of living. Lately, the increase and use of human instrumentalities of achievement have so possessed society that the issue has become crucial. The rich values of growing community are being trampled upon. Community itself is being squeezed out and destroyed. While civilization has increased, culture has declined. Many, many persons feel cynical, hopeless, released from responsibility, or threatened by some awful doom. With great new forms of power in the hands of uncultured men, individualism in the modern world has gone wild. In the absence of the dominating control of an overarching community of life, wolfish competition and monstrous acquisitiveness possess the earth.

In consequence, a vast world-wide movement toward coercive collectivism is sweeping the nations toward communism, fascism, and other forms of unification yet to be made clear. But collectivism of the dictated type cannot save the values of life. It may save society for a time. But nothing can render to mankind the cardinally great values, nothing can give dynamic stability to civilization, except a vital community. Such community is not and cannot be dictated nor deliberately set up. Rather it can and will grow when the right conditions are provided. Fascism does not provide the right conditions, for it is definitely and hopelessly destructive to any such rich and creative growth of community. Communism seems to contain some seeds of communal living favorable to communion, along with its other elements. Democracy holds great possibilities but fails where citizens are preoccupied with their own affairs or indifferent, ignorant, or traitorous.

Three alternatives seem to be before us as a society. One is coercive regimentation with impoverishment of all the high and human values of life. A second is social chaos and the disappearance of civilization and such culture as we do have. The third is the rich growth of community. Right now, a transitional period characterized by some form and degree of political, coercive regimentation seems inevitable. But it is as yet uncertain whether it will be organized and administered in such a way as to obstruct and destroy the growth of community or in such a way as to prepare for it and promote it. Should coercive regimentation prove to be a necessary transitional stage, will it lead to chaos or to that outburst of growth of more abundant community wherein human lives are consciously dedicated to the service and enjoyment of its values?

Mankind can be counted upon to move dauntlessly and unswervingly toward what they believe to be of value. They will organize their ways and resources by whatever plan and principle seem most potent in promoting the acquisition of recognized values. They will foster whatever developments they find to be necessary to promote the growth of such value, no matter how long and arduous the preparatory undertakings may prove to be. The chief problem is that of developing sound value-sense in society and of vivifying before the world the greatest values mankind can know and serve. We must make way for this development of sound value-sense by hastening that "most important change of the century," of which Dean Pound spoke, "the transference of the sense of value from property to humanity." That will be the day of the family. The only factor which can decisively move us away from chaos toward this day is the spread of human certitude that fellow feeling among men yields greater values in life than can the profit motive which must rest upon a competitive organization where man is pitted against man. The only institutions which can develop this certitude on a scale sufficiently large to be effective are the family and the church. These two, rightly organized, ardently conscious of their essential functions, and grown mature, may turn the course of historical development away from chaos and death toward life's supreme fulfillment. Through a unity generated by a new, mutual objective, universal in its magnitude and significance, these two can save the life of sensitive community to the world.

Should the growth of community again dominate the connections between all human interests, it will do so on a far more flexible and abundant basis than it has ever done before, because of the increased powers and instrumentalities which are able to serve it. At the start, civilization developed to serve culture. When the development of civilization and culture reached a balance, history revealed a full circle of constructively related human interests. But the growth of civilization recently has become so rapid that it has reached malignant proportions and is destroying culture. Family and church, the chief institutional custodians of community among men, are faced with the world-shaping challenge to convince mankind that civilization must again take its rightful place as provider of the instrumentalities of culture. If the matured church and family, working in unity, can lead men to make the growth of community again the high vocation of all human living, history will have swung once more toward a completion of the full circle.

RELATED REFERENCES

CHAPTERS I-III

THE FAMILY, ITS CONDITION AND FUNCTIONS

Annals of the American Academy of Political Science: "The Modern Family," vol. 160; March, 1932.

Briffault, Robert: *Breakdown: The Collapse of Traditional Civilization.* Scribner's, New York, 1932.

Burgess, Ernest W.: "Family Traditions and Personality," chap. VIII in Young, Kimball, ed.: *Social Attitudes.* Henry Holt and Company, Inc., New York, 1931.

Burns, C. Delisle: *Leisure in the Modern World,* chaps. III-X. D. Appleton-Century Co., New York, 1932.

Calhoun, Arthur W.: *A Social History of the American Family,* vols. I-III. The Arthur H. Clark Company, Cleveland, 1919.

Cooper, William J.: *Home and Family Life in a Changing Civilization,* U. S. Office of Education Bulletin, 5:1-5, 1931.

Counts, George S.: *The Social Foundations of Education,* part I; part II, chap. I; part III, chap. I. Charles Scribner's Sons, New York, 1934.

Elmer, Manuel Conrad: *Family Adjustment and Social Change.* Long & Smith, New York, 1932.

Fiske, George W.: *The Changing Family: Social and Religious Aspects of the Modern Family.* Harper & Brothers, New York, 1928.

Folsom, Joseph Kirk: *The Family: Its Sociological Problems,* parts III and IV. John Wiley and Sons, Inc., New York, 1934.

Gauss, Christian: *Life in College,* part III. Charles Scribner's Sons, New York, 1930.

Goodsell, Willystine: *Problems of the Family,* parts II and III. D. Appleton-Century Co., New York, 1928.

Groves, Ernest R., and Brooks, Lee M.: *Readings in the Family.* J. B. Lippincott Company, Philadelphia, 1934.

Groves, Ernest R., and Ogburn, Wm. F.: *American Marriage and Family Relationships,* part I, chap. 7; part II. Henry Holt and Company, Inc., New York, 1928.

Holt, Arthur E.: *The Fate of the Family*, chaps. III-VII. Willett, Clark and Co., Chicago, 1936.

Kreuger, E. F., and Reckless, W. C.: *Social Psychology*. Longmans, Green and Co., New York, 1933.

Lichtenberger, J. P.: *Divorce, A Social Interpretation*. McGraw-Hill Book Company, Inc., New York, 1931.

Lindquist, R.: *The Family in the Present Social Order*, chaps. IV, IX-X. University of North Carolina Press, Chapel Hill, 1931.

Lumpkin, Katherine D.: *The Family: A Study of Member Rôles*. University of North Carolina Press, Chapel Hill, 1933.

Lynd, Robert S. and Helen M.: *Middletown: A Study in Contemporary American Culture*. Harcourt, Brace and Company, Inc., New York, 1929.

———— *Middletown in Transition*. Harcourt, Brace and Company, Inc., New York, 1937.

Mowrer, Ernest R.: *The Family: Its Organization and Disorganization*, chaps. I-X. University of Chicago Press, Chicago, 1932.

Nimkoff, Meyer: *The Family*. Houghton Mifflin Company, New York, 1934.

Popenoe, Paul: *Modern Marriage*. The Macmillan Company, New York, 1926.

Report of the Committee on Recent Economic Changes of the President's Conference on Unemployment: *Consumption and the Standards of Living*, vol. I, chap. I. McGraw-Hill Book Company, Inc., New York, 1929.

Report of the President's Research Committee on Social Trends: *Recent Social Trends in the United States*. Introduction; vol. I, chaps. VIII-X, XII-XIV; vol. II, chaps. XV, XVII-XVIII, XX. McGraw-Hill Book Company, Inc., New York, 1933.

Reuter, Edward B., and Runner, Jessie R., eds.: *The Family: Source Materials for the Study of the Family and Personality*. McGraw-Hill Book Company, Inc., New York, 1931.

Schmeideler, Edgar, ed.: *Readings on the Family*. D. Appleton-Century Co., New York, 1931.

Thompson, Warren S.: *Population Problems*. McGraw-Hill Book Company, Inc., New York, 1930.

Todd, Arthur J.: *Social Trends and Their Effect on Home Life and Family Relationships*. U. S. Office of Education Bulletin, 5:21-24; 1931.

Van Waters, Miriam: *Parents on Probation*. Chaps. l-VII. New Republic, Inc., New York, 1927.

Westermarck, Edward: *The Future of Marriage in Western Civilization*, chaps. III-VIII. The Macmillan Company, New York, 1936.

Williams, Frankwood E.: *Youth, and the Present-day World*, chaps. III-XII. Farrar & Rinehart, Inc., New York, 1934.

BIBLIOGRAPHIES

Dyer, Annie I. (Robertson): *Guide to the Literature of Home and Family Life*. J. B. Lippincott Company, Philadelphia, 1924.

International Council of Religious Education, and Federal Council of Churches in America: *Bibliography on Education in Family Life, Marriage, Parenthood, and Young People's Relationships*. Federal Council of Churches, New York, 1935.

Thurstone, Flora M.: *A Bibliography on Family Relationships*. The National Council of Parent Education, New York City, 1932.

(Note: Book lists obtainable also from U. S. Office of Education, State Departments of Education, denominational headquarters, public libraries, organizations for child study and parent education, and periodicals dealing with the interests of the family.)

CHAPTERS IV-V

THE CHURCH, ITS CONDITION AND ITS FUNCTIONS

Beaven, Albert W.: *The Local Church*. The Abingdon Press, New York, 1937.

Bennett, John C.: *Social Salvation*, chaps. II, IV. Charles Scribner's Sons, New York, 1935.

Bennett, John C., et al: *The Church Through Half a Century*, chaps. XIV-XV, XVII. Charles Scribner's Sons, New York, 1936.

Brown, William A.: *The Church, Catholic and Protestant*, chaps. XI-XII. Charles Scribner's Sons, New York, 1935.

———— *Church and State in Contemporary America*, chaps. I-II. Charles Scribner's Sons, New York, 1936.

Cashman, Robert: *The Business Administration of a Church*. Willett, Clark and Co., Chicago, 1937.

Chaffee, Edmund B.: *The Protestant Churches and the Industrial Crisis*. The Macmillan Company, New York, 1933.

Coe, George A.: *What Is Christian Education?* chaps. I-IV, VIII-XIII. Charles Scribner's Sons, New York, 1929.

Devine, Edward T.: *Progressive Social Action*, chaps. IV-V. The Macmillan Company, New York, 1933.

Fry, C. Luther: *Diagnosing the Rural Church*, chaps. IV-V. Harper & Brothers, New York, 1924.

Garrison, Winfred E.: *The March of Faith*. Harper & Brothers, 1933.

Harkness, Georgia: *The Resources of Religion*. Henry Holt and Company, Inc., New York, 1936.

Holt, Ivan Lee: *The Search for a New Strategy in Protestantism*. Cokesbury Press, Nashville, 1936.

Hutchinson, Paul: *World Revolution and Religion*. The Abingdon Press, New York, 1931.

Johnson, F. Ernest: *The Church and Society*, chaps. II, VII-VIII. The Abingdon Press, New York, 1935.

————— *The Social Work of the Churches*. The Federal Council of Churches of Christ in America, New York, 1930.

————— *Economics and the Good Life*. Association Press, New York, 1934.

Journal of Social Hygiene: Church Number, vol. XXI, No. 5, May, 1935.

Luccock, Halford E.: *Christian Faith and Economic Change*. The Abingdon Press, New York, 1936.

Lundberg, George A., et al: *Leisure: A Suburban Study*, chaps. I, VI-VII, XI. Columbia University Press, New York, 1934.

Lynd, R. S. and Helen M.: *Middletown*, chaps. XX-XXIII. Harcourt, Brace and Co., Inc., New York, 1929.

Macmurray, John: *Creative Society. A Study of the Relation of Christianity to Communism*. Association Press, New York, 1936.

Mathews, Shailer: *Creative Christianity*, chaps. I-III, VI. Cokesbury Press, Nashville, 1935.

Mecklin, John M.: *An Introduction to Social Ethics*, chaps. I-III, XV. Harcourt, Brace & Co., Inc., New York, 1920.

Meiklejohn, Alexander: *What Does America Mean?* chap. XII. W. W. Norton and Company, Inc., New York, 1935.

Morrison, C. C.: *The Social Gospel and the Christian Cultus*, chaps. IV and VII. Harper & Brothers, New York, 1933.

Niebuhr, Reinhold: *Does Civilization Need Religion?* chap. III. The Macmillan Company, New York, 1927.

Rauschenbusch, Walter: *Christianizing the Social Order*, pp. 7-10, 458-476. The Macmillan Company, New York, 1914.

Robertson, H. M.: *Aspects of the Rise of Economic Individualism*. Cambridge University Press, Cambridge, England, 1933.

Royce, Josiah: *The Hope of the Great Community*, chap. III. The Macmillan Company, New York, 1916.

Sheldon, William H.: *Psychology and the Promethean Will*, chaps. III, VI (sections 23-24), and VII (sections 29-30). Harper & Brothers, New York, 1936.

Silver, Rabbi Abba H.: *Religion in a Changing World*. Harper & Brothers, New York, 1930.

Sprague, Philo W.: *The Influence of Christianity on Fundamental Human Institutions*, chap. II. Fleming H. Revell Co., New York, 1925.

Visser 't Hooft, W. A., and Oldham, J. H.: *The Church and Its Functions in Society*, part II. Willett, Clark and Co., Chicago, 1937.

Ward, Harry F.: *Which Way Religion?* The Macmillan Company, New York, 1931.

Wieman, Henry N.: *Religious Experience and the Scientific Method*. The Macmillan Company, New York, 1926.

Wieman, Henry N. and Regina Westcott: *Normative Psychology of Religion*, chaps. I-II, V-XII, XXV. Thomas Y. Crowell Company, New York, 1935.

Winchester, Benjamin: *The Church and Adult Education*, parts II and III. Harper & Brothers, New York, 1930.

Wyant, Fred B.: *Religion and the Church Tomorrow*. Cokesbury Press, Nashville, 1936.

Yeaxlee, Basil A.: *Spiritual Values in Adult Education*, vol. I, part I. Oxford University Press, Oxford, England, 1925.

CHAPTER VI

THE FOUNDATION OF RELIGION IN THE FAMILY

Allport, Floyd Henry: *Social Psychology*, chaps. VIII-XIV. Houghton Mifflin Company, New York, 1924.

Cooley, Charles H.: *Human Nature and the Social Order*, chaps. III-VI, XII. Charles Scribner's Sons, New York, 1922.

————— *Social Organization*, chaps. III-IX, XI. Charles Scribner's Sons, New York, 1920.

Dewey, John: *Experience and Nature*, chap. V, pp. 166-207. Open Court Publishing Co., Chicago, 1925.

Ellwood, Charles A.: *Christianity and Social Science*, chaps. III-VI. The Macmillan Company, New York, 1923.

———— *The Reconstruction of Religion*, chaps. VI-VII. The Macmillan Company, New York, 1922.

Hartmann, Nicolai, trans. by Coit, Stanton: *Ethics*, vol. II, chaps. XXIV, XXXIII. The Macmillan Company, New York, 1932.

Lippmann, Walter: *A Preface to Morals*, pp. 88-94 and chap. XIV. The Macmillan Company, New York, 1929.

Macmurray, John: *Reason and Emotion*, lectures 1-6, 10-13, D. Appleton-Century Co., New York, 1936.

Mc Iver, R. M.: *Community: A Sociological Study*, books II and III. The Macmillan Company, New York, 1931.

Mead, George H.: *Mind, Self and Society*, part IV, sections 32-42. University of Chicago Press, Chicago, 1936.

Reuter, E. B., and Hart, C. W.: *Introduction to Sociology*, chap. X. McGraw-Hill Book Co., Inc., New York, 1933.

Royce, Josiah: *The Philosophy of Loyalty*, lectures V and VI. The Macmillan Company, 1908.

Shaler, Nathaniel S.: *The Individual*, chaps. VI-VIII. D. Appleton-Century Co., New York, 1913.

Vlastos, Gregory: "The Ethical Foundations," chap. III in Scott, R. B. Y., and Vlastos, Gregory, eds.: *Towards the Christian Revolution*. Willett, Clark and Company, Chicago, 1936.

Ward, Lester: *Dynamic Sociology*, vol. I, pp. 662-677. D. Appleton-Century Co., New York, 1883.

Wieman, Regina Westcott. "Religion in Intimate Associations," chap. XVIII, in Wieman, Henry N. and Regina Westcott: *Normative Psychology of Religion*. Thomas Y. Crowell Company, New York, 1935.

CHAPTER VII

THE INTERDEPENDENCE OF FAMILY AND CHURCH

Coe, George A.: *A Social Theory of Religious Education*, chaps. VI-VIII, XV. Charles Scribner's Sons, New York, 1928.

Ellwood, Charles A.: *The Reconstruction of Religion*, chaps. II-III, VI-VII. The Macmillan Company, New York, 1922.

Fiske, George Walter: *The Christian Family.* The Abingdon Press, New York, 1929.

Gillis, J. M.: *The Catholic Church and the Home.* The Macmillan Company, New York, 1928.

Holt, Arthur E.: *The Fate of the Family*, part IV. Willet, Clark & Company, Chicago, 1936.

Kent, Charles F.: *The Social Teachings of the Prophets and Jesus*, chaps. XX-XXI. Charles Scribner's Sons Co., New York, 1917.

CHAPTER VIII

THE CHURCH DEALING WITH MARRIAGE

Beaven, A. W.: *The Fine Art of Living Together.* Harper & Brothers, New York, 1920.

Binkley, F. W. and P. C.: *What Is Right with Marriage.* D. Appleton-Century Co., New York, 1929.

Bridges, Horace J.: *The Fine Art of Marriage.* Chicago Ethical Culture Society, Chicago, 1930.

Butterfield, Oliver M.: *Marriage and Sexual Harmony.* Emerson Books, Inc., New York, 1934.

Calhoun, Arthur W.: *The Social History of the American Family*, vol. III, chap. 13. The Arthur H. Clark Company, Cleveland, 1919.

David, A. A., and Furse, M. B.: *Marriage and Birth Control.* The Lambeth Series. Morehouse Publishing Co., Milwaukee, 1931.

Eddy, Sherwood: *Religion and Social Justice*, pp. 152-190. Harper & Brothers, New York, 1927.

Ellis, Havelock: *Marriage Today and Tomorrow.* Westgate Press, San Francisco, 1929.

Everett, Millard S.: *The Hygiene of Marriage.* Vanguard Press, Inc., New York, 1932.

Exner, M. J.: *The Sexual Side of Marriage.* W. W. Norton and Co., Inc., New York, 1932.

Federal Council of Churches of Christ in America: *Ideals of Love and Marriage. Moral Aspects of Birth Control.* (Other bulletins.) New York, 1929, 1931.

Goodsell, Willystine: *A History of the Family as a Social and Educational Institution*, chap. VI, also pp. 192-206, 227, 246-254, 282, 313, 405. The Macmillan Company, New York, 1926.

Groves, Ernest R. and Gladys H.: *Wholesome Marriage.* Houghton Mifflin Company, New York, 1927.

364   *The Modern Family and the Church*

Harding, Esther: *The Way of All Women.* Longmans, Green and Co., New York, 1933.

Hart, Hornell: *The Science of Social Relations*, chaps. XVII-XVIII. Henry Holt and Company, Inc., New York, 1927.

Holt, Harold: *Building Family Foundations.* Morehouse Publishing Co., Milwaukee, 1930.

Hutton, Isabel E.: *The Sex Technique in Marriage.* Emerson Books, Inc., New York, 1932.

Leach, Wm. H., ed.: *The Cokesbury Marriage Manual.* Cokesbury Press, Nashville, 1934.

Mahoney, E. J.: *Christian Marriage.* The Macmillan Company, New York, 1928.

Pedersen, V. C.: *The Man a Woman Marries.* Minton, Balch and Co., New York, 1929.

——— *The Woman a Man Marries.* Minton, Balch and Co., New York, 1930.

Pope Leo XIII: *Four Great Encyclicals.* The Paulist Press, New York, 1931.

Sanger, Margaret: *Happiness in Marriage.* Blue Ribbon Books, New York, 1931.

Sherrill, Lewis J.: *Family and Church.* The Abingdon Press, New York, 1937.

Spaulding, Clarence A., ed.: *Twenty-four Views of Marriage.* The Macmillan Company, New York, 1930.

Wile, Ira S., and Winn, Mary Day: *Marriage in the Modern Manner.* D. Appleton-Century Co., New York, 1929.

Wood, Leland Foster: *Foundations of Happiness in Marriage.* 105 E. 22d St., New York, 1934.

Wright, Helena: *The Sex Factor in Marriage.* The Vanguard Press, Inc., New York, 1931.

Yarros, Rachelle S.: *The Modern Woman and Sex.* The Vanguard Press, Inc., New York, 1933.

CHAPTER IX

Working with Parents

Abell, Mary H.: *Successful Family Life on the Moderate Income.* J. B. Lippincott Co., Philadelphia, 1927.

Bott, Helen, et al: *Aims and Methods in Parent Education.* National Council of Parent Education, New York.

Carrier, Blanche: *Church Education for Family Life*. Harper & Brothers, New York, 1937.

Chicago Association for Child Study and Parent Education: *Intelligent Parenthood*. University of Chicago Press, Chicago, 1927.

———— *Building Character*. University of Chicago Press, Chicago, 1928.

Deering, Ivah E.: *The Creative Home*. Emerson Books, Inc., New York, 1930.

Fisher, Dorothy C., and Gruenberg, Sidonie M., eds.: *Our Children: A Handbook for Parents*. Viking Press, Inc., New York, 1932.

Heath, Esther: *The Approach to the Parent*. The Commonwealth Fund, New York, 1933.

International Council of Religious Education: *Christian Education in Family Life and Parenthood*, book IV, part II, of *The International Curriculum Guide*, Chicago, 1934.

———— *Home and Church Sharing in Christian Education*. Service Bulletin No. 422, 1935. *The Church's Opportunity in Family and Parent Education*. Service Bulletin No. 420, 1934.

Lindeman, Eduard C., and Thurston, Flora M., eds.: *Problems for Parent Educators*. 3 vols. National Council of Parent Education, New York, 1929 and 1931.

Myers, Garry Cleveland: *The Modern Family*. Greenberg, Publisher, Inc., New York, 1934.

National Congress of Parents and Teachers: *Parent Education*, yearbooks I, II, and III. Washington, D. C., 1930, 1931, 1932.

Nelson, Amalie K.: "Parent Education in the Church." *Religious Education*, 24, 930-934; 1929.

Parent Education: (Number given to church work in parent education) vol. I, No. 2. June, 1934.

Thorndike, Edward L. et al: *Adult Learning*. The Macmillan Company, New York, 1928.

U. S. Bureau of Education: *Parent Education, 1926-1928*. Bulletin No. 15, 1929. (See also book lists and other bulletins.)

University of Iowa: *Toward Understanding Children*. Extension Bulletin No. 261, 1931. (See also other materials.)

Verkuyl, Gerrit: *Christ in the Home*. Fleming H. Revell Co., New York, 1932.

White House Conference on Child Health and Protection: *Parent Education*, section III A, 1932. *The Home and the Child*, section III A, 1931. *The Young Child in the Home*, section III B, 1936. D. Appleton-Century Co., New York.

White House Conference (materials rearranged for use of parents): Anderson, John E.: *Happy Childhood;* 1933. Foster, Josephine C.: *Busy Childhood;* 1933. Stuart, Harold C.: *Healthy Childhood;* 1933. D. Appleton-Century Co.

Wilson, Warren H.: *The Farmer's Church*, chaps. V, VI, VIII. D. Appleton-Century Co., New York, 1925.

MATERIAL FOR STUDY COURSES

Arlitt, Ada Hart: *Our Homes*. National Congress of Parents and Teachers, Washington, D. C., 1936.

Brill, Alice C., and Youtz, May P.: *A Textbook for Child Study Groups*. D. Appleton-Century Co., New York, 1932.

Chalmers, Mary M.: *The Home Beautiful*. The Judson Press, Philadelphia, 1931.

Child Study Association: *Parents' Questions*. Harper & Brothers, New York, 1936.

Darsie, Charles: *The Christian Family. A Study of Home Ideals*. Bethany Press, St. Louis, Mo., 1924.

Eastman, Fred, and Ouellette, Edward: *Better Motion Pictures*. The Pilgrim Press, Boston, 1936. (Example of study outline in special area.)

Fiske, George Walter: *The Christian Family*. The Abingdon Press, New York, 1929.

Galloway, T. W.: *Parenthood and the Character Training of Children*. The Abingdon Press, New York, 1927.

General Council of Congregational and Christian Churches: *The Effective Church*. The Pilgrim Press, Boston, 1936.

Germane, C. E. and Edith G.: *Character Training*, part II. Silver, Burdette and Co., New York, 1929.

Gruenberg, Benjamin C.: *Outlines of Child Study*. The Macmillan Company, New York, 1927.

Hayward, Percy R. and Myrtle: *The Home and Christian Living*. The Westminster Press, Philadelphia, 1931.

Montgomery, J. H.: *Christian Parenthood in a Changing World*. The Methodist Book Concern, Chicago, 1933.

Overton, Grace Sloan: *The Home in a Changing Culture*. Fleming H. Revell Company, New York, 1935.

Strub, Celestine, O.F.M.: *The Christian Home*. Franciscan Herald Press, Chicago, 1934.

Wood, Leland Foster: *Growing Together in the Family*. The Abingdon Press, 1935.

CHAPTER X

THE GUIDANCE OF CHILDREN

GENERAL REFERENCES

Arlitt, Ada Hart: *The Child from One to Twelve*. Whittlesey House, New York, 1931.

Blanton, Smiley and Margaret G.: *Child Guidance*. D. Appleton-Century Co., New York, 1927.

Bott, Helen McM.: *Personality Development in Young Children*. Child Development Series No. 2. University of Toronto Press, Toronto, 1934.

Bower, Wm. C.: *Character Through Creative Experience*. University of Chicago Press, Chicago, 1931.

Brewer, John M.: *Newspaper Stories for Group Discussion. A Book on Problems of Character*. Inor Publishing Company, New York, 1935.

Charters, W. W.: *The Teaching of Ideals*. The Macmillan Company, New York, 1927.

Chave, E. J.: *Personality Development in Children*. University of Chicago Press, Chicago, 1937.

Chicago Association for Child Study and Parent Education: *Developing Attitudes in Children*. University of Chicago Press, Chicago, 1933.

Department of Superintendence, N.E.A.: *Character Education*, Tenth Year Book. National Education Association, Washington, D. C., 1932.

Dewey, John: *Human Nature and Conduct*. Henry Holt and Company, Inc., New York, 1922.

Faegre, Marion L., and Anderson, John E.: *Child Care and Training*. University of Minnesota Press, Minneapolis, rev. ed., 1937.

Furfey, Paul H.: *Social Problems of Childhood*. The Macmillan Company, New York, 1929.

Gesell, Arnold: *Guidance of the Mental Growth in Infant and Child*. The Macmillan Company, New York, 1930.

Glover, Katherine, and Dewey, Evelyn: *Children of the New Day*. D. Appleton-Century Co., New York, 1934.

Hartshorne, Hugh: *Character in Human Relations*. Charles Scribner's Sons, New York, 1932.

Heaton, K. L.: *The Character Emphasis in Education*. University of Chicago Press, Chicago, 1933.

Hill, Howard C.: *Readings in Community Life*. Ginn and Company, Boston, 1930.

Jersild, Arthur T.: *Child Psychology*. Prentice-Hall, Inc., New York, 1933.

Kirkpatrick, E. A.: *Fundamentals of Child Study*. The Macmillan Company, New York, 1929.

Langdon, Grace: *Home Guidance of Young Children*. John Day and Co., New York, 1931.

McKown, H. C.: *Character Education*. McGraw-Hill Book Company, New York, 1935.

Parents' Magazine, eds.: *The Mothers' Encyclopedia*. Reynal and Hitchcock Co., Inc., New York, 1934.

Patri, Angelo: *The Problems of Childhood*. D. Appleton-Century Co., 1926. (This and other books by this author are written for the beginning parent.)

Piaget, Jean: *The Child's Conception of the World*. Harcourt, Brace and Co., Inc., New York, 1929.

Proceedings of the Midwest Conference on Character Development: *The Child's Emotions*. University of Chicago Press, Chicago, 1930.

Rand, Winifred, et al: *Growth and Development of the Young Child*. New ed., W. B. Saunders Co., Philadelphia, 1934.

Renz, Carl and M. P.: *Big Problems on Little Shoulders*. The Macmillan Company, New York, 1934.

Strang, Ruth: *An Introduction to Child Study*. The Macmillan Company, New York, 1930.

Thom, D. A.: *Everyday Problems of the Everyday Child*. D. Appleton-Century Co., New York, 1927.

Wilson, Frank T.: *Guiding our Children*. Globe Book Company, Boston, 1935.

CREATIVE EXPRESSION

Hartman, Gertrude, and Shumaker, Ann: *Creative Expression*. John Day Company, New York, 1932.

Koopman, G. Robt., et al: *Helping Children Experience the Realities of the Social Order*. Board of Education, Ann Arbor, Mich., 1933.

Mearns, Hugh: *Creative Power*. Doubleday, Doran & Company, New York, 1929.

Rasey, Marie L., and Schaal, Kennetha: *Development of Character through Community Problem Solving*. Detroit Teachers College, Detroit, 1929.

USE OF MONEY

Gruenberg, S. M. and B. C.: *Parents, Children and Money*. Viking Press, Inc., New York, 1933.

Laws, Gertrude: *Money, Children, and Parents* (pamphlet). California State Board of Education, Sacramento, 1930.

READING

Moore, Annie E.: *Literature Old and New for Children*. Houghton Mifflin Company, New York, 1934.

Starbuck, Edwin D., and Shuttleworth, Frank K., et al: *A Guide to Literature for Character Training*. 4 vols. The Macmillan Company, New York, 1929.

Terman, L. M., and Lima, M.: *Children's Reading*. D. Appleton-Century Co., New York, 1931.

RECREATION

Bancroft, Jessie: *Games for the Playground, Home, School and Gymnasium*. The Macmillan Company, New York, 1927.

Blumer, H.: *Movies and Conduct*. The Macmillan Company, New York, 1933.

Lee, Joseph: *Play in Education*. The Macmillan Company, New York, 1923.

Riggs, A. F.: *Play: Recreation in a Balanced Life*. Doubleday, Doran and Company, Inc., New York, 1935.

Rogers, James E.: *Child and Play*. D. Appleton-Century Co., New York, 1932.

SEX EDUCATION

Cady, B. C. and V. M.: *The Way Life Begins*. American Social Hygiene Assn., New York, 1917.

de Schweinitz, Karl: *Growing Up*. The Macmillan Company, New York, 1928.

Gruenberg, B. C.: *Parents and Sex Education,* revised ed. Viking Press, Inc., New York, 1932.

Strain, F. B.: *New Patterns in Sex Teaching.* D. Appleton-Century Co., New York, 1934.

RELIGIOUS EDUCATION

Blair, W. Dyer: *The New Vacation Church School.* Harper & Brothers, New York, 1934.

Bower, Wm C.: *The Living Bible,* chaps. X-XIV. Harper & Brothers, New York, 1936.

Bovet, Pierre: *The Child's Religion.* E. P. Dutton & Co., Inc., New York, 1928.

Carrier, Blanche: *How Shall I Learn to Teach Religion?* Harper & Brothers, New York, 1930.

Case, Adelaide T.: "Christian Education," chap. XI in Bennett, John C., et al: *The Church Through Half a Century.* Charles Scribner's Sons, New York, 1936.

Chave, E. J.: *The Junior.* University of Chicago Press, Chicago, 1932.

Coe, George A.: *A Social Theory of Religious Education.* Charles Scribner's Sons, New York, 1928.

————— *What Is Christian Education?* Charles Scribner's Sons, New York, 1929.

Cole, Stewart G.: *Character and Christian Education.* Cokesbury Press, Nashville, 1936.

Cope, Henry F.: *Religious Education in the Family.* University of Chicago Press, Chicago, 1915.

Councilor, Homer J.: *The Junior Church.* D. Appleton-Century Co., New York, 1928.

Forest, Ilse: *Child Life and Religion.* Harper & Brothers, New York, 1930.

Fox, H. F.: *The Child's Approach to Religion.* Harper & Brothers, New York, 1930.

Gamoran, Emanuel: *Changing Conceptions in Jewish Education.* The Macmillan Company, New York, 1925.

Hartshorne, Hugh, and Lotz, Elsa: *Case Studies of Present-day Religious Teaching.* Yale University Press, New Haven, 1932.

————— et al: *Community Organization in Religious Education.* Yale University Press, New Haven, 1932.

International Council of Religious Education: *International Curriculum Guide,* book II. 203 N. Wabash Ave., Chicago.

Jones, Mary Alice: *The Church and the Children*. Cokesbury Press, Nashville, 1935.

Jones, Rufus: "Religion and Family Life," chap. XI in Rich, Margaret E., ed.: *Family Life Today*. Houghton Mifflin Co., New York, 1928.

MacLean, Angus H.: *The New Era in Religious Education*. Beacon Press, Inc., Boston, 1934.

McGucken, W. J.: *The Catholic Way in Education*. Bruce Publishing Co., Milwaukee, 1934.

Morton, Frances M.: *First Steps in Religious Education*. Cokesbury Press, Nashville, 1930.

Mumford, Edith E. R.: *The Dawn of Religion in the Mind of the Child*. Longmans, Green and Co., New York, 1915.

Munkres, Alberta: *Which Way for our Children? Handbook in Religious Education for Parents and Teachers*. Charles Scribner's Sons, New York, 1936.

Munro, Harry C.: *Christian Education in Your Church*. The Bethany Press, St. Louis, 1933.

Myers, A. J. William: *Teaching Religion Creatively*. Fleming H. Revell Co., New York, 1932.

Perkins, J.: *Others Call It God*. Harper & Brothers, New York, 1934.

Stewart, George: *Can I Teach My Child Religion?* Harper & Brothers, New York, 1929.

Sweet, Helen F., and Fahs, Sophia L.: *Exploring Religion with Eight-year-olds*. Henry Holt and Co., Inc., 1930.

Wieman, Henry N. and Regina Westcott: *Normative Psychology of Religion*, part III. Thomas Y. Crowell Co., New York. 1935.

CHAPTER XI

PROGRAM WITH THE YOUNG PEOPLE

Starred references are valuable for direct use by young people, though not all for every age level.

GENERAL REFERENCES

Arlitt, Ada H.: *Adolescent Psychology*. American Book Company, New York, 1933.

Athearn, Laura A.: *Christian Worship for American Youth.* D. Appleton-Century Co., New York, 1931.

Aubrey, Edwin E.: *Religion and the Next Generation.* Harper & Brothers, New York, 1931.

Benedict, Agnes E.: *Children at the Crossroads.* Commonwealth Fund, New York, 1930.

Boorman, W. R.: *Personality in Its Teens.* The Macmillan Company, New York, 1931.

Brooks, F. D.: *Psychology of Adolescence.* Houghton Mifflin Company, New York, 1929.

Burger, W. H.: *Growing Up With Our Children.* Association Press, New York, 1932.

Burnham, Wm. H.: *Great Teachers and Mental Health*, chaps. XII-XIII. D. Appleton-Century Co., New York, 1926.

* Cavan, Ruth S. and Jordan, T.: *Building a Girl's Personality. A Social Psychology of Later Girlhood.* The Abingdon Press, New York, 1932.

Chalmers, Mary M.: *Young Adults in Christian Fellowship.* The Judson Press, Philadelphia, 1933.

Charters, Jessie A.: *The College Student Thinking It Through.* The Abingdon Press, New York, 1930.

—————— *Young Adults and the Church.* The Abingdon Press, New York, 1936.

Coe, George A.: *What Ails our Youth?* Charles Scribner's Sons, New York, 1926.

Conklin, E. S.: *The Psychology of Religious Adjustment.* The Macmillan Company, New York, 1929.

Davis, Kingley: *Youth in the Depression.* University of Chicago Press, Chicago, 1935.

Douglas, H. P.: *How Shall Country Youth be Served?* Harper & Brothers, New York, 1926.

* Elliott, Grace L.: *Understanding the Adolescent Girl.* Henry Holt and Company, Inc., New York, 1930.

Gleason, George: *Church Group Activities for Young Married People.* Author, 715 S. Hope St., Los Angeles, Calif., 1937.

Hayward, Percy R., and Burkhart, Roy A.: *Young People's Method in the Church.* The Abingdon Press, New York, 1933.

Herriott, Frank W.: *A Community Serves Its Youth.* Author, New York, 1933.

Hogue, Helen G.: *Untying Apron Strings: The Story of Personality Development.* Character Associates, Inc., Chicago, 1936.

International Council of Religious Education: *International Curriculum Guide*, book III, *Christian Education of Youth*. 203 N. Wabash Ave., Chicago, 1932.

—————— *Youth at Worship*. Christian Quest Pamphlet No. 6, 1927.

Maus, Cynthia P.: *Youth Organized for Religious Education*. Bethany Press, St. Louis, 1925.

—————— *Youth and the Church*. The Standard Press, Cincinnati, 1923.

Mayer, Herbert C.: *The Church's Program for Young People*. D. Appleton-Century Co., New York, 1925.

Morgan, Wm. H.: *Student Religion During 50 Years*. Association Press, New York, 1935.

Office of Education, U. S. Dept. of the Interior: *Youth: How can Communities Help?* September, 1935. *Youth: A Contemporary Bibliography with Annotations*. Circular No. 152, November, 1935. Supt. of Documents, Washington, D. C.

Palmer, Leon C.: *Youth and the Church*. Morehouse Publishing Co., Milwaukee, 1933.

Pendry, Ely, and Hartshorne, H.: *Organizations for Youth*. McGraw-Hill Book Co., New York, 1934.

Sadler, W. S. and Lena: *Piloting Modern Youth*. Funk and Wagnalls Co., New York, 1931.

Schwab, S. I., and Veeder, B. S.: *The Adolescent: His Conflicts and Escapes*. D. Appleton-Century Co., New York, 1929.

Seabury, David: *Growing into Life*. Boni and Liveright, New York, 1928.

Smith, Cecil D.: *Administering the Young People's Department of the Local Church*. The Pilgrim Press, Boston, 1934.

Stock, Harry T.: *Church Work with Young People*. The Pilgrim Press, Boston, 1929.

—————— *Better Meetings for the Young People*. International Society of Christian Endeavor, Boston, 1933.

—————— *Young People and Their Leaders*. The Pilgrim Press, Boston, 1933.

Thom, Douglas A.: *Normal Youth and Its Everyday Problems*. D. Appleton-Century Co., New York, 1932.

—————— *Guiding the Adolescent*. Government Printing Office, Washington, D. C., 1933.

Thompson, James V.: *Handbook for Workers with Young People*. The Abingdon Press, New York, 1922.

White House Conference on Child Health and Protection: *The

Adolescent in the Family. D. Appleton-Century Co., New York, 1934.

Williams, Frankwood: *Adolescence.* Farrar and Rinehart, Inc., New York, 1930.

GROUPING AND FELLOWSHIP

Busch, Henry M.: *Leadership in Group Work.* Association Press, New York, 1934.

Burr, Walter: *Community Leadership.* Prentice-Hall, Inc., New York, 1927.

Coyle, Grace L.: *Social Process in Organized Groups.* Farrar and Rinehart, Inc., New York, 1930.

———— *Studies in Group Behavior.* Association Press, New York, 1937.

Elliott, H. S.: *The Process of Group Thinking.* Association Press, New York, 1928.

Elliott, H. S. and Grace L.: *Solving Personal Problems,* chap. XII. Henry Holt and Company, Inc., New York, 1936.

Follett, M. P.: *Creative Experience.* Longmans, Green and Co., New York, 1924.

* King, Henry C.: *The Laws of Friendship.* The Macmillan Company, New York, 1910.

Kreuger, E. T., and Reckless, W. C.: *Social Psychology,* chap. III. Longmans, Green and Co., New York, 1935.

Leigh, Robert D.: *Group Leadership.* W. W. Norton and Co., Inc., New York, 1936.

Lindeman, Eduard C.: *Social Discovery,* part II. Republic Publishing Co., New York, 1925.

* Martin, Herbert: *A Philosophy of Friendship.* The Dial Press, New York, 1925.

Sheffield, Alfred D.: *Training for Group Experience.* The Inquiry, New York, 1929.

Slavson, S. R.: *Creative Group Education.* Association Press, New York, 1937.

* Wieman, Regina Westcott: *Popularity.* Willett, Clark, and Co., Chicago, 1936.

RECREATION

* Breen, Mary J.: *Partners in Play.* National Recreation Assoc., New York, 1934.

* Brown, Rollo W.: *The Creative Spirit*. Harper & Brothers, New York, 1925.
* Dale, Edgar: *How to Appreciate Motion Pictures*. The Macmillan Company, New York, 1933.
* Depew, Arthur M.: *The Cokesbury Stunt Book*. Cokesbury Press, Nashville, 1934.
* Harbin, E. O.: *Phunology*. The Cokesbury Press, Nashville, 1923.
* Jacks, L. P.: *The Education of the Whole Man*. Harper & Brothers, New York, 1931.
* Overstreet, Harry A.: *A Guide to Civilized Loafing*. W. W. Norton & Co., Inc., New York, 1934.
* Rohrbaugh, Katherine and Lynne, eds.: *Handy*. 2 vols. The Church Recreation Service (A Cooperative), Delaware, Ohio.
* Symposium: Enjoying the Arts: *A Series of Essays on Appreciation*. Scholastic Publishing Co., Pittsburgh, 1926.

PARTICIPATION IN COMMUNITY LIFE

* Hanna, Paul R.: *Youth Serves the Community*. D. Appleton-Century Co., New York, 1936.
* Herriott, Frank W.: *Christian Youth in Action*. Friendship Press, New York, 1935.
Herriott, Frank W., and Wendell, Sue: *What will You do About It?* (Manual for previous listing.)
International Council of Religious Education: *Life Experiences and the New Curriculum*. Research Service Bulletin No. 6, Chicago, 1929.
Maus, Cynthia: *Youth and Creative Living*. Harper & Brothers, New York, 1932.
* Moore, H. H.: *We are Builders of a New World*. Association Press, New York, 1934.
* Nall, T. Otto: *Youth's Work in the New World*. Association Press, New York, 1936.
Reeder, Rudolph R.: *Training Youth for the New Social Order*. Antioch Press, Yellow Springs, Ohio, 1933.
Shaver, Erwin L.: *A Project Curriculum for Young People*. University of Chicago Press, Chicago, 1925.

VOCATIONAL INTEREST

* Cottler, Joseph, and Brecht, H.: *Careers Ahead*. Little, Brown & Company, Boston, 1934.

* Gowin, E. B., and Wheatley, W. A.: *Occupations.* Revision by J. M. Brewer, Ginn and Company, Boston, 1923.
* Kitson, Harry: *Careers for Young People.* Simon and Schuster, Inc., New York, 1934.
* Pitkin, Walter B.: *New Careers for Youth.* Simon and Schuster, Inc., New York, 1934.
* Proctor, Wm. M.: *Vocations.* Houghton Mifflin Company, New York, 1933.
White House Conference on Child Health and Protection: *Vocational Guidance.* D. Appleton-Century Co., New York, 1933.

SEX LIFE AND RELATIONSHIPS

* Dickerson, R. E.: *Growing into Manhood.* Association Press, New York, 1933.
* Eddy, Sherwood: *Sex and Youth.* Doubleday, Doran & Company, Inc., New York, 1928.
* Elliott, Grace L., and Bone, Harry: *The Sex Life of Youth.* Association Press, New York, 1929.
* Foster, Larimore: *Larry.* John Day and Co., New York, 1931.
* Harris, Erdman: *Twenty-one.* Harper & Brothers, New York, 1931.
* Miller, Catherine A.: *Eighteen.* Round Table Press, Inc., New York, 1933.
* Royden, A. Maude: *Sex and Common Sense.* G. P. Putnam's Sons, New York, 1928.

PRE-MARITAL PREPARATION

* Bomar, Willie M.: *An Introduction to Homemaking and Its Relation to the Community.* W. B. Saunders Co., Philadelphia, 1931.
* Burkhart, Roy A.: *Thinking About Marriage.* Association Press, New York, 1934.
* Cunningham, Bess V.: *Family Behavior: A Study of Human Relations.* W. B. Saunders Co., Philadelphia, 1936.
* Cross, Earle Bennett: *The Ideal of a Home.* Roger Williams Press, Pawtucket, R. I., 1934.
* Dahlberg, Edwin T.: *Youth and the Homes of To-morrow.* Judson Press, Philadelphia, 1934.
* Goodspeed, Helen C., and Johnson, Emma: *Care and Training of Children.* J. B. Lippincott Co., Philadelphia, 1929.

* Groves, E. R., et al: *The Family and Its Relationships*. J. B. Lippincott Co., Philadelphia, 1932.
* Hunter, L. P.: *The Girl To-day, the Woman To-morrow*. Allyn and Bacon, New York, 1932.
* Jordan, M. J., et al: *Home and Family*. The Macmillan Company, New York, 1935.
* Justin, Margaret, and Rust, Lucile: *Problems in Home Living*. J. B. Lippincott Co., Philadelphia, 1929.
* Neumann, Henry: *Modern Youth and Marriage*. D. Appleton-Century Co., New York, 1928.
* Rockwood, Lemo Dennis: *Living Together in the Family*, American Home Economics Association, Washington, D. C., 1934.
* ———— *Pictures of Family Life: Young People's Descriptions of Family Life*. American Home Economics Association, Washington, D. C., 1935.
———— *Teaching Family Relationships in High School*. Manual for teachers. (See preceding listing.)
* Trilling, Mabel B., and Nicholas, Florence W.: *The Girl and Her Home*. Houghton Mifflin Company, New York, 1932.
* Walker, Kenneth M., ed.: *Preparation for Marriage*. W. W. Norton and Co., Inc., New York, 1933.

INTEGRATION OF LIFE

* Baker, Archibald G.: *Christian Missions and a New World Culture*, chaps. X-XIII. Willett, Clark and Co., Chicago, 1934.
* Betts, George H.: *Foundations of Character and Personality*. The Bobbs-Merrill Company, New York, 1937.
* Burnham, Wm. C.: *The Wholesome Personality*, chaps. VI-VIII, X, XIV. D. Appleton-Century Co., New York, 1932.
* Cabot, Richard C.: *The Meaning of Right and Wrong*. The Macmillan Company, New York, 1933.
Cornell University Agricultural Experiment Station: *Rural Youth; Activities, Interests, and Problems*. Bulletin No. 649, May, 1936, Ithaca, New York.
* Ferris, Helen: *This Happened to Me*. E. P. Dutton & Co., Inc., New York, 1929.
* Harper, W. A.: *Youth and Truth*. D. Appleton-Century Co., New York, 1927.
* Lippmann, Walter: *A Preface to Morals*. The Macmillan Company, New York, 1929.

* Patrick, G. T. W.: *Introduction to Philosophy*. Houghton Mifflin Co., New York, 1924.

Piaget, J.: *The Child's Conception of the World*. Harcourt, Brace and Co., Inc., New York, 1929.

* Royce, Josiah: *The Philosophy of Loyalty*. The Macmillan Company, New York, 1908.

* Rudisill, Earl S.: *The Intimate Problems of Youth*. The Macmillan Company, New York, 1929.

* Stoops, John D.: *Ideals of Conduct*. The Macmillan Company, New York, 1926.

Strong, Edward K.: *Change of Interests with Age*. Stanford University Press, Palo Alto, Calif., 1931.

Thorndike, E. L.: *Adult Interests*. The Macmillan Company, New York, 1935.

Weston, Sidney A., and Harlow, S. Ralph: *Social and Religious Problems of Young People*. The Abingdon Press, New York, 1934.

* Werner, Oscar W.: *Every College Student's Problems*. Silver, Burdette and Company, New York, 1929.

* Wieman, Henry N.: *Methods of Private Religious Living*. The Macmillan Company, New York, 1929.

(See also discussion units now being published by several denominations, which guide the interests of young people into larger social consciousness.)

CHAPTER XII

Counseling in Family Difficulties

Beard, Mary: *On Understanding Women*. Longmans, Green and Co., New York, 1931.

Bernard, L. L.: *An Introduction to Social Psychology*. Henry Holt and Co., Inc., New York, 1926.

Bingham, Walter V., and Moore, Bruce V.: *How to Interview*. Revised ed. Harper & Brothers, New York, 1934.

Bogardus, Emory S.: *The New Social Research*, chaps. III-VI. Jesse Ray Miller, Los Angeles, 1926.

Burkhart, Roy A.: *Guiding Individual Growth*. The Abingdon Press, New York, 1935.

Burnham, W. H.: *The Normal Mind*. D. Appleton-Century Co., New York, 1924.

Burnham, W. H.: *Great Teachers and Mental Health*. D. Appleton-Century Co., New York, 1926.

Busch, Henry: *Leadership in Group Work*. Association Press, New York, 1934.

Cabot, Richard C., and Dicks, Russell L.: *The Art of Ministry to the Sick*. The Macmillan Company, New York, 1936.

Clouser, L. W., and Robinson, W. J.: *Educative Experiences through Activity Units*. Lyons and Carnahan, Chicago, 1932.

Colcord, Joanna C.: *Broken Homes: A Study of Family Desertion and Its Social Treatment*. Russell Sage Foundation, New York, 1927.

Culbert, Jane F.: *The Visiting Teacher at Work*. Commonwealth Fund, New York, 1930.

de Schweinitz, Karl: *The Art of Helping People out of Trouble*. Houghton Mifflin Company, New York, 1924.

Dexter, A. A. and R. C.: *The Minister and Family Troubles*. Harper & Brothers, New York, 1931.

Dresser, Horatio: *Knowing and Helping People*. Beacon Press, Inc., Boston, 1933.

Edson, Newell W.: "Family Adjustments through Consultation Service." *Journal of Soc. Hyg.*, 1932. 18:198-211.

Eliot, Thomas D.: "Current Efforts in Behalf of the American Family," *The Family*, 1928. 9: 87-94.

Elliott, H. S. and G. L.: *Solving Personal Problems*, chaps. VIII-IX, XI-XII, XVI. Henry Holt and Company, Inc., New York, 1936.

Folsom, Joseph K.: *The Family: Its Sociology and Social Psychiatry*, part V. John Wiley and Sons, Inc., New York, 1934.

Furfey, P. H.: *New Lights on Pastoral Problems*. Bruce Publishing Co., Milwaukee, 1931.

Goodenough, F. L., and Anderson, J. E.: *Experimental Child Study*. D. Appleton-Century Co., New York, 1931.

Groves, E. R.: *The Marriage Crisis*, chap. X. Longmans, Green and Co., New York, 1928.

Groves, E. R., and Blanchard, Phyllis: *Introduction to Mental Hygiene*. Henry Holt and Company, Inc., New York, 1930.

Hart, Hornell and Ella B.: *Personality and the Family*. D. C. Heath and Company, Boston, 1935.

Healy, Wm., and Bronner, Augusta F.: *New Light on Delinquency and Its Treatment*. Yale University Press, New Haven, 1936.

Horney, Karen: *The Neurotic Personality of our Time*, chap. XV. W. W. Norton and Co., Inc., New York, 1937.

Johnson, F. Ernest, ed.: *The Social Work of the Churches*. Federal Council of Churches, New York, 1930.

Kanner, Leo.: *Child Psychiatry*. Thomas Publishing Co., New York, 1935.

Kirkpatrick, Edwin A.: *Mental Hygiene for Effective Living*. D. Appleton-Century Co., New York, 1934.

Kreuger, E. T., and Reckless, Walter C.: *Social Psychology*. Longmans, Green and Co., New York, 1935.

Lee, Porter, and Kenworthy, Marion: *Mental Hygiene and Social Work*. Commonwealth Fund, New York, 1929.

Lindeman, Eduard C.: *Social Discovery: An Approach to the Study of Functional Groups*. Republic Publishing Co., New York, 1925.

Mowrer, E. R. and Harriet R.: *Domestic Discord: Its Analysis and Treatment*. University of Chicago Press, Chicago, 1928.

Murphy, Gardner and Lois B.: *Experimental Social Psychology*, chap. IX. Harper & Brothers, New York, 1931.

Murphy, Gardner, and Jensen, Friedrich: *Approaches to Personality*. Coward-McCann Co., New York, 1932.

Myerson, Abraham: *The Nervous Housewife*. Little, Brown & Company, Boston, 1920.

National Council of Parent Education: "Marriage and Family Counseling." *Parent Education*, April and May, 1936. Vol. III, Nos. 1-2.

Oliver, John R.: *Pastoral Psychiatry and Mental Health*. Charles Scribner's Sons, New York, 1932.

Pratt, George: *Morale: The Mental Hygiene of Unemployment*. National Committee for Mental Hygiene, New York, 1933.

Richmond, Mary E.: *Social Diagnosis*, chaps. VI-VII. Russell Sage Foundation, New York, 1917.

Shaffer, Laurence F.: *The Psychology of Adjustment*, part IV and Bibliography. Houghton Mifflin Co., New York, 1936.

Sheffield, Ada E.: *Social Insight in Case Situations*, chaps. II-VI. D. Appleton-Century Co., New York, 1937.

Sheldon, Wm. H.: *Psychology and the Promethean Will*, chap. VII. Harper & Brothers, New York, 1936.

Slavson, S. R.: *Creative Group Education*, chaps. I-III, XIII, XVIII, Appendix B. Association Press, New York, 1937.

Stevenson, George S., and Smith, Geddes: *Child Guidance Clinics*. Commonwealth Fund, New York, 1934.

Stolz, Karl R.: *Pastoral Psychology*. Cokesbury Press, Nashville, 1932.

Strecker, E. A., and Appel, K. E.: *Discovering Ourselves*. The Macmillan Company, New York, 1930.

Symonds, Percival M.: *Diagnosing Personality and Character*. D. Appleton-Century Co., New York, 1931.

Taft, Jessie: *The Dynamics of Therapy in a Controlled Relationship*. The Macmillan Company, New York, 1933.

Waller, Willard: *The Old Love and the New: Divorce and Readjustment*. H. Liveright, New York, 1930.

White, Wm. A.: *Twentieth Century Psychiatry*, chap. I. W. W. Norton & Company, Inc., New York, 1936.

Wieman, Regina Westcott: "Counseling Procedures," chap. XXII in Wieman, H. N. and Regina W.: *Normative Psychology of Religion*. Thomas Y. Crowell Company, New York, 1935.

Williamson, Margaretta: *The Social Worker in Group Work*, chaps. I, VI, XII. Harper & Brothers, New York, 1929.

Young, Kimball: *Social Psychology*. F. S. Crofts & Co., New York, 1931.

Young, Pauline V.: *Interviewing in Social Work*, chaps. I-VI, XII-XVI. McGraw-Hill Book Company, Inc., New York, 1935.

CHAPTER XIII

Trends in the Work of the Churches

Athearn, W. S.: *The Indiana Survey of Religious Education*, vol. I. Harper & Brothers, New York, 1924.

Brown, Wm. A.: *Ministerial Education in America*, vol. I, Summary. Harper & Brothers, New York, 1934.

Brunner, Edmund de S.: *Churches of Distinction in Town and Country*. Harper & Brothers, New York, 1923.

Coe, George A.: *A Social Theory of Religious Education*, part V. Charles Scribner's Sons, New York, 1928.

Douglass, H. Paul: *The Protestant Church as a Social Institution*. Harper & Brothers, 1935.

————— *Church Unity Movements in the United States*. Harper & Brothers, New York, 1934.

Gleason, George: *Church Group Activities for Young Married People*. Author, 715 S. Hope St., Los Angeles, 1937.

Hartshorne, Hugh, et al: *Standards and Trends in Religious Education.* Yale University Press, New Haven, 1933.

————— and Ehrhart, Earle V.: *Church Schools Today.* Yale University Press, New Haven, 1933.

Hooker, Elizabeth R.: *United Churches.* Harper & Brothers, New York, 1926.

Lotz, Philip H., and Crawford, L. W., eds.: *Studies in Religious Education,* chaps. XVIII, XX-XXII, XXIX. Cokesbury Press, Nashville, 1931.

Ward, Harry F.: *The New Social Order,* chap. XI. The Macmillan Company, New York, 1920.

See also articles in current periodicals of which the following are instances:

Homiletic Review: Wyrick, Hubert McN., vol XCV, pp. 479-481, 1928.

International Journal of Religious Education: McKibben, Alma, vol. X, no. 2, pp. 12-13, October, 1933; Wagner, James E., vol. X, no. 11, pp. 9-20, 32, July, 1934; Shields, Elizabeth McE., vol. XII, no. 2, pp. 14-15, October, 1935; Hayward, P. R., vol. XI, no. 3, p. 20; and Veith, Paul H., vol. XI, no. 3, pp. 8, 40, November, 1934; Chalfant, Ruth H., vol. XII, no. 9, pp. 8-10, 37, May, 1936.

Religious Education: Pratt, George K., vol. XXV, no. 8, pp. 703-708, October, 1930; (News Note) vol. XXIV, no. 10, pp. 907-908, December, 1929; McPherson, Imogene M., vol. XXVIII, no. 1, pp. 62-69; and Zeigler, Earl F.: vol. XXVIII, no. 1, pp. 80-87, January, 1933.

Religion and Life: Wood, L. F., Summer Number, 1934.

Journal of Social Hygiene: Tippy, Worth M., April, 1932. Wood, L. F., November, 1932, Swift, Edith H.; October, 1933, Lathrop, John H.; December, 1934.

See also files of *Family, Child Welfare, Survey,* and *Annals of the American Academy of Political and Social Science.*

CHAPTER XIV

Program for the Conservation of the Family

Beaven, Albert W.: *The Local Church: Its Purpose and Program.* The Abingdon Press, New York, 1937.

Bossard, James H. S.: *Problems of Social Well-Being*. Harper & Brothers, New York, 1927.

Bower, William C., ed.: *The Church at Work in the Modern World*. University of Chicago Press, Chicago, 1935.

Burk, William: *Youth's New Day: A Handbook for Coordinating Council Workers*. Los Angeles Lion's Club, Los Angeles, 1935.

Carpenter, Edward: *Toward Democracy*. Albert and Charles Boni, Inc., New York, 1935.

Chaffee, Edmund D.: *Protestant Churches and the Industrial Crisis*. The Macmillan Company, New York, 1933.

Cobb, Stanwood: *New Horizons for the Child*. Avalon Press, Washington, D. C., 1934.

Dawson, Christopher: *Religion and the Modern State*. Sheed and Ward Co., New York, 1935.

Dell, Floyd: *Love in the Machine Age*. Farrar and Rinehart, Inc., New York, 1930.

Ellwood, Charles A.: *The Reconstruction of Religion*. The Macmillan Company, New York, 1922.

Elmer, Manuel C.: *Family Adjustment and Social Change*. Ray Long and Richard R. Smith, New York, 1932.

Epstein, Abraham: *Insecurity*. Smith and Haas, Inc., New York, 1933.

Federal Council of Churches: *Social Ideals of the Churches*. Pamphlet. 105 East 22d St., New York, 1934.

Furnas, C. C.: *The Next Hundred Years*. Williams and Wilkins Co., Baltimore, 1936.

Garvie, A. E.: *The Christian Ideal for Human Society*. Ray Long and Richard R. Smith, New York, 1930.

Gauss, Christian: *A Primer for Tomorrow*. Charles Scribner's Sons, New York, 1934.

Groves, Ernest R.: *The American Family*, chap. VII and part II. J. B. Lippincott Co., Philadelphia, 1934.

Hargreaves, J. R.: "Reach the Unchurched." *International Journal of Religious Education*, July, 1936.

Hart, Hornell N.: *The Techniques of Social Progress*, chaps. III, IX, XI-XIII, XVIII. Henry Holt and Company, Inc., New York, 1931.

————— *Living Religion:* A manual for putting religion into action in personal life and in social reconstruction. The Abingdon Press, New York, 1937.

Hart, Joseph K.: *Education for an Age of Power*. Harper & Brothers, New York, 1935.

Jennings, H. S.: *The Biological Basis of Human Nature*, chaps. X, XIII. W. W. Norton & Company, Inc., New York, 1930.

Johnson, F. Ernest: *Economics and the Good Life*. Association Press, New York, 1934.

Kilpatrick, Wm. H., et al.: *The Educational Frontier*. D. Appleton-Century Co., Inc., New York, 1933.

Kotinsky, Ruth: *Adult Education and the Social Scene*. D. Appleton-Century Co., Inc., New York, 1933.

Leiper, Henry S.: *Christ's Way and the World's Way in Church, State and Society*. The Abingdon Press, New York, 1936.

McConnell, F. J.: *The Christian Ideal and Social Control*. University of Chicago Press, Chicago, 1932.

Merriam, Charles E.: *Political Power*. McGraw-Hill Book Company, Inc., New York, 1934.

Milne, A. A.: *Peace with Honour*. E. P. Dutton and Co., Inc., New York, 1934.

Moulton, Harold G.: *Income and Economic Progress*. Brookings Institution, New York, 1935.

Mumford, Lewis: *Technics and Civilization*. Harcourt, Brace and Company, Inc., New York, 1934.

Myers, James: *Churches in Social Action*. Pamphlet. Federal Council of Churches, New York, 1935.

Niebuhr, Reinhold, and Eddy, Sherwood: *Doom or Dawn*. Eddy and Page, Inc., New York, 1936.

North, Cecil C.: *Social Problems and Social Planning*. McGraw-Hill Book Company, Inc., New York, 1932.

Overstreet, Harry A.: *A Declaration of Interdependence*. W. W. Norton & Company, Inc., New York, 1937.

Page, Kirby: *Individualism and Socialism*. Farrar and Rinehart, Inc., New York, 1933.

Popenoe, Paul: *The Conservation of the Family*. Williams and Wilkins Co., New York, 1926.

Read, Ralph H., ed.: *The Younger Churchmen Look at the Church*. The Macmillan Company, New York, 1935.

Rorty, James: *Our Master's Voice*. John Day and Co., New York, 1934.

Rugg, Harold: *The Great Technology*, chaps. I-II, X-XVII. John Day and Co., New York, 1933.

Schuman, Frederick L.: *International Politics*. McGraw-Hill Book Company, Inc., New York, 1933.

Studebaker, John W.: *The American Way*. McGraw-Hill Book Company, New York, 1935.

Van Loon, Hendrik W.: *Tolerance*. Garden City Publishing Co., Garden City, 1933.

Ward, Harry F.: *In Place of Profit*. Charles Scribner's Sons, New York, 1933.

Whitehead, A. N.: *Leadership in a Free Society*. Harvard University Press, Cambridge, Mass., 1936.

References listed under *Grouping and Fellowship*, Chap. XI, p. 374, are fully as important here as there.

For valuable material for visual education see series of charts in folders published by

The National Forum (A Non-Partisan Movement for Social Education) 820 East 56th St., Chicago, Illinois, 1937.

Cooperation Visualized.	*International Problems Visualized.*
Farm Problems Visualized.	*Economic Problems Visualized.*
Health Problems Visualized.	*Special Problems Visualized.*

PERTINENT PERIODICALS

Group A: addressed to parents and teachers:

American Childhood	*Childhood Interests*
Character	*Junior Home Magazine*
Child Study	*Parent Education*
Child Welfare	*The Parents' Magazine*

See also the official church publications for parents or the family

Group B: addressed to special interest groups but containing articles or book reviews of interest to parents and teachers:

Allied Youth	*Journal of the National Educational Association*
Child Development Abstracts	*Mental Hygiene*
International Journal of Religious Education	*Progressive Education*
Journal of Home Economics	*Religious Education*
Journal of Social Hygiene	*Social Action*
	The Christian Century
	The Family
	The Survey
	World Youth

Group C: addressed to general public, but containing materials for home-makers in the form of articles, book reviews, special departments, or information service:

Better Homes and Gar-   *Leisure*
    dens   *McCall's*
Good Housekeeping   *Pictorial Review*
House and Garden   *The Delineator*
House Beautiful   *Woman's Home Com-*
Hygeia   *panion*
Ladies' Home Journal

Group D: Newspapers carrying departments of worthy and dependable materials; probably best illustrated by the *Christian Science Monitor*.

GUIDING OUTLINES FOR STUDY GROUPS

The Groups Who May Be Interested

REAL students of family life are not satisfied with a mere informational approach to the field. They want to discover the possibilities in regard to constructive developments. They have some degree of creative attitude toward family life, and so are interested in the normative as well as the descriptive aspects. There are at least three groups of such students:

1. Persons now themselves engaged in home-making.
2. Young people anticipating, and inquiring about, the meanings and possibilities involved in the home-making experience.
3. Persons whose vocational interests and success are inextricably connected with, and conditioned by, the effectiveness of functioning of the family.

Conspicuous among this last group are teachers and deans; counselors in public and private work; social workers; leaders of personality-fostering institutions which seek to guide youth in its leisure and other special interests; and last but very important, the pastors and religious workers of various types of churches.

It has ceased to be strange to find community leaders pressing the family to study the economic, political, and other such aspects of society. Now it must cease to be strange to require that community leaders come to understand the family for what essentially it is and can become, rather than merely as a factor that must be dealt with as an incident in vocational undertakings.

THE PLAN OF THE OUTLINES

Because of limitations of space, the outlines must be in instrumental rather than fully charted form. Therefore, there is first presented a basic outline, intended as a tool to be used in guiding the group in its study. Following this, there is a list of some of the areas of study which may be approached, which includes enough references to the text to launch the work. Since no one area could be more than superficially dealt with in one or two study meetings, it is suggested that time be allowed for study to go deep enough to release activators impelling to constructive developments.

Different subjects selected for study will emphasize different sections of the guiding outline, of course, and at times it may seem best to omit some sections of this outline. However, the general plan of the outline is very simple with its five major divisions, and it is consistent with the theme of the book. After (1) *The Problem* has been formulated and located in its settings, there come (2) *The Inquiry* and (3) *The Application,* which call for work carried on by the units of membership relatively independently (each family, individual, or vocational interest participating). During these parts of the process, the group acts as resource, constructive critic, and clearing-house. Then comes (4) *Sharing the Findings,* when the materials and projects involved become the bases of closer interaction, analysis, and fellowship, first within the group, and then between the group and the community. Here is widening of community actually under way. The last part of the group process is (5) *Coöperative Evaluation.* Through the creative fellowship of the group there takes place the crystallizing of all the beauty, truth, goodness, and community they have discovered or developed, into useful and treasured forms. Of course, these crystallizations must be on a tentative basis, subject to being dissolved and re-precipitated by further experiences and insights. Nevertheless, it is an essential part of the process that they shall clarify and formulate and appreciatively taste their findings. These may become manifest as principles, methods, norms, or techniques, as records, codes or forms of art and ritual. Group expression of appreciation of earned insights and understanding may be rendered in private or public, and may take many forms, culminating in worship. That is, if the group study has been successful, it has become for each unit of membership, a creative, progressively integrative and communally expansive experience.

GUIDING OUTLINE

I. The Problem.

    A. Selecting and formulating the problem to be studied.

> This may be facilitated by recording the questions asked by various members in connection with the field, and then arranging them in reference to the relations of the members to the field.

    B. Seeing the problem in its settings.
        1. In its relationship to the other interests of the larger society.
        2. In its relationship to everyday human living.

II. The Inquiry.

    A. Considering the basic findings.
        1. Study by each member of the selected references and of relevant research findings including statistics, supplemented where feasible by significant interviews, controlled observation, and investigation.

> The listing of annotated resources for study should be built up continuously during the whole study and made available to all members. The local library may coöperate valuably here.

        2. Pooling and sifting of the findings by the group through discussion, referring to authorities through lectures or study, and methods of critical analysis and testing.

    B. Exploring the guiding principles for making use of these findings.
        1. Discovering and formulating the principles.
        2. Examining the implications of these principles for specific kinds of situations.

III. The Application.

    A. Setting up the conditions in which these principles can function.

        1. Ascertaining what conditions are required for the functioning of these principles.

            a. General conditions—needed always by these principles.

            b. Particular conditions—called for by the characteristics of specific situations.

        2. Locating the critical or germinative occasions for the working of these principles.

            a. Those most favorable, facilitating, reinforcing.

            b. Those most unfavorable, frustrating, negating.

        3. Locating available materials and tools useful in setting up the required conditions.

        4. Selecting available methods and techniques useful in setting up the required conditions.

        5. Blocking out specific projects which hold the promise of improving individual situations through appropriate functioning of these principles.

        These will have to be discussed by the group through types and illustrative projects, supplemented with a listing of generally helpful possibilities. Then each member-unit must work out its own specific project. If the leader of the group has the time and skill for it, it would be profitable at this point to have conferences with each individual unit.

    B. Selecting the criteria by which to recognize the functioning of these principles in actual situations, and the measures by which to discover the progress in guidance being made in the projects undertaken.

        This is an essential group undertaking, for it forestalls many mistakes, much trial and error floundering and impeding discouragement, and so, obversely, facilitates, encourages and reinforces.

    C. Dealing with the sub-problems to be met during projects undertaken.

        1. Understanding the problems.

            a. Locating and preparing for those regularly to be

expected in such situations: exploring objectively the unexpected problems which eventuate.

    b. Defining constructive attitudes in dealing with the sub-problems.

        (1) Appreciation of the growth-significance of problems.

        (2) Impartial consideration from the various points of view involved, i.e., parent-child, husband-wife, member-outsider, etc.

        (3) Regarding the process as social engineering.

    c. Ascertaining the degree of solvability of sub-problems.

        (1) Considering the nature of both internal and external factors operative in the situation.

        (2) Considering the various levels upon which adjustment is possible.

        (3) Considering the probable changes regularly to be expected in the personal and social factors involved.

2. Locating appropriate and effective methods and techniques.

3. Creative treatment of each sub-problem.

This may involve ignoring certain aspects; or diverting attention to other things; or coöperative evaluation, experimentation, and exploration; or weighting of satisfactions and dissatisfactions; or providing more convincing experiences in the tastings of value, etc.

IV. Sharing the Findings.

    A. Bases for sharing the findings.

      1. Securing coöperative comparison, criticism, and evaluation.

      2. Making available to others the various achieved developments.

      3. Securing organized attention and action in regard to needed developments.

> a. On problems interrelating the interests of the local group.
>
> b. On problems pertaining to progress in the field.

B. Directions of sharing.

> 1. Between members of the study group.
> 2. Between the group and the larger community, local or larger.

C. Methods of sharing the findings.

These may include an exhibit of projects by members; a symposium; an open forum; the publishing of a bulletin; the instituting of extension groups; the maintenance of a public bulletin board in the field of study; the maintenance of a weekly column in the newspaper; the pooling and organization of valued reading notes; useful formulation of the group's records regularly inscribed with answered and unanswered questions, descriptions of projects, achievements and conclusions, together with suggestions or plans for action or further development; a panel discussion; engaging of a speaker to deal with certain difficult aspects; written reports of projects by individual units; communication of disturbing findings to proper authorities or to larger, more powerful groups; coöperation in specific ways with other community organizations; development of reading lists, annotated and specifically indicated as to matter dealt with; library service through built-up library of group or in connection with public library; expression through the various arts, especially the graphic, literary, musical, and dramatic, and through worship. Any or all of these may be arranged on either a group or a public scale, depending upon the present stage of ability of the group and the significance of the particular findings under consideration. A group demonstration day or week may combine a number of these forms of sharing and be made very contributive to the community.

V. *Coöperative Evaluation.*

A. Interpreting the outcomes.

> 1. Identifying the values and disvalues which have emerged, both those anticipated and prepared for, and those unexpected; both the direct outcomes and the indirect ones, positive and negative.
> 2. Exploring the implications of these outcomes.
>> a. For the individual member-units experiencing them.
>>
>> b. For the further study and activities of the group.

c. For the field of their study.

d. For the growth of good, of meaning, in all the world.

B. Appreciating the outcomes.

The recognitions and celebration of growth of value, of meaning, of fellow feeling, may take many forms: pageants, plays, festivals, and other forms of dramatization and musical expression; the impressive calling of the attention of the group or of the public to important issues through presentation of selections from the works of authorities and true artists, or through group-developed articles, poetry, plays, short stories, and books; recognition services and programs; the development of appropriate ritual; and significant worship services. The celebration of the growth of good, of fellow feeling *can* hold deeper thrill and significance than the celebration of the successes of organized greed and other evil.

SUGGESTED AREAS FOR STUDY

Note: T=Text; I=Index.

1. How does the genuine family grow?

   I. *Family*, definition of; biological foundations of. *Sharing*, of interests.

2. How do the conditions and the conflicts of interests in current civilization affect the family?

   T. Chaps. I and II.
   I. *Group*, instrumental; nurturing.

3. What functions must the modern family fulfill? Why?

   I. *Family*, functions of.

4. What are the conditions which foster communion in the family? How are these set up?

   I. *Communion*, specific requirements for. *Community*, requirements in development of. *Growth*, conditions of; confusions necessary to. *Love*, growth of; motivation of, in marriage; primary fact of. *Unity*, growth of, in family.

5. What are the conditions which hinder family communion? How are these avoided or overcome?

   I. *Communion*, conditions which injure. *Love*, false ideas of. *Group*, pressures on family; pressures on youth.

6. What is the basic bond between family and church? What common ground does this give these two institutions?

> I. *Church*, bond between family and; objectives of. *Family*, as germinative center of love; objectives of; religious significance of. *God*, Kingdom of.

7. How do the conditions and conflicting interests of current civilization affect religion and the church?

> T. Chap. IV.
> I. *Church*, current attitude toward; oppression of. *Religion*, current attitudes toward. *Values*, of current civilization; promoted by church.

8. What functions must the modern church fulfill? Why?

> I. *Church*, functions of; social load of.

9. How must the church and family interfunction if each is to survive and develop?

> T. Chap. VII.

10. What can be done for family life through better launching of it?

> T. Chap. VIII.

11. What is involved in effective parenthood?

> I. *Parent Education*, achieved by church; areas where needed. *Parents*, education of, by children; objectives of; failings of.

12. What guidance of the growth of meaning is most important (a) during childhood?

> T. Chap. X.
> I. *Children*, religious experience of. *Communion*, early conditioning in; lowest level of.

13. What guidance of growth of meaning is most important (b) during youth?

> T. Chap. XI.
> I. *Community*, conditions of young people in; education through participation in. *Loyalties*, as factors in self-organization. *Youth*, blank future of; community in organizations of; completions of; disorganization of; effective group pressures upon; weaning of.

14. What part do theology and the Bible rightfully have in religious education?

    T. Pp. 229-233.
    I. *Doctrines.*

15. Why can the problems of the family be best dealt with through group approach?

    T. Chap. XII.
    I. *Group,* approach through, to group problems; constructive use of.

16. What is involved in the maturing of the family?

    I. *Family,* enlargement of community in; maturing of; organizing for power in. *Children,* force in enlarging community. *Socialization.*

17. How can God be most readily experienced in family life?

    I. *God,* child's experience of; experience of, in family; as love; patterns for discerning; sense of presence of; working of.

18. What are the marks of a genuinely Christian family?

    I. *Christian. Family,* criteria for success of. *God,* highest manifestations of. *Living,* Christian way of. *Love,* as life principle of family. *Loyalty,* religious. *Marriage,* Christian. *Ritual. Virtues,* roots of. *Worship.*

19. What are the emphases and trends in the present relations of the church to family life?

    T. Pp. 189-193; chap. XIII.

20. Outline a program of church education for family life incorporating the basic essentials.

    T. Chaps. XIII and XIV.
    I. *Parent Education. Education,* methods of. *Guru. Love,* germinating center of. *Loyalties,* as factors in family unity. *Marriage,* education for.

21. What specific changes are needed in the modern church which seeks to carry out a program both Christian and socially effective?

    T. Chap. V.
    I. *Church,* bases for unity in; definition of; nurture of fellowship in; objectives of; practical procedures of; prime work of; relation to special interests; reshaping of; strategic position of. *Salvation,* for the church. *Vital Issues of Life. Wills of the Church.*

22. Concerning the contributions of the family—what is involved in speaking of the family as the source of social energy?

> I. *Emotional*, equipoise; set. *Family*, attitude toward individual members in; conditioning of later life in; religious function of; social responsibility of; jurisdiction of; values in. *Personality*, greatness of; uniqueness of. *Physical energy*, factor in relationship; as social material. *Religion*, revitalized by family.

23. Concerning the contributions of the family—how is the chief contribution (development of communion, of fellow feeling) specifically related to the solution of public problems such as conflicts between capital and labor, world peace, interracial and international relations, and control of commercialized amusements (movies, dance halls, etc.)?

> I. *Communion*, foundations of; growth in family; growth in society; type of connectedness in. *Democracy. Equality*, organic. *Group*, conflict. *Growth*, of interconnectedness. *Individual*, caught into the larger unity. *Progress. Sensitivity*, essential in communion. *Sharing*, of meanings. *Social Institutions*, types of, instrumental, personality-fostering.

24. What specific developments could be undertaken immediately by the church and other community institutions for the sake of fostering the social and religious effectiveness of the family?

> T. Chap. II; Part III.
>
> I. *Family*, recognition of achievements of. *Homemaking. Organized Minorities*, constructive direction of. *Patterns*, change in; for family living.

25. Outline a program in social reconstruction particularly directed toward increasing family effectiveness which merits the continued coöperation of church and family, together with other community institutions.

> T. Chaps. I and XIV.
>
> I. *Dean Pound. Education*, for change. *Family*, definition of; modern resources of; organizing for power in; social responsibilities of; functions of. *Freedom. Group*, constructive use of; therapy through. *Loyalties*, progression of. *Motive. Relationships*, effect of competition on; experimental approach in; trust essential in. *Salvation*, individual; modern problem of. *Slavery. Social*, ideals of church; planning; reconstruction; responsibility. *Social Institutions*, reshaping of. *Values*, as activators; convincing experiences of. *Youth*, organizations of; social responsibility of.

INDEX

333-337; medium of, 24, 50-51, 143; modern resources of, 45-46, 65, 108-109; norms in, 41-42, 59, 69-71, 183, 184, 187, 199, 209; objectives of, 143-144, 161, 194, 215, 282, 337, 340, 344-345; oppression of, 5-6, 9, 12-13, 18-20, 20-22, 29, 53, 67, 331-333; organization of, 41, 58, 90, 118, 151-152; organizing for power in, 18-20, 48, 52-53, 67, 180-181, 338-339, 348-354; problems of, Chaps. I & II, 51, 57-58, 149-150; recognition of achievements of, 50-51, 58, 66, 68, 172-173, 184, 209-210, 212; religious experience in, 65, 131-133, 137-141, 142, 173, 189, 202-203; religious function of, 139, 158-161; religious significance of, Chap. VI, 137-143, 157-160; root-age of, 6-8, 44-46; social responsibility of, 20-22, 39-40, 42-44, 56-57, 67, 68-69, 70, 150-151, 180-181, 333-337; social status of, Chaps. I & II, 5, 7-8, 9, 11-12, 45, 51-53, 209-210; social worth of, Chap. III, 52, 71-74, *see also* Community (germinal sources of); uniqueness of, 34-35, 135; unity of, 40, 52-53, 59, 63, 68, 69-70, 71-73, 136, 138-141, 150-151, 216, 219-220, 226, 282; values in, 45-46, 50-51, 56, 57-58, 330

Father, 12-13, 24-28, 43, 72, 151-152
Fear, 16, 222-224, 335-336, 338-339
Federal Council of Churches of Christ in America, 185, 295, 312, 314-315, 317
Fellowship, in church, 81, 87, 92-93, 102-103, 109-110, 122-123, 153-171, 288-289; effect of competition on, *see* Competition (effect of); as cultural neighborhood, 137-138, 146-147, 321; disciplines required in, 14, 67-68, 110, 172-173, 179-180; within family, Chap. VI, 9, 55-59, 87, 90, 118, 137-144, 193-196, 282; freedom and, 138, 265-268

Financing of Church, *see* Church

Freedom, 12, 16, 50, 136, 138, 195, 265-268
Freud, Sigmund, 16
Friends, The, (The Quakers), 88, 317
Friendship, 67-68, 128, 179-180, 247, 249-250, 257-258, 259, 261, 263
Functions, discovered, 59; *see* Family, Church, Social Institutions

Germany, 112, 331
God, child's experience of, 65, 131-133, 137-141, 142, 230-233; conditions for work of, *see* Growth, (conditions of); definition of, 143, 202; experience of, in family, 65, 90-93, 131-133, 137-141, 142, 173, 189, 202-203; family devotion to, 65, 131-133, 137-141, 190-193, 202-205; as First Value, 114; as the Great Unfamiliar, 224; highest manifestations of, 132-133, 138-141, 142-143, 281; inadequately conceived, 68, 216-217, 222-224, 230-233; Kingdom of, 190, 256, 293, 340; as love, 68, 86, 132-133, 137, 138-139, 143, 160-161, 172-173, 256, 281-282, 341-344; loyalty to, and church unity, 86, 88, 123, 295-296, 341-344; outreach toward, for completion, 247; patterns for discerning, 98-100, 113-119, 133-140, 202-203; relation of church to, 102-103, 112, 341-344; sense of presence of, 202-203; working of, 99, 128, 132, 138-141, 143, 202-203, 205, 256
Good, Nature of, 117
Group, approach through, to group problems, Chap. XII, 47, 83, 88, 119, 122, 185, 248, 267-268; conflict, 10, 24, 82-85, 92-93, 112, 122-123, 127-131, 183, 332; constructive use of, 18-20, 267-268, 345-346, 349-356; education of, Chap. XII, 62-63, 173-175; instrumental, 23, 50-51, 67, 144-145, 147, 344-345; loyalties, 40, 68, 102-103, 117-118, 268; nurturing, 71-74, 147, 249, 254; pressures on family, 9, 26-27,